Encyclopedia of
Rock

Encyclopedia of Rock

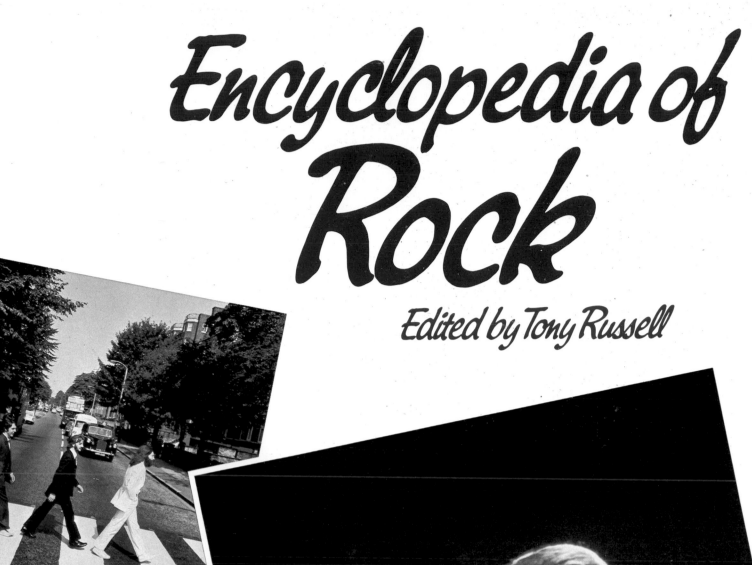

Edited by Tony Russell

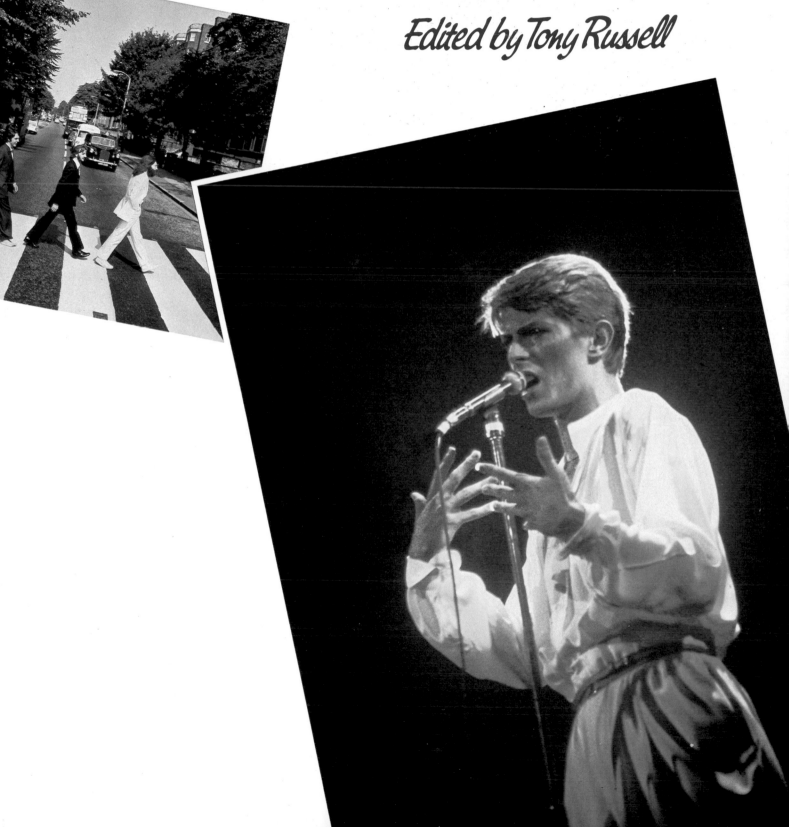

This edition published in 1983 by
Crescent Books, a division of
Crown Publishers Inc, by arrangement with
Octopus Books Limited
59 Grosvenor Street London W1

© 1983 Hennerwood Publications Limited

Printed in Spain by
Artes Graficas Toledo, S.A.
DL TO-772-83

Library of Congress Cataloging in Publication Data

The Encyclopedia of Rock

   Includes index.
   Contents: The Heroes; The Hardware; The
Business; Rock Directory.
   1. Rock music—History and criticism. I. Russell,
Tony.
ML3534.E5 1983   784.5'4'009   83-2060
ISBN 0-517-408651

HALF TITLE From the top: Fats Domino, B.B. King, Elvis Presley, Chuck Berry.

TITLE SPREAD From top, left: Jimi Hendrix, Bob Dylan, The Who, Mick Jagger, the Beatles, David Bowie.

PAGES 4-5 From left to right: Debbie Harry, Kid Creole & the Coconuts, Bryan Ferry, Dire Straits, Sting.

Contents

Introduction

Well, it looks as if it's all here in this book, from pre-Coasters to post-Clash. This is the story of rock from its origins through to the present day. At the moment all of us are kept on our toes by groups coming and going at the rate of knots — so last week's heroes may have arrived too late to find a place here. What *is* included, for those of us who like to revel in not entirely useless information, are the answers to hundreds of questions, such as 'Who wrote "Wabash Cannonball"?' After reading this book you can confidently shout, 'Roy Acuff, of course!' I've known people who get invited to parties for less, so look no further for an excuse to buy this book.

For those of us who were teenagers in the Sixties, the words *Ready Steady Go!* and *Saturday Club* strike a joyous note, and my favourite bands, such as the Beatles, the Animals, the Yardbirds and the Who, are all very well documented here. For older readers there are the 'teen idols' like Fabian and Paul Anka — or my sister's favourite, Tommy Steele. I was specially impressed with the fact that my lot, Genesis, are in this book — but don't let that put you off buying it. All the great names are here, so settle down and read it, absorb it — and just think about all those parties you'll be going to.

Phil Collins

The Heroes

Origins

When rock 'n' roll exploded upon the world in the middle Fifties, with the successive thunderclaps of Bill Haley, Elvis Presley, and Little Richard, it all seemed to come out of a clear sky – there had been no storm-cloud, no darkening, no old men shaking their heads. (There would be plenty of those later, of course.) Rock 'n' roll started, like the Universe itself, with a big bang – or perhaps with a staccato rattle of big bangs, followed by a lot of smaller ones.

Or so it seemed. Few people then were in a position to know that rock 'n' roll, far from being a miracle from nowhere, was a music with a long history – indeed, several parallel histories, for it was the result of years of foundation work by several contractors: country music, blues, gospel; bluegrass, Western Swing, rhythm &

ABOVE *T-Bone Walker, the first master of electric blues guitar, dominated the West Coast blues scene of the Forties.*

RIGHT *B. B. King was originally inspired by Walker's jazzy phrasing, succeeding him as the leading modern blues guitarist.*

blues (R&B) doo-wop, jazz. None of these forms of music *became* rock 'n' roll, and some of them were crucially different from it, even opposed to it; but each played some part in the process out of which rock 'n' roll was distilled.

'Let me tell you about the first hit Elvis Presley ever had. I think this song tells the story better than anything that he ever did.' The speaker is Charlie Feathers, a Memphis rock 'n' roll singer and slightly older contemporary of Presley, talking about one side of Elvis's first release in 1954 – which has a strong claim to be the first Southern rock 'n' roll record of all. 'Was a tune called "Blue Moon of Kentucky". I often wondered where the idea there came from, Elvis singing it that way. He had the big lips, you know, and he'd sing like a colored feller . . . then you take upright bass and a guitar hitting some blue licks. Well, there you got what they call the rock.

And that was blues and bluegrass mixed. And this went on around there for a long time.'

What Feathers says can be applied to *all* original rock 'n' roll: that it was a fusion of blues and country music. (He calls the latter bluegrass because he is thinking of the background of the song in question, but country music in general is clearly what he means.) Presley's first record was nothing if not a fusion: the other side was a blues hit of a few years earlier, 'That's All Right (Mama)', but set to a jaunty bluegrass-derived country beat. He yanked blues and country music into partnership – then he turned round and did the same thing the other way about.

There was in fact nothing original about this. Treaties had been struck between the two musics at frequent intervals for at least 15 years. Presley should be credited with the particular character he gave to the idea, not the idea itself. But before we arrive at Elvis, or even at that 15-year countdown to rock 'n' roll, we need to know the musical landscape in which it all took place.

Blacks, Whites & Blues

Country blues of the Twenties and Thirties was essentially a music of the solo singer-guitarist, and as such had an utterly basic and very widespread appeal to all embryo musicians, black and white. At that time you could buy a guitar from one of the giant mail-order houses, such as Chicago's Sears, Roebuck, for a few dollars, and it was the commonest first instrument. Every Southern kid grew up likely to be acquainted with at least a handful of blues standards – 'Match Box Blues', 'Sitting on Top of the World', 'Milk Cow Blues'. These and other country blues numbers, though they were originated by black singers, were quickly absorbed into the repertoires of musicians both sides of the colour-line, responsive alike to their universal stories and memorable tunes. This broad response to what was at first considered to be a strictly confined idiom – blues (and jazz) was marketed as 'race' music, in separate catalogues from other popular music – cannot easily be observed on records, since in those days there was no percentage in recording from white musicians what were in effect cover-versions of black records. A few white singers jumped this barrier, either by transforming the songs enough to deceive the recording men or simply by changing their titles and claiming them as their own compositions.

One artist did neither, but devised his own kind of white man's blues: Jimmie Rodgers, 'America's Blue Yodeller', 'The Father of Country Music'. A Mississippi-born singer whose voice came over on the then new

electrically recorded discs with unusual warmth and clarity, Rodgers yoked together the blues and the yodel, set them to his simple but curiously individual guitar accompaniments, and rode this crossbred all the way uptown. He was probably the first country singer with an undifferentiated appeal thoughout the South (and elsewhere in the United States, too), and certainly the first to stamp a Hollywood brand of star quality upon what was regarded as a rather impersonal music.

As the record business became more aware of its market, or rather of the several distinct regional markets, the notion of lifting blues out of their black milieu and putting them over to white record-buyers began to make good commercial sense. Moreover, white musicians themselves were more and more often looking to black music to supply ideas. White country music was an inherently conservative form, and it needed occasional shocks from the blues or jazz current to keep it lively. In particular, the bands that were springing up in the Thirties in the Southwest – Texas, Oklahoma, parts of Arkansas, and Louisiana – were avid eavesdroppers on the blues and borrowed its songs and ideas wholesale as they developed an exciting new idiom called Western Swing.

Hi-flyers & Playboys

In their devil-may-care robbery of every idiom in sight, Western Swing musicians were the first highwaymen of American music. Not only the blues were pillaged but jazz, swing, Hawaiian music, Mexican mariachi combos, even polka bands. To this magpie's nest of old and new, borrowed and blues, the Western Swing bands brought an instrumental style blended from seemingly conflicting sources. The core of the group was something like the

LEFT *Muddy Waters took the Deep Southern blues to Chicago, plugged them in, and became the father of the modern blues band.*

BELOW *Jimmie Rodgers sang an authentic white man's blues in the Thirties and changed the face of country music for all time.*

traditional country stringband of fiddle(s), banjo, and guitar(s). From conventional popular-band formation came the brass and reed sections – at least one trumpet, a saxophone or two, and a clarinet – and the piano. From the new technology of the mid-Thirties came a wholly new instrument, the amplified steel guitar. Virtually all these instruments were played not in the comparatively straight, melodic manner of earlier country band music but in a variety of 'hot' improvised styles inspired by contemporary jazz. Some of the musicians actually were Southern jazzmen, or at least orchestral players; some even came across like white bluesmen, singing in slurred, slack-mouthed fashion and using the black slang of the day. Western Swing was a refuge for musical misfits, a home for good ol' boys who yearned to be bad.

From the mid-Thirties until World War II bands like Bob Wills & His Texas Playboys, Milton Brown & His Brownies, Bill Boyd's Cowboy Ramblers, the Light Crust Doughboys, the Hi-Flyers, the Tune Wranglers, and the Modern Mountaineers kept the dance halls and juke-joints of Texas swinging. Nearly all of them, in addition to maintaining road schedules that would turn present-day bands grey-haired in a month, kept the airwaves rolling with music from powerful stations in Dallas, Fort Worth, Houston, San Antonio and, especially, in Tulsa, Oklahoma, to the north, where Bob Wills' band broadcast every day over station KVOO – sometimes directly from their steady job at Cain's Dancing Academy (a venue that 40-odd years later was to play host for one memorable night to the Sex Pistols), sometimes by a remote link-up from wherever they were on tour.

With the advent of World War II many of the Western Swing bands dissolved under the pressure of the call-up or essential war work. Of those that held on, some made the trip to the West Coast, echoing the vast 'Okie' migrations of the previous few years in which farming families of the Southwest gave up trying to raise crops in a dustbowl and followed the promise of work in the Californian fruit orchards. (Their grim and poignant story was unforgettably told by the Oklahoma singer and ballad writer Woody Guthrie – the first and most profound model for Bob Dylan.) By now, however, the work opportunities were in the huge ship-building factories. Streaming grimy and exhausted off their shifts, at any time round the clock, the war-workers needed nothing more urgently than familiar dance music, and in enormous halls holding several thousand dancers a new, bigger, and louder Western Swing evolved.

Once the war was over and there was a less frenetic drive for musical satisfaction among Western Swing's one-time audience, it became impossible to payroll such large line-ups. Around 1942-4, as well, a recording ban was imposed by the American Federation of Musicians, during which the momentum of many recording artists' careers was fatally interrupted. When the record industry began to pull itself back together afterwards, the domination of the major companies, RCA Victor, Columbia, and Decca, was broken. Small-time operators everywhere in the United States, but especially on the West Coast, grabbed the options the majors had let slip. They had the knowhow, they had the artists and they could get records cut and manufactured, but for a while they could not match the nationwide distribution painstakingly developed over the past couple of decades by the Big Three. But whether by choice or not, these new

independent labels restored to country music a character it had begun to lose: the variety of distinctive regional styles which it had possessed, in all its richness, when it first shook hands with the record industry back in the early Twenties.

Uptown & Downhome Blues

The course of the blues, meanwhile, had been somewhat similar, and in the immediately postwar years it was virtually identical with that of country music. The first generation of country blues singers had died or been made obsolete by the younger or more adaptable musicians who operated in the northern cities, principally Chicago, where a powerful clique accounted for the majority of blues recordings, on all three of the major labels, for the best part of a decade. Unlike the earlier idiom, urban blues in the North was conceived as group music. The personality of the performance remained that of the singer, but he or she was backed by a small band: piano, guitar(s), bass, drums, often with a harmonica or a horn or two to take over from the voice in instrumental breaks. The quirks of locality which had immediately distinguished one country bluesman from the rest — peculiarities of accent or instrumental technique, or the use of highly localised songs or song-types — mostly disappeared, to be replaced at best by the strong individuality of the leading singers or the studied ingenuity of the finest blues composers. This was the era of a new set of blues standards: Leroy Carr's 'Blues Before Sunrise' and 'Mean Mistreater Mama', Johnnie Temple's 'Louise Louise Blues', Roosevelt Sykes's 'The Night Time Is the Right Time', Jazz Gillum's 'Key to the Highway' — all of them remade countless times by subsequent blues-singers up to the present day, and all pressed into service many times, too, by Western Swing, country, and rockabilly artists.

The Chicago monopoly was not absolute: a few southern-based blues artists weathered the Thirties while playing in acoustic, solo-conceived styles, like Blind Boy Fuller, who played for working people around the tobacco warehouses of North Carolina and made many popular records; his 'Step It Up and Go' was to become a country and rockabilly favourite. Haunting the blues story of the Thirties, too, is the still-shadowy figure of Robert Johnson, a Mississippi singer-guitarist who seems today to stand like a colossus at the crossroads where the old loosely made country blues met the more polished and urgent approach of the North. Though his records seem not to have been widely circulated, and he died not long after making them, Johnson left a remarkably deep personal impression upon the bluesmen who encountered him; and they and others not only kept his songs alive but developed their potential to create some of the most influential music of the early postwar years.

Johnson was also one of the first blues artists to be presented to the international audience of blues enthusiasts, when a reissue compilation, *King of the Delta Blues Singers*, was released in 1961. Reviewing this LP Alexis

Louis Jordan & His Tympany Five yoked a jumping blues-based sound to urban wit and jive, straddling the territories of R&B and jazz. Idolised by black musicians all over the United States, they set the stage for artists such as Chuck Berry.

ABOVE *Bobby 'Blue' Bland united the strains of blues and gospel to become one of the great voices of what would soon be soul music.*

RIGHT *The hypnotic rhythms and slurred singing of Jimmy Reed made for a distinctive brand of Fifties and Sixties blues.*

Korner, himself an architect of the British blues scene, wrote: 'It would be impossible to over-estimate Johnson's importance, either as a performer or as a style-setter for later blues artists. . . . The entire "down-home" or country rhythm-and-blues movement (Chicago style) has been based [in part] on [his] work.' What Korner could not have anticipated was that Johnson's impact would re-echo in musicians generations later in other cultures. No other figure in the history of the blues has wielded a comparable influence upon rock music; it is doubtful if any rock musician grounded in the blues was not at some time besotted with Johnson's work. Eric Clapton, it is hardly too much to say, has built some of his life upon it. It lies hidden, but not very deeply hidden, in

the music of the Rolling Stones – not merely in the Johnson song they used to do, 'Love in Vain' – and of Bob Dylan, whose copy of *King of the Delta Blues Singers* can be spotted, two inches to the left of the cat, on the sleeve of *Bringing It All Back Home*. As one critic, Greil Marcus, has said, 'Johnson is a sort of invisible pop star'.

The Mississippi Delta blues milieu in which Johnson grew up also furnished all the major artists in one section of postwar blues, the music that took shape in the country around Memphis in the late Forties and then shipped itself virtually *en bloc* northwards to Chicago. Muddy Waters, Howlin' Wolf, Sonny Boy Williamson, Jimmy Reed, and – in Detroit rather than Chicago – John Lee Hooker, achieved a revolution that seems, on the face of it, implausible. They replaced the urbane and by now rather stereotyped band music of the Thirties generation with a style that was partly a brusque throwback to earlier rural blues, partly a joyous discovery of how that music could be transformed and energised by electricity. Roaring and strutting in steamy neighbourhood bars, to the howling of amplified harmonica and bottleneck guitar, the new bluesmen of the northern ghettos not only transformed the city blues scene but wrote the sourcebook of the British R&B revival.

Until the Chicago irruption of the early Fifties, the dominant blues styles had been those of the West Coast. Whereas Chicago drew its black population, and thus its blues musicians, from deep southern states like Mississippi and Arkansas, the exodus to California had been from the Southwest, and naturally the transported music reflected, in each case, its stylistic origins. Mississippi country blues had a heavy duple-time (DAH-dah) rhythm and a dark, even ominous vocal tone, whereas Texas was characterised by lighter triplet rhythms

(DAH-dah-dah) and voices pitched higher, often delivered almost conversationally. When southwestern blues remoulded itself in California in the mid-Forties it was, by comparison with Chicago's, a subtle and understated music: the guitarists played skipping single-string runs and jazz chords, the drummers used their brushes a lot, the vocalists adopted a confidential manner. It was a music of wit and urban flash, pleading and sardonic by turns. Its masters were T-Bone Walker, the father of modern blues-guitar playing; the wispy-voiced singer-

pianist Charles Brown; the boogie specialists like Amos Milburn.

Some of these qualities had been prefigured in the late Thirties and early Forties by Louis Jordan, a singer and alto saxophonist, who with his brisk little combo the Tympany Five made many amusing and culturally evocative records: 'Saturday Night Fish Fry', 'Ain't Nobody Here But Us Chickens', 'Choo Choo Ch' Boogie', 'What's the Use of Getting Sober (When You Gonna Get Drunk Again)?'. Jordan had the wit and verbal agility of Chuck Berry (though not his desegregated view of teenage culture), and his music has proved to be durable. British pub bands of the early Eighties have been the latest of many to go song-raiding in Jordan's banks.

Much of what has happened in the blues since the shaping postwar decade has been by way of a fusion of Chicago and West Coast styles. B.B. King had the Mississippi/Memphis background that might have taken him to Chicago, but he absorbed T-Bone Walker's guitar style early on and conceptually straddled the blues world. King's enormous impact on American music has made him the model of almost all blues guitarists and singers ever since – but this status was gained for him in part by the admiration of rock guitarists, who brought him in front of their own audiences.

The Gospel Strain

In the singing of B. B. King, and contemporary blues or soul artists such as Bobby 'Blue' Bland, the spirit of the blues dwells in a curious harmony with that of gospel music. Virtually every soul singer, and many blues singers, first sang in public with local gospel groups or in church choirs. The world of the black gospel group is rather enclosed, with its own circuit of churches and auditoriums and its own record-companies. As a matter of spiritual principle gospel people do not mix with sinful – that is, blues-playing – folk. But since gospel is also an immensely emotional, demonstrative music it has appealed to many artists as much by its showbiz glitter as by its religious precepts, and from gospel's ranks many superb singers have risen and unconcernedly cashed in their Christian union cards for the secular gravy: Little Richard, Sam Cooke, Clyde McPhatter (sometime lead singer of the Drifters), Aretha Franklin, and many others.

White gospel groups belong to their own, musically more straitlaced, tradition of quartet singing, which is a nicely balanced format but not often very exciting. The overlapping vocal lines, the abrupt contrast of high and low voices, the acceleration of fervour that typify black gospel group singing are heard in generally more muted versions in white sacred music. (An exception to this is the frenzied music of poor-white fundamentalist sects like the Holiness (Sanctified, 'Holy Roller') churches, which approve of stringed instruments and unbridled singing, but this is congregational music, not readily transferable to any recognised commercial idiom, and practised in any case by only a small fraction of white Southerners.) White gospel voices tend to be conventionally 'good' and relatively free of the accentual colour and stylistic mannerisms that enhance – you might even say define – country music singing. Nonetheless the popular white quartets of the Forties and Fifties, such as the Brown's Ferry Four, the Blackwood Brothers, and the Statesmen, made a considerable, although seldom acknowledged, contribution to rock 'n' roll; Elvis Presley was an avid fan of the last two groups and often attended 'all-night sings'.

Honkytonking

While black gospel had an uneasy, almost illicit musical relationship with blues and R&B, white gospel turned its face firmly against most country music of the Forties and Fifties, and the overlap of either artists or styles was rare. The most forceful voices of country music were the honkytonk artists like Ernest Tubb, Kitty Wells, Webb Pierce, and Lefty Frizzell, with their songs of cheating ('Slipping Around', 'Wild Side of Life'), drinking ('There Stands the Glass'), and loneliness ('Walking the Floor Over You'). It was tough blue-collar music, and it was crafted for the unpredictable speaker sound of the jukebox – very much as Phil Spector's hits, years later, were designed for the tinny sound of car radios: wailing fiddles and pedal steel guitars, thumping rhythms on guitar and bass, and strong, uncomplicated voices that could ride effortlessly above the static.

The greatest of the honkytonk singers was Hank Williams, whose short but fiery life and awesome power to touch the hearts of his audience recalled Jimmie Rodgers and went a step further. Like Rodgers, Williams had been drenched by the blues and would never dry out – but his genius was for the straight, no-fuss country song, with a true-life storyline and unforgettable refrain, and he wrote more of them, or more that will live, than anyone of his time: 'Cold, Cold Heart', 'You Win Again', 'Your Cheatin' Heart', 'I'm So Lonesome I Could Cry', 'There'll Be No Teardrops Tonight', dozens more.

Williams put the 'I' of deeply felt personal experience into an idiom that had still not quite shaken off the third-person narrative technique inherited from Old World balladry. As well as modernising country music he brought it into the world of commonplace romance inhabited by mainstream popular songs, and was the first great country-pop crossover artist. And he achieved a glamour by dying alone, in the back of a car, from a drug overdose before he was 30.

The image of honkytonk music was that of a man down on his luck, without money, deserted by lovers and friends, his only home a bar-room and his only friend a glass. Nothing could have been more distasteful to the God-fearing country singers of the era like Roy Acuff and Hank Snow, who sang instead about innocent subjects like trains (Acuff's 'Wabash Cannonball' and 'Freight Train Blues', the latter picked up later by Dylan; Snow's 'I'm Moving On' and 'The Golden Rocket') or made a pact with the Lord in country sacred songs like Acuff's 'Great Speckled Bird' – a peculiar title (from the book of Jeremiah), but one of the greatest hits and most enduring melodies in country music. The spiritual world of Acuff and Snow and their kind, who dominated the influential radio show broadcast every week from Nashville, Tennessee, the Grand Ol' Opry, was also shared by many of the leading artists in bluegrass.

ABOVE *The Ryman Auditorium at Nashville, famous home of Grand Ol' Opry until 1974, is now a stop on country music tourist trips.*

RIGHT *Hank Williams at the Opry microphone. Like Jimmy Rodgers he was a bluesman born white – and country music's greatest songwriter.*

Bluegrass

Whereas Western Swing had been the great extender of country music, squeezing its bag of tricks ever fuller with notions drawn from blues and jazz and elsewhere, bluegrass was the ultimate conservative idiom. Descended from the mountain stringband music of the Twenties and Thirties, at first it merely adapted that fiddle-banjo-guitar format by adding a bass and a mandolin. What gave it real distinction was the innovative skill of its first exponents – the snappy three-finger banjo-playing of Earl Scruggs, the bluesy mandolin and mountain-high tenor singing of Bill Monroe – and the heart-searching three-part and four-part harmonies that it introduced to country music, poignantly exemplified by the Stanley Brothers. Yet for all its traditional observances – the use of old ballads, the leaning towards old-time religion, the avoidance of electric instruments – bluegrass was in a quiet way revolutionary. Steeped in the blues, it brought back into country music the lonesome anguish of the black experience.

Despite their common mixed parentage of country music and blues, bluegrass and rock 'n' roll bore little family resemblance. Indeed, bluegrass was chased off the stage in the mid-Fifties by rock 'n' roll, much to its moral and professional chagrin. Yet early rock 'n' roll often revealed its bluegrass connections. The Everly Brothers' harmonies were almost pure bluegrass; the jumping eight-to-the-bar bass playing of Bill Black on Presley's first records matched that on Bill Monroe's first bluegrass sessions seven or eight years earlier. The crisp group-playing and tight-throated vocal styles of bluegrass also echo in rock 'n' roll's sibling, rockabilly.

Rockabilly

With a nod of apology to the purists, we can simply define rockabilly as original Southern rock 'n' roll of the middle-to-late Fifties. The name implies rock 'n' roll with a hillbilly (that is, country music) bias, and rockabilly did have more bluegrass flavour than the Northern rock 'n' roll of Bill Haley, which was inspired jointly by Western Swing and black R&B. Rockabilly was not necessarily 'whiter' than other contemporary forms of rock 'n' roll, but it had a country-boy lack of sophistication and hectic rhythms, and its singers went closer to the borderline between commitment and frenzy. Its characteristics are clipped, jittery lead-guitar playing, slapped bass, and a range of vocal mannerisms encompassing the mumble, the hiccup, the stutter, and the shriek. Presley's first recordings for the Sun label in Memphis and, even more vividly, Carl Perkins's sides that shortly followed them typify rockabilly in its glory; but it was a truly 'roots' music and had practitioners all over the South, particularly in areas like Tennessee and Virginia, where it attracted musicians restless within the musical and social confines of bluegrass. It also caught on in the upland-South and in northern cities that had large southern immigrant populations, like Detroit and Cincinnati. Someone once remarked sourly: 'Blues is a music of bare competence, and that's what blues musicians are – barely competent.' If there is any truth in that, it goes double for rockabilly, which enjoyed so localised a vogue that almost any small-town band could get a few hundred records cut and pressed. As a flood of reissues in recent years has shown, a lot of it was resolutely primitive – but it had high spirits that somehow evaporated when, as quickly happened, artists and record-companies insensible to its cultural subtleties tried to turn it into nationally marketable rock 'n' roll.

King of the Indies

All these musical tracks – blues, country music, Western Swing, bluegrass, gospel, rockabilly – converged in the great sorting-yard of rock 'n' roll and thereafter a wide, shining way stretches to the present. Putting date, location and architect to that event is the great pursuit of rock 'n' roll historians, and the current consensus seems to be 1954, Memphis, and Sam Phillips of Sun Records. (See the next chapter for more on this combination.) But there were test-runs before that, unintentional 'feasibility trials' which sorted the useful ingredients from the irrelevant and in some cases came very close to making the rock 'n' roll discovery ahead of schedule.

A recurrent motif of rockabilly was boogie-woogie, which had enjoyed a huge popularity in the late Forties. A piano-based music invented by the black house-party pianists of the Twenties and Thirties, it was effortlessly transplanted into country music, and nowhere with more dedication than on the Los Angeles label Capitol. Part-owned by Hollywood songwriter Johnny Mercer, Capitol had early success with mainstream pop acts like Nat 'King' Cole and Frank Sinatra, but its country stable

of Merle Travis, Tex ('Smoke, Smoke, Smoke That Cigarette') Williams, Tennessee Ernie Ford, and others pioneered a brash new idiom, country boogie. Saddled to the romping eight-to-the-bar beat, bristling with tearaway solos on piano and guitar, country-boogie songs borrowed the humour of Western Swing and the jive of Louis Jordan in a music both witty and stomping.

Capitol was never an independent in the classic sense – it started with money, knowhow, and class, whereas the true indie got by on overdrafts, instinct, and nerve – together, often, with a certain contractual sleight-of-hand. Certainly nobody could accuse King Records of having class, still less its proprietor, the short, fat, asthmatic, and irascible Syd Nathan. And yet King in Cincinnati was the leading indie of the Forties and Fifties, and in retrospect either the most perceptive or the luckiest company ever to throw a bearhug around American music – for King signed, and held on to, many of the leading artists in country music, Western Swing, blues, R&B, gospel (black and white), rockabilly, country boogie, and bluegrass.

More remarkable than King's roster, however, was a marketing strategy that the company seems to have pioneered. Hit records from the hillbilly section of the catalogue would be given to black artists to record. So the jocular 'Bloodshot Eyes', having sold well in joint composer Hank Penny's Western Swing-flavoured ver-

LEFT *The Stanley Brothers, Ralph (with banjo) and Carter: joint creators, with Bill Monroe, of the 'high lonesome sound' of bluegrass.*

ABOVE *Bill Monroe & the Blue Grass Boys: the classic line-up of fiddle, banjo, mandolin, bass and guitar as Monroe pioneered it.*

sion, was turned by Wynonie Harris into brawling R&B. Cross-overs in the other direction were rarer, but several of King's country acts had blues-inspired hits.

Ostensibly King was just wringing two sets of sales-figures from a single composition, chiefly for the benefit of the company's publishing wing. But the label could not help elasticating the tastes of its patrons, by offering them familiar songs in unfamiliar settings (or, of course, the reverse). Yet King never made that next logical jump, to the notion of a single artist uniting two styles, two traditions — perhaps, in part, because Nathan, unlike Sam Phillips, had no creative or musical-philosophical axe to grind. For the brainwave, or accident, of rock 'n' roll we must return to Presley — not as the planner of that stylistic and cultural alliance, but as the vivid emblem of the time, the place and the mood in which it happened.

Rock 'n' roll is a quintessentially American music — but, more than that, it is a music that could have evolved only where and only when it did. Several experiments — some planned, some entirely accidental — had to be tried and learned from, or discarded, before it became possible. It is only when we look back now that it seems that the dawning of rock 'n' roll was inevitable.

The Breakthrough

In North America the ferment that greeted the breakthrough of rock 'n' roll was fanned by racial and religious segregationists, political opportunists, self-appointed arbiters of public morality, and the previously complacent old guard of the record industry. The music itself was not their great worry, nor even the newly popularised generic name rock 'n' roll. The panic started when what had seemed to be comfortably exploitable substrata of American society and music began coalescing into an uncontrollable phenomenon of unimaginable destiny.

In Britain similar claptrap spouted from predictable mouths, culminating in May 1958 with the public pillorying of Jerry Lee Lewis. Generally, though, there was little paranoia behind the British establishment's condemnation of rock 'n' roll; there was a certain amount of public agitation about teddy boys and the unruly behaviour of postwar youth in general, but that hardly

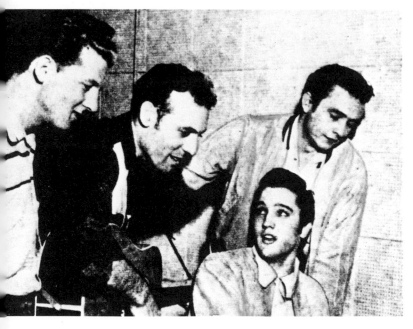

ABOVE *Sun stars, December 1956: Elvis Presley (seated) at Sun studios with Carl Perkins (with guitar) overlooked by Jerry* *Lee Lewis (left) and rising country star Johnny Cash (right).* RIGHT *Perkins, now a popular country singer, in the Seventies.*

amounted to a major upheaval of British society. As for the music, apart from a minority group, most of them jazz musicians and fans, nobody in Britain knew anything about the roots of rock 'n' roll or its social implications. Of those who did, most could not see the alien American sounds being successfully translated to Britain. Bandleader Ted Heath's view was fairly typical: 'I don't think the rock 'n' roll craze will come to Britain. You see, it is primarily for the coloured population. I can't ever see it becoming a real craze.'

By the time he said that, in May 1956, Heath was already wrong: the 'craze' had arrived. Bill Haley and the Comets already had six British chart entries, Lonnie Donegan had two hits to his credit, and on the very day that Heath's prophecy was published Elvis Presley first entered the British Top 20 with 'Heartbreak Hotel'. A week later Carl Perkins was in the chart too, shortly followed, over the summer of 1956, by Frankie Lymon and the Teenagers, Fats Domino, Gene Vincent and the Blue Caps, and the Platters. Had bandleader Heath qualified his statement, saying something like: 'I don't think rock 'n' roll will come to be much more than a craze in Britain. You see, it isn't indigenous to our nature. I can't ever see it lasting in its raw form,' in the short term he would have been substantially right.

The original invasion of Americal rock 'n' roll music irrevocably changed the lives of many British teenagers of the Fifties. But the vast majority was only briefly touched by the alien phenomenon; beneath the enthusiasm for certain hits or a temporary crush on one or other of the stars, traditional social values were largely unaffected.

Similarly, most people in the British record industry failed to take original rock 'n' roll seriously; it was an inexplicable fad, to be ignored, or temporarily exploited while they manipulated it into something more understandable and acceptable. Just as, in pre-rock times, all the most popular waves of American music had to some extent been appropriated by the British record industry, there was obviously an opportunity here to follow this latest American nonsense with more profitably marketable British artists and recordings. Some of the younger bucks in the business, a few of whom had an inkling that rock 'n' roll was more than just a freak departure from normality, set about looking for British rockers. There was none to be found.

During the latter half of 1956 the first British artists specifically promoted as rock 'n' rollers began to appear, and by 1959 there were apparently almost as many young British rockers vying for success as there were American originators. In truth, though, Britain had not yet been long enough exposed to the music to have yielded any *real* rockers – nor had the British record industry fully discovered what it was about American rock 'n' roll records that made them sound so dynamic. At best – and a few were very good of their type – the new British artists, accompanists, and producers artfully simulated rock 'n' roll. But somehow even the most inspired British efforts came out sounding cosier, more obviously manufactured, than the genuine, original, American article.

As it happened, it didn't really matter: by 1959 the original wave of American rock 'n' roll was all but washed up. Partly through accidents and coincidences,

but mainly by concerted effort, the American establishment seemed to have brought the beast under control and was busily breaking it down to a soft, wet, malleable parody of its former self – similar to the British version. Like all good monsters rock 'n' roll was soon to confound its oppressors by breaking loose again in mutant forms, primarily through American blacks and British whites – but that would be a rather more self-conscious era. The musical styles might be related, but most of the subsequent heroes could not really be compared to the originators who inspired them.

Bill Haley

First came the roots, then came Bill Haley and the Comets – as unlikely a group of rock 'n' roll pioneers as could today be imagined. A chubby-faced, avuncular character even when young, Haley was nearing his 30th birthday when he shot to 'overnight' fame; most of his band looked much older. He was not a great singer, writer, musician, or stylist, nor was the band a hotbed of musical revolutionaries. With Haley on rhythm guitar the Comets fielded a lead electric guitar, steel guitar, tenor sax, acoustic bass, and drums. They were a competent small dance combo that did not so much swing as keep time – almost strict-tempo style, in fact. In that respect

UPPER *Bill Haley and the Comets remained a popular stage act long after the hits stopped coming; here they are at a concert in the mid-Sixties.*
LOWER *Country Boy Bill, before the breakthrough.*

Sam Phillips and his recording studio would prove to be the focal point of the rock 'n' roll explosion. Ike Turner would prove to be an important force in the development of R&B and, with his later protégée and wife, Tina, a major soul star. Haley's first attempt at R&B moved no mountains, but his second R&B cover version, 'Rock the Joint' (1952), was by far his best-received record to date. Encouraged by this enthusiastic public reaction, the following year he wrote and recorded his own whimsical pastiche of R&B, 'Crazy Man Crazy', and in August 1953 found himself with a hit.

Events then moved apace. In March 1954 Haley and his band, by then named the Comets, were signed by the major label Decca and placed in the care of Milt Gabler, an experienced producer who had supervised most of R&B pioneer Louis Jordan's influential hits. Gabler fulfilled the Comets' musical potential, so that, in his own words, 'They got a sound that had the drive of [Jordan's] Tympany Five and the color of country and western.'

In May 1954 the group's first Decca release, 'Rock Around the Clock' (designated a foxtrot), sold encouragingly well. But it was the follow-up, a modified version of Joe Turner's R&B hit 'Shake, Rattle and Roll', that really set the cash-registers ringing, prompting Decca to repromote 'Rock Around the Clock' to even greater success and enabling the song's publisher, Dave Myers, who was also acting as Haley's manager, to persuade MGM to feature the record in the movie *The Blackboard Jungle* (1955), an exposé of American juvenile delinquency. Myers' move turned out to be a master-stroke.

When *The Blackboard Jungle* hit the cinema circuits, Haley, the Comets, and rock 'n' roll made the big time. Three years after the song had first been offered to Haley and a year after he had finally recorded it, 'Rock Around the Clock' became an anthem for the era, with Haley the unlikely figurehead. For a while he kept ahead of the game, starring in the first rock 'n' roll movies and in 1955-6 clocking up a dozen or so hits, whose total worldwide sales still keep his name in the all-time best-seller league of rock. By the time he first appeared in Britain, however, in February 1957, he was already an anachronism: affable and never less good in concert than on his records, but outdated by the younger studs who had appeared in his wake. One reviewer observed of his first London concert: 'Measured by the yardstick of family entertainers, (it) is as wholesome and forthright as a Billy Cotton Band Show.'

Elvis Presley

Haley and a changing line-up of Comets continued recording and touring until his death in 1981, but apart from periodic reissues of his original hits – especially in Britain and continental Europe, where he retained his most loyal following – he was never again a serious contender for chart honours. Foremost among the reasons for his rapid fall from grace was the spectacular arrival from seemingly nowhere to world-stage centre of Elvis Presley.

As a figurehead for this new phenomenon called rock 'n' roll Elvis Presley seemed to be everything that Haley was not. Ten years Haley's junior, he looked mean, moody, and magnificent. In place of Haley's winsome

Elvis Presley in his classic hip-swivelling routine on the Milton Berle television show in 1956. Behind him is Scotty Moore, Presley's lead guitarist from the earliest recording sessions.

they were probably better than all the other rock 'n' roll heroes. Unlike the more erratically structured hits of others, Haley and the Comets' releases were consistently good to dance to – guaranteed floor-fillers. The band was also loud, and by the time they hit the headlines their records were being extremely well produced to emphasize their solid beat. Most important of all, they were fortunate in being the first act to introduce rock 'n' roll music to a mass audience.

Raised in a farming family in Chester, near Philadelphia (Pennsylvania), Haley inevitably heard the urban sounds of swing but was also bred on the locally popular country music. Between 1945 and 1948 he toured many states as a small-time country singer, before settling down in Chester, working for local radio station WPWA, and forming the Four Aces of Western Swing. In 1949 the group's regular broadcasts brought them a recording contract with a small local label; but it was a change to a slightly larger company and a different sound that gave the first hint of what was to come. In 1951 Haley and his band, renamed the Saddlemen, made their first recording for the new company – a cover version of the southern black R&B smash 'Rocket 88', recorded a month or so earlier by Jackie Brenston with Ike Turner's band at Sam Phillips' studio in Memphis.

joviality, he exuded sex and a sense of rebellion; he moulded the music into a personal statement instead of reducing it to a predictable formula; his was so radical a departure that at first it was incomprehensible to a lot of his own generation, never mind the old folk. Behind the rebellious image, Presley was not in fact so dramatically different. Shy and even gauche except when among his peers or on stage, he was respectful to his elders, doted on his mother and was a natural son of the society that spawned him. He was also, however, a cauldron of untamed talent and energy. Whereas Haley had gradually developed a catchy blend of musical influences that was less than the sum of its parts, Presley almost immediately outpaced his influences and unconsciously created something new. Even so, his commanding success was not quite as overnight as it seemed.

Elvis Presley's musical roots were principally deep-southern gospel, blues, and country. Born in Mississippi, he was raised amidst the fervour of Pentecostal religion and the racially shared poverty, emotions and music of an otherwise rigidly segregationist state. When he was 13 his parents moved to Memphis where he heard the early R&B stars on radio station WDIA and became aware of Sam Phillips' recording studio on Union Avenue, the opening and growing importance of which coincided with his own adolescent development. He first used the studio in April 1953 to make a private recording for his mother, and he was soon back in earnest,

auditioning for a professional recording contract with Phillips' Sun label.

During several encouraging but unfulfilling trials Elvis was introduced to guitarist Scotty Moore and bass player Bill Black. In July 1954 it was with these accompanists that he finally excited the astute ear of Phillips with an abandoned, impromptu reworking of Mississippi-born Arthur Crudup's Forties blues hit, 'That's All Right (Mama)'. For the flip of Presley's first Sun single Phillips chose his equally personalised romp through Bill Monroe's Forties country bluegrass hit, 'Blue Moon of Kentucky': two songs from musically comparable but socially segregated roots, dynamically reinterpreted

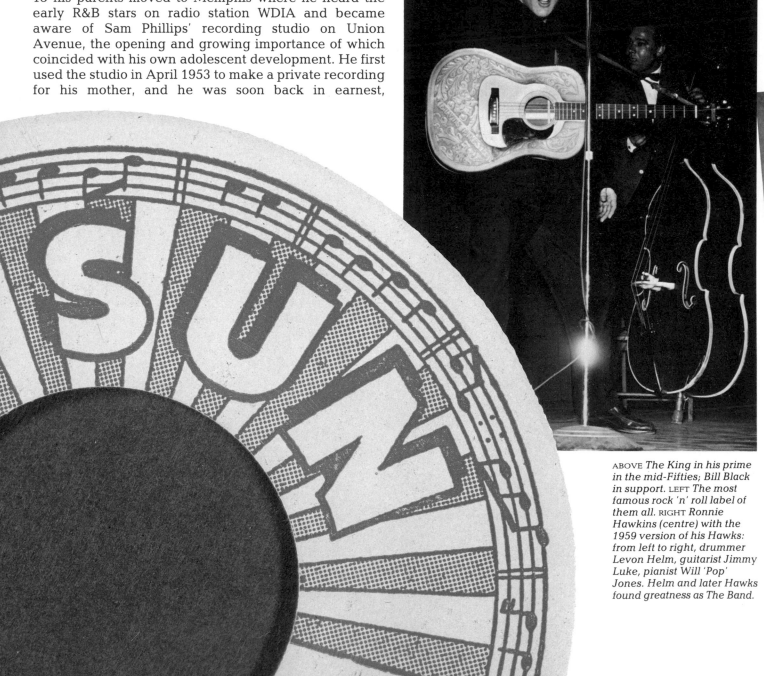

ABOVE *The King in his prime in the mid-Fifties; Bill Black in support.* LEFT *The most famous rock 'n' roll label of them all.* RIGHT *Ronnie Hawkins (centre) with the 1959 version of his Hawks: from left to right, drummer Levon Helm, guitarist Jimmy Luke, pianist Will 'Pop' Jones. Helm and later Hawks found greatness as The Band.*

straight down the middle and out into uncharted territory. After one local airing of a test pressing, public demand confirmed the release as a local hit before Phillips had even had time to get the records manufactured and delivered to record outlets.

Over the next 18 months four more of Presley's revitalised R&B/country Sun couplings met with increasing regional success, while he barnstormed around the southern country circuit, rapidly progressing from novelty status to hysterically received showstopper. He remained strictly a Confederate phenomenon, though, until autumn of 1955, when he was adopted by the grand-daddy of all hustler-managers, the self-styled 'Colonel' Tom Parker, and, through Parker, was signed by RCA Records, which had been prompted by Decca's success with Bill Haley to look out for a competitive act. Within weeks of its being recorded (in January 1956) Presley's first RCA single, 'Heartbreak Hotel', was No 1 on the national pop chart, and his first national TV appearances were causing apoplexies of disgust or delight, depending on the viewer's age and inclination.

Elvis was not the first southern white kid of his generation to innocently but potently mix musical influences in a 'revolutionary' rock 'n' roll style. Some, like

Ronnie Hawkins (born two days after Elvis, in Arkansas), were precociously boppin' the blues on stage while Presley was still in high school, but did not record until after Elvis had opened up the opportunities. Others, like Sonny Fisher (born in 1931 in North Texas), may even have influenced or at least helped to encourage the budding Presley, and first recorded in much the same style around the same time as Elvis. It was a general trend, not a one-man movement. But once he got started, on stage and record, Elvis was undoubtedly the most dynamic of the young 'hillbilly bopcats' – and his

unprecedented zoom to international fame was the key that unlocked the floodgate of rock 'n' roll.

During the two years or so between his international breakthrough in 1956 and his induction into the US Army in March 1958, Elvis was the object of massive extremes of public adulation and abuse. Despite the pressures, he maintained a remarkably consistent excitement on record. With a bigger studio, and with his two original accompanists augmented by a second guitarist, pianist, drummer, and, frequently, the vocal quartet the Jordanaires, the sound of his records was inevitably fuller, more rounded than his Sun sides. But there was little compromise in their content. Although he was now given specially written songs to record – songs that were deliberately conceived for his voice and style rather than spontaneously created rock 'n' roll – many of them came from excellent young writers such as Otis Blackwell or Jerry Leiber and Mike Stoller, and Elvis also continued to record many personalised reworkings of R&B and country songs. However, because of the pressures and at the behest of Parker, his previously hectic touring schedule was quickly curtailed and replaced by annual movie appearances. The first four, *Love Me Tender* (1956), *Loving You* and *Jailhouse Rock* (both 1957), and *King Creole* (1958) – and particularly the last three – were strong enough to confound his critics and delight his fans. But, however successful, they were not a completely satisfactory substitute for live concerts.

When Elvis went into the army he was still the undisputed King of Rock 'n' Roll, at least in worldwide popularity, sales, and influence, although several other American rockers were by then more highly regarded by their own international legions of fans. When he emerged again in March 1960 his personal standing was if anything greater than before. Time and patriotic duty had made him respectable to many who had previously found him intolerable. The music scene, however, had changed considerably; the raw rockers had disappeared, to be replaced by a softer breed of teen idol.

Immediately after leaving the army, and despite a mammoth hit with 'It's Now or Never', which had more in common with Mario Lanza's version of 'O sole mio' than with rock 'n' roll, Elvis made a group of fine recordings while it was still uncertain whether his reputation had survived his absence. Once his apparent ominpotence was reestablished, however, the Elvis Presley entourage slumped complacently back on its monumental wallet and turned a blind eye to reality.

Elvis's innate talent still occasionally wrung memorable moments from his foundering career, but for most of the Sixties his film and record output degenerated into a grotesque betrayal of everthing he had originally seemed to represent. It was not until long after a new rock revolution had been created by others that in 1968, he finally emerged from artistic torpor to test himself against the new blood.

Elvis's last 10 years were like a dramatised replay of his career to that point: triumphant return, looking and sounding magnificent; stabilisation into a successfully proven routine; degeneration. This second time around, though, the degeneration was, tragically, mental and physical. Nonetheless, when Elvis died in August 1977 he had proved himself to be not only the most influential rock 'n' roll originator but one of the very few original rockers to survive and succeed again on more than simple nostalgia.

To differentiate them from the black, predominantly urban R&B records that were originally popularised as rock 'n' roll by American DJs like Alan Freed, the more rural-rooted early recordings of Elvis and his southern white contemporaries were occasionally tagged 'rockabilly' by American trade papers. It was a reasonable distinction: the southern whites were inspired by more primitive musical roots than were the urban black R&B stars who were their immediate predecessors. At the same time, and by complete coincidence, a group of British jazz traditionalists were reviving even older American country-blues roots. They called their efforts skiffle. From their ranks came Anthony 'Lonnie' Donegan.

Skiffle

British skiffle – the term was originally used of the juicy blues parties of the American Depression years – was not closely comparable to rockabilly; among many other differences it was more a deliberately amateurish recreation of a 'folk' idiom than a rush of blood to the vitals. Nor were most of the vaguely academic revivalists remotely similar to the newly emerging American rockers; they would probably have been disdainfully amused had anyone suggested they were. It was the loose, rhythmic vitality of skiffle that was distantly equivalent to rockabilly – that, and the fact that anyone who could find three strummable chords on a cheap guitar could have a go for himself. Before rock 'n' roll crossed the Atlantic the skiffle craze was already spreading out from the jazz-club circle of its instigators. As the first shockwaves of rock arrived, Donegan was bounced into national prominence and seemingly every street in Britain suddenly boasted an amateur skiffle group.

A Glasgow-born Londoner of Irish descent, Donegan had played folk and jazz music throughout his teens before joining Ken Colyer's revivalist traditional jazz band in 1952. With Colyer's band he first started fronting skiffle interludes within the main set. The following year he moved to Chris Barber's band for a similar role, and in 1954 he was recorded as the novelty feature on a Chris Barber LP, performing a couple of pre-war country blues tunes. One of them, 'Rock Island Line – an old Leadbelly favourite – Donegan sang in appropriate train-like tempo, building from a standing start to breakneck, barely comprehensible speed. It wasn't rock 'n' roll, exactly, but it was the wildest sound on any British record of the day. Public demand eventually prompted the release of 'Rock Island Line' as a single in late 1955, and by January 1956 Donegan was in the British Top 10, four months before Elvis's first UK success.

During 1956-7 Donegan dominated the initial British response to American rock 'n' roll with many similar hits; he was the biggest British influence of the era, inspiring many young hopefuls like John Lennon to form their first groups. And skiffle in general had deeper repercussions than the Tin Pan Alley pop-rock which followed it. Alexis Korner, for instance, who replaced Donegan in the Colyer and Barber bands before launching his own skiffle group and club, would be the catalyst of the London-based R&B boom of the Sixties.

ABOVE *Roy Orbison recorded rockabilly for Sun, but broke internationally as a balladeer.* OPPOSITE *Jerry Lee Lewis may have* *donned a bow tie and dapper suit for this late-Sixties TV show but he remained the boogie-woogie Killer of old.*

Sun Stars

Meanwhile, back in Memphis in late 1955, Sam Phillips was looking for a replacement for Elvis. An ex-DJ from Florence, Alabama, Phillips had moved to Memphis in 1946 and had quickly become aware of the city's pivotal position amid the developing R&B and country-music scenes of the South. In 1950 he started his Memphis Recording Service, opening a small studio which was soon the source of many R&B hits by locally based black acts, several of whom would become major names in later years. Initially the recordings were issued by companies as far afield as Chicago and Los Angeles, but in February 1952 Phillips founded the Sun record label and began building his own roster of acts. Despite a number of local successes with R&B and country recordings, the company was not doing too well until Phillips sold Elvis's contract to RCA in November 1955.

During 1955-9 Sun attracted and recorded many fine artists. Some, like Roy Orbison and Charlie Rich, eventually found fame with different companies; others, like Billy Riley, never made much chart impact but were in fact as talented and exciting as many more successful rockers. Apart from Johnny Cash, whose first country hits were on Sun, only two of the company's finds followed Elvis up the charts during the heyday of rock 'n' roll. First in line was Carl Perkins.

Perkins joined Sun in October 1954 and came up with his breakthrough smash hit, a genuine rock 'n' roll anthem, one month after Elvis left for RCA. The song was 'Blue Suede Shoes'. Elvis quickly covered it for his new

label but it was Carl's original version that was the bigger American hit. In Britain the positions were reversed. Following the hit, Perkins was briefly touted by Sun as the next Elvis. It was not a realistic claim. Although as a writer and guitarist Perkins was by far the more talented of the two, he did not have the looks, the fire, the charisma of Elvis. He did, however, write and record many other brilliant songs, including 'Honey Don't', 'Boppin' the Blues', 'Put your Cat Clothes On', and 'Pink Pedal Pushers' – classics all.

After a desperate patch, Perkins resurfaced in the Sixties to great acclaim, particularly in Britain, and established a solid career as a moderately successful country singer and touring rock 'n' roll legend.

Jerry Lee Lewis

Virtually the same could be said of Sun's other great hero; but somehow, in his case, the words seem inadequate – like describing Muhammad Ali as a passable

boxer. For apart from the fact that he was late onto record, it is hard to refute the widely held belief that Jerry Lee Lewis turned out to be the greatest rocker of them all.

Lewis was raised in the same Pentecostal religious tradition and cultural setting as Elvis and was exposed to almost identical musical influences. From there on the two young rebs grew to be as different as milkshake and moonshine. Unlike Presley and other contemporaries, Lewis really was as outrageously extreme as his later image. By the time he rapped on Sun's door in the autumn of 1956 he had been expelled from preacher-training college for playing hymns boogie-woogie style; he had been twice married, once bigamously; and he had been resident blues 'n' boogie man in brothels and cut-throat dives along the Mississippi waterfront. He was also without the slightest trace of insecurity about the invincibility of his own talent.

The bare facts of the self-styled Killer's breakthrough are few but frenetic. After one southern regional hit, in the late summer of 1957 he smashed to international success with a lascivious rockin' boogie, 'Whole Lotta

Shakin' Goin' On', quickly followed by an even wilder affront to conservative morality, 'Great Balls of Fire'. Also in late 1957 he quietly entered his third marriage – to his 13-year-old second cousin, Myra. Such marriages were perfectly legal and not particularly unusual in Louisiana. While his next hit, 'Breathless', was climbing the charts in May 1958, he appeared in London, caught the full force of a kick from the high horse of British morality, ostensibly because of his 'unacceptable' marriage, and was effectively knocked out of the big time for the next 10 years. In 1968 he returned to establishment favour with the first of a string of American country hits. By the mid-Seventies his second wave of success had ebbed to more modest proportions but he remains a star booking, the most successful survivor of the rock 'n' roll originators.

At the time of the public outcry that felled his career, Lewis was looking set to challenge Presley's supremacy, especially as Elvis had just been called up into the army. But even without Lewis's forced exclusion from the race it is doubtful whether he would have remained top dog for long, for by 1958 rock 'n' roll was already being changed into a commercial parody that was alien to his nature. Jerry Lee Lewis has never been one to compromise his own feelings, and therefore his music, for the sake of commercial success. In his long and prolific career there have been occasional attempts by producers to modify his style, and naturally the overall sound of his records has been affected by changing technology. Throughout it all he has remained the piano-pumpin' personaliser of country weepers and riotous rockers.

In July 1981 Lewis was rushed into a Memphis hospital for emergency surgery on a stomach ruptured by many years of wild living. His condition was critical, his chances 50/50. Upon recovery and release he bought himself a $40,000 customised Cadillac, a $25,000 Chevrolet Corvette, a good long cigar, and a bottle of his favourite whiskey. 'As long as they gimme a piano I'll be out there,' he proclaimed. 'They try to take that away, I'm gonna kick some ass.' There speaks the true voice of rock 'n' roll.

Lewis's uncompromising personality and music attracted a higher proportion of male fans than most other rockers. He had masses of female admirers as well, of course, and still has, but he was never really a teen idol. Most of the younger girls found him intimidating rather than sexy. Much the same could be said of Gene Vincent, who was signed by Capitol Records as their answer to Elvis but ended up a rockers' cult hero rather than an international phenomenon.

Gene Vincent

When he started out Vincent was actually a personable young Southerner, a little rough around the edges and unfortunately disabled by a leg injury incurred in 1955 while he was a naval dispatch rider, but averagely wholesome. By the time of his death from alcoholism in 1971 he had become a travesty of his image, perman-

NEAR RIGHT *Gene Vincent at the start of his UK phase (December 1959), supported here by British rock 'n' roll guitarist Joe Brown.*

FAR RIGHT *Eddie Cochran on stage in Britain in February 1960, less than a month before his death in a car crash.*

ently fighting the physical pain of his injuries and the mental pain of deteriorating talent with a bottle. He fought long and hard, though. It was not until the end of the Sixties that he had obviously lost the voice and style that had made him special.

Vincent was unique among the original rockers in that he was internationally successful with his first record, 'Be Bop a Lula', a breathy shuffle punctuated by yelps of delight and a simple but striking guitar solo. Released in the summer of 1956, the record was immediately successful and seemed to promise a strong career. Amazingly, his next release barely touched the charts and he had only two more small hits before dropping out of the record big time once and for all.

Vincent had a major record company behind him, which recorded him prolifically without trying to compromise his style. His backing group, the Blue Caps, were an excellent band of fiery young rockers – indeed, many rate them as the first real white rock group, with their two electric guitars, bass, and drums line-up that was to become the standard format. On stage and on record they were consistently exciting, yet commercially they failed to sustain momentum.

Perhaps the reason was Vincent's appearance: he was gaunt, angular, awkward in motion – compelling to watch but not conventionally good looking. Perhaps it was his voice, a rare sound caused by his exceptionally arched palate – beautiful on ballads but weirdly distraught and frequently incomprehensible on up-tempo material. Mainly, though, it would seem that Gene Vincent and the Blue Caps were just too primitive for mass acceptance.

At the end of the Fifties Vincent moved to Britain, where he was decked out in black leather by impresario Jack Good and enjoyed renewed popularity among rock-starved European fans. After further injury in the car crash that killed his friend Eddie Cochran in April 1960 he gradually deteriorated, although back in Amer-

ica he was to record one of his greatest albums in 1967.

Haley, Presley, Perkins, Lewis and Vincent: together they encapsulate the story of the international breakthrough of rock 'n' roll, with Donegan representing the initial British response. There were many other pioneers, of course, but, excluding one vital section of the music yet to be mentioned, for one reason or another they did not have the international impact or musical significance of the famous five. There were also several artists who did share their international impact and whose careers overlapped with them, but who really heralded the next phase of rock. They naturally warrant their place in the honour-roll of heroes. But first, what of some great but often ignored originators?

The Black Pioneers

Here we come to an ironic twist. The term rock 'n' roll was lifted from the language of black America and first began to be popularised in the early Fifties as an alternative description of black American R&B. So by those terms of reference *all* black American R&B artists of the era were the original rock 'n' roll pioneers – and in fact, of course, they were. But as increasing numbers of young whites began reinterpreting black R&B and adding other influences, it was their hybrid style that came to be more generally called rock 'n' roll – especially when, inevitably, the white artists first carried the music to an international audience. Under the new term of reference there could not be any black rock 'n' roll artists unless public opinion decided otherwise.

A typical example of someone who was not at the time noticed by mass – international, predominantly white –

Of all the great rock 'n' roll originators, Chuck Berry was by far the most gifted and prolific songwriter, one of the best guitarists, and a unique stylist. His rock 'n' roll standards were a major inspiration in the 1960s rock boom in Britain.

LEFT *Little Richard was the manic extremist of rock 'n' roll for a few brief years in the late Fifties. His early Seventies suit of mirrors offered a pale reflection of his former glory.* BELOW *In the late Fifties Ray Charles wrote many hits that were covered by white rock 'n' roll stars – his own brilliant versions being classified as R&B.*

audiences was Ray Charles. After five years of modest success, during 1955-9 Charles became a leading figure in American black music, originating, among many other hits, songs recorded by Elvis Presley, Jerry Lee Lewis, the Everly Brothers and Eddie Cochran. The cover versions were generally thought of as rock 'n' roll; Charles was firmly categorised as R&B.

Only three black solo stars sufficiently ruptured the identity barrier to be internationally acclaimed among the white rock 'n' roll pioneers. Apart from the fact that they were superb at what they did they had little in common: one was a wild exaggeration of the preceding trends in R&B that had first been called rock 'n' roll; one was a unique exception to the general trend of R&B; the third was a polished but fairly typical exponent of one regional form of R&B, who recorded in much the same style from the late Forties to the late Sixties. So much for general opinion about what did or did not constitute rock 'n' roll music.

Little Richard

On the strength of about a dozen of the recordings he made in 1955-7, the wild exaggerator is a viable contender for the Greatest Rocker of All Time certificate:

Little Richard. After four or five years of tuning up with some unexceptional releases, he suddenly burst forth with a batch of mindbending records and a stage act that was never less than hysterical. Unfortunately, or perhaps wisely, at the peak of his excess in late 1957 he just as suddenly decided that he had had enough and promptly enrolled as a trainee preacher. In 1962 he was tempted back to rock 'n' roll by his British fans and launched into an erratic second phase that was intermittently as exciting as the first time around, but then slowly deteriorated under the deadening weight of his own vanity. By the mid-Seventies he was a hopeless shambles, until he smartly returned to the church, where he remains a popular minister.

Even if the brevity of his greatest moments denies Little Richard preeminence, there is no denying that the great moments were stupendous. His original recordings of 'Tutti Frutti', 'Long Tall Sally', 'Ready Teddy', 'Rip It Up', 'Lucille', and 'Good Golly Miss Molly' are among the very best rock 'n' roll records ever made. They influenced artists from Bill Haley and Elvis Presley on through the Beatles to practically every rock 'n' roll group that has ever tried to sound exciting – but has failed to equal the intensity of the originator.

Chuck Berry

Just as influential in his own way was Chuck Berry, although his international success was gradual rather than immediate. Incredible as it seems in the light of subsequent events, during the original rock 'n' roll era Berry had only one British hit, 'Sweet Little Sixteen', and that was as late as May 1958, three years after he had launched his career in America with the million-selling 'Maybelline'.

Berry was an exception to the general trend of R&B. Although he had been influenced by the West Coast blues giants and had then migrated to work with Chicago's blues clique, Berry had also absorbed a lot of white country music. His resulting hybrid style was comparable to the southern white rockabillies'.

Berry was as sharp as a flick-knife – acutely aware of which side his bread was best buttered. He sang a little blues every once in a while, but mainly he wrote and recorded perceptive observations of the all-American white teenage lifestyle. He was possibly the first of the era to make rock 'n' roll records that were specifically concerned with rock 'n' roll music and the preoccupations of the record-buyers; certainly he was the first to do it so well and so often. White songwriter/producers Jerry Leiber and Mike Stoller would soon follow his lead in their work with the Coasters and other acts. Ironically, though, when Berry got started they were still writing songs specifically about, and for, black America. Eddie Cochran with Jerry Capehart also wrote and recorded a few hits in similar vein; others did too. By that time Berry had knocked out a sizeable catalogue of songs that would become rock 'n' roll standards. Berry compositions like 'Thirty Days', 'Roll Over Beethoven', 'Schooldays', 'Rock and Roll Music', 'Johnny B. Goode', 'Carol', 'Memphis Tennessee' and others must be among the most frequently performed and recorded songs in rock history – though few versions rival Berry's own.

Together with the less lyrical tunes of Bo Diddley, a Chicago-based contemporary who never caught on as a rock 'n' roller, Chuck Berry's songbook became the standard reference work of the Sixties' British group boom, and he enjoyed renewed popularity, this time in Britain as well. By the mid-Seventies, however, he was, in the words of one of his songs, too pooped to pop anymore. He still occasionally tours but not with any great enthusiasm.

Fats Domino

The other popular black rocker, Antoine 'Fats' Domino, has had the longest career of any of the well-known rock originators – and, without much fuss or fanfare, one of the most commercially successful. But he broke no new boundaries, created no new sounds. He just happened to be there doing his thing when a new audience stumbled across him and decided that what he was doing was rockin' and rollin'.

His first rock 'n' roll hit was 'Ain't That a Shame' in the summer of 1955. It was only a small hit because the main honours went to Pat Boone's vastly inferior cover version. Nevertheless it was his first record to sell in any quantity to a white audience. It also happened to be his 25th record release since he first went on record (with 'The Fat Man' in 1949), and it was not colossally different from any of the others, most of which had been R&B hits.

Domino exemplified the postwar R&B of his home city, New Orleans: an insistent rolling or staccato piano, infectious beat, good solid horn section, and an appealing, usually jovial vocal part. All of his records had the same magic. Some were more catchy than others, and as

LEFT *Fats Domino, still rocking in the late Seventies: in 20 years only his hairstyle has changed.* BELOW, LEFT *Billy Fury, the best of his British breed.* ABOVE *James Brown in London, 1970 – an R&B superstar light-years beyond his lowly start in the mid-Fifties.*

he became more popular the beat became a little heavier. Later, a string section started appearing on his records, too. But basically his whole recording career has been one long Mardi Gras mambo. His biggest hits during the rock 'n' roll era included 'I'm in Love Again', 'Blueberry Hill', 'Blue Monday', and 'I'm Walkin'. In all he had about 50 hits before he faded from the charts in the mid-Sixties. He still tours with his band every now and again, looking and sounding much the same as he has for the past 30 years.

Rock'n'Roll: the Sequel

There was much more going on in the first great age of rock 'n' roll, of course, than just the careers of the originators. But the rest was not so much part of the breakthrough as the story of the ones-that-didn't-break-through and of the follow-through.

The American black vocal-group scene of the mid-Fifties was a ferment of change and innovation. Great lead singers emerged like Clyde McPhatter and Jackie Wilson (both from the Dominoes) and Sam Cooke (from the Soul Stirrers), who were among the first of a new breed that carried their gospel-rooted style to broader audiences, and laid the foundations for the development of soul music. Great success, too, was enjoyed by groups such as the Moonglows, the Flamingos, Hank Ballard and the Midnighters, and many more. But only in America.

In 1956-7 the pubescent Frankie Lymon and the Teenagers broke through internationally with 'Why Do Fools Fall in Love?' and 'I'm Not a Juvenile Delinquent', topped the bill at the London Palladium, and rapidly faded until Lymon's early death. The Platters, who were not as good as many groups who failed to make it, were saved by the magic voice of lead singer Tony Williams: 'The Great Pretender', 'Only You', 'My Prayer'. At the other extreme were the crazy Coasters, with 'Yakety

Yak' and 'Charlie Brown' – and a whole lot of clowning.

Of greater long-term significance within the American black-music scene was the foundation work of two immensely successful and influential personalities: James Brown and Berry Gordy Jr. A rural-Georgian contemporary of Little Richard, Brown first recorded in February 1956, but apart from one brief attempt to step into Richard's discarded rock 'n' roll shoes he ignored current trends, instead developing his own interpretation of R&B roots that would eventually make him the most individually significant black star of the Sixties and substantially affect the music and attitudes of black America to the present day. Based in the car-manufacturing capital, Detroit (Michigan), during the same period, Gordy began a successful career as a songwriter (notably in 1957 with Jackie Wilson) and part-time producer. With the aid of a great deal of local talent, he laid the foundation of the Motown empire of the Sixties (see next chapter).

After Lonnie Donegan, Britain failed to come up with much for a while, though chirpy cockney sparrow Tommy Steele successfully fooled around with a few lightly rocking hits before owning up. The next wave was better – sometimes. Impresario Larry Parnes created a whole stable of evocatively pseudonymous starlets, of whom Marty Wilde (né Reginald Smith) was especially good at covering American pop-rock hits like 'Endless Sleep', 'Donna', and 'Teenager in Love', while Billy Fury (né Ronald Wycherly) initially came closest in looks and sound to simulating the American originators, before reverting to type with a succession of classy pop-ballad hits in the early Sixties. Others of the Parnes breed included Vince Eager, Dickie Pride, Duffy Power, Johnny Gentle – and Georgie Fame, who matured into a respected stalwart of the Sixties R&B scene.

By the time these young hopefuls began to appear, Britain was already out of the first rock 'n' roll era and into something altogether different, a transition best exemplified by the most successful survivor of them all, Cliff Richard. After a typical skiffle-based but Presley-inspired apprenticeship Richard (born Harry Webb) was first recorded in August 1958, at the same time being picked to star regularly in a new TV series of pop shows, *Oh Boy!* The following month the début show neatly boosted Richard's first single, 'Move It', up the charts, and his subsequent weekly appearances quickly made him the most popular of the new British breed of pop-rockers. After only two more mock-rock hits, in July 1959 an excruciatingly soppy ballad, 'Livin' Doll', gave him the biggest British seller of the day, foreshadowing his later career as the Mr Clean of the pop world. This is not to depreciate Richard; indeed, he can only be admired for successfully surviving the many musical changes of the past 20 years and re-emerging in the second half of the Seventies as an international pop superstar, looking and sounding younger than ever with hits like 'We Don't Talk Anymore' (1979). But whatever the ingredients of his talent, they certainly have little in common with original rock 'n' roll.

The American follow-through was streets ahead of the British. The Everly Brothers emerged with a long run of consistently enchanting country-based harmony hits, beginning with 'Bye Bye Love', 'Wake Up Little Susie' (both 1957), and 'All I Have To Do Is Dream' (1958). Ricky Nelson was not so hot on up-tempo material but

LEFT *Buddy Holly: an immense posthumous influence.* ABOVE *Cliff Richard – with Bruce Welch (left) and Hank Marvin of the Shadows – dominated British pop just before the Beatles changed everything.*

proved a fine teen balladeer; there were excellent musicians on his early records, too. Eddie Cochran was erratic, but at his best was one of the most talented rock guitarists, with a strong voice and plenty of style. Some of his finest recordings, like 'C'mon Everybody', 'Summertime Blues' (both 1958) and 'Somethin' Else', were also lyrically sharper than most contemporary hits. And then of course there were Buddy Holly and the Crickets.

Perhaps Holly should really be up in front with the breakthrough heroes. He was early off the mark, and certainly the international popularity and influence of his voice, songs, and guitar work – and of the Crickets as a band – had a greater long-term effect on popular music than several of the other originators. On the other hand, the very nature of Holly's talents and the direction in which his career and recordings were heading at the time of his death in 1959 illustrate only too well how rock 'n' roll was changing.

Holly first performed and broadcast in his home town of Lubbock (Texas) about 1954, singing and playing straight country and country-bop numbers with a school friend. During 1956 he first recorded professionally in Nashville, mostly his own songs performed in roughly similar style to the first few of his subsequent hits. Some of these tracks were later rated amongst his best work, but at the time they went nowhere.

Early in 1957 Holly and the Crickets started recording in Norman Petty's studio in Clovis, New Mexico, and, with a new record deal, hit the jackpot. Because of contractual problems the first new release was simply credited to the Crickets, and thereafter they more or less alternated the credits – one release was by Buddy Holly, the next by the Crickets – and even though the same team participated in most of them until not long before Holly's death. Interestingly, though, whereas the releases credited to the Crickets were all fairly raunchy (even 'It's So Easy' had a rough edge to it, although 'Fool's Paradise' was a bit wet), several of the Buddy Holly issues were candybar-sweet. They had great charm, of course, especially to love-sick young things, but 'Everyday', 'Heartbeat', and other syrupy titles that emerged after Holly's death had precious little to do with rock 'n' roll. Once Holly had split from the Crickets this tendency was confirmed: listen to his work with the Dick Jacobs Orchestra, as heard on both sides of his posthumously released hit 'It Doesn't Matter Anymore'/ 'Raining in My Heart' (1959). In two years he had taken his music from the raw southern sounds of 'Rock around with Ollie Vee' and 'That'll Be the Day' (1957) to a blueprint of Adam Faith's British pop hits. This was progress?

The Pop Revolution

The Sixties saw a revolution in popular music, the effects of which are still being felt some two decades later. In a few short years interest switched from singles to albums, from mono to stereo, from dance music to move the body to cerebral music to please the intellect. New styles emerged out of old — girl-group pop, beat music, folk-rock, country-rock, acid-rock, soul — and the sleeping spirit of rock 'n' roll was reawakened by a succession of bright new talents, led of course by four young, self-taught beat musicians from Liverpool.

Yet the decade began with little hint of the upheavals to come. Rock music had reached a low creative ebb by 1960, not least because of the absence from centre-stage of many of its early heroes: Chuck Berry was in jail for abduction of a minor; Jerry Lee Lewis was in disgrace following his marriage to a 13-year-old cousin; Little Richard had renounced rock 'n' roll for religion; Buddy Holly was dead; Elvis Presley was on national service with the US Army in Europe. The rock 'n' roll *sound* was no longer a particular feature of teenage records — orchestral accompaniments were now common, ballads were once again much in evidence — and the very image of rock had altered radically, from rebellious and anarchic to something of which even parents could approve.

Teen Idols

The commercialisation of the teen market that rock 'n' roll inspired made such changes inevitable, and during the late Fifties the intense competition within the record industry produced a seemingly limitless stream of new faces, dances, and novelties. More young girls than ever before were buying records, and the success of Paul Anka with 'Diana' and Tab Hunter with 'Young Love' (both 1957) signalled the birth of a whole new subculture built on the tastes and fantasies of Little Miss America. Teenage magazines appeared, packed with fan gossip, love stories, and exclusive interviews with the stars, and television came into its own as a potential star-maker.

Presley's famous appearance on Ed Sullivan's show in 1956 offered an early indication of television's promotional power, but in that same year the 16-year-old co-star of a popular soap opera was invited to make a record. This was Ricky Nelson, who recorded a version of Fats Domino's 'I'm Walkin'' for Verve and was then signed by Domino's own label, Imperial, as their answer to Elvis. With Nelson in the public eye week after week, his success was assured; by 1963, he had achieved no less than 36 Hot 100 hits and had made a creditable start to a movie career.

Nelson was carefully marketed as the more acceptable face of rock 'n' roll, with greased-back hair, country-flavoured songs, and only a hint of rebellion in his manner. The teen idols who followed him were less concerned with rock content, though they too had television to thank for their breakthrough. The key show was *American Bandstand*, broadcast from Philadelphia each weekday and compèred by one-time radio announcer Dick Clark. The timing of the show — at four o'clock, just as the high schools were emptying — was perfect, and the presence of a live studio audience of teenage dancers meant that it became a launching pad not just for new stars but for new dance crazes as well. Most of all, the show offered America a sanitised version of teenage music — rock 'n' roll without its rough edges — and one of Clark's specialities was to give homilies about clean living, going to church, and showing respect for one's elders. *Bandstand* rendered rock harmless, and Clark was happy to take the credit.

A mini-industry soon sprang up in Philadelphia to 'service' the programme with artists and records. Club owners Bob Marcucci and Peter De Angelis set up their own label, Chancellor, to promote their local discovery, a former trumpet-playing child prodigy called Frankie Avalon, whose debut hit was the puerile 'De De Dinah' early in 1958. Avalon had a barely passable voice and no rock 'n' roll credentials: like most of his teen-idol contemporaries, he had a classic Italian-American ghetto background and dreamed of becoming the next Frank Sinatra, Tony Bennett, or Perry Como, not a second Elvis Presley.

Avalon's success with songs like 'Venus', 'Why?', and 'Bobby Sox to Stockings' — all tailor-made to fit his spruce image — prompted Marcucci and De Angelis to try again, this time with a pretty face quite literally pulled in from the street. Fabian Forte was just 15, could not sing, had no stage presence, and had to be taught how to wiggle his hips, yet his dark Italianate looks more than compensated as far as *Bandstand* viewers were concerned. Chancellor launched a massive publicity drive, buying space in the trade magazines for advertisements that bore the legend, 'FABIAN IS COMING! WHO IS FABIAN? FABIAN IS HERE!', and a string of growling hits resulted. The first wholly manufactured idol of the pop era, he was a puppet in the hands of whizz-kid entrepreneurs and, unlike Nelson and Avalon, lacked even the talent and ambition to carve a career for himself in the wider showbusiness world, once his days at the top were numbered.

Other teen idols emerged via the *Bandstand* route — Bobby Rydell, Charlie Gracie, Freddy Cannon, Tony Orlando, Bobby Vee, all with varying degrees of talent. Girl singers had a place, too, notably Connie Francis,

RIGHT *The Beatles in the Cavern Club, Liverpool, the spiritual home of Merseybeat. Spearhead* of the pop revolution, they inspired many of the creative developments in Sixties rock.

whose records were comic strip versions of teenage romance that told of going on vacation, walking home from high school with a new boyfriend in tow, wandering whether Johnny's intentions were honourable.

Connie's only real rival was Georgia-born Brenda Lee, who was just 15 when her first hit, 'Sweet Nuthins', reached the American chart in 1960. As a child star she had obvious novelty value, but she also possessed one of the huskiest, most tender, and most powerful voices in pop music. Although her material was for the most part teen-oriented and inconsequential ('Let's Jump the Broomstick', 'Speak to Me Pretty', and 'Rocking Around the Christmas Tree' were typical), she could tackle angst-ridden ballads like 'All Alone Am I' and 'Losing You' with a maturity and feeling that belied her tomboy image and underlined her country-music roots.

Brenda Lee's discs were among the more engaging of the *Bandstand* era, but the show's influence on pop at the turn of the Sixties was generally reactionary. Quite apart from the show's preoccupation with image and gimmicks, Dick Clark revelled too much in his self-appointed role as arbiter of teenage taste, choosing exactly who could appear and refusing to accept acts who did not conform to his safely conventional standards. The degree of power he exercised was exposed during the Congressional inquiry into payola (bribery within the record and radio business) in 1959, when it emerged that he owned stock in six different music publishing firms, three record labels, a record-distribution company, a management agency, and a record-pressing plant. He had allegedly misused his position within television to give his own acts or records preference; examples were given of how he had engineered the chart success of discs by Duane Eddy, the Crests, and others. Yet he escaped prosecution, claiming to have rid himself of all outside interests at the onset of the proceedings. Disc jockeys, including the legendary Alan Freed, were not so lucky: many were branded as corrupt and unceremoniously sacked as the record industry tried to put its house in order.

The hearings had a cleansing effect on the industry but hardly improved the state of pop. The spirit of rock 'n' roll resurfaced occasionally during the early Sixties – notably on records by one-time rockers like Roy Orbison, Del Shannon, Dion di Mucci (with his group, the Belmonts), and Bruce Channel – but an overwhelming blandness lingered in the charts. Hits like Brian Hyland's 'Itsy Bitsy Teenie Weenie Yellow Polka Dot Bikini' and Joanie Summers' 'Johnny Get Angry' followed the familiar pattern of high school pop, while *American Bandstand* – still with Dick Clark in charge – both reflected and perpetuated young America's continuing obsession with the new dance steps. *Bandstand's* particular achievement was to turn the Twist into a national institution by fostering the career of Chubby Checker and giving screen time to dozens of one-off Twist records like Santo and Johnny's 'Twistin Bells', Rod McKuen's 'The Oliver Twist', the Champs' 'Tequila Twist', and Bill Doggett's 'Let's Do the Hully Gully Twist'. Checker's 1960 cover version of Hank Ballard's 'The Twist' opened the floodgates, reaching Number 1 in America a few weeks after release and repeating its success a year later, when the media discovered that the dance craze had been taken up by the chic clientèle of New York nightclubs such as the Peppermint Lounge.

ABOVE *Brenda Lee, barely 15 years old when she first charted, was known as Little Miss Dynamite.* RIGHT, ABOVE *The Drifters (lead singer Clyde McPhatter at right); Leiber and Stoller masterminded their early hits.* RIGHT, BELOW *Chubby Checker does the Twist.*

New Sounds in America

The Twist was Philadelphia pop's last great fling: by 1963, Nashville, New York, and Detroit had taken over as the music's major creative centres. Nashville's massive growth as a business and recording community paralleled the rise in popularity of country music, which could be credited almost entirely to the influential production works of guitarist Chet Atkins. The so-called 'Nashville Sound' that he perfected was in reality little more than a diluted version of Fifties country, with the traditional fiddle and steel guitar accompaniment abandoned in favour of a rock-influenced combination of piano, percussion, and rhythm guitar, yet the change in instrumentation effectively broke down the barriers between country and mainstream popular music. The early Sixties saw an invasion of the pop chart by Nashville artists like Jim Reeves, Hank Locklin, Jimmy Dean, Patsy Cline, Bob Luman, and Floyd Cramer, while all the Everly Brothers' hits, from 'Cathy's Clown' (1960) onwards, were recorded there under Chet Atkins' able direction.

New York's pop reputation, meanwhile, was built on a white interpretation of the black R&B sound, echoing the process that had given birth to rock 'n' roll back in the mid-Fifties. Black artists often had to make severe compromises to keep their place in the pop market – Ray Charles, for instance, turned away from his revolutionary blend of gospel and R&B to record lushly orchestrated country ballads like 'I Can't Stop Loving You' and 'Take These Chains', while Sam Cooke switched from gospel-inspired material to clever pop songs like 'Cupid' and 'Twistin' the Night Away'. The Drifters, too, were typical of many black vocal groups who, with white musicians, songwriters, and producers masterminding their sessions, happily adapted their music to the requirements of white taste. Their 1959 million-seller 'There Goes My

Baby', produced by Jerry Leiber and Mike Stoller, exploited all manner of instrumental and production effects and established strings and Latin rhythms as important features of pop records.

Although Leiber and Stoller never quite matched the ornateness of 'There Goes My Baby', subsequent Drifters records followed a studied pop formula that proved equally influential. 'Save the Last Dance for Me' (1960) crystallised the group's new Latin-based sound and directly inspired the Shirelles' 'Will You Love Me Tomorrow', written by the up-and-coming songwriting team of Gerry Goffin and Carole King and produced by Luther Dixon for the Scepter label. This in turn sparked off three solid years of girl-group hits, most by all-girl trios (black and white) brought into the studios from high schools and street corners, who were only too willing to be manipulated by some whizz-kidd producer if it meant earning $100 a night touring on the strength of the resulting hit. What the success of these records showed was that teenagers were now clearly interested most in a record's *sound*: if so many discs by complete unknowns like the Cookies, the Angels, the Murmaids, the Jay-nettes, the Chiffons, and countless others could make the US chart, then obviously it had little to do with image or visual appeal. It was down to the sound, the *production* of individual records. Exactly who sang on what record was for a while no longer important: voices were generally subservient to the grand designs of the men behind the consoles.

Many new, small, independent labels emerged in New

ABOVE *Carole King, one of several young songwriters recruited from high school by New York's Aldon Music publishing house. With lyricist-husband Gerry Goffin she wrote many of the most memorable pop songs of the years immediately before the Beatles.*

York to cash in on the girl-group boom, and they provided a fertile training ground for such backroom arrangers and producers as Bert Berns, George 'Shadow' Morton, Burt Bacharach, and Phil Spector. All took the black girl-group sound as their base, and most used songs supplied by one particular publishing house, Aldon Music of Broadway, which included Goffin and King, Neil Sedaka, Howie Greenfield, Jeff Barry, and Jerry Keller in their roster of writers in the famous Brill Building at 1619 Broadway (where Leiber and Stoller also had their headquarters). Most of the Aldon staff were middle-class Jewish teenagers recruited by owners Don Kirshner and Al Nevins from the high schools: contracted on a nine-to-five basis, their brief was to produce songs to specifications provided by the various record companies. If a song for Bobby Vee was required, everyone would work on it and the best would be offered to him. This conveyor-belt system, an extension of the 'song factory' principle beloved of Tin Pan Alley in the pre-rock days, was extensively copied and produced some excellent results. Most of all, it imbued in the songwriters a strong sense of musical discipline and craftsmanship that set the standard for the rest of the decade.

The Spector Sound

The most imaginative manipulator of the girl-group sound was Phil Spector, who became a greater pop celebrity than any of the artists he recorded. He cut his teeth as a producer with Leiber and Stoller in New York and with Lester Sill and Lee Hazlewood in Phoenix, Arizona, sitting in on sessions and making contributions when allowed to. Early productions for Gene Pitney ('Every Breath I Take') and the Paris Sisters ('I Love How

You Love Me') set the tone for his later work: both were epic, ethereal, endlessly remixed and extensively over-dubbed, and both were products of weeks of painstaking effort. In 1961 he formed his own label, Philles, with Lester Sill as joint head, and signed the Crystals; a year later, with two chart successes behind him, he bought out Sill and moved his base of operation from New York to his home city of Los Angeles, where he knew session musicians would be more amenable to his ideas. Working exclusively in his favourite studio, Goldstar, he set about crafting what became known as the Spector 'Wall of Sound' — a dense, three-dimensional effect achieved by placing together layer upon layer of musical sound. 'Mine is a Wagnerian approach to rock 'n' roll', he told an interviewer in 1963. 'All I'm doing is writing little symphonies for the kids. I was looking for a sound, a sound so strong that if the material were not the greatest, the sound would carry the records. It was a case of augmenting, augmenting, augmenting. It all fitted together like a jigsaw. The records are built like a Wagner opera. They start simply and they end up with dynamic force, meaning and purpose.'

With each successive production, Spector became more and more ambitious, graduating from relatively straightforward girl-group records like the Crystals' 'Then He Kissed Me' and the Ronettes' 'Be My Baby' (both 1963) — on which the voices seemed to be competing against one of the most elaborate rock arrangements ever — to the Righteous Brothers' brooding 'You've Lost That Lovin' Feeling' in 1965. This was no sweet teenage love song but an adult ballad, written by Barry Mann and Cynthia Weill in deliberate imitation of the Four Tops' 'Baby I Need Your Loving', and the record featured a monumental three basses, three pianos, four acoustic guitars, eight horns, four saxes, three percussionists, drums, eight background singers, bongoes, vibes, and a harpsichord. The recording took three days; the remixing took nearly three weeks. The result was a near-perfect example of how a great R&B voice (Bill Medley of the Righteous Brothers was already regarded as one of America's best white R&B singers) could be married to a contrived yet disciplined pop production without any consequent loss of passion. Ike and Tina Turner's 'River Deep — Mountain High', unarguably Spector's greatest production achievement, proved the point all over again in 1966, although its comparative failure in America forced Spector into a self-imposed retirement.

Spector gave status to the role of record producer, but he was also a major commercial innovator. He had an almost paranoid distrust of the rest of the record industry and saw himself as fighting the system through his own record label. Much of his marketing policy went against accepted industry practice: just when most companies were expanding their rosters and hiring experts to handle specialised tasks like talent-hunting or publicity, Spector relied on a minuscule staff and took charge of each record at every stage of its production, from first take through to final pressing. He put instrumentals on the flipsides of his records, so that disc jockeys would not be tempted to turn the record over and disrupt sales; rather than issue up to 20 singles a week as the majors did, he released one a month and would not issue another until its predecessor's sales life was clearly on the wane. He was one of the first producers to mix his

LEFT *The Ronettes – sisters Ronnie and Estelle Bennett and cousin Nedra Talley – whose records showcased the production genius of Phil Spector. Ronnie (on the left) married Spector.*

ABOVE *Ike and Tina Turner's electrifying recording of 'River Deep – Mountain High' featured Spector's 'wall of sound'. Tina's blues-soul voice had few betters in Sixties rock.*

records specifically with transistor radios in mind – he would turn up the treble to create a ringing sound certain to catch the ear of a casual listener. His success also gave a substantial boost to the burgeoning pop industry in California, hitherto best known for having given America the short-lived surf music and hot-rod fads.

Motown

Just as Spector helped open up the Los Angeles scene, so a sharp black businessman named Berry Gordy Jr put the city of Detroit on the music map at the beginning of the Sixties, with a string of labels that were soon amalgamated into one huge corporation called Motown. Like Spector, Gordy took the black R&B vocal sound as his starting point and wholeheartedly pursued the white market. Through him, Motown developed into not only the most profitable independent label ever but also the only black-owned business organisation of any kind to make a major impact on American industry. He began by hiring local acts and copying current chart styles – Motown's 1962 hits included the Contours' 'Do You Love Me', a Twist record, and Barrett Strong's 'Money', a rock 'n' roll number – but he quickly made Motown entirely self-sufficient in material, by encouraging signings like Smokey Robinson of the Miracles, Lamont Dozier, and Eddie Holland to write and produce not only their own discs but those of other acts on the label. His music publishing company Jobete funded Motown's expansion into the album field and artist management – a key Gordy innovation was the Motortown Revue, a touring roadshow of Motown acts that played all the major stadiums in the northern United States – and he plotted the label's long-term future by nurturing the rise of a select handful of charismatic artists and groups, including the Supremes, the Four Tops, and 'Little' Stevie Wonder.

The remarkable Motown production 'sound' had parallels in the work of Phil Spector and Leiber and Stoller, but the most obvious feature of Motown records was the strong gospel element. Detroit had a particularly

LEFT *Aretha Franklin, major soul star of the late Sixties. Like many other great black singers, she began her career in a church choir, and she developed complete mastery of the gospel style.* ABOVE *The Supremes, whose lead singer Diana Ross (left) was the jewel in Motown's crown until she left in 1981, having made a* successful bid for stardom in two movies. ABOVE, RIGHT *The Four Tops (lead singer Levi Stubbs Jr at left) who charted 24 times in Britain in 1965-73.* BELOW, RIGHT *Motown's most versatile artist: songwriter/producer/singer Smokey Robinson wrote for and recorded many of Gordy's most popular stars.*

high reputation for gospel music and a nationally-known figure in Rev. C. L. Franklin, father of Aretha Franklin, who had been instrumental in getting church groups and choirs on record. Gordy deliberately introduced a gospel flavour into his productions by copying the accompaniments used in church singing and the call-and-response patterns heard on gospel records. Martha and the Vandellas' 'Dancing in the Street' and the Supremes' 'Baby Love' (both 1964) showed how well Gordy and his production team had absorbed the gospel lesson – both featured an entreating lead singer and an answering chorus, singing against a solid R&B beat. Gordy contrived to marry two separate traditions in black music, gospel and R&B, and in so doing he not only produced great dance music but a very significant strain of what was soon labelled 'soul' music.

Motown records were created to a strict, proven formula that nevertheless allowed individual talent to shine, particularly if the vocalist was as distinctive as

Smokey Robinson, Diana Ross, or Levi Stubbs (lead singer of The Four Tops). Robinson's pleading falsetto was equally suited to ballads like 'Two Lovers' and up-tempo material like the classic 'Shop Around' (1960), but it was as a writer and producer that he proved indispensable to the Motown set-up. His compositions included 'My Guy' for Mary Wells and 'My Girl' and 'Get Ready' for the Tempations, earthily romantic songs graced by impeccably sweet turns of phrase and appealingly simple imagery. Bob Dylan was even moved to describe him as America's 'greatest living poet'. In Diana Ross, lead singer with the Supremes until Gordy groomed her for solo stardom in the late Sixties, Motown had a vocalist with a light but mature style and real sex appeal. More than any other Motown artist, she personified the label's changing image as the Sixties wore on, moving from straight formula songs like 'Where Did Our Love Go' and 'Stop In the Name of Love' to classy ballads like 'I'm Still Waiting' and Las Vegas appearances. Later

writer/production team; their songs were vehicles for the booming, dramatic voice of Levi Stubbs and depicted him as a proud man suffering at the hands of some uncaring female – 'I Can't Help Myself', 'Seven Rooms of Gloom', 'It's the Same Old Song', 'Standing in the Shadows of Love'. Their greatest moment was the 1966 million-seller 'Reach Out – I'll Be There', which carried an implicit gospel message in its title and was widely interpreted as a paean to black consciousness. Marvin Gaye also recorded gospel-laced material like 'Can I Get a Witness' and 'Pride and Joy' (both 1963) before finding his own style with compulsive dance records like 'How Sweet It Is' and 'I Heard It Through the Grapevine'. The Isley Brothers happily submitted their characteristic free-flowing vocal style to corporation requirements and won an international audience that had previously been denied them. Perhaps because they were not true products of the Gordy star-making stable, the Isleys were never accorded the creative freedom that Smokey Robinson, Norman Whitfield, and others enjoyed; their potential was not fully realised until the Seventies, after they had parted company with Motown.

Berry Gordy marketed all his acts under the slogan 'The Sound of Young America', and for some years the Motown label was the prime source of dynamic, original dance music in the USA. Its dominance was not affected by the popularity in America of the Beatles and their British contemporaries – indeed, the Beatles' enthusiastic endorsement of the Motown sound in interviews gave the label renewed credibility. More significantly, Motown records were formative influences on the Beatles' early vocal sound, as cover versions of the Marvelettes' 'Please Mr Postman' and the Miracles' 'You Really Got a Hold on Me' on their second album (1963) testified. Drawing on precisely those styles of girl-group pop and black R&B that had gone largely unheard in Britain, the Beatles fashioned the first great phase of the Sixties' pop revolution.

From Skiffle to Beatlemania

still, she led Motown's successful foray into Hollywood with star roles in films such as *Lady Sings the Blues* (1972) and *Mahogany* (1975).

Other leading Motown talents during its early years were the Four Tops, Marvin Gaye, and a group well-known to black audiences prior to joining Berry Gordy, the Isley Brothers. The Four Tops, like the Supremes, worked under the wing of the Holland, Dozier, Holland

Britain seemed the unlikeliest place imaginable for a musical revolution. The cultural conditions were hardly conducive to change or innovation. The music industry consisted of a handful of major record companies with a vested interest in maintaining the status quo of heartthrobs and trad jazz bands. The radio airwaves were controlled by the BBC, who gave only cursory coverage to American rock 'n' roll and barely acknowledged the existence of teenagers. British recording stars modelled themselves closely on their American counterparts, copying everything from style of dress to repertoire and Presley-like sneer. Confronted with the gloss and glamour of all things American, Britain suffered from a gigantic inferiority complex that had its roots in the post-war years of austerity and recession.

Growing up in this kind of atmosphere, British teenagers in the Fifties automatically looked to America for excitement – on record, on television, in the cinema. Hollywood fuelled the American myth: the people in American movies looked well-to-do, the girls looked sexier, kids in particular seemed to have everything they could want – even cars! Rock 'n' roll provided a soundtrack to America's supremacy in mass culture. Teenagers saw the newsreels, read the newspapers, heard Bill Haley's 'Rock Around the Clock' and were transfixed. Most of all, the new music seemed to give identity to teenagers as a particular social group, not just as part of one amorphous mass audience. Their first inclination, as always, was to imitate – so the rock 'n' roll 'look' (inspired as much by Marlon Brando and James Dean as by Elvis) became part of the British youth scene, as teenagers took to wearing leather jackets, teddy-boy outfits, and D.A. haircuts.

The real impetus behind British rock music came not from these imitations, however, but from the skiffle boom of the middle and late Fifties. Skiffle was do-it-yourself music at its simplest: the 'authentic' three-piece line-up was guitar (three chords would suffice), washboard-and-thimbles (percussion), and tea-chest-with-strung-broomhandle (bass). Guitar sales rose phenomenally, a small number of skiffle acts reached the chart (the Vipers, Nancy Whiskey, Johnny Duncan), and for a while skiffle did indeed seem to offer a healthy alternative to rock. Yet skiffle's very success hastened its decline: those teenagers who had mastered the guitar chords found the standard skiffle line-up limiting and its repertoire inappropriate to their situation. Increasingly, the American rock 'n' roll acts offered a way ahead, with their electric guitars, anti-authoritarian lyrics, and altogether more aggressive image. Eddie Cochran and Buddy Holly were popular models.

The new British pop music was developing, independent of chart trends, in provincial cities like Liverpool and Newcastle. There, one-time skiffle groups had evolved naturally into rock 'n' roll outfits, playing not only the accepted rock classics but material from sources denied to other parts of the country – R&B records brought in by American seamen, for instance, putting in at Liverpool. Such groups were either amateur or semi-professional and played a set local network of youth clubs, jazz and blues clubs, and dancehalls. They entertained few ideas about making the big time, since to gain access to record companies or promoters required throwing in their jobs and moving down to London, where success was not guaranteed.

Liverpool's music scene was uniquely self-sustaining, partly because of the city's American connections. In the Fifties, Liverpool's life was dominated by its connections with the international shipping trade. Everyone knew somebody in the 'Merch' (the merchant navy), which was the city's principal source of employment. Liverpool boys who worked the Cunard and Blue Star lines to New York and New Orleans continually returned with American records that were never released in Britain. The regional differences in these strange new sounds – they included blues from the Deep South, hillbilly music from Nashville, girl-group records from New York – were unimportant to the teenagers who heard these discs when the sailors returned to home port. Thus Liverpool became an extraordinary musical melting pot of styles synthesised in a 'live' context – in front of young audiences who demanded good dance music – by local musicians. What the Liverpool groups produced could not easily be defined, but it came closer to the true spirit of American rock 'n' roll than anything that the London-based record companies could offer.

The regional groups generally took pride in their isolation from London and poured scorn on the slick contrivances of bands like the Shadows, whose guitar technique was flashy and mechanical and whose stage routines were blandly choreographed. By contrast, Liverpool beat music was defiantly spontaneous – what the groups lacked in finesse they made up for in energy. They were lucky, also, in having the sympathetic encouragement of a handful of club owners, local journalists, and would-be promoters. Ray McFall was one of several managers of jazz cellars who switched to beat music when the trad craze faded, and his Cavern Club became a focal point of teenage social activity in

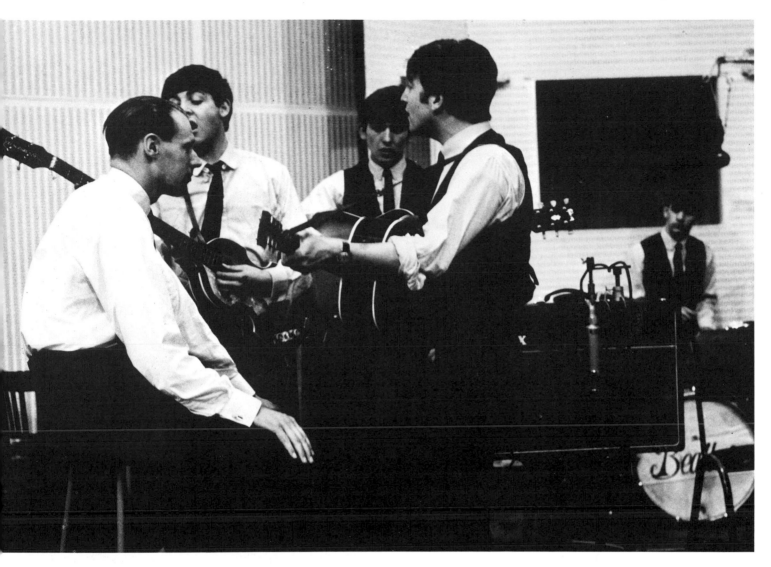

LEFT *Lonnie Donegan who led the late-Fifties skiffle boom.* ABOVE *The Beatles with producer George Martin at EMI's Abbey Road (London) studios in 1963. As their music grew in ambition, Martin helped turn their often bizarre ideas into reality.*

Liverpool. Because the club was not licensed, McFall had no age restriction to enforce and could open whenever he wanted, which meant lunch-time sessions as well as evenings. Liverpool even had its own music paper, *Mersey Beat*, which was run on a shoestring by Bill Harry and carried chatty features and straight gig information. Events like the massive beat spectacular, held at the city's 6,000-seat boxing stadium to highlight local talent, gave the local scene identity and inspired yet more kids to form their own outfits.

In 1961 *Mersey Beat* estimated that around 350 groups were operating in Liverpool. Soon after, readers elected the Beatles as the most popular local band in a poll. They were distinctive but far from unique, and their rise to local prominence had followed the classic skiffle-to-rock-group pattern. The four who made up the Beatles at this time – guitarists George Harrison and John Lennon, bassist Paul McCartney, and drummer Pete Best – all came from lower-middle-class backgrounds and had played in various skiffle and beat groups before coming together as the Silver Beatles. Under the somewhat exasperated management of Alan Williams, they secured a residency at a club in Hamburg's notorious Reeperbahn district, and served a memorable apprenticeship there before returning to the Cavern as conquer-ing heroes. Their lack of on-stage discipline and general unreliability caused Williams to drop them, and several months of uncertainty were finally ended when local record-store owner Brian Epstein took control of their affairs.

Epstein experienced at first hand the difficulties involved in getting any provincial group a recording contract. Decca, the biggest and most prestigious of Britain's pop labels, hesitated but eventually turned the Beatles down in favour of a Dagenham group, Brian Poole and the Tremeloes. The only company to show definite interest was Parlophone, a subsidiary of EMI that was best known for comedy and novelty records. Label head George Martin's first inclination – typically for the time – was to select one of the group as a front-man and to promote them as another Cliff Richard and the Shadows. He also saw no need to depart from the tried and trusted policy of using material provided by professional songwriters for single releases, although Lennon and McCartney's growing aptitude as writers soon forced him to change his mind. In October 1962 'Love Me Do', the Beatles' first release, caused a few ripples and just scraped into the British Top 20; a few months later, however, 'Please Please Me' stormed to Number 2 and heralded a new era in chart history.

The Beatles made such a huge impact because they were different. Unlike the clinically preplanned product of much early-Sixties chart pop (British and American), their music was very much self-styled and self-deter-

ABOVE *The Beatles in concert in late 1963; the backdrop is the cover picture of their* With the Beatles *album.* RIGHT *Spencer Davis Group, a major R&B band in 1964; Steve Winwood on keyboard.* RIGHT, ABOVE *The Hollies were formed in Manchester in 1962.*

mined. They started as arch purveyors of dance music, best experienced live in club or dancehall, and the beat-club environment was stamped all over their first album, *Please Please Me* (1963). It included Beatle versions of songs that had long been Cavern favourites – Arthur Alexander's 'Anna', the Isley Brothers' 'Twist and Shout', the Shirelles' 'Baby It's You', the Cookies' 'Chains' – and had sleeve notes by Tony Barrow that stressed the group's crowd-pleasing live qualities. Such covers were mostly close copies of the originals, with only the instrumental arrangements altered slightly to accommodate two rhythm guitars, but of most significance was the way Lennon and McCartney put the lessons of those records into practice in writing their own material. Not only did they base their harmony sound on that of black girl groups like the Shirelles, they closely modelled their earliest songs on those of the masters of the girl-group song, Gerry Goffin and Carole King. From them, John and Paul learned how to craft pop songs, how to construct them in terms of a complete musical arrangement, and how to write in a conversational mode. Many of the Beatles' great early songs were conversation songs, addressed to either a partner or a confidant ('She Loves You', 'I Saw Her Standing There', 'If I Fell', 'And I Love Her').

Lennon and McCartney developed rapidly as songwriters, producing vast numbers of new songs virtually to order. Theirs was a very professional approach to songwriting, often determined by commercial requirements: songs were custom-written for release as singles, flipsides, or album tracks, or for other acts in Epstein's growing management stable – Billy J. Kramer, Tommy Quickly, Cilla Black, and the Fourmost were all launched with John and Paul songs. They were not immune from looking to other currently popular artists for inspiration: 'Love Me Do' had a harmonica break inspired by Bruce Channel's 'Hey Baby' and Frank Ifield's 'I Remember

the timing was precisely right: Britain's young postwar generation was just starting to exercise its new spending power and to question the old order in morals and politics (1963 was the year of the Profumo scandal). As for America, it was no coincidence that the Beatles broke through just a few months after President Kennedy's assassination: at an all-time low point in America's history, Americans looked abroad for something new and diverting to renew their faith in youth.

The Beatle Legacy: UK

The success of the Beatles revitalised the British pop scene as never before, in both commercial and creative terms. They shattered the industry's London bias overnight: Liverpool was quickly raided by A&R managers frantic to sign anyone with a guitar and a Scouse accent, although only a handful of Merseybeat bands made a comfortable switch from live club work to the recording studio, notably the Searchers, the Swinging Blue Jeans, the Merseybeats, and those groups managed by Brian Epstein. The latter now included Gerry & the Pacemakers, Billy J. Kramer & the Dakotas, and the Fourmost, all of whose recordings were produced by George Martin. Because of its proximity to Liverpool, Manchester became the next port of call for the record companies. By mid-1964 the Manchester groups with recording contracts included the Hollies, the Mindbenders, St Louis Union, and Herman's Hermits. Birmingham offered the Rockin' Berries, the Applejacks, the Sorrows, Pinkerton's Colours, and the Spencer Davis Group.

Literally thousands of groups were formed in the aftermath of Beatlemania and between 1964 and 1966 home-grown British beat music swamped the chart. The industry was continually on the lookout for the next big group – no one really expected the Beatles to last – and there were a few false alarms. Supposedly unique 'sounds', peculiar to a particular locality, were usually the products of some publicist's over-fertile imagination. The Dave Clark Five, for example, were launched as pioneers of a 'Tottenham sound' in late 1963. In fact, they had no connection with what was happening elsewhere in London, namely the R&B movement that was gathering momentum in the city's clubs and pubs. This movement had a more intellectual base than Merseybeat, attracting more students than working-class teenagers, but it unearthed a crop of new groups whose music was superficially similar.

The London R&B scene actually dated back to 1953, when jazzman Chris Barber became the first British bandleader to play R&B in his act. Two Barber associates, Alexis Korner and Cyril Davies, formed the enormously influential Blues Incorporated in 1961 and opened their own club in a basement beneath Ealing Broadway underground station, their aim being to feature forms of blues ignored by the conservative jazz-club circuit. As the following for R&B grew, especially among young people, other jazz clubs switched over and new venues opened in London suburbs. These tended to concentrate on one of three specific streams of R&B – the 'rural' school favoured by Davies (who left Blues Incorporated within a year), the jazz-influenced 'urban' school led by Korner, and the 'soul' school

You' (both 1962 hits); 'Please Please Me' had been intended as a Roy Orbison-type ballad (hence the falsetto) until George Martin suggested that they increase the tempo; 'Misery' was written, on the Beatles' first nationwide tour, with bill-topper Helen Shapiro in mind.

The Beatles' style crystallised with each single and album. An early innovation was to turn a minor element of the girl-group style, the 'yeah' response to the main vocal line, into a Beatle trademark. They performed, recorded and wrote as a tight-knit unit, and songs tended to emerge organically – one playing ideas off the other, John composing the verse and Paul the middle eight, George embellishing the finished product with some instrumental ideas of his own. There was a kind of internal democracy within the group that was itself something new. There was no recognised leader: John and Paul shared lead vocal, while Ringo and George were given solo slots on albums. Paul once described the Beatles as 'four parts of the same person', and, in image, they were. Not handsome in the classic teen idol sense, they dressed uniformly, wore (for the period) daringly effeminate hairstyles and appealed to both sexes equally. What was more, they were obviously intelligent. They adopted a refreshingly cynical attitude to showbusiness and made a positive virtue out of their provincial background, exuding Northern wit and charm without the least hint of patronising their audience.

The Beatles carved out their own musical niche and could easily have stayed in it, had they wanted to. By the end of 1963, Britain was awash with what the *Daily Mirror* labelled 'Beatlemania'. The newspapers, entrenched in a circulation war, carried daily reports of hysterical scenes at Beatle concerts and fought among themselves for exclusive interviews. Television and radio featured them incessantly, and Beatle wigs, boots, sweaters, and suits went on sale. The Beatles were immortalised in wax at Madame Tussaud's, chosen to appear in the Royal Variety Performance, and lauded and criticised in almost equal measure by politicians. In early 1964 the whole process was repeated as the group took America by storm, something no British pop act had ever achieved. Analysing the Beatle obsession became everyone's pet hobby, but the significant point was that pioneered by Georgie Fame during his celebrated stint at the Flamingo Club in Soho's Wardour Street.

R&B followers tended to look down on mainstream pop as commercially tainted and lacking 'authenticity', and some diehards even disapproved of the newer wave of blues bands playing Chuck Berry and Bo Diddley songs. Nevertheless, when the big companies began showing interest in the club scene (as a direct result of the beat boom), many of the bands signed contracts and seemed only too willing to make commercial compromises. If there was a major difference between Liverpool beat and London R&B, it had more to do with image than music. While a group like the Searchers would discard jeans and leather jackets for suits in a quest for showbusiness acceptance, London contemporaries like the Rolling Stones were more inclined to make a deliberate point of dressing casually, wearing their hair as long and as dirty as they liked, and acting in a way that was most likely to enrage parents of pop fans. Refusal to conform was a big part of the appeal of R&B's American figureheads like Howlin' Wolf and Muddy Waters, and the Stones in particular saw themselves as upholders of this radical tradition. Yet, as they soon discovered, turning one's face against the Establishment did not necessarily have to mean turning one's back on the mass market: upsetting authority could be a great marketing ploy.

The Rolling Stones all came from safe, suburban, Home Counties backgrounds, but their command of the R&B styles popularised by Muddy Waters, Slim Harpo, and others was total. They began as imitators, but their lack of deference towards their sources, their refusal to stand in the shadow of their mentors, set them apart from their fellow R&B bands from the start. While other groups accentuated the musical qualities of R&B, earning respectful silence while their lead guitarist recreated a Muddy Waters guitar solo, the Stones played up the music's innate sexuality and gave it contemporary relevance. Mick Jagger's tom-cat strut and swagger was far less playful and much more provocative than Presley's gyrations had ever been, while the songs he wrote with guitarist Keith Richards were cold, hard slices of macho sentiment. The typical Jagger-Richards stance was one of contempt towards women – 'Yesterday's Papers' and 'Under My Thumb' (1966) gloried in male supremacy – while in other songs their targets were less specific. 'Get Off of My Cloud', '19th Nervous Breakdown' and 'Satisfaction' (1965) expressed a more general cynicism towards society and reinforced the Stones' image as anarchists and rebels.

Controversy stalked the Stones through drug busts, concert riots, paternity suits, and personal tragedies like the death of Brian Jones in 1969. They were the eccentric, threatening extreme of British pop in the Sixties, and the chief spokesmen of swinging, liberated, promiscuous London. To both parents and the younger record buyer, the Beatles represented the other, safer, and more melodic extreme, yet the two groups seemed to complement each other. There was even an agreement between their respective managements that new records would be released at pre-arranged times, so that they never had to compete with one another for sales.

After the Stones, the most ruggedly individualistic of the R&B bands was the Animals, who came from Newcastle but were 'discovered' in London. While Mick Jagger's vocal style was at heart a mannered parody of

ABOVE *British R&B pioneer Cyril Davies (left) with his partner in Blues Incorporated, Alexis Korner. Davies died in 1964 just as the R&B boom began to take off.* RIGHT, ABOVE *The Rolling Stones'* *calculatedly subversive image counterpointed that of the Beatles.* RIGHT, BELOW *The Animals were specialists in earthy R&B; Eric Burdon (vocal) is in the centre, Alan Price (organ) at left.*

black singers, Animals' vocalist Eric Burdon seemed to have black feeling in his blood. Where Jagger sounded dispassionate, detached, cynical, Burdon shouted commitment. While the Stones' music was guitar-based, the Animals built their sound around Alan Price's intense, powerhouse organ playing. They were also one of the first British groups to be directly influenced by Bob Dylan: their first record, 'Baby Let Me Take You Home', was a version of a traditional blues song called 'Baby Let Me Follow You Down' that Dylan had recorded on his debut album in 1962; their second release was an Alan Price arrangement of a song from that same LP, 'House of the Rising Sun'.

Surprisingly for such an uncompromisingly gritty R&B band, the Animals trusted their recording career to Britain's leading independent pop producer, Mickie Most, whose unerring commercial sense led to hits galore for Herman's Hermits, Lulu, the Nashville Teens, Donovan, and (much later) Suzi Quatro and Mud. It was only after Price's departure for a solo career in 1965 that the group – and particularly Eric Burdon – began rebelling against the commercial strictures that Most imposed. Once established as a chart act, they were determined to dictate their own musical direction.

Some bands, notably Manfred Mann, wavered in their allegiance to their R&B roots but produced first-class commercial records. Mann himself, an expatriate South African with an impeccable jazz-blues pedigree, saw no contradiction in playing real down-home blues at a club gig and appearing on *Top of the Pops* the next day to promote an ephemeral piece of pop fluff like 'Pretty Flamingo' or 'Do Wah Diddy Diddy'. His taste was the band's great saving grace: he made a point of covering Dylan songs ('Just Like a Woman', 'Mighty Quinn', 'With

British R&B also spawned the mod scene, albeit indirectly. Mods were working-class teenagers, mostly from London, who built a complete subculture around themselves, their fashions, their tastes, and their prejudices. Scooters, amphetamine pills (taken by the dozen to keep awake throughout the weekend), parka jackets, pork pie hats, and short, feminine hairstyles were all part of the culture, while for music they turned to West Indian bluebeat, American soul, and the records of a handful of cult bands that came closest to capturing the narcissistic spirit of mod. It was the mods who gave British pop a definite sense of style in the mid-Sixties, dominating the number one pop television show, *Ready Steady Go!*, and making Carnaby Street the centre of hip fashion long before the colour supplements discovered it.

The first great mod band was the Yardbirds, who came together at art school (like so many British bands of the time) after seeing the Rolling Stones perform at the Station Hotel, Richmond, in 1963. They were natural heirs to the Stones' R&B mantle, being young and technically efficient and with evident star quality, and they already had a live reputation that was second to none when Simon Napier-Bell became their manager. He turned their natural on-stage moodiness into a selling point and gave them mod credentials – they copied the mod look, smashed up their equipment in an orgy of mock violence for Michelangelo Antonioni's film *Blow-Up* (1966), and cut a number of Mickie Most-produced 45s ('For Your Love', 'Shapes of Things', 'Heart Full of Soul') that were gimmicky enough to win chart placings but hardly tested their abilities as R&B musicians. The relentless commercialism eventually became too much for Eric Clapton, who left in 1966, but with such distinguished replacements as Jimmy Page and Jeff

God on Our Side' and Dylan himself was said to be consistently impressed with the results. Other groups to emerge with the R&B movement made little impression on the chart but were important for giving several future superstars of rock an early break – John Mayall's Bluesbreakers had Peter Green and John McVie (later of Fleetwood Mac), Jack Bruce, Mick Taylor, and Jon Hiseman; Bluesology had Elton John (then plain Reg Dwight) and Long John Baldry; Steampacket featured Rod Stewart, Julie Driscoll, and Brian Auger; the Graham Bond Organisation featured John McLaughlin, Jack Bruce, and Ginger Baker.

ABOVE *The Who were Britain's foremost mod group. From left: John Entwistle (bass), Keith Moon (drums), Roger Daltrey (vocal), Pete Townshend (guitar/ songwriter).* NEAR RIGHT *The Kinks had mod beginnings but soon revealed a softer, quirkier side to their music.* FAR RIGHT *The Yardbirds traded on a mod image but had a solid grounding in R&B, their early style based on Chicago blues. Guitar heroes to emerge from their ranks included Eric Clapton (seen here at left), Jimmy Page and Jeff Beck.*

Beck sharing lead guitar, the Yardbirds continued to forge one of the earliest forms of progressive rock.

If the Yardbirds' status as a mod group was incidental to their music, the Who identified themselves completely with the mod cause. Their adoption of mod gear and their ritual destruction of stage equipment during live gigs were publicity gimmicks conceived by manager Kit Lambert, but Pete Townshend's songs accurately charted the attitudes and obsessions of the average pill-popping mod. If the Who began by cashing in , at least they took their role as mod figureheads seriously: 'My Generation', 'I Can't Explain', 'Substitute', 'I Can See for Miles', 'Anyway, Anyhow, Anywhere' were all lifted straight from the mod experience. They were also representative of the slightly younger bands that, rather than look to the blues for inspiration, drew instead on the rock tradition itself; Townshend's own hero (and song-writing model) was Eddie Cochran.

The Small Faces and the Kinks also come into this category. The Small Faces had what would now be called a street-punk image and a style that strongly echoed contemporary soul music – 'Whatcha Gonna Do About It' (1965) their debut hit, used a riff (a repeated musical phrase) from Solomon Burke's 'Everybody Needs Somebody to Love'. However, like the Who in their 'Happy Jack' and 'Pictures of Lily' period, they also produced quirky singles that satirised the absurdities of suburban life – their best, 'Lazy Sunday' and 'Itchycoo Park', hinted gleefully at psychedelic trips in mundane English settings. The Kinks, too, wrote with a satirical edge, though their first 1964-5 releases ('You Really Got Me', 'All Day and All of the Night', 'Tired of Waiting for You') were raw, unsubtle slices of prehistoric heavy metal. Lead singer and resident songwriter Ray Davies proved to be one of British pop's most idiosyncratic figures, painting melancholy little word pictures of swinging London in songs like 'Dedicated Follower of Fashion', 'Sunny Afternoon', and 'Waterloo Sunset'.

All these groups helped alter the face of British pop, but they had the Beatles to thank for creating a climate conducive to change. On a commercial level, the Beatles prised open the huge American market for everyone from the Rolling Stones to Dusty Springfield (and even cabaret singers like Matt Munro and Shirley Bassey), thereby turning the modest British record industry into a multi-million-dollar export business and adjusting the commercial sights of every pop artist that followed. It was the Beatles, too, who rewrote some of the standard rules of the pop-music game about choice of material and an artist's involvement in the creative process. Likewise, the Beatles' increasingly progressive approach to their music, their desire to experiment and take risks, their dislike of the star system and growing indifference to commercialism, all left an indelible mark on the musicians who followed them. The Beatles turned the dream of creative freedom into a reality and, in so doing, made pop music more than just entertainment.

The albums *Rubber Soul* (1965) and *Revolver* (1966) demonstrated just how far the Beatles had moved away from their beat beginnings. Each gave credibility to the notion that pop music could constitute art – highbrow critics in Sunday newspapers were already labelling Lennon and McCartney 'the greatest songwriters since Schubert' – and they underlined the potential of the album form as a means of making musical statements.

Even more eye-opening was the Beatles' use of recording studio resources, especially on tracks with explicit references to drugs, like 'She Said She Said' and 'Tomorrow Never Knows'. George Martin's ingenuity as a producer was taxed to the full as they laced their music with ever more elaborate effects and toyed with the possibilities of stereophonic sound. *Sgt Pepper's Lonely Hearts Club Band*, issued bang in the middle of the flower-power summer of 1967, was the culmination of this process; a gargantuan, multifaceted commentary on the times. Fundamentally, *Sgt Pepper* was a gloriously self-indulgent 'concept' album – the first of its kind in the rock field – permeated throughout by a mood of nostalgia and an ironic view of showbusiness rituals.

Sgt Pepper and their six-song score for *Magical Mystery Tour* (an hour-long television film) brought the Beatles' whimsical, pseudo-artistic period to an end. Non-musical factors – the death of Brian Epstein, their involvement with the Indian mystic the Maharishi Mahesh Yogi, the launch of Apple as an exercise in what Paul McCartney called 'western communism', John Lennon's liaison with Yoko Ono – all contributed to a collective creative breakdown within the group, although Lennon, McCartney, and Harrison had begun to move in separate musical directions as early as the

Help! album (1965). The friendly competition between the three produced some excellent results, but by the time the double album *The Beatles* was released in 1968, that rivalry had dissolved into acrimony.

Folk Rock: Dylan & After

If the Beatles were catalysts for change within British rock, their influence in shaping the American scene after 1964 was incalculable. Pre-Beatle pop in the USA was not without its bright lights – notably the Four Seasons in New York and the Beach Boys in California – but the Beatles effectively put America back in touch with its own rock heritage, reviving the dynamism of rock 'n' roll and breathing new life into half-forgotten styles. As in Britain, they sparked off a massive explosion of beat groups, the best of whom expanded further upon the Beatles' musical ideas, and forced the American record business to revalue its position towards rock. Most important of all, they attracted back to pop those former fans who had lost faith in the music around the time of the *Bandstand* era – the same fans (musicians among them) who had turned instead to the more intellectually credible field of folk music. With their return to rock, a new hybrid style emerged: folk-rock.

The appeal of folk music to America's middle-class

student generation was easy to understand. Folk was not a commercialised music, so it had integrity; it had historical roots and was the basis for much scholarly research; it was the music of the working classes, the poor, the migrant workers and immigrants, so it had political connotations. 'Ban the bomb' marches, peace drives, and demonstrations against racial segregation were very much a part of college life in the early Sixties, and the music of Woody Guthrie, Pete Seeger, the Weavers, Joan Baez and others provided a rallying cry. Guthrie was a particularly romantic figure, having spent years living out the kind of roving, bohemian existence that has always attracted middle-class radicals, while Seeger – writer of such folk anthems as 'Where Have All the Flowers Gone', 'If I Had a Hammer', and 'Guantanamera' – had been blacklisted during the McCarthy era of the Fifties for his espousal of left-wing causes (the successful career of the Weavers, of which Seeger was a member, was effectively blighted for more than a decade by the blacklisting).

The folk-music community was centred on Greenwich Village in New York. Among the many new names to win recognition there were Judy Collins, Ramblin' Jack Elliott, Dave Van Ronk, Phil Ochs, Tim Hardin, and young Robert Zimmerman, who changed his surname to

ABOVE *The Byrds, the first group to merge folk and rock styles, first charted (1965) with Dylan's*   *'Mr Tambourine Man', although only Roger McGuinn (centre) actually played on that session.*

Dylan in tribute to poet Dylan Thomas. Dylan was soaked in the mythology of folk and claimed to have travelled the highways with Woody Guthrie, on whom his singing and songwriting style was closely based. At a time when it was unusual for folk singers to write their own songs – traditional material was regarded as more 'authentic' – Dylan made his mark with a string of deftly constructed mock-folk songs that ran the gamut of all the social and political subjects with which the folk audience concerned itself. His second and third albums, *The Freewheelin' Bob Dylan* (1963) and *The Times They Are A-Changin'* (1964), established him as the angry young man of the folk scene, a master of the polemical song; but all this concealed a deep distrust and dislike of the folk establishment. Dylan's instinct was to rebel against the expectations of his folk followers, and from 1964

onwards he cut down noticeably on the number of political songs in his concert repertoire.

He replaced them with much more personal material like 'It Ain't Me Babe', 'My Back Pages', and 'All I Really Want to Do', songs born of his own experiences and written as self-expression. His fourth album, *Another Side of Bob Dylan* (1964), confirmed his new direction but infuriated the folk purists, many of whom labelled him a traitor to the folk tradition. He took most of his old fans with him, yet no one was prepared for the next startling change in Dylan's music, which became evident on his *Bringing It All Back Home* album (1965) and (most starkly) in his appearance at the 1965 Newport Folk Festival. Dylan had switched to rock – and the Beatles were his inspiration. 'They were doing things nobody was doing', he told his biographer, Tony Scaduto 'their chords were outrageous, just outrageous, and their harmonies made it all valid ... I knew they were pointing the direction where music had to go ... in my mind, the Beatles were it.' Rock versions of his songs by the Byrds, the Animals, Manfred Mann, and others convinced him that the time was right to take what would be an irrevocable step. Rightly, he judged that rock accompaniment would add new dimensions of energy, attack, and power to his songs.

His understanding of the rock idiom stemmed from his own adolescence, when he was as much a rock 'n' roll fan as any other Midwestern teenager. Rock 'n' roll formed his new stylistic base: 'Subterranean Homesick Blues', the hit single taken from *Bringing It All Back Home,* was a clever update of Chuck Berry's 'Too Much Monkey Business'; but the most gripping features of his newer recordings were the blues-inflected backings and the intense, searing organ sound of sideman Al Kooper (echoes here of the Animals and Alan Price). His songs were more vitriolic than ever, with a level of invective that was totally new to rock, and his targets ranged from society itself ('Maggie's Farm', 'Desolation Row') to unnamed individuals ('Like a Rolling Stone', 'Positively Fourth Street'). In 1966 the *Blonde on Blonde* album introduced a mellower and more mystical Dylan, much taken with the philosophy of Zen. As his lyric writing advanced from the savagely direct to the metaphysically complex, so his music incorporated longer, lusher instrumental passages that echoed the studio work of the Beatles and his fellow folk-rock innovators, the Byrds. A serious motorcycle accident in 1967 put him out of action for almost a year, but he re-emerged with an album (*John Wesley Harding*, 1968) that again marked an abrupt change of course: this was Dylan in a much more basic vein, singing homespun country melodies to the accompaniment of some of the best session musicians in Nashville. Never one to simply follow trends, Dylan's great contribution to rock was to explore surprising new avenues and extend the music's frame of reference – not once but several times.

Dylan's influence was important, too, in other key respects. He changed the very nature of the pop song, eschewing its traditional subject matter. When he wrote about love his approach was profoundly anti-romantic. He questioned whether relationships could ever be permanent ('Don't Think Twice, It's Alright', 'One Too Many Mornings') and derided the conventions of courtship in songs such as 'It Ain't Me Babe' and 'Just Like a Woman'. He took social and political comment into the record charts for the first time and introduced a new realism into rock lyrics. He changed the *language* of pop songwriting, making brilliant use of literary devices like irony and metaphor and bringing a poetic quality to songs. The very fact that lyrics did assume such an importance within rock was partly due to Dylan. He also proved that a rock singer didn't necessarily require a 'good' voice to make an impact – Dylan's rasping, strident, in some ways unmusical voice had power because of his command of nuance and intonation, and the point was not lost on the generation of singer-songwriters who followed him – though few if any had his gifts as a writer of lyrics.

Dylan was far from alone in seeing the potential of a folk-rock marriage. He was one of many folk musicians who were re-converted to rock at the hands of the Beatles around 1964, though he had more confidence than most to make the break. Next to Dylan, the most influential figures in folk-rock were the Byrds, who were formed by ex-Chad Mitchell Trio member Roger McGuinn after seeing the Beatles in *A Hard Day's Night*. His approach was clinical: he sought to match folk harmonies and material with rock instrumentation, thereby imbuing rock with some of the melodic, ethereal qualities of folk music. Their first disc was a version of Dylan's 'Mr Tambourine Man', which McGuinn had completely rearranged and all but rewritten – and, to make sure the Beatle-like guitar sound was precisely right, he called in three vastly experienced ex-Phil Spector session men, Hal Blaine, Larry Knechtel, and Leon Russell, to complement his own twelve-string guitar work. The result was a complex, dream-like record that inspired a hundred imitations, all created to an extraordinarily impact-laden commercial formula.

What the Byrds synthesised was a folk-rock *sound*, finely textured and graced by breathtaking three-part harmonies. They continued to record Dylan songs, and even occasionally a more conventional folk item like Pete Seeger's 'Turn! Turn! Turn!', but their desire to experiment eventually cost them their 1965 status as 'America's Beatles'. Moving from folk-rock to experiments with electronics on their albums *Fifth Dimension* (1966) and *Younger Than Yesterday* (1967), and finally in 1968 to country-rock, the Byrds lost a sizeable section of their audience – but not their influence on the folk and rock scenes. The strange, cosmic nature of their music during their *Fifth Dimension* phase, and in particular its association with the drugs sub-culture, predated the extravagantly experimental (some might say pretentious or at least over-praised) sounds of San Francisco bands such as Jefferson Airplane and the Grateful Dead, most of which had folk beginnings.

Other artists to appear under the folk-rock banner included the Lovin' Spoonful, the Mamas and the Papas, Sonny and Cher, and the Turtles, as well as a handful of folk-style duos and soloists. The Spoonful were basically a Greenwich Village jugband with rock instruments, whose amiable good-time style had antecedents not just in Beatle music of the 'Good Day Sunshine' ilk but in the songs of jazz singers Fats Waller and Hoagy Carmichael. The Mamas and the Papas also started in the Village but found success in Los Angeles, after they had teamed up with producer Lou Adler, a one-time West Coast representative of Aldon Music and a songwriting partner of Sam Cooke and Herb Alpert. Adler masterminded the

protest-music craze in California in 1965, launching the former New Christy Minstrel singer Barry McGuire somewhat over-optimistically as a 'second Dylan' with the hit single 'Eve of Destruction'; and he paved the way for hippy acts like the Sonny and Cher duo. These two were ex-Phil Spector sidekicks who grew their hair long and wore sleeveless sheepskins and bell-bottoms. Their sound was more Spector-ish than folk-rock, and their songs mostly concerned parental problems; but shrewd marketing placed them firmly in the protest bag with which folk-rock was at first confused.

Strangely few of the original Greenwich Village folk set benefited directly from the upsurge of interest in folk-rock, though one-time residents like Neil Young, Steve Stills, Gordon Lightfoot, Joni Mitchell, and James Taylor did make a huge impact later in the decade. Solo singers generally fared less well than groups in the Beatle-obsessed atmosphere of the mid-Sixties, and those who did gain big record deals tended to suffer in the shadow of Bob Dylan. One such was Tim Hardin, composer of such bitter-sweet love songs as 'Reason to Believe', 'Misty Roses', and 'If I Were a Carpenter', whose world-weary, jazz-tinged vocal style was slightly ahead of its time. More successful in the long term was Paul Simon, whose songs accurately mirrored the insecurities and liberal concerns of mid-Sixties middle-of-the-road student America. A former high school friend of Carole King in New York, he once tried to deter her from joining Aldon Music because of the relentless commercialism of the pop scene. Yet a few years later, in partnership with Art Garfunkel, he created a commercial 'monster' of his own in the 10 million-selling album *Bridge Over Troubled Water* (1970).

ABOVE *New York's Four Seasons.*
RIGHT, ABOVE *Joni Mitchell, a Greenwich Village folk-singer, now a leading singer-songwriter.*

The Beatle Legacy: USA

Despite the style's prominence, America's response to the Beatles and the 'British invasion' did not begin or end with folk-rock. The Young Rascals, a four-man group from the Italian quarter of New York, mixed black R&B with a Latin sound to produce a style that was described as 'blue-eyed soul'. The Four Seasons, with a similar Italian-American background, maintained the early Sixties form that had brought them hits like 'Rag Doll' and 'Big Girls Don't Cry' without adapting their style at all. Their record company, Vee Jay, who also owned the rights to some early Beatle recordings, even issued an album in 1964 of tracks by both groups with the provocative title *The Beatles Versus the Four Seasons*. Over in California, meanwhile, where most of America's major record companies now had their national offices, a string of groups were launched as American 'answers' to the Beatles – Paul Revere and the Raiders, Gary Lewis and the Playboys, the Seeds, the Beau Brummels. The most spectacular success of all was achieved by the Monkees, four young actor-musicians hired through an advertisement in the trade paper *Variety* to star in a

weekly comedy-with-music television series. The lessons of Ricky Nelson's success back in the late Fifties were clearly not forgotten – and the songs for the series were provided by none other than Goffin and King, Neil Sedaka, and the Aldon Music crew of the pre-Beatle days. There was a nice irony in this, as the Beatles – propagators of the virtues of writing one's own material – had seemed to be making even the best of the 'song factories' all but redundant.

But if there was one group that encapsulated all the changes within American rock in the Sixties, it had to be the Beach Boys. Formed in 1961 by three brothers, Dennis, Brian, and Carl Wilson, a cousin, and a friend, their style was at first a cross between the Four Freshmen and Chuck Berry – high harmonies and teenage lyrics set to a clanky guitar backing. They established the surf-music genre with obsessive Brian Wilson songs about the joys of riding the waves; then, once that craze had died down, they turned to emulating the Spector sound. Brian's particular genius was for production, and between 1963 and 1967 he took his admiration of Spector, the Beatles, and other experimentalists in sound to fantastic extremes, overdubbing endlessly and creating kaleidoscopic sound pictures full of light, space, meticulously mixed harmonies, and rococo lyrics. Wilson's aim seemed to be to take rock music on to a higher mystical and academic plane, though the Beach Boys' first 'artistic' album, *Pet Sounds* (1966), was misunderstood by many and unfairly compared to the Beatles' *Revolver*. Their true masterpiece was the single 'Good Vibrations' (1966) an intricately constructed exercise in vocal and production style and the vocabulary of hippydom. In 1967 Wilson scrapped what was to be the group's consummate musical statement, an album called *Smile*, in its final stages, scared by competition from *Sgt Pepper*. From then on Beach Boy music became increasingly disjointed, as the group drifted into flirtations with transcendental meditation, acid, doubtful hippy sects, and the ecology movement. Nevertheless, they have stayed together, occasionally producing work of unequivocal greatness, and today rank among the elder statesmen of rock.

Soul

There was one area of American rock that drew only fleetingly on British influence: soul music, which underwent a revolution of its own in the Sixties. Soul was born of two hitherto unrelated black styles, the gospel music of the churches and the raunchy R&B of the clubs and bars: to mix the two, as Ray Charles did on records like 'What'd I Say' and 'I Got a Woman' (1954) was to outrage both musical communities. Gospel, after all, was sacred music; as bluesman Big Bill Broonzy said of Charles, 'He's mixing the blues and spirituals and I *know* that's wrong'. Yet the gospel influence grew steadily with the rise of Tamla Motown and, particularly, the popularity among black and white audiences of the former gospel star Sam Cooke. His smooth, precise vocal style was much copied and, as the epitome of successful, sophisticated black youth, he became a figurehead and model for all subsequent soul stars. The other godfather of the soul movement was James Brown, a fiercely individualistic performer who first emerged in 1956. His aggressive, pleading style and on-stage histrionics made him the greatest live performer in soul, and none knew better the power of soul as dance music.

While Motown in Detroit specialised in formula product, the Stax label in Memphis had a less refined commercial approach and gave its singers freer rein. Stax also had a recognisable 'sound', rooted in the instrumental work of the Mar-Keys rhythm and horn section, whose guitarist, Steve Cropper, also co-wrote and arranged for many of the company's artists. These included Otis Redding, on whose records the Mar-Keys' horns were used in call-and-response style, like a chorus, and whose chief innovation was to improvise on the lyrics and depart from the melody at the right emotional moment. This added intensity and a note of unpredictability to his records and performances, though, as the label's biggest-selling soul artist, he worked so much in this style that his discs eventually verged on self-parody. He was killed in an air crash late in 1967, by which time he had gained the largest following of any soul singer among white fans in America and Britain.

Other Stax acts included Wilson Pickett, Sam and Dave, Eddie Floyd, Rufus Thomas and William Bell and Judy Clay. In the same mould were a number of black soul performers contracted to Atlantic, Ray Charles'

ABOVE *Wilson Pickett, whose hits included an epic version of the Beatles' 'Hey Jude'.* RIGHT, ABOVE *Stevie Wonder, perhaps the major* creative force in Seventies soul. RIGHT, BELOW *Otis Redding, whose huge world following came only after his death in 1967.*

former label, which had close recording connections with Stax. Chief among these was Aretha Franklin, who was groomed as a gospel queen in the tradition of Clara Ward and Mahalia Jackson but made a deliberate move into the white jazz/middle-of-the-road market around 1960, when she signed with Columbia. Dissatisfied with life on the night-club circuit, she moved to the sympathetic musical environment of Atlantic's studio at Muscle Shoals, Alabama, and recorded there under the direction of producer Jerry Wexler. Despite the brassy accompaniments and tight, spare production, her new records were closer to gospel than anything yet heard in the charts. Aretha explored the celebratory and devotional aspects of gospel in discs like 'Respect', 'Natural Woman', and 'Chain of Fools' (all 1967) though the lyrics were secular. Indeed, one of the great strengths of soul music was that it expressed, in its lyrics, the pride and defiance of black society at a time of change. Music always had offered blacks an escape route from the ghetto; now those musicians and singers, instead of simply giving the white man what he wanted, could truly be said to be performing for their own people. They were visible exemplars of 'black power' in its most positive sense.

Changes in white rock were also felt within soul, especially in the move towards a more progressive outlook around 1967. Motown, feeling the competition from Stax and Atlantic most keenly, relaxed its formula approach and became specialists in what was labelled 'psychedelic soul'. The Temptations, working with writer/producer Norman Whitfield, adopted a heavy, guitar-based rock sound and dabbled in self-consciously meaningful lyrics, seeming to draw on everything from West Coast acid-rock to the raw style of Jimi Hendrix. Stevie Wonder switched to a similarly progressive path a little later, suddenly dropping the cabaret-singer guise

that Berry Gordy had encouraged him to adopt in favour of moog synthesiser, Muslim philosophy, and social comment. He was instrumental in persuading Motown to give its artists more direct control over their own output, from which the Jackson Five, Smokey Robinson, and Marvin Gaye would all benefit in the Seventies. The post-1967 period also produced a new crop of soul stars from other labels, including Curtis Mayfield (ex-leader of the Impressions), Sly and the Family Stone, the Chi-Lites, and the Philadelphia-based Delfonics.

As the rock world entered the late Sixties, so many of the changes set in motion earlier in the decade came to fruition. Rock became more socially aware, more experimental, and musicians attained a degree of artistic control over their music that would have been unthinkable a few years before. Perhaps most significantly – thanks especially to the efforts of Bob Dylan, the Beatles, and the Rolling Stones – rock was coming to be seen as an instrument of change – not just as a soundtrack to leisure activity but as something of social value in itself.

The American Scene 1965-75

The later Sixties were a period of great social and political upheaval, a time when traditional values were being questioned or discarded altogether. A new spirit of affluence and optimism engendered a liberal atmosphere which the youth of the Western world could embrace and exploit; but this sense of freedom led to a clash with authority in the shape of parents, laws, and governments. Popular music of the era underwent a

ABOVE *Mike Bloomfield was a star of Paul Butterfield's Blues Band, which backed Bob Dylan at the 1965 Newport Folk Festival.*

RIGHT *Carlos Santana and his band swept from Fillmore auditions to stardom as a Sixties Latin-rock group. He remains active as ever.*

change which was both a reflection and an essential ingredient of the social revolution. Important issues became magnets of discontent. Thus America's position in Vietnam, disputed drug laws, modes of dress and speech were all rallying points of the Sixties movements. Entertainment and politics were no longer regarded as unrelated entities. As a confidently self-aware youth culture became widespread it found a sparking-point in the new clubs, festivals, records, and art of the time. A new language was spawned, the language of the underground movement with its happenings and love-ins. A new tribal spirit seemed to have been born.

This groundswell of alternative culture cannot be considered without looking at the major groups of the Sixties. While some of the music was made to be experienced in a state of drug-induced euphoria, was

thus totally escapist, much else was designed to reflect and even to nourish the spirit of rebellion. In 1965 folk-rock and protest-pop were contemporary with the burning of draft cards and the desecration of the American flag on the steps of the Pentagon.

West-Coast Revival

Musically, as we have seen, American fashions were very much influenced by what was happening in England with the British beat groups and with the adventurous excursions of the Beatles. America's biggest pop group was still the Beach Boys, but something else was stirring in California now. Surf music and folk protest songs were soon to be replaced by a more strident electric rock, whose volume and intensity were in themselves causes of alarm in the establishment. The significant gathering-places for the emerging talents of this period were on the West Coast, most importantly Los Angeles and San Francisco.

The Mamas and the Papas epitomized the marriage of Los Angeles' pop-rock sound and the new production expertise. Their beautifully constructed close harmonies and hippy image placed them neatly between the surf bands and the new West Coast personalities. They achieved great commercial success with singles like 'Monday, Monday' and 'Dedicated to the One I Love' (1967) but internal disagreements and an inability to shake off the more glib associations of folk-rock and Scott McKenzie-style flower-power marred their progress and led to their early dissolution in 1968.

While Los Angeles remained the centre of the entertainment industry, San Francisco's more cosmopolitan environment encouraged a greater variety of artistic expression. Its older elegance and compact size were in marked contrast to the slick modern scale of Los Angeles. As the beat generation of the Fifties had congregated there, so too did the beats' successors, the hippies, or, as they were somewhat coyly termed, flower children.

Early entrepreneurs like Chet Helms and his Family Dog Organisation and Bill Graham, founder of the Fillmores, played a vital role in providing the first clubs and halls where the new music could be heard, a music often fuelled and inspired by the hallucinogenic drug LSD, not yet outlawed in California. In 1965 Ken Kesey and his Merry Pranksters held their infamous acid tests

at the Fillmore West to a background of sounds provided by the embryonic Grateful Dead and a kaleidoscope of strange stroboscopic lighting and electronic gadgetry contributed by the LSD chemist Stanley Owsley III.

A whirl of psychedelic noise ushered in the 'summer of love'. As word spread, there was a sudden migration of young people to San Francisco. The Haight-Ashbury area was thronging with those curious to experience the hippy lifestyle first-hand. What began as a series of disconnected events assumed the proportions of a scene, one which was not yet commercialised.

The Grateful Dead and the Jefferson Airplane were in the forefront of the new music, but there were many others whose style contributed to the broad sound of San Francisco. Amongst the first generation of bands were the Charlatans, Big Brother & the Holding Company, the Beau Brummels, Country Joe and the Fish, and Sopwith Camel. As an audience for these groups grew, so did a need for bigger venues. Bill Graham and Chet Helms could fill concert halls like the Avalon, Fillmore West, and Cow Palace, while on special occasions the musicians would perform for nothing in Golden Gate Park

Bill Graham

The musical explosion that rocked San Francisco in the middle Sixties, earning it the title of the Liverpool of America, could never have reached fruition without the acumen and vision of Bill Graham. A displaced European emigré, former actor and co-founder of a San Francisco mime troupe, Graham began his promotional life putting on benefit concerts in the Bay Area. As the scene burgeoned he noticed a need for bigger venues capable of housing the new talent, ones that encouraged dancing and multimedia happenings.

Graham opened the Fillmore West on 10 December 1965 with the Jefferson Airplane, and for the next five years managed to provide imaginative bills incorporating three or more bands. The sister venue in New York, Fillmore East, was run on similar lines, with Graham featuring all the major acts of the time as well the top British groups. There was theatre, comedy, and jazz too, including appearances by Lenny Bruce, Benny Goodman, and Miles Davis. One innovation was a cheap Tuesday-night audition spot, which helped to break Tower of Power and Santana for the first time.

As the scene expanded Graham took on more ambitious venues and extended his expertise to management with the Airplane and It's A Beautiful Day. He encouraged the groups to record live albums, and some of these were seminal West Coast sets, the Dead's *Live Dead* (1970) and Quicksilver Messenger Service's *Happy Trails* (1969) among them.

Although he closed both Fillmores in the early Seventies Graham's ambitions remained – to provide high-quality entertainment at reasonable prices. The trust he had built up enabled him to promote shows across the world. He is the favourite promoter for the Who, the Rolling Stones and, always, the Grateful Dead, for whom he arranged four shows in 1978 in front of the pyramids of Giza in Egypt.

or even off the back of a truck parked in the Haight itself.

Los Angeles was also enjoying an explosion of new groups and clubs. Fundamental to the scene were the Byrds, whose work has been described in Chapter 3. Their records were artistic successes, but as live performers they were notoriously erratic. This and the friction between founding members Roger McGuinn, David Crosby, and Gene Clark, led to the departure of Clark for a partnership with Doug Dillard and a series of rows between McGuinn and Crosby, which were resolved only when the latter left after receiving a substantial financial settlement. But the importance of

the Byrds in the middle Sixties can hardly be exaggerated. Not only did they record a body of beautifully constructed melodic and harmonic work; they were also innovators who broke British dominance of the American rock scene.

In terms of the music business the Byrds were a catalyst that sent the record executives scuttling for their cheque books. As rock music became a significant money-spinner it revitalised an industry in search of new rising stars. Jac Holzman's Elektra label was among the first to spot the trend, and signed the group Love in 1965, while Capitol signed the Leaves and Atco took on

The Jefferson Airplane became an institution in 1965 as America's first subversive acid-pop band.

From left: Paul Kantner, Skip Spence, Grace Slick, Jorma Kaukonen, Jack Casady, Marty Balin.

Buffalo Springfield. All these bands were characterised by the twelve-string guitar sound, close harmonies – and the distinctive Byrds haircut.

Love were unfortunate in being slightly ahead of their time. The brilliance of their leader Arthur Lee counted against them: at a time when band democracy was still taken for granted, he tended to clash with the other members, with Elektra, and with the Los Angeles scene-makers. Nevertheless the band's debut album

63

Love (made in 1965 but released in 1966) was remarkable for beating the Byrds to the punch in covering 'Hey Joe' (the Chester Powers song which became the anthem of the LA punk groups) and for the quality of the original writing and playing. This was at a time when even the Byrds were happier doing cover versions and still had to rely on the talents of session sidemen like Hal Blaine, Leon Russell, and Glen Campbell (all veterans of the Shindig TV show) to polish their sound. Love ceased to be regarded seriously as part of the mainstream after Da Capo (1967), although both that album and its successor, the extraordinary Forever Changes (also 1967), have given them, in retrospect, a legendary status and Arthur Lee an enduring reputation.

Meanwhile San Francisco's gathering rock community was also experiencing the fruits of commercial interest. Jefferson Airplane secured a large deal with RCA and

Sly Stone

Sylvester Stewart, or Sly Stone as he is better known, is a veteran of the West Coast scene. Sly first entered the business as producer for San Francisco's Autumn label, which he ran with DJ Tom Donahue. Autumn had local hits with the Beau Brummels, Vejtables, and Mojo Men, while Sly gained a name as one of the area's best DJs.

In 1966 he formed the Stoners, who evolved into Sly and the Family Stone, a hybrid rock-and-soul outfit notable for their multiracial line-up. Their first single, the exhilarating 'Dance to the Music' (1968), was a worldwide hit, and its follow-ups 'M'Lady' and 'Everyday People' (both 1968) established the group at the forefront of a revitalised Californian soul movement.

Sly's increasingly political material gave him the status of a superstar among the radical Black Panthers, and the albums *Stand!* (1969) and *There's a Riot Goin' On* (1971) perfectly captured the mood of a tense society. After an epic performance at Woodstock it seemed that the Family Stone could do no wrong, but this proved to have been their pinnacle. Afterwards Sly's disenchantment with touring, and crucial personnel changes (such as bassist Larry Graham departing to form Graham Central Station) only dissipated their vitality.

Throughout the Seventies the formerly flamboyant Sly became a recluse, recording to less effect than in the Sixties. It wasn't until 1979's *Back on the Right Track* that he could hint at the good times. Ironically, a collection of his older songs remixed for disco came out at the same time and sold better. Then in 1983 *Ain't But the One Way* marked a fine return to his roots.

Sly Stone is still justly regarded as a vital element in the conscious development of sophisticated funk, and the modern stars of disco have undoubtedly plundered many of his original ideas.

LEFT *Country Joe McDonald satirised the American political scene in the Sixties through a psychedelic haze; he remains active today.*

ABOVE *The Grateful Dead were the undisputed masters of acid rock in the 1960s, and still play. From left: Jerry Garcia and Bob Weir.*

provided the Bay Area with a sex symbol in singer/writer Grace Slick, recruited in 1966 from a disbanded rival band, the Great Society, to replace Signe Anderson. Airplane were formed by Marty Balin, who rehearsed the group in his Matrix club and persuaded Bill Graham to give them special prominence at the Fillmore West. Balin's seamless singing with Slick, and the Airplane's ambitious live sets, enabled them to tour America to spectacular effect. The singles 'Somebody to Love' and 'White Rabbit' were national hits, while the albums *Surrealistic Pillow* and *After Bathing at Baxter's* (all 1967) were evidence of the diverse creativity of the West Coast groups.

The Band

Although the Band were of seminal importance to the Sixties scene, their existence was something of an anomaly in that era. As the Hawks, Robbie Robertson, Richard Manuel, Levon Helm, Rick Danko, and Garth Hudson (all, except Helm, Canadians) had been an accomplished rock 'n' roll outfit backing Ronnie Hawkins and others.

The Band achieved real prominence as Bob Dylan's backing group for his ground-breaking electric tours of 1966, including the infamous date at London's Albert Hall, and the following year their partnership resulted in the making of the legendary *Basement Tapes*, a collection of songs (cut in 1967) officially released only in 1975.

Music from Big Pink (1968) – this was the name of their house in Woodstock – was the band's own début, a highly evocative treatment of American rural and folk tradition, and this character immediately set it apart from the acid-rock norm. Just as inventive were the individual talents of the Band, all of whom seemed capable of treating their instruments afresh. *The Band* (1969), *Stage Fright* (1970) and *Cahoots* (1971), which featured Van

Morrison on one track, continued to develop the rural motifs, while *Moondog Matinee* (1973) was an exciting return to rock 'n' roll roots.

Always highly regarded critically, the Band never managed to make a similar commercial impact, though they did perform at the massive Watkins Glen Festival in 1973. Usually they were happier in the studios. In 1974 they worked once again with Bob Dylan, both live (*Before the Flood*) and in the studio (*Planet Waves*), but their own creativity was less in evidence. Dylan repaid the debt he owed to their part in his career when he guested on their final concerts at the Academy of Music. Aside from Dylan the Band attracted the support of several other highly regarded musicians who had come to pay their respects and participate on the triple album *The Last Waltz*. These included Joni Mitchell, Van Morrison, Neil Young, Dr John, Ron Wood and Ringo Starr – testimony to the Band's enormous integrity and the awe in which they were held by people who gained greater success with less talent.

Since that time the Band have kept to their promise of retirement, although several of them have made excellent solo albums. The timeless quality of their music makes the possibility of their reuniting a genuinely attractive prospect.

LEFT *The Band in concert in the late Sixties. Foreground, from left: Garth Hudson, Rick Danko, and Jaime Robbie Robertson.*

ABOVE *Captain Beefheart and his various Magic Bands have been playing country- and jazz-based rock since the mid-Sixties.*

operated outside the mainstream and would later be regarded as an anachronism.

While critics have often spoken of a West Coast sound, it would be more accurate to say that California was responsible for a variety of sounds. For example, Country Joe and the Fish were psychedelic *and* political, combining the musical form with some well-aimed swipes at Lyndon Johnson's Vietnam policies and conservative Middle America. Conversely, a group like the Steve Miller Band concentrated on delving into their blues origins, Miller having served his apprenticeship with such notables as Chuck Berry and Otis Rush. The Miller Band was also indicative of the influx of musicians to California. Their roots, like those of San Antonio's Sir Douglas Quintet, lay in the blues and country heritage of Texas. As musicians such as the Quintet's Doug Sahm introduced different strains, including those of the 'Tex-Mex' border musicians, San Francisco became acknowledged as a melting-pot of many styles.

By 1966 Haight-Ashbury was a thriving artistic community, and a second generation of bands had emerged. As well as local outfits like Quicksilver Messenger Service and the soulful Sons of Champlin there were now frequent visits by up-and-coming Los Angeles celebrities such as Spirit, the Doors, and Buffalo Springfield, as well as Eastern groups like the Youngbloods, Paul Butterfield's Blues Band, and early jazz-rock combinations such as Chicago Transit Authority, Blood, Sweat and Tears, and Electric Flag.

San Francisco also boasted two of the most influential

Airplane were noted for their instrumental prowess, and the bass playing of Jack Casady and inventive guitar work of Jorma Kaukonen were perfect foils to the vocal strengths of Slick and Balin. In Paul Kantner, too, the group possessed an overtly political writer and singer who would eventually ursurp Balin's position as leader.

The Grateful Dead did not sign to Warner Brothers until 1966, although their musical experience stretched back farther than Airplane's. As a jugband and then as the Warlocks the prototype Dead perfected their style of acid rock. Their long improvisations denied them chart success but guaranteed them a large and fanatically devoted live following. Their leader, Jerry Garcia, was a veteran of the Kesey acid tests and an accomplished blues and bluegrass guitarist. Alongside him the 17-year old prodigy Bob Weir on rhythm guitar and the classically trained bassist Phil Lesh formed the basis of an electric conception that had little to do with pop music. The Grateful Dead were among the first bands to experiment with synthetic treatments and to use more complex studio instrumentation than the established guitars-bass-drums line-up. Their live sets would run as long as four hours, and a song like 'St Stephen' or 'Dark Star' became the basis for some wildly original playing. The height of their attempts to interpret the LSD experience can be heard in *Anthem of the Sun* (1968) and *Aoxomoxoa* (1969). But the Dead's unique approach meant that they

Psychedelia

While the most famous examples of acid rock emanated from bands like the Grateful Dead, Quicksilver Messenger Service, and Moby Grape, there was much other worthwhile if obscure music being recorded under the banner of psychedelia between 1965 and 1968.

Psychedelic garage rock was a form of American punk that rarely made any national impression but helped to establish local scenes. Generally combining R&B with treated guitars, tape loops, backwards effects, and lyrical and verbal excesses, these groups stayed on the right side of insanity by virtue of their humour and flair for the absurd. Bands like the Standells, Leaves, Seeds, Electric Prunes, and 13th Floor Elevators concentrated on the extreme aspects of hallucinatory music, though their appearance and belligerent attitude often belied the 'peace-and-love' slogans touted by psychedelia's promoters.

A quick glance at some band names and song-titles indicates that they were either deranged or enjoying an involved joke with their audience. For instance Seattle's Electric Prunes enjoyed brief notoriety with 'I Had Too Much to Dream (Last Night)' (1967), while the Barbarians could boast a one-handed drummer.

A first-time listener can gain an immediate insight into the genre from the compilation *Nuggets*, a lovingly balanced set of weirdness gathered together by critic (and singer Patti Smith's guitarist) Lenny Kaye.

radio stations in KSAN and KMPX, which were forerunners of the FM radio boom and spokesmen for the underground network. KSAN and their respected DJ, the rotund Tom Donahue, could break a local group into the national charts, as happened in 1967 with the Doors' first No 1 hit, 'Light My Fire'.

The Doors epitomised all the possibilities of Californian rock. They were excellent musicians, capable of expanding a commercial repertoire into longer improvised pieces like 'The End' and 'When the Music's Over' (1967). In their singer Jim Morrison they had a figurehead who fused a poetic flair with a potent sexual and rebellious image. Morrison took his audience further than any of his contemporaries, inciting an adulation that bordered on teen-appeal hysteria. When he tired of these manimpulative practices he entered a 'mystical' phase, advocating anarchic rebellion and urging his audience to think beyond the solace of mere vinyl. Deliberately provocative songs like 'Five to One' and anti-war numbers like 'The Unknown Soldier' were accompanied by on-stage cries of revolt. In the process Morrison earned a notoriety that overshadowed the Doors' music. Several Doors shows were disrupted by baton-wielding policemen, and Morrison was arrested twice for alleged obscenity. On the second occasion, in Miami, he was called to stand trial for indecent exposure, an offence that carried a maximum sentence of five years imprisonment. Although he was acquitted, incidents like this

Allen Toussaint

Although the attention of the rock industry necessarily focussed on the East and West coasts during the Sixties, much good and lasting music was created in other parts of America.

New Orleans' musical tradition had a lineage that stretched back to the early days of jazz and forward to the epoch-making R&B of the Forties and Fifties. In particular New Orleans is noted for its stylists. The most important today is arguably Allen Toussaint, a direct descendant of the Dave Bartholomew production stable, who is equally gifted as a pianist, composer, and singer, and who has managed to uphold the standards of the great Professor Longhair (Henry Roeland Byrd) and the rock giant Fats Domino while bringing his own stamp to soul.

Toussaint began his career in 1960 as producer and bandleader for Minit and, later, other labels in New Orleans. His early credits before his army service (1963-5) indicated a strong sense of local

sound and he notched up several hits with Ernie K-Doe (whose 'Mother-in-Law' was a national No 1 in 1961), Jessie Hill, Aaron Neville, Chris Kenner, Irma Thomas, and sundry others. At the same time Toussaint recorded solo for RCA and established his own studio company with another veteran of the New Orleans scene, Marshall Sehorn.

Toussaint's most popular work in the Sixties was accomplished with Lee Dorsey and the Meters. Dorsey's enthusiastic and effervescent vocal style, allied to the producer's combination of elegant piano and raw rhythmic backing, established him as a household name with a string of American and European hits like 'Ya Ya' (1961), 'Ride Your Pony' (1965), and 'Holy Cow' (1966), while the Meters' bag of assorted instrumental numbers possessed a charm and novelty that they could expand upon during the Seventies.

Toussaint's ability to combine his native grasp of melody and expertise with whoever he works with gained him the respect and patronage of musicians around America and beyond. His credits include working with Dr John (on the vintage *Right Place, Right Time* album, 1973), the innovative disco funk band Chocolate Milk, and notables like John Mayall (1972), the Band (1972), Wings (1975), and Joe Cocker (1978).

Though mainly known as a production wizard and songwriter of the highest class, Toussaint's own solo ventures like *Southern Nights* (1975) and *Motion* (1978) have proved that as an interpreter of his own songs he is second to none. He is responsible for a huge body of hit material and is recognised as a superb arranger, a New Orleans pianist of repute, and a soulful master of that strain of Louisiana music which remains untouched by the wilder excesses of the rock business.

destroyed Morrison's faith in America's freedom of expression, and in 1971 he moved to Paris. His mysterious death there – apparently he drowned after suffering a heart attack in a bath-tub – seems if anything to have conferred a romantic gloss on his reputation.

As the underground became the norm for American youth, the forces of law and order were compelled to recognise that the very fabric of conventional life was under attack. So-called subversion seemed rife, not just from the long-haired peace marchers but from the intellectuals who sided with the hippy rejection of customary values and found their mouthpiece, if not in music, in the first outpourings of a radical free press. Publications such as *The Realist* and *The Oracle* expressed views that outraged America's political elders, engaged in a war they could not win in Vietnam and a battle they were now losing on the home front.

In 1966 LSD was declared illegal, an event followed by violence on the campuses and even more radical rock music. In 1968 there were full-scale riots at respectable universities like Columbia in New York City and Kent State (Ohio), and at the Democratic Convention in Chicago. As the violence escalated young people were beaten up, and some were killed, by over-zealous police officers. Many parents finally began to wonder if everything

was right with the America they thought they stood for.

Musically, too, America had started to absorb the talent that first surfaced on the West Coast: Bill Graham opened a second Fillmore in New York City and found no shortage of bands willing to fill his ever-ambitious bills. While Airplane and the Dead were established veterans of the scene, others like Santana and Creedence Clearwater Revival were ready to take their place. Santana signed to Columbia Records on the strength of being the first group to headline at the Fillmore West without having a major record contract. They played a fusion of West Coast rock and Latin-influenced rhythms, traceable to the mariachi origins of their founder Carlos Santana and their ebullient percussionists, on albums rather than singles. Santana shot to national prominence after their part at the Woodstock festival (1969), perhaps the best remembered festival of all. Santana's performance in front of almost half a million people was also immortalised in the film of the event.

Woodstock (in upstate New York) was one of many festivals held throughout America, evidence of a music too popular now to be restricted to club appearances. Although its devotees were not aware at the time of any creative decline, the festival circuit began a trend that culminated in the stadium-playing, platinum-selling acts and the heavy metal sound that replaced the Sixties' alternative culture.

By now the disturbing level of drug casualties and

LEFT *Frank Zappa has purveyed puzzlingly eclectic rock sounds for almost two decades.*

BELOW *The Doors, 1969. From left: Robbie Krieger, Ray Manzarek, Jim Morrison, John Densmore.*

social dropouts was something that not even the most devoted radical could defend. Violence marred another festival, held at Altamont Speedway (south-east of San Francisco) in 1969, where a young black man was stabbed to death in full view of the stage on which the Rolling Stones were performing. This kind of incident seemed to validate the authorities' claims of youthful irresponsibility, and the sordid deaths of Jimi Hendrix and Janis Joplin in 1970 added force to that argument.

Janis Joplin was one of rock's most tragic figures. Her talent as an interpreter of the blues and as a dynamic live performer with San Francisco's Big Brother and the Holding Company was sadly dissipated by her increasing dependence on and final destruction by heroin. She

ABOVE *Jimi Hendrix re-created rock guitar style – a legend and an inspiration to a whole generation of groups.*

RIGHT *Janis Joplin, a great interpreter and almost an embodiment of the blues; destroyed by heroin in 1970.*

made her name when appearing at the Monterey Pop Festival in 1967 with Otis Redding and Jimi Hendrix, and her popularity continued to grow even after her death. Her importance led to a documentary movie of her ill-starred life, *Janis*, and she was subsequently compared to her own idols, Bessie Smith and Billie Holiday.

The camaraderie of the West Coast bands proved impossible to sustain into the Seventies. It came under attack from the police, owing to the association of the bands and drugs; but it was also destroyed from within by the fragmentation of the original groups into new ventures. Some, like Frank Zappa and the Mothers of Invention, questioned the entire basis of the flower era, accusing its leaders of naivete. Zappa himself was an adept exponent of jazz and avant-garde rock, using it to express a brand of satire that dared to poke fun even at the Beatles. On a more positive note Zappa was one of the first independent studio owners in Los Angeles and, in conjunction with his manager Herb Cohen, he set up the Straight label, which gave valuable help to artists, such as Captain Beefheart and Tim Buckley, who might otherwise have remained relatively unknown.

The pretentiousness and artifice which Zappa saw arising from the ashes of Haight-Ashbury were at their most prevalent in the early Seventies, a period when musical excellence became equated with technical arrogance, supergroups formed and disbanded as if by rote, and singer-songwriters dispensed well-intentioned inanities. There was plenty of good music still to be found, but there was no longer any discernible unifying factor between the practitioners and the listeners.

Some bands still transcended the limitations of simple rock 'n' roll by their energy and commitment: one such was Creedence Clearwater Revival, who in John Fogerty had the advantage of a very gifted writer, singer, and musician. Creedence were the last of the Californian bands originating in the Sixties to make a sustained impact on the charts. They valued the hit single and could make even a large concert hall seem intimate, while Fogerty had an endless supply of classic songs with which to captivate a mass audience: 'Proud Mary', 'Bad Moon Rising', and 'Green River' (all 1969) were equally popular in America and Europe, and their album sales topped the million mark. Like other groups Creedence were undone by an internal insistence on group democracy. When Fogerty handed over control to

Little Feat

One of the more interesting and offbeat bands to emerge in the Seventies, Little Feat have left a catalogue of memorable material and provided, in Lowell George (above), one of the decade's finest songwriters. George's early career with punk group the Standells and a brief 1970 stint with Frank Zappa's Mothers of Invention are of little importance; though it was during this period that he wrote 'Willin'', a sardonic truck-driver's lament that would become the Little Feat anthem. Zappa encouraged him to go solo and George departed, taking Mothers bassist Roy Estrada with him. An eponymous debut for Warner's (1970) revealed some fine blues and country playing.

Despite a lack of company support Little Feat persevered with their infectious approach, reaching a creative peak on *Sailin' Shoes* (1972), *Dixie Chicken* (1973) and *Feats Don't Fail Me Now* (1974). Lack of commercial success had persuaded the members to concentrate on sessions, George adding his slide guitar to John Cale's *Paris 1919* and Van Dyke Parks' *Rediscover America* while pianist Bill Payne assisted the early Doobie Brothers.

The group re-formed to play on a European showcase for Warner's, together with the Doobies, and capitalised on a healthy cult following to steal several shows from their partners. Thus reconstituted the band finally earned some reward for their excellence, *Their Last Record Album* (1975) charting in Britain and America. This success, however, was tempered by George's ill-health. After contracting hepatitis he was unable to fulfill touring schedules, and the band functioned and developed without his idiosyncratic song-writing to guide them. This enforced democracy resulted in a dilution of their strengths and led to internal bad feeling. George was not happy with the jazzier departures of *Time Loves a Hero* (1976) and refused to play certain songs on stage.

After a rather drab double live album George pursued a solo career with more conviction, and his *Thanks I'll Eat It Here* (1978) was a clear return to old form. Tragically, this rejuvenation was halted by his death after a show at Washington, D.C. in 1979. In deference to him the other Feat members agreed that without George there was no group and bowed out with *Down on the Farm* (1978), parts of which were finished after his death.

his partners Creedence's music became diluted. He eventually dissolved the group, and made two solo albums which indicated his ability to handle country, gospel, and rock standards – but at their peak Creedence were writing those standards themselves.

Another early Seventies band to taste mass success were the Allman Brothers from Macon, Georgia. Their lead guitarist Duane Allman was one of the hottest young session musicians in Muscle Shoals. He played with Wilson Pickett and Aretha Franklin and was one of the few white players to gain the trust and respect of the blues community. The Allmans were in some ways a Southern equivalent of the Grateful Dead, renowned for their lengthy sets and guitar-based jamming. After the distinction of heading the closing concert at the Fillmore East, however, they were dogged by personal tragedies: Duane Allman in 1971 and drummer Berry Oakley in 1972 were killed in virtually identical motorcycle accidents. Nevertheless the group survived these setbacks, the gifted Richard Betts taking over lead guitar, and became America's biggest live attraction by 1973. Even after his death Duane Allman continued to be acknowledged as a master of bottleneck guitar. He was a major influence on the heavy-metal groups who followed in the wake of the British band Cream, while the Allmans were certainly the blueprint for the immensely popular but short-lived southern group Lynyrd Skynyrd.

Anyone taking stock of the years between 1965 and 1970 could not fail to notice how mutually dependent the

Crosby, Stills, Nash & Young took members from Buffalo Springfield, the Byrds, and the Hollies and became a hugely popular supergroup in the early Seventies.

musical scenes of Los Angeles and San Francisco had become. For example, a version of the Byrds was still in operation, but the group's progeny had spread in several directions. One temporary member, Gram Parsons, persuaded the Byrds to record a country-flavoured departure, *Sweetheart of the Rodeo* (1968), before he left on the eve of a South African tour to form the Flying Burrito Brothers with another ex-Byrd, Chris Hillman. The Burritos were influential on a grand scale only after Parsons' death in 1973. Before that time their *Gilded Palace of Sin* (1968) and *Burrito De Luxe* (1970) were minor cult sellers; even *Sweetheart of the Rodeo* had not been well received by Byrds fans or the critics.

Parsons himself was an intriguing individual, Harvard-educated but with a Deep South upbringing. His penchant for fraternising with wealthy rock stars, notably the Rolling Stones, contributed to his poor health and eventual demise, but he was responsible for writing some of the most compelling modern country music outside the confines of the Johnny Cash and Merle Haggard mainstream. The attention granted to his solo records *GP* (1973) and *Grievous Angel* (1974) led some to foist on him the tag of founder of country rock, but this is a difficult claim to sustain. The embracing of country-music traditions was inevitable for many of the bands who found their initial sources drying up. Besides, country was as much part of America's musical heritage as rock 'n' roll or the blues, providing new material to cover and more instruments to play, such as the banjo, mandolin, and steel guitar. By 1970 everyone from Bob Dylan (with *Nashville Skyline*) to Steve Miller and the Grateful Dead (on *Workingman's Dead*) had recognised these possibilities and made a country album.

Emmylou Harris, who had been Gram Parsons' partner and vocal foil on his solo albums, continued to keep his memory and influence alive after his death and also developed her own solo career working with the Hot Band. Albums like *Pieces of the Sky* and *Elite Hotel* (both 1975) enhanced her reputation — as did a guest appearance on Bob Dylan's *Desire* (1976) — and helped to establish the place of country-styled women singers in rock. Another such was Linda Ronstadt, whose early band included Glenn Frey, later with the Eagles.

Another former Byrd, David Crosby, in conjunction with Stephen Stills (late of Buffalo Springfield) and expatriate Englishman Graham Nash (late of the Hollies) formed the first American supergroup in 1969, adding one of Stills' partners in Buffalo Springfield, Neil Young, a year later. Crosby, Stills, Nash & Young made two phenomenally successful records, *Deja Vu* (1970) and *Four Way Street* (1971), which, if nothing else, served to highlight the differences between them. While Stills and Young were still excellent guitarists and writers, Crosby's hippy patter and self-pitying whines, like 'Almost Cut My Hair', were to many an embarrassment. A series of reunion concerts in 1975, and an outdoor appearance at Wembley Stadium (London), demonstrated rock's increasing reliance on nostalgia.

Neil Young, at least, emerged from the Sixties with honour intact. He made one of 1970's better albums, *After the Goldrush*, and with various versions of his backing band Crazy Horse continued alternatively to delight and perplex a devoted following. His *On the Beach* (1974) and *Tonight's the Night* and *Zuma* (both 1975) sets were as artistically courageous as the latter efforts of Crosby, Stills and Nash were moribund. Stephen Stills enjoyed a brief respite as a solo artist and founder of Manassas.

Ry Cooder

Ry Cooder is one of American music's most distinguished stylists, an acknowledged master of bottleneck guitar and a modest believer in the benefits of good music whether it be jazz, mariachi, or rock 'n' roll.

A native of Los Angeles, Cooder learnt directly from folk-blues singers like the Reverend Gary Davis and Sleepy John Estes, perfecting a technique that was academic at first but soon acquired a strikingly expressive individuality. His first band, the Rising Sons (formed 1966), featured a similarly inclined blues singer/guitarist, Taj Mahal. They recorded one unreleased record for Columbia, and Cooder worked on Mahal's debut LP in 1967.

As a noted session player he played with Captain Beefheart, Randy Newman, and Little Feat before his virtuosity brought him to the attention of the Rolling Stones. After assisting them with *Let It Bleed* (1969) it was rumoured that Cooder might join the Stones, but at that time he professed little interest in rock showmanship.

After meeting arranger Jack Nitzsche, Cooder helped him score the films *Candy*, *Performance*, and *Blue Collar*. More recently he has branched out on his own to score *The Long Riders* and Jack Nicholson's *Border*.

As a solo artist Cooder recorded several excellent albums for Reprise, showing an ability to interpret a good song and uncovering a rich vein of blues, country, and jazz numbers with authenticity and humour. He is responsible for bringing the public's attention to a wider range of ethnic music than they might otherwise have encountered, though he has always belittled this worthy side of his work. Nonetheless, his integrity has ensured that neglected figures like Sleepy John Estes received their first substantial royalties for many years.

In the later Seventies and early Eighties Cooder concentrated on his own writing and stepped up live performances, with the result that *Bop Til You Drop* (1979) and *Borderline* (1980), both digitally recorded, finally brought him a level of popularity to match his talent. This has been particularly true in Europe, where Cooder is now a star — an irony that is not lost on him. A surprising and adventurous musician, articulate raconteur, and gifted showman, Cooder is one of America's most mature artists.

Steely Dan

Steely Dan are perhaps more of a concept than a band. The brainchild of two New Yorkers, Walter Becker and Donald Fagen, the Dan have always been concerned with instrumental and lyrical sophistication, with leanings towards horn charts and refined soloing; essentially a recording-studio enterprise, they have little ambition to be a fully fledged touring rock group.

Becker and Fagen worked as songwriters for ABC Dunhill in the early Seventies before their producer Gary Katz persuaded them to form their own band.

It was soon obvious that Steely Dan's literate writing and urbane attitudes were out of the rock norm, but they hit success with the singles 'Do It Again' (1972) and 'Reelin' in the Years' (1973). Well-received albums like *Countdown to Ecstasy* (1973) and *Pretzel Logic* (1974) developed their chief themes – college reminiscences and East Coast put-downs of plastic California – and to their great surprise the band found themselves with a growing audience.

By now Becker and Fagen were moving into studio sophistication and adopting specialist musicians to play certain tricky solos. Their first line-up dissolved, and, freed from the pressures of live concerts, Becker and Fagen could concentrate on lengthier, jazz-inflected songs. With the managerial assistance of Irving Azoof they secured filmscore work for *FM*, and Becker contributed the title song to the film *Heavy Metal*. Fulfilling their ambition to work with the jazz élite, including horn players Wayne Shorter (of Weather Report) and Tom Scott (a top session man), and enjoying a huge following of fans prepared to indulge their albums-only policy, Steely Dan went on to have Top Ten albums with *Aja* (1977) and *Gaucho* (1980). They then promptly split up.

The ever-unpredictable duo have since been engaged in a long-running battle between their former record company MCA and their new label, Warner's, for whom Donald Fagen recorded *Nightfly* (1982); this album continues their baffling trend by being entirely in the mould of former Dan sets. It seems that Becker is quite capable of functioning in his own – which may be bad news to Steely Dan purists but ultimately seems to make little real difference.

ABOVE *Allman Brothers Band. From left: Gregg Allman, Dickie Betts and Berry Oakley. Betts played lead after Duane Allman died.*

RIGHT *Commander Cody and His Lost Planet Airmen were country favourites until they split in late Seventies, Cody going solo.*

Country Rock

Meanwhile country-rock was continuing to expand and to find an audience that had never heard of Ernest Tubb or Hank Williams. By 1970 country-rock was being practised in earnest by groups like Poco and the New Riders of the Purple Sage – but Poco, with their pedal-steel guitarist Rusty Young, and NRPS, abetted by Dead's Jerry Garcia, were merely the Californian equivalents of a music essentially of the South.

It was to Nashville (Tennessee) that the rock stars came to learn their new craft or to hire expert musicians.

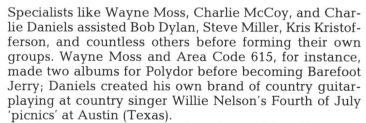

Specialists like Wayne Moss, Charlie McCoy, and Charlie Daniels assisted Bob Dylan, Steve Miller, Kris Kristofferson, and countless others before forming their own groups. Wayne Moss and Area Code 615, for instance, made two albums for Polydor before becoming Barefoot Jerry; Daniels created his own brand of country guitar-playing at country singer Willie Nelson's Fourth of July 'picnics' at Austin (Texas).

Other contemporary bands included West Virginia's Asleep At the Wheel, who combined novelty and humour in their act and were adopted as honorary Californians; the humorous, truck-driving Commander Cody and His Lost Planet Airmen; and Dan Hicks and His Hot Licks, a vaudevillian harmony group.

The country vogue which had begun with the Byrds had by the early 1970s been fully assimilated by rock culture, and it reached its commercial peak with the Eagles. Composed of former members of Poco, the Dillard and Clark Expedition and the Flying Burrito

Brothers, the Eagles were at first excellent in records like 'Take It Easy' (1972) and the adventurous concept (thematic) album *Desperado* (1973), but they were eventually weakened by the pressures of a business that was as much based on a star hierarchy as had been the movie industry of the Thirties. Their popularity, after the huge-selling *One of These Nights* (1975), was not matched by the quality of their material.

The early success and eventual failure, musically, of the Eagles were echoed by many other West Coast acts who became mass-market entertainers and then tended to lose contact with both their musical roots and popular taste. There were innumerable songs telling of the 'authenticity' of life on the road or glorifying a semi-mythical lifestyle whose high-points seemed to be drug-induced ecstasy or oblivion. It took an exceptional talent to rise above such pretentious mediocrity, and most of the better music of the middle Seventies was made by artists who at that time failed to achieve a breakthrough into stardom.

LEFT *Steve Miller gave psychedelia a blues edge.* UPPER *The J. Geils Band brought back high-voltage R&B.* LOWER *Alice Cooper combined the grotesque with heavy metal.*

Heavy Metal

True, the years between 1970 and 1975 did produce several relatively fresh styles in America — but once again the most durable was British-influenced. Heavy metal, or hard rock, had its roots in the sounds created by the post-beat groups, particularly that seminal R&B outfit

the Yardbirds and the guitar pyrotechnics of their three lead-guitar virtuosi, Eric Clapton, Jeff Beck, and Jimmy Page. The success of Page's Led Zeppelin in Britain was followed in America by scores of similarly inclined though less-gifted bands anxious to bludgeon their audiences with sheer volume and posture. Groups like Grand Funk Railroad, Iron Butterfly, and the reformed Blue Cheer played this essentially retrogressive music with varying degrees of subtlety, made a lot of money very quickly, and for the most part disappeared into deserved obscurity. Other, tenacious guitar heroes like Ted Nugent, Ronnie Montrose, and Wayne Kramer, resurfaced on heavy-metal bills in the Midwest, indulging in displays of fretboard flash held in gladiatorial circumstances. These guitar contests or battles of the bands enjoyed a brief heyday.

Not all hard rock was totally devoid of finesse: groups like Bob Seger's Silver Bullet Band, Blue Oyster Cult from Long Island, and Boston's J. Geils Band made their own, distinctive contribution to the genre. In the Blue Oyster Cult's case, a flair for lyrics and melody was enriched by the band's gift for parody. On the other hand, they were perfectly prepared to compete for commercial acceptance: their mid-Seventies hit 'Don't Fear the Reaper', was a classic single — and impressive proof that the devil still had some of the best tunes.

The J. Geils Band took its leads from homegrown R&B, Motown, and the jukebox jive of the late-night DJs who had surfaced on the renegade airwaves of the Fifties. Lead singer Peter Wolf had himself been a DJ and added authentic highspeed rapping and superfast, stylish vocal dexterity to J. Geils' clever updates of a black heritage. (Wolf gained notoriety in the gossip-columns when he married the actress Faye Dunaway, an event which gained the band much media exposure. The band's early albums contained its most inventive reworkings of the American soul tradition, as well as plenty of blues and original numbers that easily held their own in that company.

Perhaps the most popular (though hardly the most gifted) heavy-metal outfits were Aerosmith and Kiss. Aerosmith chose an image that was visually Stones, aurally Zeppelin, and very little else. Kiss opted for gimmickry, theatrics, and grotesque make-up in the style of Alice Cooper. Although they fulfilled a function as surrogate teenyboppers their attraction wore off rather quicker than their mascara.

Rock Balladeers

Heavy metal apart, the most enduring musical feature of this period was the singer-songwriter, an extension of the folk tradition that had antecedents in the work of Pete Seeger, Woody Guthrie, Leadbelly (Huddie Ledbetter), and the Weavers. Bob Dylan, of course, had revitalised the tradition most forcefully and had given the singer-songwriter musical respectability and prominence in mainstream circles. As a matter of convenience rather than of accuracy, many of the new writers were labelled Dylan imitators, a tag that was calculated to damage only the genuinely original talents (the others were glad of such reflected glory).

Not that many of these songwriters *were* particularly original. For every gifted writer like Joni Mitchell or Laura Nyro there were scores of balladeers like James Taylor and Don McLean, many of whose songs seemed

to invite the listener into a world of obscure misery or melancholy confusion; though Taylor's sometimes striking lyric images at least set him apart from some of the others. James Taylor himself perhaps summed up these singers best with a catalogue of introspective material drawn from several periods in mental institutions. His first recordings were for the Beatles' Apple label, but his work on Warner's, notably *Sweet Baby James* (1970) and *Mud Slide Slim and the Blue Horizon* (1972), sold much better on both sides of the Atlantic. Taylor's laid-back autobiographical style and slight, tense, yet melodic voice set the tone for a host of imitators.

Other singers, such as Loudon Wainwright, Jim Croce, and Jim Stafford, leavened their repertoires with the occasional burst of sardonic humour; while Tom Rush and Eric Anderson mined a more poetic vein. The crossover singer-songwriters Lobo and John Denver escaped the coffee-club circuit altogether by concentrating on overt sentimentality and lush arrangements that marked them as a new breed of middle-of-the-road pop stars. They had more in common with the enduringly popular Simon and Garfunkel than with, say, the angry voice of the young Dylan.

To Paul Simon's credit, he was prepared to experiment with diversions into jazz and gospel settings for his new solo material, which was a good deal more adventurous than that of his partnership with Art Garfunkel. His songs on *There Goes Rhymin' Simon* (1973) and *Still Crazy After All These Years* (1975) exhibited a new maturity of writing and musical execution, and the arrangements employed the talents of jazz musicians like the gifted saxophonists David Sanborn and Toots

ABOVE, LEFT *Randy Newman, composer of sharp-edged ballads sung by many, but best of all by himself.* ABOVE *Van Morrison progressed from blues shouter through R&B vocalist to singer of a* vast stylistic range from Celtic folk to way-out jazz. RIGHT *One of rock's great session men, Al Kooper has played with Bob Dylan, the Rolling Stones, Chuck Berry, Jimi Hendrix, and many others.*

Thielemans while still managing to find a wide public.

Joni Mitchell was equally inventive with her work in the Seventies. Indelibly associated with the Woodstock generation, for a while she overcame that limitation by concentrating on coming to terms with the aftermath of the hippy dream. While *Blue* (1971) was a suite of mature love songs rooted in reality, her later albums *For the Roses* (1972), *Court and Spark* (1974) and *The Hissing of Summer Lawns* (1975) took greater risks, with their jazz arrangements and complex lyrics. Joni Mitchell broke out of the acoustic mould by writing songs that could be interpreted by her backing band, Tom Scott's L.A. Express; and in later years she worked with the Burundi Drummers (an African group), jazzman Charles Mingus, and members of Weather Report (see below).

Artists of wildly differing backgrounds and merit sheltered behind the comprehensive label of singer-songwriter. Van Morrison, for example, had nothing in

common with any of the people mentioned above. A Dubliner who settled in Boston and later California, Morrison had been the singer and rhythm guitarist with the Northern Ireland Sixties group Them – charting with singles such as 'Baby Please Don't Go', 'Here Comes the Night', and 'Gloria', all released in 1965 – and had gone solo in 1968. His mature vocal dexterity gave fresh impetus to the form for a while. He was never afraid to set his poetic sensibility against a background that might be vintage R&B one moment and refined jazz the next. As a modern blues singer of great interpretative skill, Morrison produced a string of expertly crafted albums like *Astral Weeks* (1963), *Moondance* (1970), and *Tupelo Honey* (1971), ambitious in arrangement and showing a romantic rural bent. A succession of excellent backing bands, from the Street Choir aggregation to the Caledonia Express and often including topflight jazzmen, secured his status as a dynamic live performer who would continue to surprise and would survive his period.

The acceptance of the solo artist ensured that, as well as the deliberately independent performers, there were now hundreds of already established figures anxious to prove that they too could go it alone. For them, solo work might be a departure from their previous setting – as with John Sebastian (of the Lovin' Spoonful), Country Joe McDonald, John Kay (of Steppenwolf), or Stephen Stills – or just a sabbatical from group work. Thus the time came when every member of the Grateful Dead, the Jefferson Airplane, and the Byrds made a solo album. Sometimes a member of one of these bands, rather than go solo, would form his own band for a while. Members of the Dead and the Airplane alone accounted for the groups Kingfish, Hot Tuna, Grootna, Jefferson Starship, and Rolling Thunder. The complicated permutations of the West Coast fraternity resulted in a lineage the unravelling of which would best be left to the genealogist.

LEFT *The Eagles (Glen Frey and Joe Walsh here) were America's top group in the mid-Seventies.* ABOVE *Urban rock hero Bruce*

Springsteen, seen at his best in live shows. He achieved stardom in the mid-Seventies backed by his E Street Band.

spheres of his friend and partner Larry Beckett. The problem about Buckley, as far as the public was concerned, was that he kept so far ahead of the mainstream that his ethereal vocals, stretching over an amazing five and a half octaves, kept him at more than arm's length from commercial acceptance. After moving to the Straight label, Buckley became more way out still, experimenting with extremely avant-garde jazz and 'singing in tongues'. The result of this experimental phase was *Starsailor* (1970), regarded by many as his masterpiece.

One singer-songwriter who was beset by the Dylan tag was Bruce Springsteen. His early albums for Columbia disguised the direction that suited him best, but he finally settled on the raucous, energetic update of black R&B that found its first expression on *Born to Run* (1975). He managed to outlive both the Dylan label and the preposterous claim of his then producer, Jon Landau: 'I have seen the future of rock and roll and its name is Bruce Springsteen'. He would later be regarded as a super-hero, especially in live shows, but until 1975 even he was just another singer-songwriter.

City Sounds

The most popular black music of the period managed to combine commercial success with fruitful progression, while still maintaining the high standards of the early Sixties' soul explosion. Although Stax/Volt records ceased to influence the scene directly (at least in America) after 1967, Motown grew from a position of strength. Outside Detroit, however, Berry Gordy's monopoly of black talent was refreshingly broken in New York, Memphis, Chicago, and Philadelphia. The radical departures of artists as diverse as Sly Stone and Jimi Hendrix – the latter breaking first in the UK – encouraged a new approach, reflecting the profound changes in social attitudes.

At the forefront of the new Motown sound were Stevie Wonder and Marvin Gaye, established artists who nevertheless managed to develop their own talents and their importance within the company. In 1971 Stevie Wonder surprised his long-time devotees with the album *Where I'm Coming From*, adapting his mastery of classic pop to embrace longer material and more sophisticated lyrical expression. This turning-point was given a dramatic emphasis a year later by the praise that greeted his *Music of My Mind* album, a milestone in contemporary black art. Wonder played most of the instruments himself, experimented with different vocal techniques and incorporated the Moog and ARP programming of Robert Margouleff and Malcolm Cecil into a unique tapestry of sound. The influence of this record, and of its successors *Talking Book* (1972), *Innervisions* (1973), and *Fullfillingness' First Finale* (1974), marked Wonder out as a major figure. His developments would be heard in funk for years, and the catchy refrain of his massive selling 'Superstition' encouraged changes throughout the rock world. Artists from the Stones and Paul McCartney to Todd Rundgren and the Rascals made use of his instrumental innovations.

Marvin Gaye also progressed from being a polished balladeer and duettist on records with Diana Ross, Mary Wells, and Tammi Terrell to becoming a musician with something relevant to impart. He refined the 1968 soul sound of that classic single 'I Heard It Through the

Some of the most undervalued solo players were to be found in the Southern states. Just as the most natural country-rock came out of Tennessee, Louisiana, and Georgia, so the most accomplished songwriters were often those who, having been raised in the unfashionable milieu south of the Mason-Dixon line, had the most success with the genre. They also tended to sound less affected. Writers and musicians such as Delbert McClinton, Dennis Linde, Mickey Newbury, J. J. Cale, and Mac Gayden crossed effortlessly from blues and R&B to contemporary country with a grace and flair that was alien to most of their northern peers.

Occasionally a figure did rise above the stultifying norm of the influential studios of New York and Los Angeles. Jackson Browne and Tim Buckley started their careers on the folk circuit but possessed the talent to break into more adventurous territory. Browne moved from California to New York in order to concentrate on writing for other people. His first successful effort, 'Take It Easy', was covered by the Eagles (among others) and earned him enough in royalties to pursue his solo career while bringing him to the attention of a growing number of lesser talents eager to find a good tune.

Tim Buckley recorded several albums for Elektra during that company's golden period in the late Sixties, many of the tracks featuring the complex lyrical atmo-

Grapevine' into a body of work that could encompass political and social comment – *What's Going On?* (1971) – as well as the supreme sensuality of *Let's Get It On* (1973). Like Wonder, Marvin Gaye remains a complete artist, capable of appealing to every kind of audience.

Meanwhile Motown lost its image of being solely under the avuncular and muscular control of Berry Gordy. The label moved from Detroit to the West Coast and even incorporated a white rock offshoot, Rare Earth Records. Motown artists began to determine their own careers in a way that could not have been envisaged in the early Sixties. The new breed of acts like the Jackson Five actually became even bigger than Motown itself.

Other strains of soul in the early Seventies were heard coming from Memphis, where Willie Mitchell's Hi label helped establish the talents of such as Al Green, Syl Johnson, and Ann Peebles. Mitchell's introduction of horn and string sections as a backdrop to the subtleties of his artists brought the ballad back into favour and at the same time established the instrumental Memphis sound of Al Jackson, Andrew Love, and the Hodges family.

Similarly, in Philadelphia, Kenny Gamble and Leon Huff put the Philadelphia International label's style into the rock vocabulary, with the lush orchestration and highly developed funk of the O'Jays, Harold Melvin, and the Three Degrees. Their Sigma Sound studios produced a new texture of soul that reverberated through the industry: David Bowie was to record his *Young Americans* album there in 1975.

By the mid-Seventies the diverse success of the Stylistics, Barry White, Donny Hathaway, Curtis Mayfield, Roberta Flack, Earth, Wind and Fire, Isaac Hayes, and the Isley Brothers proved that while there might no longer be such a thing as soul music, *black* music was thriving across America.

Jazz-Rock

The avenue of Seventies musical expression that most inspired pretentiousness was that vaguely described as jazz-rock. The label had first been applied to outfits such as Chicago and Blood, Sweat and Tears, for whom the mere use of brass was sufficient for them to claim the status of jazz musicians. The term jazz-rock could also be adapted to suit bands on the outskirts of disco, like Oakland's Tower of Power, or to describe the work of John McLaughlin, Carlos Santana, Billy Cobham, or Chick Corea.

The tremendous popularity of jazz-rock provided lucrative rewards for traditionally trained jazz musicians whose livelihoods have been subverted by rock. Now even the gurus, such as the great trumpeter Miles Davis, could experiment with electronics – indeed, many of his former sidemen created the trend. Drummer Tony Williams, who formed Lifetime, had played with him, as had British guitarist John McLaughlin, who formed the Mahavishnu Orchestra in 1971. But it was left to two of Davis's more mature protégés, Joe Zawinul and Wayne Shorter, to form the definitive jazz-rock group, Weather Report. Shorter's saxophone and Zawinul's keyboards had been integral to many of Davis's best Sixties bands, and both men had been encouraged to contribute original compositions. These two fine musicians formed the constant basis of Weather Report, introducing avant-garde jazz and evolved funk to a new audience. By constantly subverting expectations – for instance by crossing traditional Western music with synthesised variants on African or Japanese forms – Weather Report

Proto-Punk

LEFT *John McLaughlin played jazz-rock with Miles Davis in the late Sixties.* UPPER *J. J. Cale, gifted singer-guitarist, plays laidback country-rock style.* LOWER *Singer Lou Reed co-founded American painter Andy Warhol's Velvet Underground in 1967.*

The radical change that many thought overdue was beginning to make itself felt in Britain. America took longer to feel the effects of the new wave, yet there were glimmerings of punk's second coming in New York City, where people were returning to the clubs to dance again and catch the new young outfits. In 1975 the first murmurings of Richard Hell, Talking Heads, Tom Verlaine, the Ramones, the Dictators, the Stilettos, and Patti Smith were being heard in seedy clubs and Lower East Side lofts. These groups professed no allegiance to the historical, nostalgic perspective of rock music, or if they did they preferred the flippant charm of the Sixties garage bands — those obscure punk combos that were condemned to live outside the accepted structure by their anti-hip stupidity. If these bands had any contemporary heroes they were usually people like Todd Rundgren or David Bowie, people who possessed glamour and touted a more space-age image than the long-haired boogie bands that were threatening to suffocate high-energy rock for ever.

Bowie himself championed the causes of two American singers, Lou Reed and Iggy Pop. Their groups had made little impact in the Sixties but their past achievements were now being viewed more favourably. Reed, a native New Yorker, had been the singer and rhythm guitarist with the Velvet Underground, the house band for Andy Warhol's East Coast extravaganzas and one of the most innovative groups to emerge anywhere in America. Their songs had nothing to do with the atmosphere of Haight-Ashbury and their sound was harsh black and white, characterised by feedback and projecting a seedy twilight world of urban misfits. In the Sixties their music could only have been an anomaly, but for the exponents of the New York new wave the Velvets were seen as a seminal riposte to Californian cosiness.

John Cale, who had played on the Velvet Underground albums with Reed and whose discordant viola had been a part of their unique sound, had left the group in 1968 to become a solo artist and producer. His first venture away from the Velvets was to oversee an album made by Detroit's Stooges, whose own lead singer, Iggy Pop, was to become as important to the new wave on both sides of the Atlantic as Cale's former band. The Stooges were a quintessential hard-rock outfit who signed to Elektra in 1969. Although their style of music was ridiculed at the time, their anarchic punk energy took on the aura of legendary exploits among the growing number of people seeking a new direction.

The circle was completed when David Bowie produced albums for Lou Reed (*Transformer*, 1972), and Iggy Pop (*Raw Power*, 1973), finally bringing them to wider public attention. So, as news of their revival filtered back from England, it found a receptive hearing once again in New York.

While the rock business was slow to admit the change, and the hierarchy was not about to admit defeat, the period was ripe for a different sound with a fresh impetus, a sound that would have as great an impact on the consciousness of the American media as did the West Coast pioneers in 1965. Something vital was stirring once again in the heart of American music. The alternative cultures of the Sixties were no longer applicable. It was time for something new.

made a mockery of the limited jazz-rock niche; and they nurtured distinctive talents such as Miroslav Vitous, Alphonso Johnson, and Jaco Pastorius.

Such virtuosity, however, was rare in the mid-Seventies: the tendency was towards safety and radio-orientated music that would soothe rather than stimulate. Rock itself was a leisure industry now, a kind of sport that was most profitably executed in vast soulless stadiums. Whereas in the Sixties the music had often undermined consumerism, it had now become a consumer product and was dictated to by the studios and the record companies. Whatever sold was necessarily good. There was no need to challenge the status quo. Genuinely gifted stylists such as Ry Cooder were considered uncommercial, and the better groups — Steely Dan or Little Feat, say — were filed as 'minority appeal'.

The British Scene 1965-75

The mid-Sixties welcomed in a golden age of British music. It was solid gold, not merely gold-plated – the quality ran right through it, from the charts to the clubs, from the overtly commercial music to the wilder grassroots. This quality and spirit were matched by a new attentiveness among pop's overseers: radio, TV, and the press became aware of the music's dominating effect upon its consumers' lives. Rather than preach about it or laugh at it, they learned to take pop on its own terms.

ABOVE Radio Caroline, first of the pirates, inspired a new school of pop radio in Britain based on brash American models.

RIGHT David Bowie, an inventor of styles both as performer and as producer, has been a towering force in rock for over a decade.

The Media

The media, in any case, were themselves changing. The old radio and TV establishment was under siege, both within its gates and outside them. Iconoclasts on the inside conceived a new style of pop programme, the ITV series Ready Steady Go!, while more bluntly commercial rivals created a new, direct opposition: the pirate radio stations.

Ready Steady Go!, which ran from August 1963 to December 1966, was the brainchild of Elkan Allen, who drew heavily upon Jack Good's innovative ideas of the Fifties, specifically his Oh Boy!, in presenting a program-

me with immediate and intentionally chaotic impact and with a live audience. The original concept of a TV magazine, incorporating fashions, films, and music, gave way by the second series to unlimited music. At the same time the avuncular presenter Keith Fordyce, a DJ on the BBC's Light Programme (forerunner of Radio 2), was phased out to leave the young Cathy McGowan in full control. She might fluff her lines or announce the acts wrongly, but she looked like the girl next door – if the girl next door could afford all the latest fashions.

Ready Steady Go! was the epitome of all that was exciting about British pop. It used many club acts, and ultimately acknowledged their importance, in 1965, by going live to capture them at their best and, often, uniquely. There were many brilliant, spontaneous moments: Jack Bruce and Paul Jones (then both in Manfred Mann) playing a two-harmonica rave-up on what would become a Cream favourite, 'Train Time'; Mick Jagger and Chris Farlowe performing 'Out of Time' – written and produced by the former, a hit for the latter – together, live. On one occasion RSG even devoted a whole programme to the mods' hero James Brown. With its excellent direction and camera-work, RSG stood far ahead of traditional TV competition like Thank Your Lucky Stars. A year after RSG began, the BBC offered competition by launching Top of the Pops, then, as now, a mere rundown of the Top Twenty. RSG, by comparison, directly influenced what would be in the charts months later.

Pirate radio provided the perfect backup. Before the pirates arrived British pop radio consisted of the evening broadcasts on Radio Luxembourg, with their poor reception and habit of fading most records about halfway through, and weekend pop shows on the Light Programme, the best of which were Saturday Club and its Sunday equivalent, Easy Beat. The first pirate station to establish itself was Radio Caroline, which began quite humbly on Easter Saturday 1964. Before long – for the first time in British broadcasting history – a choice of radio stations was available: Caroline, Atlanta, City, 390, and (most stylish of all) London. Operating from ships anchored offshore in international waters, the stations modelled themselves on the style of American radio.

By a happy coincidence, at the very time the pirates ruled the airwaves, pop music, both British and American, and especially soul music, was at its peak and was feeding the stations with unlimited good sounds. Motown, Stax, and Atlantic singles received massive airplay; classics like Wilson Pickett's 'In the Midnight

John Mayall

John Mayall has sometimes seemed to change his musicians as often as his socks. Though he has the reputation of a hard leader and paymaster, many of the greatest British instrumentalists have been members of his volatile Bluesbreakers unit, and almost all have gained much from the liaison.

Mayall put his first group, the Powerhouse Four, together in 1955, while he was at college after leaving the army. By the early Sixties they had evolved into the Blues Syndicate and found support from Alexis Korner — who, if Mayall is the father of British blues, is arguably its godfather. Once the Mayall crew arrived in London as aspiring semi-professional blues musicians, Korner put whatever work he could their way. The first Bluesbreakers were formed in March 1962 and by 1964 had released their first album for Decca, *Mayall Plays Mayall*, recorded live at London's Klook's Kleek club. Mayall played guitar, piano/organ, and har-

Hour' or Percy Sledge's 'When a Man Loves a Woman' might never have been hits but for the pirates. British soul, until then essentially a club phenomenon, now found an outlet on radio too. The horn-toting British soul bands tended to have little chart success because their covers of American soul records, though exciting in the clubs, were on record less appealing than the originals. Nevertheless, when these groups did produce something distinctive, the pirates gave them ready exposure. Georgie Fame's 'Yeh Yeh' and 'Get Away' were hits largely owing to the pirates, as were the only chart hits enjoyed by Chris Farlowe ('Out of Time') and Zoot Money ('Big Time Operator').

The slightly later singles success enjoyed by the early Underground groups can also be mostly attributed to pirate radio airplay. Pink Floyd's first single, 'Arnold Layne' (1967), was banned by the BBC because of its transvestite implications but it was heavily played by Caroline, while both Caroline and London plugged their Top Ten hit 'See Emily Play' until its success made it impossible for the BBC to go on ignoring it.

The pirates even broadcast specialised programmes, like Mike Raven's blue sessions on 390, Johnny Walker's soulfood on Caroline and John Peel's highly influential midnight-to-2am Underground show *The Perfumed Garden* on Radio London. It is no coincidence that with the scuttling of the pirates in 1967 after the passing of the Marine Broadcasting Offences Act, and the advent of the more limited Radio 1, with its needle-time restrictions and strict Top 40 format, pop became excessively indulgent, and music prospered that would never have survived continuous exposure on the pirate stations.

The pirates' readiness to encourage new ideas in music also contributed to the setting up of Britain's first significant independent record labels in the Sixties. There had been independents before, such as Transatlantic (specialising in folk) and Oriole (which had originally licensed Motown in Britain), but none was noted for breaking new British talent. Two important labels were established in 1965 – Andrew Oldham's Immediate and Shel Talmy's Planet. Both were headed by producers who had earned reputations with leading groups, Oldham with the Rolling Stones and Talmy with the Kinks and the early Who. Another producer, Larry Page, who had masterminded the then highly successful Troggs, started the Page One label a year later. Immedi-

FAR LEFT *Only 19 when he formed Traffic in 1967, Steve Winwood was already a gifted singer, guitarist and, pre-eminently, organist. Traffic broke up for two years in 1969 (Winwood forming the short-lived Blind Faith with Eric Clapton and Ginger Baker), then recorded again until 1975. As a session player he has worked with Joe Cocker, Jimi Hendrix, Muddy Waters, George Harrison, Alvin Lee and others.*
NEAR LEFT *Georgie Fame fronted the eclectic, jazzy Blue Flames, a good club act that got into the charts in the Sixties.*

monica, with Hughie Flint (drums), John McVie (bass) and Roger Dean (guitar).

It was in the following year, when Eric Clapton joined from the Yardbirds, that the group began to make an impact. Clapton's reputation as a blues guitarist was already growing rapidly and Mayall's group provided the perfect vehicle to consolidate it. The *Bluesbreakers* album with Clapton (1965) was a remarkable commercial success since it was due mainly to their high standing on the club circuit.

Peter Green replaced Clapton on guitar when the latter left to form Cream, and Aynsley Dunbar took over from Flint – a line-up first heard on record with *A Hard Road* (1966). This was as creative an album as its predecessor and earned Green a guitar-hero's reputation, enabling him to go on and form his own group, Fleetwood Mac, the following year.

The Bluesbreakers' ever-changing line-ups are almost too detailed to document. Mayall's patronage continued to enhance the careers of his musicians after they left him: Mick Taylor, for instance, who replaced Green in 1967, went on to join the Rolling Stones. But Mayall's importance lay not merely in his ability to spot and secure potentially brilliant musicians; he also evolved his styles to suit his musicians, and the results profoundly influenced others. The next phase of the Bluesbreakers introduced jazz elements, even horns (which in the notes to *A Hard Road* Mayall had vowed he would never use). In the course of the next two years, on the albums *Crusade* (1967), *Diary of a Band* (two volumes) and *Bare Wires* (1968), another extraordinary procession of musicians passed through the Bluesbreakers: drummers Keef Hartley and Jon Hiseman (both later to front their own groups), bass player Andy Fraser, later to join Free, saxophone players Dick Heckstall-Smith and Chris Mercer.

In 1969 Mayall called a halt to the Bluesbreakers, having pioneered the blues (as opposed to R&B) for more than a decade. He took a long vacation in Los Angeles and made a rather self-indulgent album about his experiences there, *Blues from Laurel Canyon* (1969) – Mick Taylor's final effort with the band.

ate had the greatest success, scoring at once with the McCoys' 'Hang On Sloopy'. Its British hits, however, were with relatively established names: Chris Farlowe, the Small Faces, Amen Corner; the last two had been lured from Decca, Farlowe from EMI.

Such independents were valuable additions to the British pop scene, but they scarcely revolutionised it. The beginnings of real change came when Island Records – a company set up by Chris Blackwell in 1962 to distribute Jamaican records, and subsequently a licensee of the prestigious New York label Sue – signed its first progressive group, Traffic, in 1967. By then, though, other changes were well under way.

Underground Rock

It is hard to pinpoint the exact origins of the London Underground. Certainly it borrowed much of its spirit and content from kindred movements in San Francisco, Los Angeles, and New York, but the London scene had its own distinct character. Richard Neville, one of the editors of *OZ* magazine, in his book *Play Power* suggests the earliest reference point: 'The seeds of London's first psychedelic circus go back as far as June 1965 at the famous Albert Hall ''Cosmic Poetry Visitation Accidentally Happening Carnally'', where London's incubating hippies tuned in to Allen Ginsberg, Christopher Logue, Lawrence Ferlinghetti, etc. and discovered much to their surprise that 7,000 others were in a similar state of gestation.' Perhaps the key event was the launching of the Underground paper *International Times* (*IT*) in October 1966 – after which, as Neville continues, 'over the next few months the directors and friends of the paper, a hippie mafia, engineered the most spectacular of London's Underground happenings'.

The key members of this 'hippie mafia' in terms of the Underground's music were John Hopkins ('Mr Underground'), who organised the first Underground club, UFO; *IT* music journalist Miles; Peter Jenner and Andrew King, of what became Blackhill Enterprises, the management company for Pink Floyd; and John Peel, then a pirate DJ on Radio London.

No one was more central to the London Underground than its 'official' band, Pink Floyd. They first transformed themselves from an R&B to a psychedelic group at the Spontaneous Underground Club, held at the Marquee in Wardour Street (London) every Sunday from February 1966 onwards. Here they met King, Jenner, and Hopkins. 'Hoppy' organised a series of Sound/Light Workshops at the London Free School (an alternative university) held at the All Saints Hall, Notting Hill Gate (London). In performances here throughout the summer of 1966, Pink Floyd's music became increasingly experimental – and alongside it evolved the light show, an idea that had filtered through from the San Francisco psychedelic scene.

The disparate elements of the London Underground were fused when Hopkins, inspired by a benefit gig for *IT* at the Roundhouse theatre on 15 October 1966, started the underground club UFO (Unidentified Flying Object or, in underground terms, Unlimited Freak Out), at an Irish dancehall in Tottenham Court Road. UFO, opened in December, enabled Underground happenings to take place regularly, and it was soon followed in early 1967 by the Electric Garden, later Middle Earth.

Originally the 'house band' of the London Underground, Pink Floyd became one of the most successful rock acts in the world. Planning their career with great care in the Seventies, they became almost as well known for their light shows as for their music.

An event that characterises what UFO and the later Underground clubs were trying to do was the 14-hour Technicolour Dream, held at Alexandra Palace (London) on 19 April 1967. This too was a benefit for the often-busted *IT*; it attracted over 5,000 longhairs and featured virtually every Underground group in Britain:

Pink Floyd, Soft Machine, the Crazy World of Arthur Brown, the Social Deviants, the Purple Gang (best known for their hippie classic 'Granny Takes a Trip'), the Bonzo Dog Doodah Band, and many more, with, of course, lights, films, crazy actors, and poetry recitals. Soft Machine's appearance sums up the lunatic spirit: Daevid Allen wore a miner's helmet, Kevin Ayers a cowboy hat which sprouted giant model-glider wings; Robert Wyatt rode a motorcycle on stage and left it running through at least part of their set.

Folk & Jazz Influences

By 1967, with two Underground clubs well established and the Roundhouse at Chalk Farm as a frequent third venue, London became the focal point of a new kind of music, which encompassed ideas both within and outside the normal sphere of pop. Both folk and jazz found a home in the Underground.

The new spirit of broadcasting and experimenting with styles is well illustrated by two essentially folk-based groups. Pentangle were formed in late 1967 by some of the key talents on the British folk scene. Bert Jansch and John Renbourn, who already had firm reputations, came together with singer Jacqui McShee, bassist Danny Thompson, and drummer Terry Cox – Thompson and Cox being session musicians and ex-members of Alexis Korner's Blues Incorporated. After trial sessions in a North London pub they moved on to the college and concert circuit with a strong debut album in hand. *The Pentangle* showed their ability to blend folk, blues, jazz and classical music – at first a somewhat clinical operation, but by the time of their second double album, recorded half in the studio and half live at London's Royal Festival Hall, they were mixing their idioms with great ease. This was *Sweet Child* (1968), which ranged over jazz – Charles Mingus's 'Goodbye Pork-Pie Hat' – Elizabethan classical music, traditional folksongs and Jansch and Renbourn's contemporary folksongs and instrumentals.

Fairport Convention, one of the earliest and best of the Underground groups, were probably more widely influential, but unlike Pentangle did not come from a folk background. Their music in 1967 was much more a recreation of American West Coast styles, and they often played superb arrangements of songs by then little-known contemporary writers, such as Leonard Cohen, Tim Buckley, and Joni Mitchell. This American inflection is most apparent on their first album, *Fairport Convention* (1967), whereas its successor, *What We Did on Our Holidays* (1968), showed them in transition, mixing traditional material like 'She Moves Through the Fair' with Dylan's 'I'll Keep It with Mine'. (Dylan's influence on the Underground was immense, particularly the albums *Highway 61 Revisited*, 1965, and *Blonde on Blonde*, 1966.) Continually changing their personnel, by their third album, *Unhalfbricking* (1972), Fairport had brought in fiddler Dave Swarbrick, whose influence on the group became stronger and stronger.

Fairport's former bassist Ashley Hutchings, who left the group in 1969, followed a fascinating line of more traditionally oriented electric folk music when he formed Steeleye Span. The initial line-up incorporated two from a 'traditional' folk-club background, Tim Hart and Maddy Prior, and Gay and Terry Woods, and they recorded the seminal *Hark! the Village Wait* (1970). As with Fairport, the line-up never stabilised. Gay and Terry Woods soon left and were replaced by Martin Carthy – a key figure in the 'folk revival' – and fiddler Terry Knight. This formation made what was perhaps their most successful blend of traditional and electric folk styles, *Please to See the King* (1971). Hutchings and Carthy left the following year, Hutchings forming a similar group, the Albion Country Band, while Hart, Prior and Knight continued as the nucleus of Steeleye and even achieved a hit single in 1973 with their unaccompanied version of the Latin hymn 'Gaudete, Gaudete'.

Both Fairport and Steeleye still exist, despite repeated changes of line-up, occasional splits and considerable overlapping of personnel. Between them they comprise a virtual 'Who's Who' of the new British folk movement. But not a monopoly: another innovator in the new British folk music of the late Sixties, certainly, was John Martyn. His most compelling work was in the 1973 albums *Solid Air* and *Inside Out*, where, with former Pentangle bassist Danny Thompson, he moved further towards jazz, both in his vocal technique and in an extraordinary acoustic guitar style, amplified through an echoplex, which built up swirling, repetitive, free-form melodies.

Martyn has a dedicated and ever-growing following but commercial success has, so far, eluded him. The other key British folk-rock group, Lindisfarne, enjoyed considerable, if brief, chart status. Formed in Newcastle and led by singer/guitarist Alan Hull, they became Lindisfarne in 1968 and built up a strong following on the post-underground club/college/festival circuit. Mixing good-time pop with more traditional folk elements, and never disguising their Geordie origins, they notched up several Top Ten hits, notably 'Lady Eleanor' and 'Fog on the Tyne' (1970), before Hull left the group in late 1972. Their most accomplished albums were their first two, *Nicely Out of Tune* (1969) and *Meet Me on the Corner* (1970).

Jazz performers, particularly the more avant-garde, were not uncommon at underground events, but it was the ideas and techniques of jazz, notably improvisation,

ABOVE *Donovan moved from folk and protest to flower-people songs typified by 'Sunshine Superman' (1966). He occasionally tours.*

RIGHT *Pentangle, drawing their line-up from many schools, built a repertoire on folk, blues, jazz, and baroque idioms.*

The Yardbirds

Originally a Kingston art-school band called the Metropolitan Blues Quartet, the Yardbirds changed their name and shifted the emphasis of their style to R&B after seeing the Rolling Stones at one of their then regular performances at the Railway Hotel, Richmond (London) early in 1963. They made their debut at Eel Pie Island on the Thames with a line-up of Keith Relf (vocal/harmonica), Chris Dreja (rhythm guitar), Paul Samwell-Smith (bass), Jim McCarty (drums), and 'Top' Topham (lead guitar), and soon took over the Stones' residency at the Crawdaddy Club. Topham left, to be replaced by Eric Clapton, whose remarkable guitar virtuosity set them apart from other R&B bands. They signed to EMI/Columbia in early 1964, but their first singles, 'I Wish You Would' and 'Good Morning Little School Girl', made little chart impression.

Remarkably for the times, and with no hit single behind them, the Yardbirds' first impact was made by an album, *Five Live Yardbirds*, recorded live by their manager Giorgio Gomelsky at London's Mar-

quee Club in mid-1965. The album sealed the fate both of Clapton, by confirming his status as an authentic guitar hero, and of the group, because he was soon to leave as a result of this critical acclaim. *Five Live Yardbirds* remains as definitive a statement of British R&B as the first Rolling Stones album. On a second live album which appeared the following year, the group did little more than back Sonny Boy Williamson.

In February 1965 the Yardbirds scored their first major singles hit with 'For Your Love', a song by Graham Gouldman (who also provided their next two hits) which reached No 2; but its overt commercialism caused Clapton to quit the group and join John Mayall's Bluesbreakers. Jimmy Page was approached to replace him but on that occasion declined, recommending in his place Jeff Beck. Beck fitted admirably into the more pop-oriented Yardbirds, with his penchant for dazzling electronic effects and less-puristic blues leanings. With Beck's innovative soloing bringing each cut to life, the Yardbirds had four further hits through 1965-6, 'Heart Full of Soul', 'Evil Hearted You'/'Still I'm Sad', 'Shapes of Things', and 'Over, Under, Side-

ways, Down', all of which made the Top Ten. These were highly inventive, as was their vastly underrated first studio album, simply called *The Yardbirds*, released in mid-1966, which with the singles won them considerable favour in America as psychedelic-rock pioneers.

Soon after the album's release, bassist Samwell-Smith left the group and Jimmy Page this time agreed to join; Dreja switched to bass. For a few months the Yardbirds boasted the twin lead-guitar sound of Beck and Page. Only one single commemorates this remarkable pairing, 'Happenings Ten Years Time Ago', but they are seen together in Antonioni's 'swinging London' movie *Blow Up* (1967). The dual-guitar pyrotechnics survived less than six months: during their ninth US tour Beck had a nervous breakdown and left the group.

The Yardbirds epitomised all that was brilliant in British rock in the Sixties and committed it to record on *Five Live Yardbirds* and that string of five classic singles. It hardly needs saying that any group that has boasted Eric Clapton, Jeff Beck, and Jimmy Page as lead guitarists has earned an honoured place in rock history.

that the Underground brought into British rock. Pink Floyd pioneered this on their long space-rock epics like 'Interstellar Overdrive'; but more important champions of avant-garde ideas were the Soft Machine. They had their origin in Canterbury (Kent) and a local group called Wilde Flowers; taking their name from William Burroughs' novel, the Soft Machine came into being in 1966. If the Underground scene had not existed then, it is doubtful whether they would have survived, given the strong jazz and avant-garde leanings of the group's members. At this time, however, LSD-inspired Undergrounders saw the Soft Machine pursuing a more pop (if bizarre pop) line, though with considerable scope for wilder tape-loop experiments, improvisation, and general weirdness. The original line-up included three strong, quirky characters in guitarist Daevid Allen, bassist Kevin Ayers, and drummer Robert Wyatt. The more serious Mike Ratledge (keyboards) welded the group together; significantly, when Wyatt departed after the *Fourth* album (1971), the wit and humour in much of the group's music till then virtually disappeared. Only their first LP, *The Soft Machine* (1967), reflects the spontaneous lunacy of their live performances at all accurately.

The Soft Machine's greatest popularity and influence have been in continental Europe. The British Underground, and particularly the Machine and (until the late Sixties) Pink Floyd, were highly inspirational forces on the burgeoning European rock scene.

Once the improvisational techniques espoused by the British and American Underground became acceptable, European rock was able to draw on its own traditions, which had previously been unacceptable to rock audiences. Electronic music, and the work of composers like Cage and Stockhausen; earlier 20th-century European composers like Satie, Messiaen, Varèse, Webern, and Stravinsky; avant-garde jazz players like Ornette Coleman and John Coltrane (whose music had always found more favour in Europe than in their native United States): suddenly all these influences poured into rock, and European groups were often more inclined, and better equipped, to exploit them than British and American bands. Accordingly the late Sixties saw the emergence of groups like Can (from Cologne), Amon Duul II (from Munich), Tangerine Dream (from Berlin), and Magma and Gong (led by ex-Soft Machine Daevid Allen) from France; all of these played electronic music or a kind of heavy rhythmic rock which at the time was utterly alien to British musicians and record buyers.

The cult grew only slowly but the chart success of Kraftwerk — originally called Organisation and initially heavily indebted to Pink Floyd — with 'Autobahn' in 1973 proved that European rock was commercially viable. This was confirmed by the success of Tangerine Dream, who had signed to Virgin Records in 1972: their first two British LPs, *Phaedra* (1974) and *Rubycon* (1975), did well in the English album charts.

The effect of jazz upon British music of the late Sixties can be discerned chiefly on the fringes of British blues, and particularly within the band-leading orbit of John Mayall. Mayall added horns to his band the Bluesbreakers on the road as early as 1966, but it was not until the 1968 album *Bare Wires* was released that a genuine jazz emphasis could be identified. How much of it was instigated by the jazzmen then in the group, Dick Heckstall-Smith, Jon Hiseman and Tony Reeves, is arguable. They later left to form Colosseum and went on the road simultaneously with another, earlier, Mayall alumnus, Keef Hartley, whose band also sported a horn

ABOVE *One of the more quirkily creative Underground groups, Soft Machine began with psychedelia, later moved on to free-form improvisation and (after Robert Wyatt left in 1971) to jazz-rock.*

RIGHT *At his best a brilliantly inventive guitarist, Jeff Beck replaced Eric Clapton in the Yardbirds in 1964. His first group, formed in 1967, included Rod Stewart and Ron Wood.*

Rod Stewart

For a long time it seemed that Rod Stewart would provide the classic example of an artist with a perfect grounding in British Sixties pop, who was highly regarded by his peers, but for whom success would always be elusive.

Stewart's first passion was football — for a while he was on the ground-staff of Brentford Football Club — but art college set him on a different path. In the early Sixties he hitched around Europe with folksinger Wizz Jones, but was deported for vagrancy in time to return to the burgeoning London R&B scene. For the next five years he served his apprenticeship with a variety of groups, getting his professional break as harmonica player and singer with Jimmy Powell & the Five Dimensions in 1964.

He went on to join Long John Baldry's Hoochie Coochie Men with whom he first became known as 'Rod the Mod'. He later rejoined Baldry when he put together Steampacket. They split up in 1966, at which point Stewart joined Shotgun Express, sharing vocals with Beryl Marsden. Shotgun Express made two (now highly collectable) singles for Columbia while Stewart himself made five solo singles between 1964 and 1967 for Decca, Columbia, and Immediate ('Come Home Baby' was produced by Mick Jagger).

In 1968 Stewart joined the Jeff Beck Group as featured vocalist and made his first major break-though. The combination of Beck's extraordinary guitar work and Stewart's soulful, guttural vocals took America by storm. Stewart spent 18 months with Beck, releasing two albums, *Truth* (1968) and *Beck-Ola* (1969), and frequently touring America.

Continuing the relationship with Beck's bassist Ron Wood, now playing lead guitar, he teamed with former Small Faces Ian McLagen, Ronnie Lane, and Kenny Jones to form the Faces, which built a healthy following through good-time live performances, Stewart now coming into his own as a showman. The Faces released four albums, but it was Stewart's solo LPs, mixing his own songs with impeccably selected material by other writers, that were the more successful, both critically and commercially.

'Maggie May', from his third solo album *Every Picture Tells a Story*, became a worldwide No 1 hit in summer 1971, propelling Stewart to superstardom. At first the Faces provided the perfect vehicle for him, but it was inevitable that he would eventually go it alone, as his solo albums and singles continued to overshadow his recorded work with the Faces. The *Never a Dull Moment* (1972) album and 'You Wear It Well' single clinched his superstar status. The standard of his albums thereafter dwindled, although they were rarely without their high points and continued to yield hit singles.

line-up of respected jazz players. Both bands were highly popular on the club and college circuit, together with other jazz-rock combinations like If and Nucleus. Colosseum and the Keef Hartley Band were fellow-travellers with a long procession of blues outfits, which had grown from a handful in 1966 to several hundred by 1968. Two groups in particular helped to inspire the proliferation of blues bands: Cream and the Jimi Hendrix Experience.

Blues Bands

Cream – Eric Clapton (guitar), Jack Bruce (bass), and Ginger Baker (drums) – had a thorough grounding in British blues and R&B, having served variously with the Yardbirds, John Mayall, and the Graham Bond Organisation. Though their first album, *Fresh Cream* (1966), was noted for its musicianship rather than its originality, their second, *Disraeli Gears* (1967), developed the less blues-based ideas that had appeared in *Fresh Cream*. Their vocal and textural strengths were highlighted and they displayed an original sense of melody on songs like 'Tales of Brave Ulysses' and 'Sunshine of Your Love', while their playing was matched by poet Pete Brown's colourful lyrics. The band's greatest impact, however, was in live performances, where they engaged in long improvisational jamming and virtuoso solos. Taken to extremes, or in the hands of less able musicians, their approach could, and did, turn into a brash heavy-metal manner; but if Cream had something to answer for – the excessive soloing, particularly the obligatory drum solo – they at least did it well.

Hendrix, too, saw his innovative playing distorted into banality and tedium by those who tried to copy him. Like Cream, his métier was playing live and experimenting on albums, but in this enlightened period both groups

ABOVE *Tangerine Dream from Berlin were inspired by electronic music and avant-garde jazz.*
ABOVE, NEAR RIGHT *Alvin Lee became a superstar at Woodstock.*
ABOVE, FAR RIGHT *'People's hero' Rory Gallagher found fame with Taste in 1966, went solo in 1971.*

enjoyed singles success, Cream with 'I Feel Free' and 'Strange Brew', Hendrix with 'Purple Haze', 'Hey Joe', 'And the Wind Cried Mary', and 'Burning of the Midnight Lamp' – all hits in 1967. Hendrix's appearances on traditional TV programmes like *Top of the Pops* sent shock-waves through many a parent's heart.

Another Mayall alumnus, Peter Green, who left him in 1967, formed his own group, Fleetwood Mac (derived from the surnames of drummer Mick Fleetwood and bassist John McVie, both also Mayall alumni). The line-up was completed by Jeremy Spencer, slide guitarist and co-vocalist with Green, and a devotee of bluesman Elmore James. They signed to the new independent British blues label, Blue Horizon, set up by Mike Vernon.

There is no doubt that David Bowie was one of the most significant and innovative rock performers of the Seventies. Aside from the brilliance of his recorded output and the quality of his live shows, his influence upon others has been profound; he has also directly inspired whole genres like glam rock, punk, and disco, and many individuals and groups from Marc Bolan, Peter Gabriel, and Brian Ferry to later artists such as the Associates, Gary Numan, Echo & the Bunnymen, and the Human League.

Yet little Bowie had done by the onset of the Seventies prepared one for his work since. In the early Sixties he had recorded under a variety of guises, culminating in the quaint LP *David Bowie* (1967), and only the 'Space Oddity' single and that intermittently excellent album suggested anything extraordinary.

It was with *The Man Who Sold the World* (1970) that he made his first impressive statement. Largely ignored at the time, this bleak work prefigured the dark vision of subsequent albums through to *Diamond Dogs* (1974). *The Man Who Sold the World* also initiated his fruitful liaison with guitarist Mick Ronson and drummer Woody Woodmansey, as well as with producer Tony Visconti. With Trevor Bolder on bass, they also started a series of low-key dates around Britain in 1971, going on to record the vastly acclaimed *Hunky Dory* the following year.

In 1972, too, the public caught up with him, with the release of *Ziggy Stardust and the Spiders from Mars*. The album, and its stage presentation, caused a sensation: to his fans, Bowie 'became' Ziggy Stardust. *Aladdin Sane* (1973) gave Bowie the first of his string of hits, including 'Starman', 'Jean Genie', 'Drive in Saturday' and others. At this peak of his career he also found time to produce Lou Reed's *Transformer* album and to write and produce 'All the Young Dudes' for Mott the Hoople.

On his temporary 'retirement' in 1973 Bowie moved to the United States where he produced the apocalyptic *Diamond Dogs* and the reflective *Bowie Pinups*, and then he confounded everyone with the R&B/soul-tinged *Young Americans* (1975) and *Station to Station* (1976), providing further hit singles with 'Young Americans', 'Fame', and 'Golden Years'. In 1976 he played the starring role in Nicholas Roeg's film *The Man Who Fell to Earth*, a touching performance, and he has continued to pursue an acting career with *Just a Gigolo* (1978) and, in 1981, a TV production of Brecht's *Baal*. He also won critical acclaim in the Broadway production of *The Elephant Man* in 1980.

In 1976 Bowie moved to Berlin, where he drew inspiration from European electronic music in three collaborations with Brian Eno: *Low* and *'Heroes'* (both 1977) and *The Lodger* (1980). The *Baal* soundtrack and the theme for the movie *Cat People* (1982) aside, his only recording since then has been the highly successful *Scary Monsters* album (1980), the source of yet another classic single, 'Ashes to Ashes', and a return to the vision first unveiled on *The Man Who Sold the World*.

(Formerly an A&R man at Decca, Vernon had signed to that label both Mayall and another early British blues outfit, Savoy Brown.) Building up a large club and college following, the group's first two albums, *Peter Green's Fleetwood Mac* (1967) and *Mr Wonderful* (1968), mostly of traditional or traditional-sounding blues, were highly successful. By late 1968, though, they had begun to move away from straight blues, adding a third guitarist, Danny Kirwan, and stunning everyone by releasing a wistful instrumental, 'Albatross', which topped the British charts around Christmas. It was the first of a clutch of inventive singles: 'Man of the World', 'Oh Well' and 'Green Manalishi' followed before Green left in May 1970 to retire from the music business. The group floundered, going through a number of line-up changes, but gradually evolved a more mellow style which helped them to popularity in America, where they concentrated their efforts. By their 1975 eponymous album they had become one of the most successful groups there, with a line-up now two-fifths American and a style that was the epitome of hip easy listening, FM rock.

Most of the other British blues outfits were hard-working but few were inspired. Among the best were Free, distinguished by Paul Rodgers' throaty singing, who enjoyed surprising singles success in the early Seventies with tracks like 'All Right Now' and 'My Brother Jake'. Taste, from the Republic of Ireland, led by the 'people's guitar hero' Rory Gallagher, were known for their inexhaustible gigging. Jethro Tull, fronted by

the eccentric fluteplayer Ian Anderson, have gradually been transmuted into a vehicle for his highly personalised and conceptualised writing. The Jeff Beck Group was powered by the former Yardbird's outrageous hard-rock guitar and featured Rod Stewart, making his first major step towards Seventies superstardom. Among other leading exponents were Ten Years After (with lead guitarist Alvin Lee), the Groundhogs, Aynsley Dunbar's Retaliation, Steamhammer, and Chicken Shack, who enjoyed one hit single in 1969, 'I'd Rather Go Blind', sung by Christine Perfect, later the wife of John McVie and from 1970 with Fleetwood Mac. By the late Sixties blues-band music had become one of the staples of the club and college circuit.

The Underground, at least defined according to its original meaning and spirit, was a very short-lived affair. Though its last vestiges lingered on until 1968, it was essentially all over by the summer of 1967. Its more sensational aspects – beautiful people, flower-power, love-ins, the drug culture – had provided easy targets for the popular press's sense of outrage. The Underground was soon exploited within the music business, too: the 1967 hit 'Let's Go to San Francisco', credited to the Flowerpot Men, was actually the work of an English vocal group, Edison Lighthouse (or White Plains), who donned kaftans and false moustaches.

Pink Floyd

Pink Floyd were probably the archetypal British psychedelic group. The initial line-up, in 1966, comprised architecture students Roger Walters (bass), Rick Wright (keyboards), and Nick Mason (drums), and art student Syd Barrett (guitar).

Originally an R&B group playing standards like 'Roadrunner' and 'Louie Louie', Pink Floyd were led by Barrett towards the nascent London Underground scene, and gradually replaced their R&B repertoire with Barrett's whimsical compositions. Through a series of benefits for *International Times* they began to attract wider attention, especially once they had taken up residency at London's premier Underground club, UFO in Tottenham Court Road. Employing the light shows from the Sound/Light workshop, their music expanded in length, making effective use of guitar feedback and Wright's eerie organ effects. Their cult following increased following their first single, in March 1967, the controversial 'Arnold Layne', which crept into

In that same year, though, aided by pirate-radio airplay, a number of genuine Underground groups did reach the charts with a series of classic singles. As well as the already mentioned Floyd, Hendrix, and Cream successes, there were Traffic's 'Paper Sun' and 'Hole in My Shoe', Arthur Brown's 'Fire', and Procol Harum's 'Whiter Shade of Pale'. More traditional pop groups embraced psychedelia: the Move, for example, with 'I Can Hear the Grass Grow' and 'Fire Brigade', and the Herd, led by Peter Frampton, with 'From the Underworld' and 'Paradise Lost'. Nor were the longer-established groups left behind: the Beatles, the Stones, the Kinks, the Small Faces, the Who, even the Hollies produced some of the finest singles of the period in addition to albums.

The Underground era saw the passing of regional British rock, as it had been known during the beat and R&B eras. It had become necessary, once again, to make a mark in London. The brilliantly inventive Family moved from Leicester; Skip Bifferty were forced to leave their native Newcastle; aspiring groups everywhere gravitated towards the metropolis. The Underground had never established itself as a provincial phenomenon – as Ray Jackson of Lindisfarne commented, 'In Tyneside, the environment didn't really lend itself to flower power. It somehow didn't relate to the smell coming from the shipyards.'

The new era gave fresh opportunities to many of the struggling club bands. The Nice, for instance, came together from various club outfits: Keith Emerson from the T-Bones, David O'List from the Attack, Brian Davison from the Mark Leeman Five. Before indulging in the pretentious classically-inspired rock that Emerson took to some kind of culmination with Emerson, Lake and Palmer, the Nice had been one of the most excitingly fresh groups to come through in 1967, as was demonstrated by their excellent debut album, *The Thoughts of Emerlist Davjack*.

It was curious, nonetheless, how old blues players like Tony McPhee, Zoot Money (who briefly led the brilliant Dantalian's Chariot), or the Pretty Things found new

LEFT *The first British supergroup, Cream was formed in 1966 by (from left) drummer Ginger Baker, bassist Jack Bruce, and Eric Clapton. Exhilarating in live performance, the group was famed for its collective improvisation and long, sometimes self-indulgent solos by Clapton and Baker. Cream disbanded at the end of 1968.*

ABOVE *After an apprenticeship in Birmingham-based beat groups, Roy Wood fronted the Move through well-crafted psychedelic-pop hits in the late Sixties before forming the first Electric Light Orchestra. He left ELO under ex-Move alumni Jeff Lynne and Bev Bevan in 1974 to purvey a zanier kind of pop with Wizzard.*

the Top 30. The follow-up, 'See Emily Play', earned them the unlikely distinction of a Top Ten record – their last until 1980's 'Another Brick in the Wall'.

Further singles success was irrelevant, in any case. Their reputation was consolidated by their first album, *Piper at the Gates of Dawn,* in the summer of 1967 – a remarkable collection of 10 of Barrett's bizarre songs, including two evocative space-rock pieces, 'Astronomy Domine' and 'Interstellar Overdrive'. Early in 1968 Dave Gilmour was brought in, initially as a fifth member, but soon to replace the acid casualty that Barrett had become.

Barrett went on to record two eccentric solo albums with the aid of his former colleagues, while Pink Floyd themselves went from strength to strength by realising their limitations and astutely planning their career to capitalise on their better qualities. They had already won over the more discerning critics, and they further fostered critical respectability by their involvement in film soundtracks: *More* (1969), *The Body* (1971), *Obscured by Clouds* (1971), and their contributions to Antonioni's *Zabriskie Point* (1970).

A new album, *Atom Heart Mother*, was unveiled

with a spectacularly staged show at the Bath Music Festival in 1970. Such careful timing served to disguise their deficiencies – to which the public anyway seemed oblivious. *Atom Heart Mother* propelled them to superstardom.

The Dark Side of the Moon (1973), a cycle of songs rather than the instrumental pieces that dominated earlier albums, proved an extraordinary triumph for the group. The album quickly reached No 1 on both sides of the Atlantic and maintained a high chart position for months afterwards.

Wish You Were Here, their next, did not appear until 1976 and met with a mixed reception. The key track appeared to be 'Shine On You Crazy Diamond', dedicated to the long-departed Syd Barrett. *Animals* (1977) restored many people's faith in the group, but it was with *The Wall*, in late 1979, that they found themselves at a new peak. It had been preceded by a single, 'Another Brick in the Wall', their first in the Seventies, which saw them through into the Eighties with a No 1 single. *The Wall* was later staged, premièred at London's Empire Pool, Wembley, and in 1981 turned into a well-received film.

acceptance. As Phil May of the Pretty Things recalled: 'When we found ourselves adopted by the Underground we had come full circle. We thought, "Here we go again, branded collectively as dirty, leery, unwashed, and so on", just like in 1964.

The Great Survivors

Meanwhile, what of the aristocracy of the Sixties groups? The Rolling Stones may have slipped into a trough about this time with their patchy psychedelic album, *Their Satanic Majesties Request*, but in the end they rocketed back, doing again brilliantly what they had always done best. Once they gave up trying to compete with *Sgt Pepper*, they reestablished themselves with a definitive slice of rock 'n' roll, 'Jumpin' Jack Flash', and *Beggar's Banquet*, at the end of 1968, was arguably their best album since their first in 1964. It was also Brian Jones's last with the group; he left in 1969 and shortly afterwards died in a swimming accident. Recruiting Mick Taylor (formerly with John Mayall), the Stones reaffirmed their rock 'n' roll status yet again with 'Honky Tonk Women' in July 1969. They ended 1969 with their first American tour in three years and, despite the horrors of the Altamont Festival, their future was sealed. They were 'the greatest rock 'n' roll band in the world', a reputation they have successfully flaunted ever since.

The main contenders, of course, had ceased to exist. The Beatles' demise had been foreseeable since the late-1968 *White Album*, and in 1970 they separated, never to team up again. Their importance in shaping the rock scene in Britain and America, even after their break-up, is immeasurable, but that of their subsequent solo careers is more difficult to determine.

John Lennon reacted abruptly to the years of Beatlemania with records that were at first avant-garde – the 1968/9 *Unfinished Music, Nos 1 & 2* – and later stark and introspective: *John Lennon/Plastic Ono Band* (1970), *Imagine* (1971). Even the 1975 *Rock 'n' Roll* album reflected the same dismissive attitude to the glories of the past. Paul McCartney, by contrast, invited comparisons with that past. After a couple of patchy solo albums he formed the group Wings in 1971, and since then has

RIGHT *Sometimes seeming to lose their way in the later Sixties, the Rolling Stones had returned* *to fresh triumphs by the end of the decade. Ron Wood, at left, replaced Mick Taylor in 1974.*

Led Zeppelin

When the Yardbirds broke up in 1968, Jimmy Page formed the New Yardbirds, later to become Led Zeppelin. He first contacted John Paul Jones, another respected session player (bass/keyboards). Initially they had Terry Reid in mind as the singer, but when he declined a friend recommended Birmingham-based Robert Plant, who played in a locally touted group, Band of Joy – which also provided drummer John Bonham.

Their first British tour won them few friends, and they immediately decided to focus on the American market, where Page's reputation had greater cachet and other British bands like Cream and the Jeff Beck Group had made considerable impact. By

their second tour there they had an impressive début album in tow. Recorded only months after they were formed, *Led Zeppelin I* (1968) set a standard in high-energy hard rock that has been rarely surpassed but often imitated. By early 1969 it was in the American Top Ten album chart, and since then the band have never looked back.

Led Zeppelin II (1969) and *III* (1970) were in much the same vein. Zeppelin created definitive hard-rock statements in songs like 'Dazed and Confused', 'Communication Breakdown', and their ultimate blockbuster, 'Whole Lotta Love'.

They planned their Seventies career most carefully, releasing one album a year and timing their tours to build anticipation for it, never performing on TV (apart from one appearance in their first year), and never (officially) releasing a single. Their

rise, rapid and phenomenal, attracted the disdain of music critics, who never acknowledged the excellence of some of their ensuing albums, particularly *IV* (1971) and *Physical Graffiti* (1975), which were surprisingly diverse in content. By the mid-Seventies they were arguably the most successful group in the world. Led Zeppelin offered a blueprint for all the successful British heavy-metal acts, such as Black Sabbath, Deep Purple, Ten Years After, and, more recently, Rainbow.

No other group has sustained for so long so huge and devoted a following by repeatedly withdrawing from the limelight, and as suddening returning with a near-perfectly conceived masterplan. By the time of John Bonham's death in 1981, however, it seemed that the band had, creatively, shot their bolt at last.

been as prolific a writer and performer as during his years with the Beatles.

Of the other Beatles Ringo Starr chose a different path, in films, while George Harrison, at least for a time, surprised everyone with his first post-break-up album, the Phil Spector-produced *All Things Must Pass* (1970). Critically well received, it was also a huge commercial success, spurred on by the even more hugely successful single 'My Sweet Lord'. Harrison then organised a concert in New York's Madison Square Garden, in August 1971, in aid of famine relief for the people of Bangla Desh. With its host of rock legends, including Eric Clapton, Bob Dylan, and the Indian sitar virtuoso Ravi Shankar, the project, which also led to a triple album and film, was the most profitable 'rock-for-charity' event ever staged.

The New Indies

This new pattern demanded a change of attitude among the record companies, and at first it was the new indie (independent) labels that showed themselves to be appropriately flexible. The British beat/R&B boom had occurred, to some extent, in reaction to the major labels' stranglehold on the quality of output, but it was through those majors – Decca, EMI, Philips, and Pye – that the groups of the early Sixties' pop explosion had released their records. The early British independents like Immediate and Planet made the mistake of trying to compete with the majors in their own backyard, with standard pop. The new independents, notably Island and Virgin, but also others spawned about this time – Chrysalis, Charisma, and Blue Horizon – took an entirely different approach, geared to the album-oriented progressive market. They could offer artistic freedom in every department, from choice of producer to final approval of sleeve artwork.

The two key independents of the late Sixties and early Seventies were Island and Virgin. Island had been slowly expanding beyond their original function of distributing Jamaican records. Founder Chris Blackwell had had some minor R&B successes with licensed American material in the mid-Sixties, but his initial singles hits had been through Philips' Fontana label, with Millie's 'My Boy Lollipop', the first major ska (bluebeat) hit in Britain, and then the Spencer Davis Group, whom Island managed. When the Davis group broke up and one of its members, Stevie Winwood, formed Traffic, Island were launched in the progressive market and had their first hit single with the group's 'Paper Sun' (1967), followed by the album *Mr Fantasy*.

Island's handling of Traffic enabled them to develop a progressive image and attract the best of the new groups: Fairport Convention, Spooky Tooth, Free, and – before their management company set up its own label, Chrysalis – Jethro Tull. By the end of the Sixties Island were the most successful independent in Britain, and they continued to nurture their progressive ideal with further careful signings: Mott the Hoople, King Crimson,

Island's initial success caused the majors to strike back with their own progressive house labels – Decca with Deram, EMI with Harvest, Pye with Dawn, and Philips with Vertigo. Where appropriate, acts were shifted from the parent labels: Pink Floyd switched from EMI's Columbia to Harvest and Ten Years After and the Moody Blues from Decca to Deram. But the majors could never fully represent the new ideals, as became apparent when Island began to distribute other indies and eventually set up their own pressing plant.

One of the new labels Island part-distributed was Virgin. Like Island, Virgin was the brainchild of one man, Richard Branson. A born entrepreneur, Branson founded *Student* magazine while still in his teens. Then in 1970, following the abolition of retail-price maintenance, he moved into record retailing, opening his first Virgin shop in January 1971 and selling records at up to 25 per cent less than the recommended price. Within a few years Virgin Records were the leading retailers of rock, and Branson's next step was to set up a label. He signed the then almost unknown Mike Oldfield and in May 1973 came Virgin's first release, Oldfield's *Tubular Bells*. It was a phenomenal world-wide success, one of the best-selling records of the decade. Branson then carefully nursed the label, using the retail outlets as indicators of public taste. Virgin thus scored early with European rock groups like Tangerine Dream and Faust and, seeing the growing cult for avant-garde music, took on Robert Wyatt and Henry Cow. By the mid-Seventies Virgin had discovered the growing cult of reggae and a separate label, Front Line, for reggae and other Third World music was created in 1978, releasing records by leading Jamaican artists like Tapper Zukie, Culture, and Big Youth. Earlier their Virgin Rockers campaign in 1976 had brought out records by U Roy, the Mighty Diamonds, Peter Tosh, and Keith Hudson.

Reggae

Reggae, which the majors were slow to discover, is one key to Virgin and Island's continued growth. Its roots lie in African and traditional Caribbean music, but it was transformed by American R&B, particularly New Orleans styles. The proximity of the Caribbean to the southern United States allowed exposure to R&B stations, while migrant West Indians also brought home American R&B records. The key elements were the emphasis on the off-beat, possibly derived from the music of artists such as Fats Domino, and the horn-dominated music of Forties and Fifties R&B 'jump' bands. The off-beat became more accentuated, and the brass playing, among less accomplished West Indian practitioners, rougher and weirder. This new beat became known as ska (in Britain bluebeat) and was popularised by travelling DJs, the 'sound system men', like Duke Reid and Coxsone Dodd. Key early performers were Byron Lee, Laurel Aitken, and Prince Buster. Their original Jamaican recordings were leased to British labels like Melodisc, Bluebeat, Island, and B&C, and by the mid-Sixties the British West Indian community had become well acquainted with the new idiom. So too had the mods.

The transition from ska to reggae began in the mid-Sixties as the emphasis shifted from horns to bass and rhythm guitars. At the same time the lyrics began to reflect social conditions. The 'rude boys' (outlaws) of the

LEFT, ABOVE *John Lennon with Yoko Ono and Phil Spector, who helped record Lennon's 'Imagine' (1971).* LEFT, BELOW *Paul McCartney was* *as prolific as ever with Wings.* ABOVE *Peter Tosh, once a member of the Wailers, took time to emerge from Bob Marley's shadow.*

Roxy Music, Cat Stevens and Bad Company.

Island's Jamaican product, meanwhile, had been assigned to Trojan, which Blackwell owned jointly with Lee Gopthal of B&C Records. Island finally sold their interest in Trojan to B&C, but retained the progressive reggae acts, notably Bob Marley and the Wailers and Toots and the Maytals. Realising that reggae would not catch on overnight, Blackwell carefully invested money in these acts, enabling the Wailers to produce their most sophisticated album, *Catch a Fire* (1972), a key record in the broadening of reggae's appeal to white audiences. Island also financed the film *The Harder They Come*, with Jimmy Cliff, which gave reggae a much wider acceptance in Britain.

Since then Island have investigated other ethnic idioms. In the mid-Seventies Blackwell made a licensing deal with Fania, the leading New York salsa label, while more recently, and perhaps more promisingly, Island have begun to expose African pop, by figures like Sunny Ade, which is already showing signs of being more widely accepted. Island seem to be using their reggae blueprint to develop yet another growing market.

shanty towns began to record – the Wailers' 'Rude Boy' (1966) was one of the first to celebrate the Kingston (Jamaica) rebels – and this music was rougher still and heavier. The electric line-up and sound immediately made the music more accessible to white audiences. This new style, 'rock steady', was championed by, among others, the Maytals and Derrick Morgan.

By that time rock-steady and raggae singles had begun to make an impact on the charts, at first because of West Indian record-buyers and the brief skinhead patronage of the music, then through the novel appeal of the unusually complex rhythms and singing style. Among these early landmarks were Prince Buster's 'Al Capone', Desmond Dekker's 'Israelites' (a No 1 in 1969) and 'It Mek', Jimmy Cliff's 'Wide World', Dave and Ansell Collins' 'Double Barrel' (No 1 in 1970), and the Pioneers' 'Let Your Yeah Be Yeah'.

Reggae was established, but it was the American Johnny Nash who brought it to a new level of commercial acceptance. He had had a hit in 1968 with 'Hold Me Tight' but it was the 1971-2 hits 'Stir It Up' (written by Bob Marley), 'I Can See Clearly Now', and 'There Are More Questions Than Answers' that had real impact, with their more sophisticated production and, always, Nash's superb singing. The album *I Can See Clearly Now* (1972) was partly recorded in Kingston, where Nash worked with Marley, and Nash's assistance helped to launch Marley in Britain. He had begun to preach the doctrine of Rastafarianism in the early Seventies, as was evident on *Catch a Fire*. Marley and the Wailers made some tentative British tours, and when the 1973 album *Burnin'* provided Eric Clapton with the hit 'I Shot the Sheriff', Marley's breakthrough was well under way. The 1975 album *Natty Dread*, with classics like 'Lively Up Yourself', 'Natty Dread', and 'No Woman No Cry', clinched his success; a live version of the last, recorded at London's Lyceum theatre, gave him his first hit.

Marley was on his way to becoming reggae's first superstar, breaking the ground for other Jamaican acts – Toots & the Maytals, Peter Tosh (previously in the Wailers), Burning Spear, Big Youth. By now reggae was firmly established in Britain and increasingly influencing

ABOVE *Jimmy Cliff, whose role in the film* The Harder They Come *(1972) launched reggae worldwide.*

RIGHT *Rastafarian Bob Marley, reggae's first superstar until his untimely death in 1981.*

Roxy Music

Roxy Music was essentially the vision of Brian Ferry, an art student who could see his ambitions being more widely realised in a rock band. The nucleus of Roxy Music formed in 1971 with Ferry (vocal/keyboards), David O'List (guitar), Andy Mackay (saxophone/oboe), Paul Thompson (drums) and Graham Simpson (bass). Mackay, a student of avant-garde music, was responsible for bringing in Brian Eno, originally the group's sound engineer, who soon found himself on stage with the group playing synthesizer, treating instruments and creating various taped effects.

They signed to Island Records and amidst almost unprecedented critical acclaim their first album, *Roxy Music*, was released in mid-1972. Not overtly commercial but strikingly eclectic and spontaneous, the album was a surprising success, consolidated by two Top Ten singles, 'Virginia Plain' and 'Pyjamarama', later that year. In the meantime,

O'List had been replaced by Phil Manzanera; the group began its policy of 'guest' bass players when Simpson was replaced by Rik Kenton, then ex-Big Three member Johnny Gustafson.

Their second album, *For Your Pleasure* (1973), which began the long association with producer Chris Thomas, lived up to the expectations of the first. It was to be Eno's last with the group. Reports of personality clashes with Ferry were substantiated when Eno departed and was replaced by ex-Curved Air violinist/keyboard player Eddie Jobson. Jobson's presence gave the group a more melodic air which seemed more appropriate to Ferry's maturing writing. Manzanera and Mackay were contributing more to the compositions and these three, with Paul Thompson, have remained the core of the group since. *Stranded* (1973) reflected the group's more refined, less avant-garde direction following Eno's departure. Roxy were becoming more sophisticated, particularly Ferry, who began to develop a career outside the group. *These Foolish Things*, his first solo album, offered his interpretations of some of his favourite songs.

Despite the expected rumours of a split, Roxy Music continued to make group albums – *Country Life* (1974), *Siren* (1975) – while the individual members explored solo projects. Ferry made a second LP, *Another Time, Another Place* (1974); Mackay released a quirky solo album, *In Search of Eddie Riff* (1974) and collaborated in 1976 on the score of the hugely successful TV series *Rock Follies*; Manzanera explored both the darker and the more colourful sides of his musical personality on two albums, *Mainstream* (1976) with his former group Quiet Sun, and *Diamond Head* (1975). Roxy's members needed these offshoots to try out the many diverse ideas that no longer fitted into the context of the group.

Siren (1975), their least eclectic (and perhaps least satisfying) album, saw them finally break in America with the hit single 'Love Is the Drug'. The freshness and inventiveness of the early Seventies had now largely been replaced by cool, polished professionalism. This is particularly true of *Manifesto* (1979) and *Avalon* (1982), which were released after a trial separation in the late Seventies.

the emerging home-grown reggae groups in Britain.

Originally reggae had been one of the few true Underground styles in Britain. The Underground rock scene had come out into the open in the new era of Seventies progressive rock; indeed, it was beginning to take itself very seriously, becoming at times too intellectual and losing sight of its original meaning and function. There was a continuous search for critical respectability. A form of genre rock came into being; that is, rock musicians sought to re-define what they were doing in terms of other mainstream styles in the hope that this would elevate the status of their music to that of jazz, folk, blues, even classical music. Robert Wyatt, then with Soft Machine, summed up the process (*Creem*, June 1972): 'In the old days when Teds used to take off my Dizzy Gillespie records and put Elvis on, there was, even so, a thing about values in music. One knew where the real worth was. The barriers were very rigid but it wasn't confused like it is today. Now, the pop press is always telling me that the barriers are down and someone who used to get off on Marmalade celebrates his coming of age by going over to the Other Chart, and thinks he's digging jazz or classical music when he's listening to the new Keith Emerson album. He's not – it's just pop in another form.'

The Superleagues

The leading progressive groups included some from the tail-end of the Sixties – Pink Floyd, in their post-Syd Barrett period; the Moody Blues, after their symphonic *Days of Future Past*; Emerson, Lake and Palmer – and new groups like King Crimson, Yes, and Genesis who were to make their mark in the Seventies. Their forte was long numbers often inspired by jazz or classical music, with extended instrumental passages and ponderous or bogus-mystical lyrics. King Crimson, with their acclaimed 1969 album *In the Court of the Crimson King*, provided an early model but soon shifted to weightier music, masterminded by Robert Fripp. Unfortunately, however, they were unable to make the same impact as, say, Yes or ELP because of the instability of their line-up. The Fripp-compiled King Crimson primer, *A Young Person's Guide to King Crimson* (1976), has glimpses of a truly progressive music.

Yes, though they suffered from constant line-up changes, had their most productive period in 1972 after Steve Howe (guitar) and Rick Wakeman (keyboards) joined the nucleus of Jon Anderson (vocal), Chris Squire (bass), and Bill Bruford (drums) and they cut the album *Close to the Edge*. Bruford joined King Crimson soon

LEFT, ABOVE *Deep Purple (here in 1974 guise): heavy metal ancestor of both Gillan and Whitesnake.* LEFT, BELOW *King Crimson were the* *early Seventies' top progressives.* ABOVE *Slow to please the rock pundits, Genesis progressed from mid-Sixties cult to superstardom.*

after, Alan White replacing him for the live triple album *Yessongs*. Thereafter Yes became increasingly cliché-ridden – even to the point of self-parody – and Wakeman left to pursue sub-classical projects like *The Six Wives of Henry VIII*. But the masters of 'classical' pretentiousness were ELP. The Nice had dabbled in rocking-up the classics, but Keith Emerson, joined by Greg Lake (from King Crimson) and Carl Palmer (from Atomic Rooster) to form ELP in 1970, took this to extremes. They recorded a live version of Moussorgsky's *Pictures at an Exhibition*, and called their final LPs *Works Vols I and II*.

A superleague had come into being; hit singles were irrelevant and promoting the album was the order of the day. A supergroup made an annual album, backed it with a world tour, and carried on in this fashion year after year. Behind it, a well-organised business machine kept everything running smoothly and efficiently.

The successful heavy-metal groups operated on the same principles. Inspired initially by Cream, Jimi Hendrix and the Jeff Beck Group, Led Zeppelin set the pattern for hard-rock groups and were followed by Black Sabbath, Deep Purple, Nazareth, Status Quo, and Uriah Heep. But heavy metal, with its thunderous rhythms, brash soloing, and near-Teutonic lyrics, at least retained some contacts with its denim-clad audience. More a working-class phenomenon than progressive rock, it still inspires a fierce passion among its followers. Most of the Seventies metal groups survive: Deep Purple disbanded but begat Rainbow, Gillan, and Whitesnake, while most

of the others carry on in one form or another. Heavy metal has never lost its appeal, and the band roster has been swelled by American groups like Rush, Kiss, and Ted Nugent, as well as the Australian group AC/DC, who used Britain as a springboard to worldwide success. The punk revolution of the later Seventies would also indirectly inspire a new generation of heavy metal groups, such as Iron Maiden, Def Leppard, and Saxon.

The early Seventies were prolific, too, in interesting undercurrents and in artists who belonged to no identifiable genre: Elton John, Rod Stewart, Roxy Music, David Bowie. Genesis, though originally in the progressive mould, seemed to fit it less and less well as they concentrated upon songs rather than instrumental display. Hawkwind, formed in the late Sixties, gave their brand of heavy metal science-fiction overtones, and had a hit single in 1972 with 'Silver Machine'. The Welsh group Man, who released 10 albums between 1968 and 1976, embodied the attitudes and philosophy of the American West Coast bands. Their 1975 live album, *Maximum Darkness*, even saw them accompanied by John Cippolina (guitar) from Quicksilver Messenger Service, for long one of the leading San Francisco groups.

The Pop Revival

The early Seventies also saw a rebirth of pure pop, and an extension of the pop market into the pre-teen population. There were blazes of glory for Mud, Sweet, the Rubettes, Showaddywaddy, Gary Glitter, David Essex, T Rex, Suzi Quatro . . . and the Bay City Rollers,

who for a while created something akin to Beatlemania. These artists dominated the singles charts between 1972 and 1974. Their music was simple and superficial, sold by glam-and-glitter presentation, and most of the performers were puppets, their strings pulled by old hands from the Sixties – pop specialists who wrote and produced the songs and thought up ever more outrageous images that could be sold through *Top of the Pops* and Mike Mansfield's TV show *Supersonic.*

In retrospect, Seventies pop is not as ephemeral as it seemed. Singles like Gary Glitter's 'Rock 'n' Roll', T Rex's 'Get It On', Slade's 'Coz I Luv You', and the Sweet's 'Ballroom Blitz' are now revered, not least by the punk generation. The skilful presentation of a glam or glitter image was also tastefully adopted by, among others, David Bowie and Roxy Music, while both Rod Stewart and Elton John, at their best, matched some of the period's classic songs with discordantly ridiculous images. Elton John was well aware of the joke in presenting such tender songs as 'Your Song', 'Rocket Man', and 'Daniel' while wearing ludicrously flamboyant costumes.

Certain other groups went their own idiosyncratic way. 10CC were veterans: Eric Stewart had been with

Genesis

Genesis, like Roxy Music, were essentially a Seventies creation. They rose to prominence in the early part of the decade, sharing an audience with such groups as Yes and ELP but lacking their instrumental virtuosity.

The original nucleus of the group at Charterhouse School comprised Peter Gabriel (vocal), Mike Rutherford (bass) and Tony Banks (keyboards). Their desire to write songs brought them together and to the attention of pop entrepreneur Jonathan King – an unlikely patron, it would seem, though King too had been at Charterhouse. He went on to produce their first album for Decca, *From Genesis to Revelation* (1969). It found little favour with either the public or the critics, who were particu-

larly dismissive of this and their subsequent album, *Trespass*, released by Tony Stratton-Smith's independent label Charisma. After *Trespass*, Phil Collins (drums) and a little later Steve Hackett (guitar) were brought in to add musical muscle to the group.

Their third album, marking the debut of Collins and Hackett, was the more fully realised *Nursery Crime* (1971), in which Genesis' unusual style began to take more concrete form. Their following, despite indifference or hostility in the music press, continued to grow with *Foxtrot* (1972).

With the release of *Selling England by the Pound* (1973), a first British hit single, 'I Know What I Like', and the ambitious concept album *The Lamb Lies Down on Broadway* (1974), Genesis became a force to be reckoned with. Gabriel, though introspective off-stage, had become a remarkable performer, acting out each song and wearing outrageous masks and costumes to depict the bizarre characters he created. Success enabled the group to stage

LEFT *An unlikely superstar, Elton John demonstrated that talent, a flamboyant theatrical sense, and self-mockery make a good mix.*

ABOVE *Pub rock represented the reaction against pretentiousness and size. Dave Edmunds' Rockpile was a typical Seventies pub band.*

Pub Rock

One final phenomenon of the early Seventies came as a reaction against massive concert tours, pomposity, and glitter – pub rock. Music has long been an important part of pub life, particularly jazz, but whereas many leading Sixties venues had used pub annexes or back rooms, the pub rock of the Seventies was played in the pub itself. Pub rock was at its peak between 1972 and 1974. The Tally Ho in London's Kentish Town was the first to open its doors to pub rockers – the now-forgotten American country-rock group Eggs Over Easy started the idea there – and soon other London pubs followed: the Nashville in Hammersmith, the Kensington, the Hope & Anchor in Islington, and others. The first rush of groups included Bees Make Honey, Brinsley Schwarz, Ducks DeLuxe, Kilburn and the High Roads, and Ace; a later wave included Kokomo, Dr Feelgood, and the Kursaal Flyers. It was music that went back to the roots – rock 'n' roll, country, and R&B – and it had an entirely different character from progressive rock and heavy metal.

Pub rock also provided an unlikely foothold for the punk bands. Stiff Records, one of the key new independent labels, drew much of its inspiration from pub rock, and its early roster included Ian Dury from Kilburn and the High Roads, Nick Lowe from Brinsley Schwarz, and Sean Tyla from Ducks DeLuxe. Indeed, Stiff's creators Jake Riviera and Dave Robinson were steeped in pub rock too: Riviera had worked with Dr Feelgood and Robinson had managed Brinsley Schwarz and done the booking for the Hope & Anchor. Other ex-pub rockers who became successful in the post-punk era were Dave Edmunds and Graham Parker & the Rumour (essentially the remnants of the Brinsleys and Ducks). Although punk music had nothing in common with the good-time pub rock style, both parties at least shared a disdain for the Seventies' 'serious' pretentions.

Punk music did, then, have strong connections with some strands of Seventies rock and was not, as is often argued, just a reaction against everything that the Seventies represented. But, more importantly, punk reached further back, and in its spirit and brash vitality rediscovered the forgotten spirit of the Sixties.

the Mindbenders, and Graham Gouldman had written classic hits for the Hollies, Yardbirds, and Herman's Hermits. Initially on Jonathan King's UK label, they found the new pop climate to their liking and made some of the freshest, cleverest pop of the period in singles like 'The Dean and I', 'Rubber Bullets', and 'I'm Not in Love'. The more cultish Mott the Hoople also saw the importance of pop. An early progressive signing of Island's, they rose to prominence with a hit written and produced by David Bowie, 'All the Young Dudes', and for a few years enlivened the scene with exciting live shows and a musical style that was a hybrid of Bowie, the Velvet Underground, Dylan, and contemporary hard rock.

Queen were initially a heavy metal group who appreciated that singles were the lifeblood of pop. During the decade they crafted an ingenious series of singles and were never afraid of self-mockery, least of all their singer Freddy Mercury. Their *Greatest Hits* (1981) would be a reminder of why they were still so successful, containing as it did such inventive singles as 'Somebody to Love', 'Another One Bites the Dust', 'Crazy Little Thing Called Love', and, of course, 'Bohemian Rhapsody'. This last launched the rise of the promotional video that would be exploited by Adam Ant and the New Wave groups in the later Seventies.

their tours more extravagantly, the presentation accompanying the *Lamb* tour being wildly over the top. It did, however, create considerable interest in America for the first time and finally won over the music critics.

Having, it seemed, achieved this major breakthrough, Gabriel – who *was* Genesis as far as most people were concerned – left the group to pursue a solo career in late 1975. For many it signalled the end of the group. After auditioning hundreds of likely replacements, Phil Collins stepped out to take over the lead vocal role with apparently remarkable ease. The first post-Gabriel album, *A Trick of the Tail* (1976), was also remarkably well received and Genesis as a rejuvenated trio (Steve Hackett had also departed) have since reached greater commercial peaks than during the Gabriel years. Ironically, Phil Collins's solo career, both in the commercial sphere and with his jazzier spin-off Brand X, has been more successful than Gabriel's.

The New Sounds

On the afternoon of 1 December 1976 an as yet little heard but already notorious group called the Sex Pistols crashed into British living-rooms. Four nervous and agitated youths responded to a merciless bating by TV interviewer Bill Grundy with a stream of four-letter invective that caused one viewer to boot in the screen of his TV set, got Grundy laid off for two weeks, and, more importantly, gave a nationwide boost to the most visible upheaval in youth culture since *Blackboard Jungle* made the name Bill Haley synonymous with misery for cinema managers back in the late Fifties.

Judging by the way Fleet Street splashed shocked headlines amongst the cornflakes and marmalade the following morning, you might have been forgiven for thinking that rock 'n' roll had until then never been anything but the perfect bedfellow of the establishment.

ABOVE *The Ramones: all leather jackets, split-level jeans, B-movie mentality, and 100mph distortions of surf and other Sixties rhythms.*

RIGHT *Johnny Rotten, a reluctant figurehead of punk and lead singer of the Sex Pistols, who were in the van of the New Wave.*

Elvis Presley, of course, was never banned for overt sexuality in his stage act, the Rolling Stones had never been caught urinating against a garage wall, and teds would never have dreamed of beating the celestial blue blazes out of mods every time the sun shone on Brighton's August beaches. Yet punk rock, with its ghoulish alliance between a brain-numbing nihilism and a glorification of all things ugly and shocking, was destined to cause the gap between the generations to yawn, once more, miles apart.

By the mid-Seventies rock was no longer the property of the teenager. It no longer reflected or provided a unifying identify for the very youth it was supposed to represent. Rock had developed a middle-aged spread.

The gap between musician and audience had reached ludicrous proportions with the advent of stadium rock.

Vast exhibition halls and cinemas – or, in the summer, the open-air festival venues – might have been the only places the rock aristocracy could conceivably have played, but their sheer size reduced the heroes, for most of their audiences, to little more than animated garden gnomes. In an effort to reduce the gulf, bands introduced ever-more-sophisticated hardware: elaborate sound systems, videos, animated films, inflatable objects that would zoom into the audience.

Pub rock had gone some way towards reversing the trend. The circuit of cellars and bars had encouraged and fed on bands such as Dr Feelgood and Eddie & the Hot Rods, from Southend, and Bees Make Honey and Brinsley Schwarz from London. These mainly R&B-based outfits banished the 20-minute guitar solo and replaced it with a gem-hard melody line hooked to a fat rhythm inside the confines of a three-minute song. Not only did the pub-rock circuit provide ready-made venues for the new groups, it also convinced them that they did not need a fleet of trucks to get up on stage in the first place. All you needed was the minimum of equipment and the maximum of dedication. Pub rock brought back the experience of listening to music and responding to it first-hand in a convivial and communal atmosphere.

America came up with its own remedy for the decay. While most of the country was sticking to its customary diet of hip-easy-listening – Jackson Browne, Fleetwood Mac, James Taylor, country crooners like Kenny Rogers, and heavy-metal or glam-rock merchants like Kiss – Manhattan looked to the nightlife and centred its attention on the club scene. The years 1974-6 saw a growing reaction against the overdressed hyperbole of glam-rockers in the proliferation of bands like Television, Jonathan Richman & the Modern Lovers, Patti Smith, Talking Heads, Blondie, and the Ramones. Captured on compilations like *Live at CBGB's* and *Live at Max's, Volumes 1 and 2*, these bands were the direct descendants of the garage bands of the Sixties who had flourished in response to the first British invasion. Taking from them a deliberately amateurish approach to music-making, they had a glorious disregard for sophistication, infusing their crudeness with a raw power. They drew their thrashing buzz-saw attack from Detroit's MC5 and Iggy Pop & the Stooges, and inherited from the Velvet Underground the three-chord rhythmic drone that would underpin their two-minute songs.

The Ramones – four 'brudders' from the New York borough of Queens – represented one aspect of this scene. Distorting the Velvet's blueprint even further, they worked with an energy that sought to make incompetence unimportant. A comic-book mentality inspired near-moronic lyrics fused with speeded up versions of classic pop cliches. With their roots firmly in the Sixties, however, it would come as no surprise when they teamed up with Phil Spector for their *End of the Century* (1980) album.

The Punk Explosion

Hung over from the glam-rock days of the early Seventies were five casualties called the New York Dolls. Trashy, decadent, over-generous with the make-up and splish-splash-coloured garb, these so-called (and mis-named) poor-man's Rolling Stones unwittingly provided the link between the American and English punk phenomena. Having witnessed a London gig by them at Biba's, a young(ish) art-student-cum-boutique-owner named Malcolm McLaren was sufficiently impressed to follow them back to the New York clubs to become their manager. A committed left-wing activist in his student days, McLaren tried to arrest the inevitable downward spiral of the Dolls' career by stuffing them into red patent-leather gear and packaging them as peddlers of what later was called Marxist chic. But the hammer-and-sickle backdrop convinced no one, least of all the Dolls, whose love affair with the sleazier side of rock 'n' roll they took too seriously. As their prophetically titled 1974 album proclaimed, it was all *Too Much Too Soon*. In 1975 guitarist Johnny Thunders left to form the Heartbreakers with Richard Hell, and hoping to renew his career by coming to London when his heroin addiction prevented the group from being signed by US record companies. Bassist Arthur Kane was lost in the Bowery, struggling with alcoholism; vocalist David Johansen and

LEFT *Malcolm McLaren, whose deft manipulation of the media earned him the title of punk's éminence grise.* ABOVE *Jordan, first lady of punk and manager of McLaren's boutique 'Sex'.*

guitarist Sylvain Sylvain survived to pursue solo careers.

It was while McLaren was trailing the Dolls around New York that he was swept up by the ground-swell of energy in the clubs, and he returned to London and his King's Road shop with his head packed with the things he had witnessed. His shop, 'Let It Rock', stopped selling teddy boy memorabilia and drain-pipes, instead stocking T-shirts that were ripped and shredded, fastened together with safety-pins, and imprinted with outrageous logos. Peddling bondage-wear that was more shocking than sexy, the shop, now renamed 'Sex', began to attract London's bored youth. Never quite giving up the idea of using rock 'n' roll to perpetrate his Situationist tactics, McLaren was more than willing to give advice to the four young blades who hung out in his shop and called themselves the Swankers. Lifting the idea of spiked-up hair (greased with Vaseline so that it looked as if an electric current had passed through it), the ripped T-shirts, as well as the 'Blank Generation' motto, from New Yorker Richard Hell (then of Television, later of his own Voidoids), McLaren moulded the Swankers into the Sex Pistols.

The original line-up included one Wally, who was replaced by a green-haired, mad-eyed youth from Finsbury Park (London) called John Lydon. Earning a new name because of his state of dental disrepair, the sneering, arrogant Johnny Rotten had just the right amount of magnetism to make him the perfect frontman. The Sex Pistols played their first gig at the St Martin's School of Art on 6 November 1975. They

LEFT *Little known in their own day, glitter rockers New York Dolls were one of the few influences acknowledged by the New Wave.*

ABOVE *Almost as media-wise as McLaren, the Stranglers rode the wave to the top; unlike most punk bands, they outlasted the Seventies.*

of *Sounds*, and the majority that openly derided or ignored it.

In the face of such hostility, fanzines sprang up such as Mark P's *Sniffin' Glue*. Combining illiteracy with an infectious enthusiasm, these xeroxed home efforts were the essence of the do-it-yourself punk spirit. On one occasion Mark P printed a page with diagrams of three guitar chords and the words 'Now Start Your Own Group'. That he was taken at his word by hundreds of aspiring musicians, ranging from the good through the bad to the abysmal, must have been something of a surprise even to him.

Punk Venues

What national media coverage the punk bands received was of the sensationalist kind that focused on the violence and amplified it. It was significant that the first time the Pistols had their photo in the *Melody Maker* was in a front-page spread depicting a brawl in the Nashville – a fight, according to one photographer who was there, that had been painstakingly re-enacted after the club closed. One by one the venues began to close their doors to the groups: the Nashville, the Marquee, and finally the 100 Club. (By September 1976, there had been enough bands to warrant a two-day festival. Held at the 100 Club, it was supposed to be the punks' coming-out party, but when a fragment from a broken glass (aimed at the band) blinded a fan in one eye, the party spirit curdled. Punk's last respectable haven in central London was lost.)

As the doors of the conventional venues closed on them, London's punks turned elsewhere for places to convene. The Screen-on-the-Green cinema in Islington offered its premises for one or two nights, but it was not until Andy Czezowski, an ex-mod and former manager of the Damned, stumbled upon an old gay club in Covent Garden called Chaguarama's that the punks had a place where they could puke in peace. After a two-week trial run, Czezowski opened the Roxy Club on 1 January 1977 with the Clash headlining. Into this subterranean home flocked the amphetamine-neutered tribe, dripping with the nastier accoutrements of sado-masochistic fashion.

massacred Small Faces and Who tunes with a hitherto unheard-of degree of amateurism, and the combination of indecipherable noise and Rotten's continuous riding of the student audience got them thrown off-stage within 10 minutes.

This was to become the familiar pattern – the Pistols would blag their way on to a bill, play for 10 or 20 minutes, depending on the tolerance of the crowd, and after trading insults have the plug pulled on them. The more they played the more the cult prospered. A full-grown following developed around them. Hippies, with their ideals of love and peace, were treated with the utmost disdain, their futility thrown in their faces like refuse. Rotten would wear 'I Hate Pink Floyd' T-shirts (the first two words being his own addition). To qualify for acceptance by the group's fans it became necessary to have 'street credibility' – which meant being under 20, having little or no education, and being a member of the working class. If your dad happened to be an accountant, tough.

Throughout 1976 bands began to flourish, taking the example of the Pistols to heart and setting up with little money but lots of fun. As bands like the Damned, Siouxsie & the Banshees, and the Buzzcocks began to get a following, so the New Wave movement (as it was dubbed) had to find an outlet for information. The music press had been caught unprepared by the onslaught of the New Wave, and it was sharply divided into the few writers who took it seriously, notably Caroline Coon in *Melody Maker* and Jonh Ingham and Giovanni Dadomo

Pogo-dancing on each other's feet (and heads), the fans would pack together to watch a procession of good, bad, and unspeakably dreadful bands power out three-chord, two-minute, fuzz-toned anthems. Between sets Don Letts, a black DJ, would fill the club with dub and reggae, forging a link between the two musics that was to be fruitful for both. Upstairs, the scene's equivalent of the music press would be on offer: the fanzines.

It was to this den of endurance that the A&R men began to flock, throwing contracts around like confetti. EMI had pipped most of them to the post by signing the Pistols in November 1976, and had planned release of their single 'Anarchy in the UK' on 26 November. But after the Grundy affair on TV EMI got cold feet: having paid them a £40,000 advance, EMI cancelled the contract on 7 January 1977.

Punk Labels & Outlets

The Pistols were not the first punk band to release a single: that achievement was the Damned's, who had signed to Stiff Records after the 1976 Mont-de-Marson Punk Festival in France. It was on this tour that pub rockers Nick Lowe, Dr Feelgood, and Eddie & the Hot Rods first came into contact with the punk contingent. So successful was their relationship that Nick Lowe agreed to produce the Damned's first single, 'New Rose'. Recorded in six hours at Pathway Studios, it shifted 4,000 copies on mail-order alone, and reached the lower rungs of the charts after the major United Artists had taken over distribution.

Stiff was an independent company moulded in the pattern of the American Beserkley label, which in 1976 had been responsible for Jonathan Richman's classic 'Roadrunner'. Beserkley's Matthew Kaufman had put his racetrack winnings behind several artists whom the major record companies would not touch with a barge-pole. Stiff, likewise, opened its doors to the punks who could not persuade any major to sign them. The independent label scene became the life-line of the new wave. All over the country, labels were being set up to accomodate the music's need to be captured on vinyl. In the true spirit of punk's decentralising campaign, little pockets of city-based activities erupted, organised along the same do-it-yourself lines as the bands themselves: labels like Factory (Manchester), Fast (Edinburgh), and Zoo (Liverpool). These were among the few that got as far as establishing stables of artists: most of the early independent labels were created by the bands themselves. Stiff and Chiswick had demonstrated that you did not need access to Fort Knox to get your songs recorded; all that was required was those all-important items of collateral, enthusiasm and access to a studio.

These mostly one-off labels relied heavily on a vast underground network of shops like Rough Trade in London's Kensington Park Road. Catering to the tastes of the New Wave fan by selling the best of New York and French imports (and Jamaican pre-releases) as well as the home-grown stuff, Rough Trade began to evolve a distribution service alongside its retailing activities. More than just a record shop, it was a meeting place where the fanzines and the advertisements for gigs and replacement drummers were sure to reach the people they were meant for. Geoff Travis, co-founder of the enterprise, maintained a strict code of discrimination, refusing to stock records which he and his staff con-

ABOVE *First a shop then a record label, Rough Trade was punk's most sensitive outlet and centre of its independent-label scene.*

RIGHT, ABOVE *The Clash sang the workers' praises.* RIGHT, BELOW *Bow Wow Wow sang about not working, to a chic jungle beat.*

sidered grossly distasteful, sexist, or in any way politically biased towards the right.

As distributors Rough Trade and its ilk were invaluable, but they could never compete in volume with the majors or longer-established indies such as Island, Virgin, and Chrysalis. At first seen by the majors as a threat, the new independent scene gradually came to a compromise satisfactory to both artist and company: the small independent label should be licensed to the major. Bands began to sign not themselves but their labels to larger companies. Thus Two-Tone and Reformation became subsidiaries of Chrysalis, F-Beat of WEA, GoFeet of Arista. The bands retained artistic control and had their records professionally marketed, while the majors took their percentage.

By 1977 most of the more promising punk bands had signed to one major or another and product was beginning to appear in the national charts. The Stranglers, older than their peers, were at first the most commercially successful of all the new wave acts. Heavily influenced by the keyboard sound of the Doors and imitating the super-snide lyrics and atonal vocals of Lou Reed, they were amongst the most competent of bands owing to their rounds of heavy gigging. Their determinedly offensive lyrics also brought them loads of publicity, from feminists and clerics alike, which gave a huge boost to singles like 'Grip' and 'Peaches'. Manchester's Buzzcocks followed the Stranglers to UA, polishing and refining their style through a dozen singles. Their

droning, repetitive chorus-lines, strung under beautifully simple melodies on tunes like 'Love Bites', were the nearest the British new wave ever got to pop music.

The Clash, on the other hand, were the most politically motivated of all the punk combos – in fact, when they signed to CBS they had to face accusations that they had sold out to the establishment. Joe Strummer's inarticulate diction, made incomprehensible by the combination of a speech defect and fury, injected their 'White Riot' (1977) with an intensity that the charts had never made room for before.

Despite bans by both radio and TV, the Pistols' 'God Save the Queen' had reached the No 2 spot (though it mysteriously failed to make No 1) in June of the Jubilee year. Having been picked up by A&M in March for a reported £150,000 and dropped a few days later for a further £75,000, the Pistols spent a few months without a record company before Virgin signed them for £50,000. But having dropped their tune-maker Glen Matlock in March in favour of the inept Sid Vicious, the Pistols found their storehouse of good songs rapidly emptying. 'Pretty Vacant' made No 7, but 'Holidays in the Sun' failed to do much more than dent the Top 20. Moreover, a split had widened between McLaren and Rotten over the film *The Great Rock and Roll Swindle*, and in January 1978, during a disastrous American tour, the band called it a day. From San Francisco, Steve Jones and Paul Cook flew down to Rio to record with train-robber Ronnie Biggs; Sid Vicious and his girlfriend Nancy Spungen

went to New York, where both of them died; Rotten went to Jamaica and later, as John Lydon again, formed Public Image Limited.

Meanwhile, the Roxy Club was suffering from raised rents, the departure of Czezowski, an influx of tourists and voyeurs and general over-exposure. When Zandra Rhodes began flogging haute-couture imitations of the punk slash-and-safety-pin look to rich dilettantes, it spelled the end for most of the original coterie. True, there was a second wave of punk, heralded by Jimmy Pursey and his football-terrace-chanting yobbos Sham 69, who made their home in the Wardour Street (London) disco the Vortex; but the driving force had, by the beginning of 1978, been largely spent.

Punk's Legacy

Naturally, a pendulum that swings so far in one direction must swing back equally far in the other. At least, that was the reasoning behind the faint-hearted affair that went under the loose title of Power Pop. The early months of 1978 saw bands with names like the Pleasers, the Yachts, the Boyfriends, and the Banned, who attempted to bring back cute, melodic pop songs while maintaining the thrash-rated tempo of punk. Instead of insulting and sneering, they actually had the temerity to try and please the audience – but neat haircuts, Beatle

numbers, and stage uniforms were not what the punters and media really wanted.

Not only had punk swept away for ever all illusions about the mysteries involved in making and distributing music, and pumped new life into rock's tired torso; it had also helped to re-invigorate the British reggae scene. Indigenous groups like Aswad, Black Slate, Steel Pulse, and Matumbi emerged in response to the ever-increasing demand for live entertainment. Punk being (as its members liked to believe) the music of rebellion, it felt kinship with the black man's response to Babylon. When the Clash recorded Junior Murvin's 'Police and Thieves' it served to confirm a growing bond between the two movements. Denis Bovell, a member of Matumbi, became greatly in demand as a producer, working with bands like the all-girl outfit the Slits and the Pop Group. It was not unusual to spot white folk sporting the sacred dreadlocks of the Rastafarian faith.

It also became common for bands like Misty, Tribesman, Pressure Shocks, and Merger to appear on the same bill as the Ruts, the Clash, and Gang of Four under the Rock Against Racism banner. Set up in 1977 in response to some ill-advised mouthings by Eric Clapton, Rock Against Racism organised multiracial gigs that reawakened rock's political consciousness. Tom Robinson, once a member of a trio called Cafe Society who recorded on Ray Davies's Konk label, assailed rock's last bastion – its machismo. Proclaiming his gayness in anthems such as 'Glad to Be Gay', Robinson regularly

Post-punk scenes in Britain. FAR LEFT *Aswad and* ABOVE, LEFT *Steel Pulse breathed new life into home-grown reggae.* LEFT *Siouxsie and the Banshees made Gothic howls.* ABOVE *Gary Numan offered David-Bowie-inspired pop to an electro-disco beat.*

muscle, and it was directly responsible for the wave of bands that mixed both rock and reggae in their sets, the most successful being the Police.

After the deliberately blinkered vision of the early days of punk, sophistication reappeared. Gradually, being dumb became passé; being smart was the new thing. Even in the Roxy days, self-taught minimalists like Wire were discovering compositional techniques such as William Burroughs' and Brion Gysin's concocted cut-ups, which David Bowie had been first to introduce into rock lyrics. Bands like the Cure were fitting into their lyrics what they had learned in their A-level English lessons. Siouxsie & the Banshees carved great blocks of sculptured sound and built them, piece by piece, into bold, cold, almost epic melodies. Out went black leather and safety pins, in came Albert Camus, army greatcoats, and shanks of henna-dyed hair.

Once again New York led the way. With the arrival in Britain of Patti Smith, the doors were flung wide open for stream-of-consciousness verbalising. New American outfits like Père Ubu (named after the pudgy anti-hero of plays by the Frenchman Alfred Jarry around the turn of the century) made serious exploration respectable in its own right. Akron's Devo, given the sign of approval by Bowie, came on with bouncy pop jingles, wacky outfits, and hilarious promotional videos, all wrapped in a witty pseudo-philosophy that celebrated what they assumed to be the inevitable decline of the West.

Disco Rock

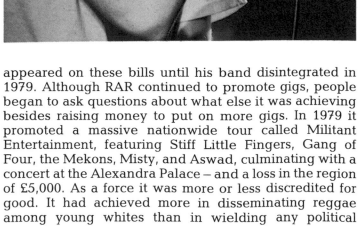

appeared on these bills until his band disintegrated in 1979. Although RAR continued to promote gigs, people began to ask questions about what else it was achieving besides raising money to put on more gigs. In 1979 it promoted a massive nationwide tour called Militant Entertainment, featuring Stiff Little Fingers, Gang of Four, the Mekons, Misty, and Aswad, culminating with a concert at the Alexandra Palace – and a loss in the region of £5,000. As a force it was more or less discredited for good. It had achieved more in disseminating reggae among young whites than in wielding any political

None of this made the smallest impression on the charts in 1978-9, since both Britain and America were under the sway of disco. Between them the film soundtracks *Saturday Night Fever* (1977) and *Grease* (1978) garnered the top two placings for the largest-selling albums in record history.

The years 1977-8 were a peak for singles sales, and several new-wave superstars shot to fame. Blondie's mix of the Sixties girl-group sound and garage-band precocity swept the board with 'Denis', 'Rip Her to Shreds', 'I'm Always Touched by Your Presence, Dear', 'Picture

This' and 'Hanging on the Telephone'. In 1979, on the strength of 'Heart of Glass', 'Dreaming' and 'Sunday Girl' and the LP *Parallel Lines*, they were the top-selling album and singles act in Britain – and they got there simply by combining pop with disco. From now on, if you wanted to have a hit single, you had to be able to dance to it.

The Police, a trio of dyed-blond punks, failed to make any impression until they had refined their blend of white reggae and pop. Contrary to the usual pattern, whereby British bands would make it at home and then attempt to break in the US, the Police operated in reverse: having released their debut *Outlandos D'Amour* (1978) in Britain to lukewarm response, they went on a low-budget tour of America. Imported copies of 'Roxanne' were at once in demand and both single and album edged their way into the US Top 30 – upon which 'Roxanne' and 'Can't Stand Losing You' were reissued and made their mark on the home charts in 1979. Simultaneously, the film of *Quadrophenia* was released with Sting (Gordon Sumner) in the role of Ace Face, his cool good looks establishing him as a teendream idol. 'Message in a Bottle' gave the Police their first No 1, in September 1979, quickly followed by its parent album *Reggatta de Blanc*. 'Walking on the Moon' repeated the feat in December, and a world tour in 1980 established them as the world's biggest-selling group.

Another rocket-to-stardom fairy-tale could be told by Gary Numan. He was quick to realise the potential that the American disco market had opened up – but he looked rather towards the Euro-disco sound popularised by the Munich-based producer Giorgio Moroder, whose use of the drum machine and synthesiser had revolutionised the disco and dance markets. Openly admitting his influences, Numan melded his introspective lyrics with an electro-disco beat culled from bands like Kraftwerk, Can, La Düsseldorf, and Neu. But his main inspiration was David Bowie, whose style during the period of his *Low* and *Heroes* albums provided Numan with the model for his stage clothes and attitudes as well as for his music. With little or no ground-level support (he had played very few live gigs) his 'Are Friends Electric?' single and *Replicas* album each shot up to No 1 in June 1979, a trick he repeated with 'Cars' and *The Pleasure Principle* in September.

In the absence of a single source of fashion, rock culture splintered into an array of tribes, each with its own mode of behaviour, dress and music, and each with its idols and icons.

Heavy Metal Reawakens

Whether it had gone away or just gone into hiding in the northern parts of England is a moot point, but in 1979-80 heavy metal began to shake its unwashed locks again. In America, certainly, the charts had always had their head-banging contingent: REO Speedwagon, Rush, and Kiss, as well as the British Led Zeppelin and Deep Purple. In Britain, however, heavy metal had never been supported by most of the rock press. Nevertheless, with the opposition now in abeyance, the denims and phantom guitar-players came out of the woodwork all over the country. Rainbow, with Deep Purple's Richie Blackmore, made the most of Graham Bonnet as their new lead vocalist and slammed the Top Ten twice. David Coverdale's Whitesnake and Ian Gillan's Virgin-signed band Gillan all made healthy impressions on the charts and even healthier appearances on the live circuit. Motorhead continued to deafen everyone as Lemmy's toothless grin appeared on *Top of the Pops*, where the band joined forces with Girlschool, an all-girl heavy-metal outfit, for their chart-topper 'Please Don't Touch'.

Assured of full houses every time a heavy-metal band played, promoters were willing to book any band with long enough hair, and, not surprisingly, there arose a new crop of home-grown bands. The British New Wave of heavy metal consisted of bands like Def Leppard, Saxon, Iron Maiden, and Angelwitch, who would pour

FAR LEFT, BELOW *The Police – from TV ads to world success.* LEFT *Def Leppard and* ABOVE *Iron Maiden perforated ear* — drums in heavy metal's own new wave. LEFT, BELOW *Older hand Ian Gillan, late of Deep Purple, crashed on too.*

themselves into hip-clutching trousers, wrap studded leather bands round their wrists, and play at ear-shredding volume while their vocalists yelled about sci-fi fantasy heroes, magic, and motorbikes. Regulars at the Marquee in London, the new heavy-metal bands virtually took over the annual Reading (Berkshire) Festival on August bank holiday.

The August bank holiday was traditionally the time for that other tribe to emerge en masse – the mods. The year (1979) that the film of the Who's *Quadrophenia* was released was one that saw a fledgling revival of the cult of cool. Most of the fans who donned green or khaki parkas, sewed badges of the Who and the Jam all over them, and flocked to Scarborough or Brighton were far too young to remember the original mod era. By and large, these were fans who had lost their interest in punk or the floating vote of the skinhead. They had none of the original mods' deep love of clothes, partly because they hadn't the money the Sixties versions enjoyed.

Formed in Woking, the Jam had crested the punk wave by possessing the necessary manic energy, yet they were set apart from the mainstream by their short-back-and-sides haircuts, Rickenbacker guitars – on which they were comparatively proficient – and an all-too-apparent allegiance to Sixties heroes like the Small Faces. Paul Weller's undoubted talent as a song-writer (as distinct from his skill at imitation) began to show itself, and 'Going Underground' went straight to No 1 in March 1980; a feat not accomplished since Gary Glitter's 'I Love You Love' in 1973, but one they repeated twice more before their demise in November 1982. Their astonishing string of hit singles placed the Jam in a league all their own, but there was a slew of lesser mod bands which promised great things but rarely produced them. Much was made of groups like Secret Affair, the Lambrettas, the Purple Hearts, and the Chords, but apart from the first (whose I-Spy label was linked to Arista) they saw little chart action. The music press made too much noise too early and smothered the movement.

Rockabilly, Mark 2

The music press made the same mistake with another insular tribe that flourished in the shadow of the new decade. Bands like Rocky Sharpe & the Replays and

ABOVE *Paul Weller's group Jam headed a Seventies-style mod revival and charted every time.*

BELOW *The Stray Cats, from New York, helped to lift Seventies rockabilly into the U.K. charts.*

Matchbox had been around the pub-rock circuit for ages, but when the American trio the Stray Cats settled in London, creating a hullabaloo within months of their arrival, pots of Black & White hair-gel suddenly began to disappear from the shelves of old-time barber shops and chemists. Sporting ludicrous quiffs piled on top of their heads, the Stray Cats played a strutting rhythm with a strong emphasis on the romance of rebellion. The Cats enjoyed the patronage of the Rolling Stones; but others managed to get by without it – notably the Polecats, the Blue Cats, and voodoo punkabillies such as the Meteors.

Two-Tone Rock

Fragmented the rock scene may have been, but there was one music that appealed to all – that of the Two-Tone stable in Coventry. The instigators were the

Specials AKA (as they were originally called), who had listened throughout their youth to recordings of Otis Redding and the best of the Stax and Motown outfits in the Midlands clubs and dancehalls. Combine that tradition with a love of ska, bluebeat, and reggae, and the anyone-can-do-it legacy of punk, and you have a basic formula that would spell much danceable fun.

Set up by Jerry Dammers, keyboards-player with the Specials, the Two-Tone label originally came into being to accommodate the band's own releases. The Specials' debut single 'Gangsters' was so successful, however, that they were quickly signed to Chrysalis. Furthermore, audience reaction soon indicated a market far larger than a single group could satisfy, and there was a swift onrush of acts with a ska/bluebeat grounding. With the Selecter, and also the Beat and the all-girl Bodysnatchers, Two-Tone placed each of their first 10 releases firmly in the charts, an unprecedented instant success. The Specials' live EP 'Too Much Too Young' also became a chart-topper, one of the very few EPs to do so. Eventually it became obvious that not even Two-Tone could contain all the action: Madness and the Beat (as Dammers' game-plan had intended) negotiated major deals of their own, going to Stiff and Arista (thinly disguised as Go Feet) respectively. Bad Manners, fronted by a character, half Yul Brynner and half Fatty Arbuckle, known as Buster Bloodvessel, mixed a similar brew, albeit with a leaning towards comedy; signed to Magnet they quickly

LEFT *The Specials hit the charts with a new approach to bluebeat and ska. The racial mix in their line-up inspired Jerry Dammers to call their own label Two-Tone.*

ABOVE *Duran Duran, purveyors of pop polish and seductive videos, climbed aboard the New Romantic bandwagon to cruise safely and infallibly into the charts.*

became regular entrants in both LP and singles charts.

Madness, from North London, at first dealt in fast paced cockney anthems that owed something to Ian Dury, but they quickly established themselves as a distinctive band with strong hooks, catchy lyrics, and a happy-go-lucky humour, emphasised by the videos produced for them by Stiff boss Dave Robinson.

Others did not last nearly as long. The Bodysnatchers were perhaps the least successful of all, finding hits only after line-up and name changes transformed them into the Belle Stars. As for the Specials themselves, a major schism left the group without their front-men – who, as Fun Boy Three, enjoyed a string of successful singles in the early Eighties. The Selecter bowed out, citing the success of the label as the reason for their departure. It was no longer possible for bands to be creative, they claimed; they had to be more Two-Tone than the originals. By the middle of 1980, it was virtually all over – the distinctive black-and-white Dammers-designed logo, the pork-pie hats, and mohair suits left the dance-floor to make room for an utterly different genre.

The New Romantics

As recession began to bite and economic gloom spread, the youth market turned its other cheek and put a spot of

rouge on it. The old axiom, that in times of extreme poverty and large-scale unemployment escapist entertainment will flourish, found new expression with the arrival of The Cult With No Name or – the Blitz Kids, the Futurists, the New Dandies. Never definitively labelled, the club scene that had evolved out of the electro-disco circuit dominated the first years of the decade. It was begun by Rusty Egan, a one-time drummer with the Rich Kids, who had become a dancehall DJ and promoter after he had hosted a Bowie Night at Billy's Club in Wardour Street (London). The evening proved so popular he had to employ Steve Strange, formerly a toilet cleaner at the Roxy Club and a shop assistant at PX, to act as doorman and turn away unsuitables. After all, who wants gatecrashers at his party?

A party was what the scene turned out to be – a costume ball for extroverts who dressed in ever more outrageous but always sophisticated guises. The space cadet, the pierrot, the cowboy, the Lawrence of Arabia rubbed padded shoulders with Sherwood Forest merry-men or big-white-hunters. The accent was on image – no matter what image, as long as it was elegant, outrageous, and exclusive. And there was a small coterie of London clothes designers, milliners, and hairdressers who catered to the needs of the new crowd. Strange and Egan moved their clubs almost as frequently as the styles changed: St Moritz, Hell, Le Kilt, Le Beat Route, Barracuda's 'Club for Heroes' – all played host at one time or another to the longest fancy-dress party in history. Although primarily a disco scene, the movement threw up its own music-makers. Spearheaded by Spandau Ballet, a group of five Islington-bred clothes-horses, bands such as Visage (featuring Egan, Strange, and bits

of Ultravox and Magazine), Duran Duran, and Landscape all found their way into the charts.

This was a coterie that fed on publicity, and when the media eventually became bored with Steve Strange's wardrobe, the whole enterprise seemed to run out of steam. The twin entrepreneurs took over the defunct Music Machine in Camden Town and turned it into a laser-decorated cocktail joint nostalgically called the Palace, with a different theme for the disco every night.

Rock Videos

What the New Romantics had made plain was that the Eighties would at least begin, if it did not end, as the decade of the visual image. No one saw this more clearly than Adam Ant, often tagged as a New Romantic but actually something rather different. Born Stuart Leslie Goddard, Adam began his career peddling pseudo-erotic decadence to a second-rate punk backing, consistently sneered at by the music press for his plagiarism and general hackdom. Adam never made any bones about his influences: he just borrowed the bits that appealed and stuck them together in a hotch-potch fashion. However, the hit formula came only after his brief period of tuition by Malcolm McLaren. In exchange for the Ants, McLaren shared with Adam his blueprint for Bow Wow Wow – 'Sun, sea and piracee'. Stowing the

Burundi tribal-drum sound, first made popular by Gary Glitter, under a chant calculated to appeal to the adolescent, he concocted images for each of his massively successful hit singles. From the Red Indian brave (with the characteristic white strip across the bridge of his nose) to the ornate figure of Prince Charming, Ant would punctiliously construct a wardrobe, hairstyle, and makeup and package them in a promotional video. Mini-feature films in ambition, these lavish affairs were directed by producer Mike Mansfield, who employed stars to add an extra touch of glamour. Glamour and image also played a huge part in the success of the Human League. When the original group broke up in

1980, Phil Oakey and Adrian Wright (the non-musician section of the band) recruited two schoolgirls in a Sheffield night club and added Ian Burden and later Jo Callis to bolster their instrumental capability. Once this mixture of electro-disco, commercial pop, faintly trashy glamour, and ever-necessary promotional video clip had coalesced, 'Don't You Want Me' and its parent album *Dare* topped their respective charts from December 1981 to January 1982, finally achieving its five-year goal.

The New Rock Market

The commercial success of the League created a high-point in domination of the charts by the new pop generation. The largest-selling music paper was *Smash Hits*, a colour-splashed fortnightly aimed at the teenage market, which printed the words of hit tunes. *Smash Hits* featured the new pop queens: the cute, squeaky-clean Altered Images, who sang about being happy and whose lead singer Claire danced like a wooden puppet in a ra-ra skirt; and the winsome, bland, glossily-produced Kim Wilde. What they all had in common was mass appeal: Soft Cell's 'Tainted Love', an electro-disco version of an old Northern Soul favourite, done out in Marc Almond's mincing camp style; Haircut 100's candy-striped, yellow sou'westered 'Favourite Shirts'; August Darnell's cocktail of Latin flora and fauna spiced with soul, R&B, reggae, or disco — all these, however they differed in their roots and influences, were united in the common appeal of the dancefloor.

In the Eighties rock's tribal edges often blurred in response to the demands of the pop market. LEFT, ABOVE *Culture Club and* LEFT, BELOW *panto-prince Adam Ant offered invitations to the dance that would be taken up by* ABOVE, RIGHT *Linx, who created an inventive version of disco-pop.* ABOVE *Kid Creole mixed danceable Latin cocktails of wit and style.*

For groups like these it was the age of the producer. To get the right gloss finish on their sound, they abandoned the Seventies attitude of bands who, with little or no experience of 32-track studios, would produce their own albums, justifying themselves by claiming that no producer could possibly construct a sound that existed only in the minds of the musicians. The attitude of the Eighties was that bands bowed to the superior knowledge and direction of the producer, who would add that extra dimension which would mean the difference between a hit and a miss. Martin Rushent and his Genetic Studios were responsible for the improvements in the sounds of the Human League and Altered Images; Trevor Horn directed ABC, masters of the new pop-funk brigade, and the sophisticated Abba impressionists Dollar; Daniel Miller masterminded Depeche Mode and its offshoot Yazoo.

Rock still managed to throw up the odd new trend, such as the jazz-funk fusion of 1981-2, spearheaded by British-bred bands like the brilliant Linx, Shakatak, and Imagination. The dislocated dance-set took jazz-funk as its basis and added a little New York avant-garde, learned from the likes of James Chance & the Contortions or the Lounge Lizards. The outcome was a fascinating blend of James Brown and Charlie Parker, laced with African polyrhythms. These white boys on funk consisted of Pop Group alumni Rip Rig & Panic, Maximum Joy, the Higsons and, most successfully, Pigbag, whose 'Papa's Got a Brand New Pig Bag' finally scored a year after release.

Less successful, perhaps, was the metropolitan-based 'new psychedelia'. Seemingly unwilling to let the Sixties go out of fashion altogether, this movement, based on the club circuit, had a lot of people wearing Byrds-type granny glasses, frilly shirts, and *Sgt Pepper* dandy uniforms, and listening to bands with names like Mind Over Matter and Mood Six. But as a movement it was doomed: it was over-exposed as a cult even before it had thrown up a central figure (promoter or band) around which it could coalesce and thrive. So 'new psychedelia' disappeared, almost as quickly as it had arrived, in the summer of 1981.

After the sweeping, frontal onslaught of the new wave, which had provided youth culture with an enduring source of inspiration, rock fragmented into different tribes, each with its own form of nostalgia, repackaged for the recession-strafed Eighties. The last two or three years have seen the blurring of those tribal edges, all barriers assaulted by the common drive of pop.

Guitars

The guitar forms the backbone of rock music and its continuing influence owes as much to its looks and style as to its musical potential. Certainly it is easy to play simple things on a guitar, and most people can get some kind of pleasing sound out of the instrument without too much knowledge of technique. However, like any musical instrument the guitar is difficult to play well, and it has over the years thrown up its fair share of virtuosi. But its attraction still lies in its simplicity, and it will always lend itself to live rock: It is much easier to *pose* with a guitar than with a keyboard or a drum kit.

The electric guitar has become a dominant force in rock music, amplified and distorted until it seems remote from its acoustic origins. Yet the principles of playing remain basically the same for every kind of guitar. Equally adaptable to both chordal and single-line melodic work, it can be used either for accompaniment or in a lead role, whether solo or as part of a group.

ABOVE *Asia's Steve Howe strums a semi-acoustic Gibson from among his extensive guitar collection.*

RIGHT *Ry Cooder, supersession-man, with an acoustic 12-string guitar, its strings arranged in six pairs.*

Acoustic Guitar

Acoustic guitars are sometimes tricky to slot into the amplified mix of electric rock on stage, and are more often associated with the singer-songwriter and the quieter undertakings of folk and country-flavoured rock. In the recording studio an acoustic guitar can be a more useful tool, lending a percussive rhythmic feel to certain tracks, or perhaps exploited to more melodic ends.

But on stage the acoustic guitar is a rarity, as it is difficult to amplify accurately and powerfully. In recent years the Ovation electric-acoustic guitars and their imitators have given ostensibly acoustic guitars a firmer place on the live stage, but these instruments tend to sound quite different from the genuine article.

The acoustic guitar most used in popular music is steel-strung, with a deep, hollow body made of wood, and a soundhole to project the sound of the vibrating strings and sympathetically vibrating top. Some acoustics have nylon strings, but these tend to be small-bodied flamenco or classical guitars, which are infrequently used in rock music.

The popular steel-strung acoustic guitar was largely developed in the United States in the early part of this century, the Martin Company being the most significant makers. They are primarily known for having invented, in the late 1910s, the large-bodied acoustic called the Dreadnought, which was originally designed in an attempt to give a bottom-heavy sound to help accompany singers, but has since found many applications in all varieties of popular music.

The two main shapes of acoustic guitar are the slightly smaller 'folk' shape, and this bulkier Dreadnought, also sometimes referred to as the Jumbo, after an instrument made by the Gibson Company of Kalamazoo, Michigan in the late Thirties. Gibson are also largely responsible for the popularity of another rather different kind of acoustic guitar, the 'arched-top' type. This has a top carved into an arch, rather than the flat or almost flat top of the much more common folk and Dreadnought types.

Acoustic guitars are made from a variety of woods. The top, or soundboard, is usually of spruce or cedar; the sides and back are mainly from rosewood, mahogany or walnut; the neck from mahogany or maple; and the fingerboard from rosewood or ebony. The steel strings are held in position by a bridge which transmits their vibrations to the soundboard, and on the end of the neck at the headstock by the machine heads, with which the player brings the strings into tune. The standard EADGBE tuning, from lowest pitched of the six strings to highest pitched, has been standard for the guitar since the late 18th century, although some guitarists use adapted tunings for different kinds of playing, particularly for slide and bottleneck styles.

Acoustic guitars normally have these six strings, but a popular variety has 12, arranged in six pairs, or courses, each pair tuned in unison or in a pre-arranged harmony. This gives the 12-string instrument a distinctively rich, full-bodied sound effective in chordal rhythm playing.

A strange variant on the acoustic guitar which first appeared in the Twenties in the United States is the ampliphonic resonator guitar, generally called a Dobro after its major manufacturer. It attempted to make the acoustic guitar louder and more cutting by attaching a vibrating metal plate to the top of the soundboard. Such instruments have a very bright sound with, not surprisingly, a rather metallic quality.

Electric-Acoustic Guitar

Ovation brought two significant new ideas to acoustic guitar design in the Sixties and in effect created a hybrid

instrument, the electric-acoustic guitar. Ovation was founded by Charles Kaman of the Kaman aerospace organisation. He applied to the guitar techniques developed in the production of helicopter rotor blades, and came up with an instrument with a back made of a glass-fibre-like material Ovation have patented as Lyrachord. This material, and the rounded shape of the back, gives Ovations a high-level, crisply projected sound.

The company's second innovation came later in the Sixties with the addition of a bridge-mounted pickup. This was connected to an internal pre-amplifier and body-mounted volume control, thus creating the electric-acoustic guitar. The theory is that here is a guitar with the general shape of an ordinary acoustic, apart from the rounded back, and an acoustic guitar's sound, but with the facility to be plugged into an external amplifier or PA system and amplified just like an electric guitar.

The Lyrachord bowl, as it is called, is based on the assumption that conventional acoustic guitar bodies will by their very nature trap elements of the sound in their sharp corners, sound that would otherwise be projected through the soundhole. This entrapment consequently makes ordinary acoustic guitars less efficient in sound projection than they might be. The smooth curves of the Ovation's bowled back ensure much more efficient, punchier projection of sound.

Electric Guitar

The electric guitar has had a surprisingly long history. It first emerged in the early Thirties in a curious guise, when a Californian company, Rickenbacker, made an odd-shaped instrument designed to be played while resting on the musician's lap. The shape of this first electric guitar earned it the nickname 'frying pan'. It was amplified by a crude, horseshoe-shaped, magnetic pickup. Much has changed since then, and electric guitars have been produced in many shapes, sizes and design configurations. But the essential mechanics are the same for all electric guitars, based on the simplicity of the magnetic pickup which is at the heart of the electric guitar's characteristic amplified sound.

Vibrating strings struck by the player are changed into electrical energy by a pickup or pickups on the body of the guitar. The strings vibrating in the pickup's magnetic field induce a current in coils of wire wrapped around the magnet, and this electrical signal is fed out of the guitar to be amplified. The electric guitar pickup is a 'transducer': that is, a device converting one form of energy (in this case vibrating strings) into another form of energy (an electrical signal).

There are two main kinds of pickup: the single-coil pickup, which has a coil of wire wrapped around either a single magnet or six individual magnets ('polepieces') for each string; and the humbucking pickup, invented in the United States in the late Fifties and featuring two wire coils and associated magnets next to each other. The coils are wound in opposite directions and are wired with opposing magnetic poles. This effectively cancels hum and feedback. There is some loss of treble in the amplified sound of a humbucking pickup, giving it a 'warm' sound when compared to the sound of single-coil pickups, which tend to have a brighter tone.

Since Rickenbacker made their first 'frying pans' in 1931 many different approaches have been adopted

BELOW *Original 1948-model Fender Broadcaster now belonging to Pink Floyd's Dave Gilmour.* RIGHT *Rory Gallagher and his well-worn Fender Stratocaster.* RIGHT, BELOW *Some of Paul Weller's collection of Rickenbacker electric guitars.*

which combine the magnetic pickup with a six-string design. Semi-acoustics are hollow-bodied guitars with pickups added for amplification. Various attempts were originally made to ally the ordinary acoustic guitar with amplification systems in the Twenties, but a notable achievement was Gibson's first electric semi-acoustic guitar, the ES150, introduced in 1935. Semi-acoustic guitars, popular with jazz and blues guitarists for their mellow tone, often feature f-shaped soundholes on either side of the pickup mountings.

More popular with the rock guitarist is the other kind of electric guitar, the solid-body type. The first commercially-produced solid-body electric guitar was the Fender Broadcaster – later renamed the Telecaster – developed by radio repairman Leo Fender and others in California and first put on the market in 1948. Guitarist Les Paul collaborated with Gibson to produce another notable solid-body electric guitar, the Gibson Les Paul model, in 1952, and two years later Fender launched his second six-string solid, the stylish Stratocaster. These three paved the way for all the rest.

Electric guitars are primarily wooden. Bodies are often made from solid or laminated alder, ash, mahogany or maple. The necks tend to be of mahogany or maple, and fingerboards are either of rosewood or the more expensive and denser ebony. The neck and body can be made in one piece, or the neck can be bolted or glued (or both) to the body. Sometimes the neck section will travel all the way through the body, enabling the strings to vibrate on one piece of wood, supported by the bridge at one end and the tuning heads at the other.

Pickups are located under the strings on the body, and associated controls nearby enable the player to adjust volume and tone, and, if the guitar has several pickups, to select combinations of these. The controls and pickups are wired together, and feed an output socket on the front or side of the body. A lead connects this socket to an external amplifier and loudspeaker.

One way of expanding the tonal control on an electric guitar is by the addition of 'active' electronics. This means that the guitar has a small pre-amplifier wired

ABOVE *Another collector, Micky Moody of Whitesnake, shows off some gems: on his lap a 1953 Gibson Les Paul Gold Top; below* *(from left) a Tokai Stratocaster copy, a National Resonator, a 1955 Gibson ES355, and a 1958 Gibson Les Paul standard.*

into its circuitry, powered either by mains or (more commonly) batteries stored inside the guitar body. This allows the guitarist to increase or decrease bass and treble sounds to a far greater extent than is possible on ordinary guitars (which are therefore termed 'passive' to distinguish them from the 'active' types).

A common mechanical effect seen on some guitars is the tremolo arm. (In fact it would be more accurate to call this device a vibrato arm, since vibrato means rapid changes of pitch; tremolo means rapid changes of volume. But the term 'tremolo arm', for all its inaccuracy, has stuck.) The most common version is that fitted to the Fender Stratocaster, altering the pitch of the string or strings being sounded by means of a handle attached to a rocking block under the bridge. It lowers or raises the pitch of the strings as the handle is pressed down or pulled up, and springs return the strings to normal pitch (more or less) after the handle is released.

The aspiring guitarist today is bombarded with every shape and colour of guitar imaginable, churned out mostly by large factories in the United States and Japan. Some players favour old, discontinued instruments for their sound and craftsmanship, and many argue that older instruments generally sound better than newly produced guitars. Others point out that only the better old instruments survive, and that the high prices of many vintage instruments are based on rarity.

Still other guitarists shun mass-produced guitars and choose to have an instrument built to their requirements

ABOVE *Richard Thompson with his Rickenbacker electric 12-string, reputed to have once belonged to Roger McGuinn of the Byrds, who popularised its jangling sound with 'Mr Tambourine Man', the group's monster hit of 1965.*
RIGHT *A Gibson Les Paul Cherry Sunburst; the colour effect is due to a special paint finish.*

VOLUME

ONE

TONE

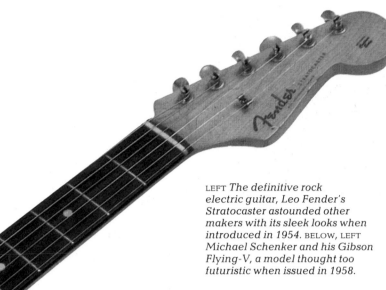

LEFT *The definitive rock electric guitar, Leo Fender's Stratocaster astounded other makers with its sleek looks when introduced in 1954.* BELOW, LEFT *Michael Schenker and his Gibson Flying-V, a model thought too futuristic when issued in 1958.*

by one of the guitar makers, or luthiers, who specialise in this sort of work. The advantages for the guitarist are personal attention and (usually) an assured level of craftsmanship, balanced against the the disadvantage of perhaps not being able to resell a relatively obscure make quite as readily as a better-known brand.

A recent trend is for players themselves to make a guitar from spare parts which are offered by makers specialising in producing custom bridges, pickups, bodies, necks, machine heads – everything, in fact, necessary to construct a guitar. This stems from the replacement fad of the late Seventies which appears to have originated with the New York company DiMarzio, one of the first to offer replacement pickups. The idea was that a cheap 'copy' guitar – that is, a guitar, usually of Japanese make, that attempts to copy the looks and design of famous guitar types – could be made to sound better by substituting a higher-output pickup or pickups for those supplied with it. The notion caught on rapidly, and spread to players who began to change the pickups of more 'respectable' guitars for the 'hot' – more powerful – replacement pickups.

Other companies were then influenced to produce replacement components to satisfy the screwdriver-wielding guitarist. Makers like Mighty Mite (who have since gone out of business) and Schecter began to make a complete range of replacement parts. The attraction was not necessarily economic, as it had been initially, since some of these guitars cost as much as conventional American and Japanese models, if not more.

Another recent trend among some electric guitar makers has been to experiment with plastic materials instead of the traditional guitar-making woods. Ovation have used what they describe as a 'high density foam material' over a rigid aluminium frame for the body of their solid electric guitar, the UKII. Gibson and Peavey have also experimented with and produced guitars made from plastic materials, and the up-market American makers Alembic have started to use a graphite fibre in their neck construction claiming that it increases rigidity and reduces weight.

Guitar Synthesizer

A few manufacturers, principally those already involved with keyboard-based synthesizers, have attempted to establish a working link between the guitar and the synthesizer. Despite the popularity of a keyboard as the control medium for synthesizers, it is by no means necessary for a keyboard to do the job.

An electric guitar (and to some extent any instrument) can be made to provide a synthesizer with control voltages by means of a pitch-to-voltage converter. This changes the pitch information produced by a guitar's vibrating strings into voltages, which a synthesizer needs to drive its voltage-controlled oscillators (making the pitch of the synthesizer's resulting notes), voltage-controlled filter (controlling the tone qualities), and voltage-controlled amplifier (shaping the notes).

But problems emerge when the synthesizer is made to try to 'track' – that is, follow accurately – the subtle playing techniques employed by rock guitarists, like varying picking strength with the right hand, bending the strings to change their pitch with the left hand, and so on. On a keyboard a key is pressed and that's that. But guitar players make notes and chords by combining various left-hand and right-hand techniques and tricks, resulting in a sound densely packed with subtle inflections and nuances.

Some of the early guitar synthesizers of the mid-Seventies avoided these facts. For example, Hagstrom's Patch 2000 system, which the Swedish company made in collaboration with American amplifier-makers Ampeg, entirely ignored right-hand picking information in the creation of the synthesized sound, and treated the guitar's fingerboard like a keyboard, each fret becoming a touch-sensitive switch that provided a control voltage on contact with a string. Only single notes could be played, not chords, and the system was not a success.

Designers have gradually come to realise that they must make the guitar element of the guitar synthesizer respond accurately to the guitarist's normal range of techniques, from both hands. Japanese electronic music-al instrument makers Roland have been among the few to attempt a practical solution. Since the late Seventies they have been working on a guitar/synthesizer combination which aims to suit guitarists' playing techniques while bearing in mind that they may not have a working knowledge of synthesizers.

The most recent Roland guitar 'controllers', loosely based on Fender and Yamaha shapes, feature a 'hex-

George Duke (right) playing what at first glance seems to be a cross between a guitar and a keyboard. It is in fact a remote keyboard controller for Duke's off-stage synthesizer set-up.

Alembic pioneered use of exotic wood and pre-amplifiers in basses. ABÓVE *John Entwistle and* RIGHT *Stanley Clarke are two notable users of Alembics.* BELOW, RIGHT

The Fender Precision was the first commercially made electric bass. ABOVE, FAR RIGHT *A newer development is the fretless bass; this Ibanez is played by Sting.*

aphonic', or six-way, pickup in addition to the standard guitar pickups on-board that are amplified in the usual fashion. The hexaphonic pick-up collects discrete information from each string, including all the inflections mentioned earlier. Chords or single notes can be played and treated with the synthesizer, and various options are open to tune the synthesizer's oscillators in harmonies with the fundamental pitch of the guitar strings. Other controls on the guitar include voltage-controlled filter switches for tonal changes, a balance knob for levels of normal guitar sound against synthesized guitar sound, and vibrato on/off touch-switches. The Roland machine is at present one of the few serious, commercially available guitar synthesizer systems, and attempts to bring to the guitarist the sort of sounds and manipulation potential which have previously been exclusive to the keyboard-based synthesizer player.

Some guitarists want future guitar synthesizers to give them the wider control facilities of most keyboard synthesizers, and a likely development will be a guitar synthesizer which can memorize and recall particular sounds set up on the control panel. Other guitar players want basic synth sounds from a very simple unit with minimal controls, and these too are likely to appear in greater numbers.

Bass Guitar

The electric bass guitar is one of the younger musical instruments used in rock. It is a four-string guitar, tuned EADG an octave lower than the six-string counterpart. It was invented by the man who can quite accurately be called the father of solid electric guitars and basses, Leo Fender. The electric bass was intended to replace the rather unwieldy upright orchestral double bass, the only instrument available to bass players at the time. Not only was the double bass awkward to use in any kind of mobile stage show, but its sound would not cut through that of the louder surrounding instruments.

Fender realised that the next step had to be electric, and the Precision electric bass guitar came on sale in 1951. The first electric bass guitar in the world, it was based on his already successful Telecaster six-string solid: the shape was similar and the overall visual impact reminiscent of the earlier model. Electric basses have permeated rock music ever since, providing a deep, solid basis for the rhythm section, working in tandem with the drums to fire the rhythmic drive of the music. The electric bass is essentially a four-string version of the six-string electric guitar, although there are minor design differences which make it slightly stronger in order to withstand the tension of the heavier strings.

A few of the earlier makers who moved in to exploit Fender's invention thought it was enough merely to make a four-string version of their popular six-string models. But in the early years of the bass guitar's existence, few rivalled Fender's success with the Precision and, in 1960, the Jazz Bass, a slightly larger and tonally more complex instrument. Fender remained *the* bass guitar for much of the Sixties and Seventies, with only occasional effective competition.

This came primarily from Rickenbacker, whose large and distinctive 4000 Series basses were characterized by their trebley tone and, visually, by their bright colours and triangular position markers on the fingerboard. The other big American maker, Gibson, fared less well, their EB Series and Thunderbird basses making little impact, and the later Rippers, Grabbers and Victorys were also largely overlooked by bassists.

Later in the Seventies a trend developed for using the fretless bass – exactly the same as a normal model – except that the frets are missing from the fingerboard, leaving it smooth as on a cello or double bass. The advantage comes from the unusual sound possible on this bass – notes can be slid along the fingerboard, and individual notes have a mellower character than those produced by a normal fretted bass. The fretless bass guitar's notes also seem to grow and die away more slowly.

To help the bass player who is used to a fretted instrument, some makers' fretless basses have fret markers on the fingerboard in the positions where the frets would normally be, forming a visual guide to the positions of the notes. Other makers put marker dots on the side of the neck facing the player, to give an idea of the fret positions, and still others produce totally clear necks and fingerboards for the confident and experienced fretless player. The American Kramer company has produced a few half-fretted, half-fretless basses, giving the best of both worlds.

Active electronics (explained in the Electric Guitar section) have seemed more at home in the electric bass. Some players find the extra tonal range offered by active circuitry useful, particular in the funky 'slapping' bass sounds common in soul and disco music. Alembic were one of the first makers to apply active electronics to their bass guitars, which are expensive and hand-crafted, made from exotic woods, and feature such oddities as light-emitting diodes in the neck as position markers.

Japanese bass makers have been very successful with their instruments in the late Seventies and early Eighties, and now produce many original designs, having moved on from a period when they tended to copy the major American makers' instruments, as they had with six-string electric guitars. Popular makes from Japan include Yamaha, Aria, Ibanez, Westone and Tokai.

The synthesizer manufacturers Roland have teamed up with Ibanez to produce a bass version of the guitar synthesizer described earlier. This converts the pitch of the bass guitar 'controller' into a voltage that drives the synthesizer circuits and produces electronic sounds not available from a normal amplified bass guitar.

But the bass guitar causing the most interest among players in the early Eighties is the all-plastic Steinberger Bass, designed by Ned Steinberger in New York. This instrument looks utterly unlike any bass made before, having no headstock on the end of the neck and a tiny body barely large enough to take the pickups and the controls. But it combines an inherent strength, a pleasing playability and strong visual qualities, enough to endear it to most rock bassists. What will deter many is the incredibly high price – but cheaper imitations of the instrument are already in production from rival companies.

The bass guitarist in the Eighties can choose between traditional wooden instruments, all-plastic newcomers, and even synthesizer control. But no one would deny that, without Leo Fender's master-stroke in 1951, rock music would certainly not sound the way it does today.

Keyboards

Keyboards are now strong contenders for the title of most used instrument in rock music, almost entirely as a result of the leap in popularity, over the past ten years, of the keyboard-based synthesizer. Synthesizers are as complicated or as simple as the manufacturer cares to make them – some are still similar to the huge telephone-exchange-like instruments that started the whole synthesizer boom, while others are starting to use the benefits of computer control, and still others are easy-to-use preset models not much bigger than the actual keyboard itself. But not all keyboard instruments in rock are synthesizers. There is still room in the studio and on the rock stage for the occasional grand piano, electric and electronic pianos, organs, and a few hybrids.

Keyboard instruments have developed quickly in the last decade – and here we are again talking primarily of the keyboard-based synthesizer. The speed with which relatively untrained musicians can obtain reasonable sounds from these instruments is increasing rapidly, while at the other end of the musical spectrum some extremely talented players are exploiting new keyboard instruments in fresh and exciting ways.

ABOVE *The Minimoog, the first compact performance synthesizer, was developed by the American Robert Moog.* RIGHT, ABOVE *Moog pictured with an earlier, larger modular system custom-built for Roger Powell.* RIGHT, BELOW *One of the first British synthesizers was the EMS VCS-3, here being used by members of Hawkwind.*

Synthesizers

The synthesizer has become almost exclusively associated with keyboards, yet a synthesizer need not be 'played' by a keyboard – indeed, synthesizers have been linked to all kinds of controlling instruments, including drums, guitars and wind instruments.

To understand how synthesizers work, we should first do some simple listening to the way in which sound is made up, and why we hear music the way we do. The synthesizer is essentially a device for taking sound down to its basic building-blocks and then putting it back together as desired.

When we hear a musical sound as being at a particular pitch, this is caused by a certain frequency, or vibration, in the air – in other words, sound waves. The more frequent these vibrations, the higher the note. Frequency is measured in cycles per second (called Hertz, or 'Hz' for short), and humans can theoretically hear a range of sounds between 20Hz and 20,000Hz. In practice, this range tends to be nearer 40Hz to 16,000Hz.

The other characteristics that define a musical sound when we hear it are the relative strengths of the harmonics above the fundamental. The fundamental is the main frequency of the note; the harmonics are multiples of this basic frequency, weaker overtones which contribute to the timbre, or tonal quality.

There are other factors which influence the way we hear a sound – its intensity or volume (sometimes called amplitude), its duration, and the way that the fundamental and harmonics alter in relative intensity over the period for which the musical note lasts.

The synthesizer at its simplest is designed to recreate these ingredients of a musical sound individually, by electronic means, and to mix them together and help them to interact in a way that simulates the production of acoustic sounds. The operator can in this way mix sound sources and modifications of these sources, deploying them in any order required.

The system that the vast majority of synthesizers use to recreate these sounds is called voltage control. It was first used by Robert Moog in the early Sixties. He applied it commercially later in the decade to his first modular synthesizer system, in which all the individual components of the synthesizer are separate and available for interconnection as required by the operator. Moog later popularized the system more widely by marketing a Minimoog, a small ready-wired synthesizer.

Each key in a synthesizer keyboard is made to produce a different voltage, called the control voltage, in a series of mathematical steps. These control various functions of the synthesizer, including the resulting sound. There are three main sections in the synthesizer: the *voltage-controlled oscillator* (VCO), controlling the pitch of the note pressed; the *voltage-controlled filter* (VCF), controlling the tone quality; and the *voltage-controlled amplifier* (VCA), creating the 'shape' of the note.

At the VCO, different wave forms can be selected for imitative qualities, the sounds of these waveforms depending on the combination of fundamental and harmonics that they contain. These include *square wave* – odd harmonics only, sounding hollow and rather like a clarinet; *sawtooth wave* – odd and even harmonics, often used for brass instrument impersonations; *sine wave* – pure fundamental only, with a soft flute-like tone, unique to synthesizers; and *triangle wave* – some odd

ABOVE *Sky's Steve Gray on stage with piano, harpsichord, and various keyboard synthesizers.*

BELOW *Landscape's Richard Burgess models Roland's memory machine, the Microcomposer MC4.*

harmonics used to substitute for sine wave because easier to create electronically. Synthesizers equipped with more than one oscillator give a fatter sound.

The VCF is a sophisticated type of tone control, and four main types are found in synthesizers. They are: *high-pass filter*, taking out frequencies below a particular level; *low-pass filter*, taking out frequencies above a particular level; *band-pass filter*, taking out all but a particular frequency; and *notch filter*, taking out frequencies at a particular level. The level around which the removal of the frequencies starts is called the cut-off frequency; the slight differences in certain makers' filter designs give each a characteristic sound quality.

Other functions vary with the make and type of synthesizer, but generally include a low-frequency oscillator (LFO), producing vibrato-like effects; a noise generator, which helps to create percussion-like and other harsher sounds; performance controls, for creative manipulation by the musician of the sounds once produced; and an envelope shaper.

The envelope shaper controls the way the note produced behaves while it is sounding, and usually contains at least two of the four basic ingredients. These are *attack* – the time at the very start of the note's life when the volume builds to its loudest; *decay* – the time, once the note has reached a maximum level, when it falls to a lower volume; *sustain* – a voltage controlling the volume of the sound while the key is pressed; and *release* – the time during which the note's volume decreases completely once the key is released.

There are many different makes and types of keyboard synthesizer, the principal manufacturers being based in the United States and Japan. The names you are most likely to see on stage and hear on record are Moog, ARP (now out of business), Sequential Circuits and Oberheim from the United States, and Roland, Korg, Casio and Yamaha from Japan.

There are two main divisions of keyboard synthesizer types: *monophonic synthesizers*, which will sound only one note at a time, no matter how many notes are pressed down on the keyboard; and *polyphonic synthesizers*, which will sound many notes at a time. The earliest instruments were monophonic and are still widely used, either as 'lead-line' synths for playing melodies and fill-in lines or for overdubbing in the studio.

Polyphonic synthesizers began to appear in the mid-Seventies. Moog's innovative Polymoog, one of the first, was based largely on organ technology and able to sound every single note on the keyboard simultaneously. Oberheim's four-voice synthesizer was another early polyphonic which in effect combined four monophonic synthesizers, enabling the musician to sound any four notes on its keyboard at once.

One of the most significant developments in keyboard synthesizers came in the late Seventies when Sequential Circuits launched their Prophet-5. This uses microprocessor control to remember every relevant part of a particular 'patch', which is what synthesizer players call the control settings needed to get a certain sound from their instruments. These memorized settings can be instantly recalled on the five-note polyphonic Prophet-5, and this facility (now shared with many other synthesizers) makes it a popular keyboard for live stage work.

A useful tool developed for interconnection with synthesizers is the sequencer. This enables the player to store sequences of notes and play them back through the synthesizer, modifying the overall sonic effect if necessary with the synthesizer controls, but retaining the overall melodic flow memorized by the sequencer. This can be in either 'step-time', a rigid, on-the-beat sequence, or 'real-time', exactly as played on the keyboard with timing and phrasing reproduced precisely. The number of notes stored in this way is limited by the sequencer's electronic capacity, but the machine does nonetheless offer a means of storing and replaying melodic lines, and is used for things like repetitive bass lines and repeated melodies and rhythm passages.

One of the most interesting recent developments in keyboard instruments has been the teaming up of computers and synthesizers. Computers, because of their ability to store and organise information, can be employed effectively to control synthesizers. They may be used as units separate from ordinary synthesizers, stor-

ing musical information as a series of numbers – the digital language that computers use to store information – and then translating them back to the analogue voltages and triggers understood by the synthesizer. Or a whole synthesizer may be entirely computer-based, with all the sound generation, storage and creation handled in digital information within the one system.

An innovative gadget in the first category was Roland's Microcomposer, introduced in the late Seventies and based on a system used by Canadian composer Ralph Dyck. It is something like a more versatile sequencer, storing all the information about a musical passage – the length and individual character of each of the notes – by layering melodic lines together in digital form in a memory. In effect, it replaces a musical keyboard with a series of knobs and switches, and the musician sends the relevant information to the synthesizer in this way, rather than by pushing keys on the musical keyboard.

In a similar way, other musicians have adapted home computers to control and provide sequencer facilities for synthesizers, using specially written programmes. Once again, these computers convert their digital information to the analogue information needed to fire ordinary synthesizers.

Completely digital synthesizers are a relatively new breed of musical instrument. Some look much like ordinary synthesizers, having a keyboard with a line of controls above it. They are different in the way they store and treat the basic building-blocks of synthesis: they have digital information about various sounds memorized and available for recall as required by the musician. Other digital synthesizers look much more like the computer systems they are, coming with a Visual Display Unit (VDU) screen and sometimes a typewriter-like keyboard for talking to the computer, along with a musical keyboard and a unit for storing the information.

One of the first commercially produced systems of this type is the Australian-made Fairlight CMI (Computer Musical Instrument), first marketed in 1979 and now becoming a popular if extremely expensive addition to some top studio set-ups. Sounds are generated, stored and processed by completely digital means, the information being stored in a separate unit using eight-inch floppy disks. Perhaps the most startling of the Fairlight's many talents is its ability to 'sample' natural sounds. It can listen to a sound through a microphone or coming off recording tape (anything at all, from a tuba to a tube train), analyze it digitally into its harmonic constituents, show you the waveform on the VDU, and regenerate this sound. The musician can then, using the keyboard, 'play' the sound back with total control over its pitch and phrasing. As well as being played on the keyboard, the sounds thus stored can be put into sequences which can be memorized and recalled as required.

The VDU has various functions, and the wave-forms displayed can be altered using a 'light-pen'. This device is pointed at the VDU, 'drawing' changes on to the display, and is rather quicker to use than the cursor, or moving dot, normally used to change information called up on computer screens. The system will also function like an oscilloscope in reverse: a waveform can be drawn from scratch on to the screen, and the synthesizer will play the sound back. Some other digital synthesizers have this sampling facility, like the Emu Systems Emulator, while others include what amounts to a built-in digital multi-track recording system, like New England Digital's Synclavier II.

UPPER *Microprocessors enabled the Prophet-15, here used by Phil Collins, to store sounds – the first synthesizer to achieve this.*

LOWER *This computer-synthesizer stores sounds digitally, displaying waveforms on a screen for modifying with a 'light pen'.*

Pianos

The traditional piano is generally referred to in rock as the acoustic piano, to distinguish it from the more recent electric and electronic simulations of the instrument. The acoustic piano is not used very widely by bands on tour, for obvious reasons: as well as being large and bulky, it can be easily damaged by careless road crews. If one is used, it tends to be hired locally for each concert. A local piano tuner will also be brought in, as pianos need to be tuned after they have been moved around.

The other problem facing those using acoustic pianos in live rock is that of amplifying the instrument with any degree of precision. Its enormous frequency range, coupled with its construction, means that straight close-miking in the PA system can often result in a rather lack-lustre 'small' sound. A few specialist pickups have emerged for live piano amplification, perhaps the most common being the Helpinstill, an American pickup which is attached to the soundboard of the piano, and the C-Ducer, a British strip-pickup, both of which give reasonable reproductions of the piano's wide dynamic range once put through a good PA system.

In the studio, the grand piano is a more common instrument. Its exposed construction, once the lid is removed, makes it easier to mike-up in the studio than the enclosed upright piano. But the piano is still regarded by most recording engineers as the most difficult individual instrument to record accurately – another

consequence of its range, which extends from below 30Hz for the lowest notes to over 400Hz for the highest.

The piano is most commonly used as a supporting accompaniment to the singer-songwriter performer, and is thus most likely to be a reasonably prominent element in the instrumental picture. There is still no convincing electronic replacement for its complex acoustic sound.

The two main types of synthetic piano are the electric piano and the electronic piano, and the difference between them lies in the way in which they produce their sounds. An *electric* piano uses a mechanical method for making the sound, often working in a similar fashion to the hammer/string action of an acoustic piano. This mechanically produced sound is then turned into an electrical signal by a pickup, the signal being fed to an internal or external amplifier and speaker set-up. An *electronic* piano, a rather more recent innovation, produces its sound by totally electronic means.

Electric pianos are the most commonly found types, and the two most popular are the Fender Rhodes piano, seen widely both on stage and in the studio, and the Yamaha electric grand. As the Yamaha's name implies, it makes more of an attempt to adapt the acoustic piano to amplified rock use.

The Fender Rhodes was invented by Harold Rhodes, who, during military service in the Second World War, was asked to devise a piano-like instrument on which hospital patients could learn to play while sitting up in bed — a therapy designed to improve the morale of injured soldiers. Rhodes originally made his bed-piano out of whatever he could get his hands on, including army surplus equipment and even otherwise unusable aircraft parts, but after the war he developed and modified it. The result was the Rhodes electric piano, eventually marketed by Fender; it began to achieve marked success in jazz and rock groups of the Sixties.

It includes a pickup system which feeds the signal from depressed keys to the output. On certain models this is fed to an internal amplification system which provides a characteristic shifting vibrato sound. This type of Rhodes piano is called the Suitcase model, while the Stage model requires an external backline amplifier. There are five models in the Rhodes range at present, the numbers in the model names indicating the number of keys in the keyboard: the Stage 54, the Stage 73, the Suitcase 73, the Stage 88, and the Suitcase 88.

The Yamaha electric grand is intended to provide a reasonably portable instrument capable of producing an amplified acoustic piano sound, and in this it is largely successful. Musicians' criticisms tend to centre on the sound quality of the lower notes: to aid portability Yamaha have adapted the string lengths of these notes, with a resulting lack of fidelity at the bottom end of the sound spectrum. Nevertheless the electric grand is a popular stage instrument, ideal for the touring band that requires a piano sound without the acoustic piano's physical and amplification problems. The Yamaha model splits in two to increase its portability, the section holding the action coming apart from the section containing the strings. The pickups are placed where the soundboard would be on a standard acoustic piano, resulting in a pleasing sound when amplified. Volume and tone controls are located just above the keyboard.

The other electric piano seen in rock bands is the Wurlitzer EP200, which also grew in popularity in the Sixties. It produces its mechanical sound differently from the Rhodes, the keys vibrating metal reeds when pressed. As with the Rhodes, some Wurlitzer models have internal amplification systems, others require a backline amp set-up.

Another popular instrument which is neither an electric nor an electronic piano but is most closely related to this kind of keyboard is the Hohner Clavinet. It produces a funky, percussive sound that mixes well with guitar and boosts the effectiveness of strongly rhythmic music. Strings under each key vibrate against metal plates to produce the sound, picked up by individual bar magnets below the strings. This instrument needs external amplification – like an electric guitar it does not need mains power, the pickups themselves producing sufficient power to drive the amplifier.

Several makers have produced electronic pianos, including Yamaha, Korg and Roland. These instruments rarely come close to simulating the sound of an acoustic piano, despite the advertising claims of the manufacturers. Electronic pianos, which produce their sounds totally electronically by a series of oscillators, do have a slightly clinical quality of their own. Some players, unencumbered by thoughts of imitating pianos, have simply used them as another keyboard-sourced musical tone colour.

Organs

The organ has diminished in popularity among the majority of rock keyboard players – another victim of the preponderance of keyboard-based synthesizers, many of which can simulate an organ sound quite convincingly. But the electric organ has played a part in the sound of rock at various times and still appears up in some keyboard setups. One name looms from the Sixties and early Seventies: Hammond.

Laurens Hammond invented the Hammond organ in the United States as far back as the Thirties, and developed the electric instrument from another of his many inventions, the synchronous electric motor. This was based on the principle that alternating current – that is, mains electricity – works at a fixed, constant frequency. So running an electric motor directly linked to this frequency ensures a perfectly constant number of revolutions per minute. Hammond combined this fixed-speed motor with a keyboard instrument, using the motor to drive small 'tone wheels' within the organ. These produced different pitches by presenting a slightly varying cogged pattern to each of the magnetic pickups in the mechanism. The pitches produced in this way were relatively pure in tone, and the instrument enabled the player to add various harmonics, or other tone

colours, to this pure fundamental tone generated by the tone wheels. These extra harmonics were added by a series of handles above the keyboard called 'draw bars', operated by the organist.

The Hammond Tone Wheel organ, as it was first called, was originally produced in 1935 and intended as a replacement for pipe organs, thus finding an early home in many churches throughout the United States. But the organ gradually came to infiltrate other musical areas as musicians discovered its powerful and rich sound, helped by a special speaker system called the Leslie. This consisted of a cabinet within which a loudspeaker was made to rotate at varying speeds, operated and regulated by the player and producing very effective tremolo sounds from the Hammond organ. Some guitarists even linked their electric instruments to the Leslie to benefit from its extraordinary swirling sounds.

The Hammond model most widely used in rock has been the American model B3 (in Europe the C3), now no longer made, although the company is still in operation, despite its founder's death in 1973. A later development was the split Hammond, a model which could be broken down into two sections for portability – otherwise, a Hammond organ was enough to give rock roadies severe back-strain, at the very least.

Other electric organs used in the Sixties have also largely died out, although there are occasional revivals of one of the most popular, the thin-sounding Vox Continental. Some electronic organs simulate the sound of the Hammond/Leslie combination and, as mentioned earlier, it is possible to get a reasonable approximation from some keyboard-based synthesizers.

Replay Keyboards

A strange instrument was the Mellotron, still produced today under the name Novatron. It is in effect a tape playback system operated by a keyboard, and has some parallels with the current computer systems (see under Synthesizers) which can 'sample' a natural sound, pitched and played back by way of a keyboard. The instrument, with its various names, has always been produced by an English company in the Midlands. The first Mellotron – whose name was derived from MELOdic elecTRONics – was made in the mid-Sixties. In the original system, each note of the keyboard activated pieces of tape with various passages of real instruments recorded on to them, at the correct pitch for the associated keyboard note pressed. Each note thus played a pitched sound of the chosen pre-recorded instrument – flutes, violins, a choir or whatever.

The renamed Novatron company still makes a single-manual model (with one keyboard, rather than the original instrument's two) called the 400, and will transfer owners' master tapes on to the special $\frac{3}{8}$ in wide tape, enabling the instrument to play back any sound, musical or otherwise. This facility attracted the BBC to buy an early model for sound effects use, and the instrument has also enjoyed wide rock music applications. Computer systems' natural sound sampling has begun to make some aspects of the Novatron sound a little old-fashioned. But the instrument, by virtue of its mechanical production of sounds, creates a musical atmosphere all its own that computer technology alone cannot replace.

Drums & Percussion

Drums are perhaps the simplest and the oldest instruments to survive in the rock band in a form related to their ancient ancestors'. Indeed, the basic make-up of the drum has changed little: there is a head, attached either to the top or to both top and bottom of the drum, and a cylindrical tube contains the vibrations and resonances of the drum. The actual note, or pitch, produced by the drum depends on a number of factors, including its overall size and the thickness and tension of the drum head or heads.

In Eighties rock the acoustic drum kit is often supplemented in the studio and on stage by electronic percussion devices, some of which aim directly to replace the conventional kit by providing accurate electronic simulation of the acoustic sounds. These can be presented in such a way that the operator need not necessarily be a drummer.

Basic Kit

There is really no such thing as the average drum kit – each drummer has his or her own preferred drum set-up and combination of drums, cymbals, stands, hardware and percussion, often dramatically changing the line-up from studio to stage work. But there are certain arrangements that have become relatively standard, at least in the eyes of the manufacturers who supply kits in specific formulations.

The most basic acoustic drum kit has altered very little since the earliest rock bashers of the late Fifties, and consists of a 22 in diameter bass drum; a small tom tom mounted on this bass drum (probably of 13 in diameter and 9 in depth, written as 13x9); a floor-mounted tom tom (probably 16x16); and a snare drum on a separate stand to the drummer's left (probably 14x5½). There would also be a couple of cymbals on separate stands, and a hi-hat (a pair of foot-pedal-operated cymbals) on another stand to the drummer's left. All these directions, are based on the assumption that our drummer is right-handed.

Adornments to this most basic of kits have appeared everywhere in rock. In the late Sixties there was a brief flirtation with the use of two bass drums, providing a hammering, insistent rhythm at the basis of the percussive pulse. More recently drummers have added multiple tom toms to their kits, where the drums will be set out around the drummer with large toms at one end ranging down to tiny toms at the other – this enables the drummer to execute spectacular rolls around the kit. Some drummers also use a type of tom called the Rototom which can be tuned and detuned, even while playing, by rotating the drum head; the whole thing looks like a shell-less head.

The bass drum, the largest drum in the standard kit, is played on its side and rests on metal spurs at the front to prevent it from creeping forward from the force of being hit by the bass drum footpedal. Drummers differ on how they prefer to arrange the heads on the bass drum, depending largely on whether they like a 'dead' or 'live' bass drum sound. A dead sound is obtained by leaving the front head off and, often in the studio, putting towels or other material inside the drum shell.

The bass drum is played by the action of the footpedal, which rocks a beater back and forth on to the playing head facing the drummer. One of the best regarded of these pedals is the American Ludwig 'Speed King' model, but each player has a personal favourite which gives a particular feel and sensitivity. Tom toms very often come without a bottom head.

Perhaps the most important invention that sets modern rock drums apart from the instruments produced before the Fifties is the plastic drum head, which is generally credited to Remo Belli, now head of the Remo drum company. The advantage of the plastic head is that it is unaffected by temperature changes and humidity levels. It is also stronger, more durable, has greater reliability and is easier to tune than animal skins – all important factors for the touring and recording rock drummer.

The snare drum produces its characteristic crack by virtue of the wire snare which runs along the bottom head of the drum. This can be turned on or off by a lever on the side of the drum which alternately brings the snare into and out of contact with the lower head. When it is in contact, and the batter head (as the top head is called) is struck, the snare vibrates in sympathy.

As well as the standard 5½ in snare drum, some snares are made deeper, with a consequently bassier sound. These deeper models can give drummers a greater range of sounds from the snare, and some players have been known to use two snares of different depth in their kit for songs requiring contrasting effects. A playing technique commonly employed on the snare drum is the 'rim shot': the raised rim around the top of the drum is hit with the

RIGHT *Cobham with his acoustic drum kit. One of the finest jazz-rock drummers,* *Cobham has played with many rock greats; his 'drum clinics' are famous among fellow musicians.*

ABOVE *King Crimson's drummer Bill Bruford uses a mixture of traditional acoustic hardware and modern electronic percussion.*

BELOW, RIGHT *John Keeble of Spandau Ballet also has a mixture: Simmons electronic drums, plus acoustic snare and cymbals.*

drumstick at the same time as the batter head, producing a distinctive 'thwack' sound.

Cymbals come in various types and sizes and thus with varying sounds. While a few drummers seem almost to specialize in obtaining percussive effects from a vast array of metal plates, others have abandoned cymbals to concentrate wholly on drums. There are two fundamental types of cymbal: the *crash* type, used for sudden accents, usually of thin or medium thickness and measuring between 16 in and 24 in in diameter; and the *ride* type, for continuous, supportive rhythm-keeping, usually measuring between 18 in and 24 in in diameter. There are many other types, often using exotic or more straightforward onomatopoeic names, and varieties exist offering versatile effects between those of ride and crash cymbals. Cymbals are usually supported on individual stands, some with an angled section or boom (as on microphone stands) to enable the cymbal to be placed more conveniently for the drummer.

The hi-hat is a development of an American device, originally called the low-boy or lo-hat. This pair of cymbals was eventually moved up above (or level with) drum height so it could be played with sticks, combining this sharp attack with the sounds of the cymbals opening and closing, operated by a footpedal.

Percussion

Percussion is a very general term in rock: properly it refers to any instrument struck or beaten or scraped to obtain a rhythmic sound, and therefore includes the drums and cymbals of the standard kit. It tends, however, to be used for acoustic instruments other than the kit which are struck, beaten and so on, and can range from Latin American percussion instruments through to bits of old metal or beer bottles.

The Latin percussion instruments appear and reappear in rock largely according to musical fashions or the geographical origin of the percussionist. Congas and bongos are probably the instruments most seen on the rock stage that come into this category, and these, combined with the occasional cowbell attached to the bass drum or held in the hand and struck with a

drumstick, are used more as a gimmick than as a standard rock sound. We should also include in percussion those instruments known as 'tuned' percussion – the marimba, xylophone, and vibraphone – played by both pianists and drummers, though rarely in rock.

All sorts of instruments are hit in the name of percussion. The *guiro* is a long cylindrical container with grooves around it which are scraped with a stick. The *tambourine* is a thin, single-headed, drum-like instrument with metal shakers set around the shell and is usually played by being held in one hand and struck with the other. The *cabasa*, a stainless steel cylinder around which beads are strung, is shaken in the hand. *Boo-bams* are long tuned drums, which have been simulated by recent modern imitations called Octobans.

Drummers also sometimes use large percussion instruments like the *gong*, hung on a stand behind the drummer's stool and hit with a mallet. *Timbales* are sometimes added to the tom tom complement of a kit to lend a harsher, slightly hollow-sounding tone to the range offered by standard drums, and a player may have a pair of timbales set up elsewhere on stage to be featured on a particular song.

Electronic Percussion

Electronically produced drum and percussion sounds have become a strong force in the rock music of the Eighties. In a sense the rise of the instruments producing these sounds has been something of a surprise, when one considers most musicians' previously low opinion of electronic percussion. In the past such devices were occasionally useful for home recording or demo work, but rarely employed as fully-fledged constituents of a group's live or recorded sound.

The first drum synthesizers, appearing in the late Seventies, were set up almost exclusively to produce a simple sweeping sound, which became associated with disco records – despite the potential of many of the drum synth units to produce quite varied sounds.

Now, however, two main types of electronic percussion have surfaced, and both are extensively used by groups in many of rock's varied factions. Partly we have the benefits of electronic technology to thank for the acceptance of these gadgets, and, some would argue, we must look to drummers' own introverted musical attitudes, and record producers' needs for a universally acceptable drum sound, to explain the current predominance of electronic percussion, especially on record.

The two types of electronic percussion now in use can be termed 'player-activated' and 'player-programmable'. While in some instances the two categories become rather blurred, most commercially produced units fall into one or the other of these two types.

Player-activated devices include items like the Simmons SDS-V electronic drum kit, made in Britain, where it was invented by Dave Simmons, and first sold in 1980. It is at first sight a rather unconventional-looking drum kit, but in layout and general playing technique is at least recognisable as a drum kit. The standard 'drums' in the Simmons kit are rather thin hexagonal boxes with a black or white playing surface on top. They are just over a foot in diameter, although the unit used as a bass drum is a few inches larger. These 'drums' – it would probably be more accurate to call them pads – have a 'trigger', or pickup, mounted inside and screwed to the playing head so as to vibrate when hit. This trigger sends an electronic signal to a separate 'brain', or control box, which offers complete control over the eventual sound of each pad, when amplified through an amplifier or PA system or fed to a recording mixer.

Some players set the Simmons kit up like a drum kit, and there are now pads which simulate cymbal and hi-hat sounds. This 'kit' set-up is how it is usually used on stage. In the studio, players often employ what is referred to as 'the suitcase', a case containing a number of plain Simmons pads which feed the brain in the same way as the kit-type pads, but without the visual impression of an acoustic kit.

The brain features a factory-preset sound for each pad, simulating the sounds of a conventional drum kit. Many players stick to these sounds. But the brain also has the facility to produce three more sounds for each pad of the operator's own making, offering control over various aspects of the drum sound to produce these individual sounds which can be stored and recalled at will.

Player-programmables, the other type of electronic percussion, include gadgets like the Linn drum computer, Roland's drum machines, and various other programmable units. These are simply electronic devices, and do not in themselves have any of the physical characteristics of drums or drum kits (although it is possible with some to use conventional acoustic drums to trigger the devices, an example of the blurring of definitions mentioned earlier). A player-programmable drum machine allows the user to set up layers of drum-like electronically-produced sounds and make

convincing simulations of conventional drum kit and percussion patterns. With some models, however, it is possible to achieve unusual sounds, an attraction to certain rock players.

Different machines employ varying methods to achieve these simulations and patterns and to 'write' the percussion compositions into the machine. Some of the Roland drum machines, for example, feature a scan of LED lights which tell the operator where certain beats of a particular drum sound occur within the pattern being written, presenting a visual equivalent of the resulting drum sound. This can be useful for operators who are not drummers. Other machines, like the Linndrum, a very successful Californian device found in many top studios, reproduce sounds by using real drums, digitally recorded and stored in memory chips within the machine.

Simpler drum machines may merely provide preset rhythms – particular types of beat that have been worked out and stored in the machine by the maker, and are played back simply by pressing a button. These are more usually associated with cabaret and home-organ use than with creative rock music.

It seems unlikely that the drummer at the live rock show, seated behind a barrage of drums and percussion devices, will be ousted by the electronic and computer-controlled rhythm units which have invaded rock recently. In the studio, where sound has precedence over visual effect, this gadgetry will take a firmer hold. Certainly the rock drummer will continue to hit things for a long time – what is changing is the way in which the energy of that impact is being treated.

The Business

In the Studio

The average musician is becoming more and more aware of studio recording techniques. Relatively inexpensive systems have brought 4-track and 8-track recording into the reach of the average home musician or semi-pro band. But it is important to remember that 'semi-professional', these days, applies more to the user than to the equipment. Modern home recording gear is at least as sophisticated (often more so) and offers at least as high a quality as the equipment in top-flight studios during the late Sixties – and is considerably cheaper.

The one thing that does not come in the box with a new home multitrack, however, is the expertise that characterises today's commercial recording studios. Like any skill, including musicianship, this has to be developed with time and effort. Music and recording require two factors in balance: something to communicate to others, and the expertise and techniques required to make that communication effective.

These home recording systems are fine for demos, or for recording gigs for reference and practice. But sooner or later a musician needs something more: generally a record deal. This may place the band in a 'real' studio for the first time, and the sight may be somewhat daunting. To begin with, there will be at least two, possibly three,

ABOVE *A typical recording console at a modern studio. Note the sound-processing equipment beside* the console. RIGHT *A Neve 8108 console in EMI's famous Abbey Road studios in London.*

people involved in the recording process. One will be the producer, whose job it will be to help the band get its ideas on to tape in a suitably commercial way. Most producers are not technical people, and many do not have operational knowledge of the studio and its equipment – that is the engineer's job – but a good producer will know what he wants to hear, and will be able to relate a band's musical needs, as well as his own, to the engineer in a way he can understand. In control of the equipment will be the engineer, who, unlike the producer, will probably not have heard the demos. Part of his job is technical – getting a good representation of the

music on to tape – but he is equally experienced in the art of getting along with musicians, and understands the problems of a band in the studio for the first time. In some larger studios he will have an assistant, an apprentice engineer who will be responsible for setting up microphones, finding the right place on the tape, setting up effects and making the tea. As operating the tape-recorders is one of his primary tasks, he is often referred to as a tape operator or tape-op.

So much for the personnel. The first thing that a studio newcomer will notice on entering the control room, however, is the mass of sophisticated, high-technology hardware. In the centre of the room, dominating the surroundings, is the mixing console. This is positioned centrally, often facing the double-glazed window looking into the studio itself, affording a good view of the musicians within. Most importantly, it faces the monitor speakers, which are set up to give the best possible stereo image, or 'sound picture', to the engineer and producer.

Although the console may look daunting, it is in fact quite simple, once you begin to understand what it does. There is a vast array of knobs, buttons and other controls, but they are arranged in *channels* – generally at least a couple of dozen, and often many more – which are all virtually identical. This is because modern multitrack recording involves recording individual instruments on separate tracks of a special tape recorder, 24-track systems being the most common, using 2 in wide recording tape. Each console channel is designed to give complete flexibility of control over the sound of the instrument which is passing through it. Let's follow the signal path through a typical console channel during a recording session to see the kind of possibilities offered by such a system.

First of all, the signal from the studio – generally a microphone placed in front of, say, a guitar amp, although the sound may come from an electronic instrument like a synthesizer, plugged into a direct-injection (DI) box – comes in at the top of the channel. Here we find a gain control, which enables the volume to be set so that the signal is not so loud that it causes distortion, nor so low that objectionable noise (hiss) results. The gain level set, the signal passes to an equalizer – basically a more complex form of tone control – which enables the engineer to modify the sound if required. High, medium and low frequencies (treble, mid and bass) may be boosted or reduced; generally at least four specific frequencies may be selected out of a wide range, as against the two or three frequency controls usually found on a hi-fi system. Just after the equalizer (and sometimes just before as well) is often what is known as an 'insert point', where lines run to a jackfield or patchbay – a set of connectors – which enables extra signal processing ('outboard') gear to be patched into the signal path for extra signal modification or special effects. Typically, such an outboard device might be a compressor or

limiter, which enables a sound's level to be controlled to even out large variations in volume that might otherwise cause distortion. The signal then passes to an area of the channel from which subsidiary signals may be generated, for example to send the sound back to the musician's headphones – this is known as a cue mix, or fold back – or to add echo. After this comes the final volume control, which determines the actual level sent to the tape machine. This volume control is a high-quality linear fader, placed directly in front of the engineer, so that he can adjust the level exactly for the best result, reading the signal on a meter corresponding to the appropriate tape-machine channel. From the fader, the signal is routed by way of a series of buttons or switches (typically a row of 24 pushbuttons) to the appropriate tape-machine channel, generally using another fader, called a group fader. This is because it is often necessary to place the output of more than one channel on to a single track of the tape: the correct balance is obtained with the main faders, and the overall level going to the tape machine can be adjusted with the group fader without upsetting the balance.

Most of the console is a set of exact copies of the channel described above. In addition, there will be a 'monitor panel', often placed near the group faders, which enables the engineer to hear the signals as they go to the tape machine. Here, a rough balance can be set up which will enable everyone to hear what is going on to tape, and also, during playbacks, what has been recorded. On some consoles the monitor faders are incorporated in the main channels. A master module on the console enables the engineer to control the loudspeaker volume, talk to the musicians in the studio through their headphones or a 'talkback' loudspeaker, record the track title and take number on tape ('slate'), and line up the tape machine with an inbuilt oscillator.

Pair of Tannoy Super Red monitor speakers; the one on the left has its cover removed to show the loudspeaker itself. The monitor allows the engineer to hear the signals as they are being recorded.

Recording & Overdubbing

The recording of a title in the studio takes place in three stages: recording, overdubbing and mixing.

The first stage involves getting the band in the studio to play what is known as the 'basic track'. This will generally involve, for example, recording bass, drums, rhythm guitar or keyboard, and perhaps a rough vocal track for guidance (often therefore called a 'guide vocal'). The purpose is to produce a really solid and accurate rhythm track, and it is important that all the musicians play in the studio together so that they can work together, as the music must not only be played accurately, but 'feel' right as well.

Very seldom are solos, backing vocals and the like recorded at this stage. The basic track may take several attempts before everyone agrees it is right, and this is where good rehearsals prior to the recording are most important. If the musicians are well-rehearsed they will know the track very well, and will be able to get a master basic track in a few takes. Without that rehearsal, the band will virtually be learning the track in the studio – a very expensive rehearsal room! – and will be too tired, by the time they know it, to play it with any real 'feel'. A favourite story in the industry is that the Animals' hit 'House of the Rising Sun' was recorded for a little over £1.50. As it happens, the story is true, but it was only possible because they were thoroughly rehearsed before they ever stood in front of their microphones.

For the basic track, each instrument will be assigned its own track of the tape. Very often drums are recorded on a number of tracks, the bass drum especially being assigned its own tape track to give the engineer plenty of flexibility in the mixing stage later on. Some engineers take this track splitting to illogical extremes, allocating as many as a dozen tape tracks to the drum kit, with hi-hat, bass drum, snare, each tom tom and each cymbal separately miked, and a couple of overhead microphones to catch the ambience.

At the end of the basic recording stage, somewhere between a third and a half of the available tape tracks will have been used, leaving the others for the next stage of the process: the adding of other instruments, solos, lead and backing vocals, and perhaps a string or brass section (or both). It is usual to record first all the basic tracks for all the numbers of an album, but sometimes some extra instruments will be added after each basic track has been recorded.

Before going on to the next stage of the recording process – 'overdubbing', or adding the extra elements that make up the whole performance – it is important to note the difference between a recording session and a live gig. They are quite different art-forms, and many bands new to the studio do not realise this. On a live gig, the band has to play everything at once: there is no way of adding extra sounds except with a tape backing track (which is often done by a number of top bands whose music is too complex to be played all at once). Bands used to gigging without the benefit of backing tracks will obviously develop their songs for the live environment, performing a musical arrangement which gives the fullest sound without running out of musicians. In the studio it is a different matter: there are plenty of tape tracks, and multitracked harmony guitars, multiple backing vocals and the like are all possible. Some bands

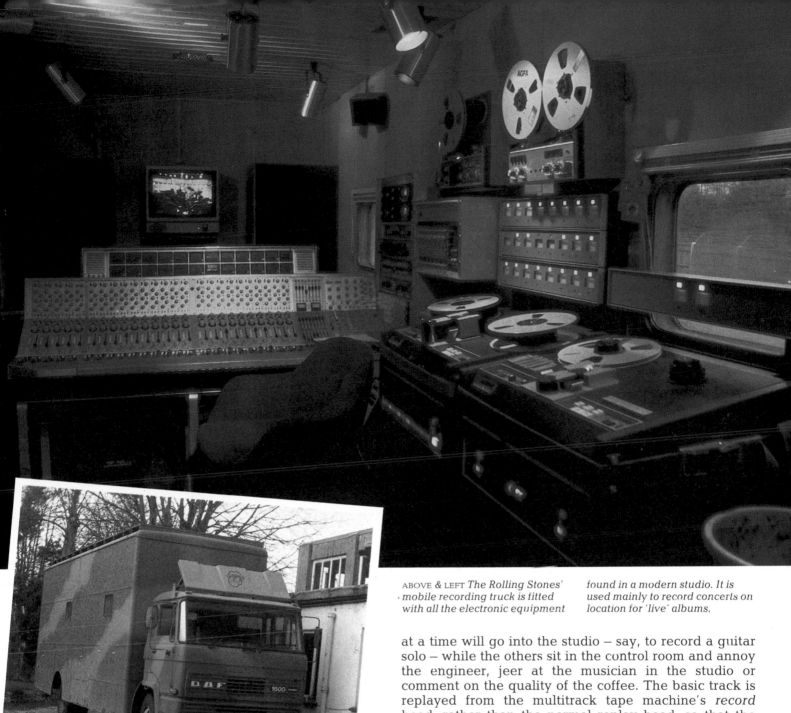

ABOVE & LEFT *The Rolling Stones'* *mobile recording truck is fitted* *with all the electronic equipment* *found in a modern studio. It is* *used mainly to record concerts on* *location for 'live' albums.*

refuse to use the possibilities of the studio because they are worried that they 'won't be able to do it live' – but once they acknowledge that live and studio music are different forms of expression, they avoid that problem. In the studio, it is true to say that if the music would benefit from extra instruments, they should be added. (That does *not* mean adding extra sounds for the sake of it!) The problem of rearranging the music for live performance should be tackled later, using taped backing tracks if necessary.

During the overdubbing stage, the basic track is brought up on the monitor panel and fed to the musicians in their headphones. Generally one musician

at a time will go into the studio – say, to record a guitar solo – while the others sit in the control room and annoy the engineer, jeer at the musician in the studio or comment on the quality of the coffee. The basic track is replayed from the multitrack tape machine's *record* head, rather than the normal replay head, so that the overdubs will be synchronised with the basic track which is already on tape: this is called 'sync replay' and is an important function of studio tape-recorders that is not often found on domestic machines.

Of course, it is often difficult to play a complicated solo in one go. On stage, if you play a duff note, you cannot go back and re-do it, but in the studio this is quite possible. By playing the track back and entering the record mode at the place required ('dropping in'), a wrong note can be re-recorded without affecting good bits before that point. It is difficult to drop *out* accurately, however, so duff notes must either be corrected when they occur, or a new take must be made, perhaps on another track. In the latter case, it is possible to pick the good parts from a couple of attempts at a solo, and the engineer can then mix between them, by switching or cross-fading one into the other at specific points, recording the result on a third track to give a complete solo. This is called 'track bouncing'. However, in the case of a solo, it is preferable to record a complete attempt, rather than construct a solo out of lots of little bits of tracks, as a genuinely complete performance will hang together better and sound more musical. However accurately the 'bouncing down' is done, there is a distinctive feel to each attempt that does

ABOVE *A disc-cutting suite at the CBS studios, London, one of the most advanced in Europe. The console next to the tape machine* *allows each track to be equalised and compressed during the cut.* BELOW *An engineer examines the master lacquer with a microscope.*

not always fully survive track-swapping in midstream.

Studio atmosphere is an important aspect of the recording process, and nowhere is this more true than in the overdubbing stage. Most studios are equipped with sympathetic lighting which may be dimmed subtly to lend a more creative atmosphere. The importance of studio atmosphere should not be underrated.

Indeed, vocals are usually left until last, so that the vocalist can get a complete understanding of the track, and can work on the vocal part so as to avoid clashing with obstinately screaming guitar lines which, perhaps, were added by the lead guitarist when drunk at three o'clock the previous morning.

All the overdubs having been completed to the satisfaction of the producer (and, with any luck, the band as well), the next stage is to mix all those 24 or so tracks down to stereo. There is usually a thankful pause at this point, and a 'rough mix' is done by the engineer to enable the producer and the band to go away with cassettes to think about what they have committed to tape. (This also gives the vocalist the chance to notice that he didn't sing quite what was on the lyric sheet, so it will need to be done again.) The rough mix is generally what is known as a 'faders-up job' – the engineer just pushes up the faders to more or less the same level and records what comes out. All that is needed is a guide so that everyone can hear all the parts of the recording and make judgements about what should be featured, held back, or obliterated with echo on the final mix. Rough mixes are thus generally not good things to play to the record company; they are not *that* far from what the final mix will be (they do have all the instruments on them), but the balance is often rather curiously bad and might give the wrong impression. Engineers are very sensitive about this. Of course, sometimes the opposite happens and everyone spends many long hours trying to make the master as lively as the rough mix (which was unfortunately recorded on a cassette and thus can't be used as a master for cutting). This is a variant of the 'demo problem', in which everyone wonders why the final master is nowhere near as good as the demo.

ABOVE *Digital processes now rule in the recording studio. This tape recorder is the prototype* of *a new eight-track digital model produced by Studer. Other models provide up to 24 tracks.*

Mixing

And so to mix. The mix (otherwise known as the mixdown or remix) requires the tape-machine tracks to be brought back through the console channels as before, allowing further equalisation and sound-bending to be performed, the levels being balanced with the faders and the results sent to a stereo tape recorder, generally using ¼ in wide tape running at 15 inches per second. Each tape track can be positioned in the stereo sound-stage with a knob known as a 'pan-pot', which can also be used for dynamic effects. Echo and reverberation can also be added at this point, and often need to be, since modern studios are quite 'dead' acoustically, in order to avoid one instrument's mike picking up the sound from another instrument which happens to be playing at the same time in the studio ('leakage'). Reverberation is simulated by various devices, which may consist of steel plates with transducers on them, spring lines, or digital reverberation simulators. Very seldom is the classic 'echo chamber' – a room not unlike a bathroom in acoustic character – used in modern recording because most studios do not have the space for one. Other effects used on the mix include repeat echo – where a sound is delayed for a short time and then heard just after the original, as on many Elvis Presley records – and its variant, automatic double tracking (ADT), where the original and the delayed sound are so close together in time that they sound like two identical instruments playing in unison, but can be split in the stereo (say hard left and hard right) to give a fuller sound. This is an easier process to perform than true double tracking, which requires the musician to repeat a performance virtually exactly during the recording process. Then there is the familiar 'swooshing' sound of phasing or flanging, as used on the Small Faces' 'Itchycoo Park' and many other recordings. All these effects are used (or overused) in efforts to make the sound more exciting.

Modern recording is very complex, and the mix is especially so. Having at least 24 tracks (and sometimes twice as many) coming off tape, as well as numerous effects returned to the console faders, the engineer (and virtually everyone else in the control room, in earlier days) has to move a number of faders gently and subtly during the course of a mix, to feature instruments where needed, and to hold back lines which are supposed to be behind lead lines. To help in this task, so-called 'console automation' has been developed. In its basic form, this consists of a computer system which looks at the faders all the time and memorises the movements made. This allows the engineer to make each movement once only, until ultimately all of a complex set of fader movements have been memorised and the engineer can sit back and listen to see if it was really such a good idea after all. Such aids are indispensable in studios becoming ever more complex and sophisticated.

The mix may still take several takes to complete, however, and often there will be some parts of one take which are 'right', and other parts of other takes which are 'right', especially on a long and complex number. These parts can be pieced together by the process of *editing*. The engineer locates the 'right' bits on the tape, cuts them out with a razor blade and edits them together with special adhesive splicing tape to form a whole. When the mix is decided to be right, the master is copied for safety purposes and the job is done. If the performance is destined for record release, the tape is then taken to a cutting room, where a cutting engineer transfers its contents to an aluminium 'blank' coated with lacquer, using a cutting lathe, whose heated stylus cuts the familiar concentric grooves in the surface. Cutting is a fine and difficult art and represents the culmination of the creative parts of the recording process. After that it is all downhill; the pressings are often of poor quality, sounding nothing like as good as the original. You may be annoyed when you spend a lot of money on a record that turns out to be warped, eccentric, or noisy; artists, engineers, and producers get even more upset.

All this may soon change, however. Now on the scene is the Digital Audio Disc, a small shiny silver disc carrying over an hour of music of very high technical quality. It is the domestic end of the new digital recording process which is sweeping the recording world, a process which promises a virtually direct link between the studio and the listener at home. Digital recording equipment in the studio is eliminating noise, distortion and other untoward effects which have dogged the industry for years, and the DAD promises a new, near-perfect home sound quality that will replace conventional records – which have not changed in their basic production process for almost half a century. The future looks – and sounds – good.

Some have said that all the sophistication and complexity of the recording process is an enemy to musical expression – that the recording process has become more important than the music. In some cases this may be true, but in general, modern recording offers the artist an unparalleled ease of expression and control over his music. There will always be a place for live music, for acoustic music and for simpler forms of musical expression. But as with any art-form, there must be an idea to communicate, and an effective means of communication to bring that idea to people. The modern recording process, for all its complexity and sophistication, provides that means of communication, for the benefit of all those who care to listen.

Selling the Group

The record industry has evolved in an extraordinary way over the past 30 years. Just a few of the fads that have caught the public's imagination are show tunes, romantic-ballad singers, skiffle groups, rock 'n' roll idols, British beat, psychedelia, Glam Rock, Power Pop, Punk Rock, New Wave, New Romantics . . . whatever the craze, the industry somehow carries on, blissfully ignoring recession or world crisis. Today's slick TV rock presentations reflect this buoyant, carefree outlook on life – encouraged, of course, by the record companies themselves. Promotional rock videos costing thousands of pounds to produce – mostly paid for by the record companies – have already revolutionised the market

Charts & the Media

The process of 'selling' a new group, however, is still dependent on more familiar strategies, and a key factor is the role of the charts. All major companies and independent distributors are geared to a weekly listing of top-selling singles and albums. At 9 am on a Tuesday, when details of the new singles charts are released to the companies by Prestel, it's always a harrowing moment; careers can rise and fall in one fell swoop.

In 1952, when the *New Musical Express* published the first British chart of best-selling singles – a Top 12 – no one dreamed that it would become a crucial marketing tool. In those days there were four music weeklies – the long established *Melody Maker*, *NME*, *Record Mirror* and the now defunct *Disc*. Each went on to compile and publish a list of best-selling records. When the BBC launched *Top of the Pops* in 1964, they worked on an average of all four charts. It wasn't until 1969 that the BPI (British Phonographic Industry) appointed an official body to compile a weekly list of best-sellers. The BMRB (British Market Research Bureau) drew up a list of approximately 750 stores to participate in the compilation. After endless stories of chart 'hyping' the system was eventually changed. In January 1983, Gallup was given responsibility for conducting the research operation, which took on an entirely new approach. Press-button technology had taken over from pen and paper. Each of 250 record outlets had a specially designed 'data-capture' unit installed, into which would be fed the details of all records purchased at that outlet. Each unit is connected to Gallup's own master computer by conventional telephone link. Every Saturday night, at two centres – one in London, the other in Oxfordshire – another specialist unit automatically 'telephones' the outlet units to draw off the recorded data. London works from the top of the dealer list, Oxfordshire from the bottom, thus providing a fail-safe system. The data are then processed overnight. With the old system, only two charts were compiled, of singles and albums. The Gallup method allows for six charts, covering 7 in and 12 in

ABOVE Music Week's *Top 75 Singles and Airplay pages; the latter is a guide to singles played on local or national radio during the week.*

RIGHT, ABOVE *Videos are central to record promotion; this still is from Duran Duran's video for 'Rio'.* RIGHT, BELOW Top of the Pops *is devoted exclusively to the Top 40.*

singles, a combined singles chart, LPs, prerecorded cassettes, and a combined LP/tape chart.

The charts first appear in print in *Music Week*, which is the leading trade magazine. These are the charts used by the BBC, especially for *Top of the Pops*, and consequently they are recognised by the industry as a whole. The advent of BBC Radio 1 and the emergence of local radio stations have given great importance to airplay patterns especially in more recent years. *MW* also publishes an Airplay Action report, divided into several sections. Of prime importance are two charts logging the number of weekly plays a record receives on the BBC's national outlets, Radios 1 and 2. A third chart logs the 75 most played records on local radio. This chart is broken up into ten areas, listing each station separately, and will indicate a Hit Pick/Record of The Week, and whether plays originate from the main 'A' list of prime-time shows or the secondary 'B' list. A final chart covers 'Breakers',

the most popular new records appearing in the Report for the first time.

Returning to the singles and albums charts, the only information that remains classified is the actual weekly sales figure for each record. This confidential information is, however, supplied separately to the record companies in the BARS (British Analysis of Record Sales) Report. It will often reveal some interesting facts; for instance, one of 1982's biggest hits, 'Pass the Dutchie' by Musical Youth, was selling at its peak more records than all of the singles in the rest of the chart put together!

As soon as the new charts are released, each record company scrutinizes the fluctuations of its product at a weekly marketing meeting. A list of priorities is drawn up, depending solely on the new chart positions and the previous day's dealer demand. If a single crashes into the charts at, say, No 30, the act is virtually guaranteed an appearance on *Top of the Pops*. The record company will then risk pressing several thousand more copies of the record in anticipation of demand. A band on tour will quite often cancel a date, perhaps feigning illness, if the chance arises for a *TOTP* appearance. With a successful act, a record company will have already spent thousands of pounds making a promotional video, weeks before the record's release date. Copies of the video are then placed with TV stations and record stores around the country, providing an initial boost for the single.

Members of the band will also be expected to undertake a promotional tour of the leading radio stations throughout the country. These include Capital in the South East, BRMB in the Midlands, Piccadilly in the North West and Clyde in Scotland. The promotion department will set up interviews on various chat or rock shows in each area. This type of promotion is always encouraged; a friendly group can switch from a station's 'B' list to the 'A' list after just one visit.

The most important priority for any London-based promotion person is BBC Radio 1. If a record gets on to the station's unofficial playlist, it stands an excellent chance of hit status. The competition is cut-throat, and many companies run a bonus scheme to give staff extra incentive. The promotion person, or plugger, has to convince the producers of key rock shows to programme his or her particular priority single. This can often be a desperate job, and a plugger's best qualification is a likeable personality. *What* you know may not matter; *whom* you know is crucial. The most prestigious programme to conquer on Radio 1 is the morning breakfast show, which has the highest audience rating of any radio show in Britain.

The general public, of course, assumes that the DJ of a high-rating show chooses the records that are played. This is not so; the DJ may well bask in the public limelight, but it is the producer who controls the programming format. If a record fails to make the Radio 1 playlist a plugger will try again the following week, and if necessary, the week after. If met with total rejection, a record company will usually regard the single as 'lost'. When this occurs, the group's manager will often consider hiring independent promotion people.

The TV department's main concern is *Top of the Pops*, televised from the BBC Studios at White City. But on the night, the studio bar is the focus of music business activity. Managers, their bands, publishers, agents, rival record company executives, all rub shoulders in what is affectionately considered one of the last bastions of British rock music tradition. The job of a TV plugger is, again, to sell the band to the producer. *TOTP* only accepts bands with singles climbing the Top 40, and as such is exceptional. *The Old Grey Whistle Test* and others are wide open to the selling principle.

The record company's press office, too, will swing into action when a new band is launched. Its job is to obtain maximum publicity in the most advantageous publications for each act on the roster.

Creating an Image

When assigned a new band, the press officer's first task is to hold a meeting with the group and its management to discuss 'image': lifestyles, hairstyles and the type of clothes the group prefers. Eccentricities are always encouraged; for example, Boy George of Culture Club became a household personality almost overnight because of his bizarre feminine appearance, which was

accentuated at the suggestion of his PR adviser. It is also quite common for a record company to finance a shopping spree for a new group, so that they appear in the most up-to-date fashions dictated by the clutch of shops around Chelsea's World's End. Many acts, of course, develop their own fashion ideas: Adam Ant's pirate look certainly helped his publicity on its early stage, while the all-girl group Toto Coelo came to prominence by wearing dustbin liners converted into mini dresses. But for image-consciousness few have matched David Bowie, whose enormously popular self-styled creation of the early Seventies, Ziggy Stardust, reached a pinnacle of showbiz flamboyance.

When the right image has been chosen, the group will be asked to attend a publicity photo session. There are several dozen established photographers who specialize in rock personalities. A PR will often try to match the 'personality' of the photographer with that of the group in order to get the best possible rapport. Once the session is completed, the group will be interrogated by a press office staff writer, who extracts enough factual information to prepare a biographical sheet for reference purposes.

With the biography and a set of publicity photographs in hand, the PR will commence the press launch. This entails setting up a series of interviews for the group, which ideally will be divided into the following categories: a national popular daily (*Daily Mirror*, *The Sun*, *The Star*, *Daily Express*, *Daily Mail*), a 'heavy' national (*The Times*, *Guardian*, *Observer*), all the leading rock weeklies and a selection of 'teenybop' magazines (*Jackie*, *Blue Jeans*, *My Guy*). The national popular dailies are in intense competition, so the PR can go for only one of them. Most Fleet Street journalists are too busy to think up unusual ideas, and will just ask 'What's the angle?'

The last few years have seen significant changes throughout the rock press. Gradually declining circulation figures for the established weeklies *Melody Maker* and *NME* prompted the launch of *Smash Hits*, *The Face*, *Flexi-Pop* and others. The attractive combination of good, snappy copy and quality colour shots has quickly captured the youth market. Even the long-established *Record Mirror* changed format to compete with the new look. Of the newspaper-styled weeklies only *Sounds*, with its faithful heavy metal following, has survived with any degree of success.

A popular trend among the rock weeklies is to elect a journalist to travel on the road with a band. The writer infiltrates the entourage, travelling on the band coach with road crew, friends and groupies, observing and noting the odd quirky anecdote. Entertainment after the show comes into its own on this kind of assignment; many a hilarious story had its beginnings at a midnight feast in a Leeds curry house, or a sordid Merseyside drinking club at 3 am. The hotel bar is another favourite gathering point; in fact, most groups carefully choose their hotels, making sure that drinks are available all night, if necessary. One well-known rock guitarist keeps a pocket-book listing hotels with 24-hour bar service, as well as an equally lengthy list of all-night drinking clubs. Often several bands will spontaneously gather in one club on the same night, particularly if several are touring within the same area: one evening Liverpool's Club Zoo acted as host to the Human League, Altered Images, Echo & the Bunnymen and The Teardrop Explodes. Regular London club-goers include Marc Almond of Soft Cell, Boy George of Culture Club, Siouxsie of the Banshees and Lemmy of Motorhead. New bands often

FAR LEFT *Mike Read, whose BBC Radio 1 Breakfast Show attracted the U.K.'s biggest radio audience.* ABOVE *Adam Ant as a pirate and*

RIGHT *David Bowie in the character of Ziggy Stardust: a colourfully presented stage identity can fix a star's image in the public mind.*

complain about lack of press publicity, yet many have only themselves to blame. A band can create its own press following simply by making regular appearances at the more popular clubs. It is surprising how a few name-checks in gossip columns can suddenly start a 'buzz' on a band. All it takes is vast stamina and the ability to consume an endless supply of fancy cocktails – also, of course, a financially buoyant manager!

The Hard Sell

A & R, Promotion and Press have always been considered the creative side of the industry. The degree of creativity, however, often leaves a lot to be desired, and invariably depends on the talent and enthusiasm of each individual. The other side of the business is dominated by the marketing department, which also includes advertising and merchandising. This is the department with the hard-sell ideas, conjuring up anything from an extravagant in-store merchandising push to a £100,000 TV advertising campaign. However, with the onset of the recession, record companies had to tighten their purse strings drastically. One result has been the rise of the 'direct response' method of TV advertising. This involves the collaboration of a commercial TV company

ABOVE *Rusty Egan plays electro-pop hits at the Camden Palace (London), the hugely successful dance club run with his partner Steve Strange.*

RIGHT, BELOW *Bryan Ferry at an autograph session. Meeting the fans is an integral part of concert tours by many of the major groups.*

is in the preparation that surrounds a major concert tour. Whenever a national tour is announced it is the job of the sales force to make sure that the chart-return stores in each town on the tour are well stocked with the act's latest release and back catalogue. It is common practice for a group's manager to check out the main stores, so this task is usually completed with a high degree of efficiency. Occasionally a group on tour will be called upon to sign copies of their new album — inevitably, at the largest chart-return store in each city centre. The cycle is successfully completed when the chart store in question wins the concession to sell the band's records in the foyer at the local concert hall.

One of the most lucrative spin-offs of the record industry has been the comparatively recent growth of the independent merchandising companies, who are officially licensed to use a band's name and logo for reproduction on T-shirts, tour jackets, patches, badges and so on. The idea of linking the selling of T-shirts with a rock act, and following its tours with the approval of the group's management, came about in the early Seventies with teenybopper groups like the Bay City Rollers and the Osmonds. Before that, merchandisers were looked upon as back-street pirates, selling low quality T-shirts emblazoned with designs on which the makers paid no royalty.

Today, the competition to obtain the concession on a band's merchandising is intense. Many of the companies — there are hundreds — run a national network of full-time reps, servicing record shops, chains of music retailers, video shops and gift shops, as well as the traditional outlet of the theatre foyer. The profit margin on merchandising paraphernalia can be quite substantial. The Rolling Stones' 1982 tour was reported to have been the highest-grossing merchandising tour in British rock history. Even so, much top-selling merchandising is of the lesser-known but much-followed bands whose fans enjoy their cult status and like to advertise their membership of an exclusive club. Many of these are heavy metal bands: Motorhead, AC/DC, Saxon, Gillan, the Michael Shenker Group and Iron Maiden are among the current favourites.

Groups on Tour

While merchandisers fight it out over major tour concessions, the new record-company signing is in a similar predicament. There are several ways of breaking a new band — getting it initial recognition — and touring is, of course, one of them. An endless string of club dates is all very well, but with a new album or single to promote, the record company is going to be more demanding. One strategy is to try for 'support act' on a major concert tour. If there are, say, eight dates with an average of 2,500 people at each, there is a captive audience of 20,000 before the band even walks on stage. The group's manager or record company will have already approached the dozen or so major concert promoters to see if any 'suitable' artists are touring at the appropriate time. Naturally, the group's sound must complement that of the headlining act, in order to attract people in from the bar.

A continuous problem with support acts is that they may upstage the headliners. Jimi Hendrix booted Ted Nugent off a tour in the Sixties after witnessing the Mad Axeman's rabble-rousing performance. In 1975, Little

and a specialist marketing organisation such as Tellydisc or Telly Shop. The TV company offers cut-price advertising rates (since the commercials are unusually long, often lasting several minutes) in return for a percentage of the sales. The record can be obtained only by mail-order, from an address announced at the end of the commercial. As well as making a guaranteed profit, the record company is left with a valuable list containing thousands of names and addresses of people interested in a certain type of music — very useful for an advertising mail-out.

Whenever hhe new group is signed to a major record company, the marketing department estimates an advertising budget from which to work. This information remains strictly confidential as far as the group and its management are concerned, since budgets vary enormously according to the status of the band. If a group insists on additional press advertising, for instance, the extra cost will often be recouped from their royalties.

The record company's links with the record dealer are their 'tele-sales' — people taking dealers' orders over the telephone — and the travelling sales force. Every record company has a fair idea of the chart-return shops, though this is always hotly denied. All these stores receive a weekly call from the sales representative of their area. They will also be the first to receive copies of 12 in singles, picture discs and any amount of merchandizing paraphernalia. In addition, they are offered attractive monthly discounts — nothing illegal about that, but it does incur the wrath of the nearby non-chart shop. The 'tele-sales' team complements the sales force, by making regular 'phone calls to chart shops, either reminding them of special new releases or, perhaps, informing them of an act appearing on *Top of the Pops*.

Another area where the sales force comes into its own

Feat caused a similar sensation when they supported the Doobie Brothers on their debut British tour. A year later, the Sex Pistols caused something of a riot at London's Lyceum when they played support to the West Coast sounds of Climax Blues Band. Heavy metal outfit Saxon came to prominence only after completing a lengthy British tour as support to Motorhead. The list goes on. Many headline acts today prefer to check out their potential support act first, and many actually suggest a suitable band themselves.

As far as the record company is concerned, there is just one stumbling block – money. Promoters don't put a support band on tour out of the goodness of their hearts – the record companies have to pay out thousands of pounds for the privilege, and competition is extremely tough. But with enough foyer displays and promotional aids a group can very often win through.

The principles of concert tour promotion have evolved over the years. Back in the Sixties the role of the promoter was far more easily defined and there were fewer names to contend with. The list was headed by Harold Davison, Robert Patterson, Arthur Howes and Don Arden (now manager of the Electric Light Orchestra and boss of Jet Records). Both Howes and Arden pioneered the 30-date rock tours of the early Sixties, organizing a string of concerts featuring artists like Chuck Berry, Bo Diddley, Carl Perkins, Little Richard, the Everly Brothers and Sam Cooke. Davison and Patterson were associated with Frank Sinatra and an altogether more sophisticated kind of performer, but also introduced Britain to Ike and Tina Turner and Creedence Clearwater Revival, among many others. In those days the promoter was something of an insular force, and contact with the record companies was negligible. There were no in-house press departments, and today's common practice of servicing the media with free concert tickets – paid for by the record companies – was absolutely unheard of. Major groups of the era would hire their own publicists to work in tandem with the promoter. Tony Barrow and Derek Taylor were responsible for the Beatles' PR on any number of world tours, while Les Perrin handled publicity for the Rolling Stones until his untimely death.

Attitudes changed completely during the early Seventies, at least as far as Britain was concerned. This was the age of the affluent American conglomerate, spearheaded by Warner Communications-owned Kinney Records (now WEA), home of Warner-Elektra-Atlantic. The company's hip, laid-back image was something new to Britain. Managing Director Ian Ralfini ran the show with a devil-may-care flamboyance. Parties, champagne and lavish press receptions were the order of the day. If the sun shone, it was not uncommon to shut up shop and take the staff on a picnic or perhaps a trip down the river.

The extravagance continued into the mid-Seventies – and the entire industry is now paying the consequences. But at best it did draw the music business closer together. Suddenly everyone seemed to know everyone else. This was not really surprising, as there seemed to be a different champagne press party every night; then, of course, there was always that institution of music-business excess, the Speakeasy Club in London's Oxford Circus.

This small revolution stretched beyond the record

Rock as theatrical extravaganza.
ABOVE *ABC in 'Poison Arrow' – a scene from their video* Mantrap.
RIGHT *Alice Cooper, an early dabbler in heavy-metal theatrics,* peaked with the grisly Welcome to my Nightmare *world-tour show.*
FAR RIGHT *Deep Purple, Seventies heavy-metal cult, anticipated U.S. Eighties stadium-rock bands.*

companies; there was also a new breed of publishers, agents and promoters. As far as major concert tours, European and British, were concerned, 1975 saw the biggest, brightest and costliest of the period – the Warner Brothers Music Show. It took six bands – the Doobie Brothers, Little Feat, Tower of Power, Graham Central Station, Montrose and Bonaroo – on a 26-day trek through Europe, as well as dates in London and Manchester. Including the crew, record-company executives and others, there were 72 people 'on the road'. Logistically the tour is remembered as perhaps the most complex ever to play Europe.

The tour, however, was not the artistic success that everyone had hoped for, at least not in Britain, arriving as it did on the eve of the punk explosion. As already mentioned, Little Feat were the hit of the entire show, though for their only London appearance they were relegated to a Sunday-afternoon slot, supporting the Doobies.

In its own way, the Warner Brothers Music Show *did* introduce a new sense of urgency and sophistication into major concert touring and its many problems. Although not on such a grandiose scale, most major tours today run smoothly and efficiently, thanks partly to the increasing acceptance of the tour manager as an integral part of the entourage. His job is to make sure the band arrives in time for sound checks, the road crew are in order, the hotels are correctly booked and the band is up in time to travel to the next city. As every major band today appreciates, an experienced tour manager should be highly prized.

'Stadium rock' has been perhaps the biggest grossing phenomenon in the American music market over the last decade. An audio-visual spectacle, complete with smoke-bombs, dry ice, laser beams, strobes, back projection and so on, has become the very essence of American rock. Bands such as Journey, REO Speedwagon and Styx have captivated thousands with their earth-shattering approach to rock music. They are perhaps the last real rock heroes, though they have little or no support from much of the music press. Journey is one of CBS's hottest American acts, with platinum albums like *Evolution* (1979). REO Speedwagon, who have been on the road for over 10 years, topped the charts in the early Eighties with the single 'Keep On Loving You' and the album *Hi Infidelity*, while Styx have also maintained a good score of hit records.

Looking at early influences, Alice Cooper was the first

to crash the scene of the late Sixties with a subtle combination of music and theatre that was to culminate in the pioneering 'Welcome to My Nightmare' world-wide tour. In 1973, New York-based Kiss retaliated with a show of alarming theatrical excess. Lead singer/bass player Gene Simmons, resplendent in a two-tone painted face and high-heeled glitter boots, soon became the darling of the Glam Rock set. Although a big hit single eluded them in Britian, Kiss went on to play several bizarre nights at London's Wembley Arena in the latter part of the Seventies.

The Warner Brothers Music Show may well have highlighted the complexities of tour logistics, but the Rolling Stones' 'Tour of the Americas' that same year is still regarded as the most prestigious overland trek in rock history. It was certainly the biggest and most elaborate, commencing on 1 June in Baton Rouge, Louisiana and ending in late August in Caracas, Venezuela. In three months of travel the Stones played 55 concerts to over two million people. The Stones' line-up – Mick Jagger, Keith Richards, Ron Wood, Bill Wyman, Charlie Watts – was augmented for the occasion by keyboardist Billy Preston. The tour, which took nearly a year to plan, was announced at a New York press conference that saw the Stones rolling down Fifth Avenue one lunch hour on a truck, playing 'Brown Sugar'. Times Square unveiled the world's largest billboard, announcing the tour schedule; it had been painted by an army of workmen the night before. Across America, over a million tickets went on sale at the same moment; by 8 pm on the same day the concerts were 50 per cent sold out.

Months earlier, stage technicians began assembling and testing, in an aircraft hangar in upstate New York, the most elaborate stage ever designed for a concert tour. Jules Fisher, production supervisor and lighting designer, and Robert Wagner, scenic designer, were given the task of creating a performance area that would utilise sound and light to link the performers with the vastness of the halls in which they played. The outcome was a stage based on a lotus-petal design, with highlights of chrome laminate on ornately patterned shiny decking. Fitted with a centrally located floor drop lever, the stage was 26m (71ft) in diameter, weighed 25 tons and was transported in six semi trucks. The lotus petals could be raised and lowered by hydraulic ramps; the floor was highlighted with inlaid neon. The stage was cleverly illuminated so as to give the appearance of light moving with the performers. The total power output was half a million watts, conducted through 65km (40 miles) of copper conductor cable runs. A portable flying sound system, consisting of 32 cabinets weighing 225kg (500lb) each, was transported to all dates. Two main PAs were used in front and one in the rear. All sound was monitored to a digital relay system, ensuring that the sound was emitted in front and at the back simultaneously to avoid distortion.

In order to move these 45 tons of equipment, a crew of 22 technicians and handlers coordinated a transport caravan consisting of seven semi trucks; three for the stage, two for electrical equipment, one for PA and one for group equipment. An average of 50 staff travelled throughout the tour, headed by Tour Commander (as he preferred to be known) Peter Rudge.

The Rolling Stones' 'Tour of the Americas' came, like the Warner Brothers Music Show, at a time when the recession was just beginning to bite. Although both tours initially lost thousands upon thousands of dollars, which

was to be expected, the Stones at least made up for it by selling millions more records all over America. Calculating the logistics of touring is often a risky business, especially when launching a big-selling US act for the first time in Europe. The band will often play to less than capacity houses at a far smaller fee than it is used to in America; it also stands to lose a great deal of potential earnings if it stays away from the United States for several months.

In 1983 the charts were as confusing and complex as ever before, offering an enormous diversity of sounds, especially between Britain and the United States. The British singles market is certainly less discriminating, bogged down with a batch of electro-pop bands such as Flock of Seagulls, Tears for Fears, Blancmange and Blue Zoo, though Culture Club has introduced some degree of individuality. The Americans are still up for that clean, slick sound, typified by John Cougar, Hall & Oates, Chicago and Survivor. The British album charts are dominated by TV-advertised albums (from such companies as K-Tel, Arcade and Ronco), with the occasional breath of fresh air from Madness, Siouxsie & the Banshees and Dire Straits. The US album charts keep the superstars in business: Fleetwood Mac, Crosby Stills & Nash, Neil Diamond, Billy Joel, Asia and so on.

And what of the future? The British majors will continue to lose money with an endless stream of inconsequential, laid-back American product that sounds fine if you are driving down the Santa Monica

Boulevard but offensive and dull to the listener caught up in a Brixton traffic jam. The companies cannot really be blamed: the small print of virtually every US recording contract guarantees British release. Until someone finds a way around that one, the flood-gates remain wide open.

The rock superstars – shrewd and business-orientated in the Eighties – will continue the trend to form their own record labels. Eric Clapton's Duck Records is one of the newest, taking its place alongside George Harrison's Dark Horse Records, the Beach Boys' Brother Records, Elton John's Rocket Records, and Rolling Stones Records, all influenced, of course, by the Beatles' ill-fated venture, Apple Records. The major record company will always be with us, because of its worldwide dominance, but in Britain, at least, the indie will continue to encroach upon its territory of lucrative profit margins. Audio-visual technology has introduced a new threat, of course, but one factor remains constant: there will always be a weekly list of best-selling records.

Rock Directory

A brief guide to the work of the most important names in the evolution and development of rock from the Thirties to the present. The list includes not only individual artists and groups but also producers, songwriters, and others, and also some of the independent record labels. In the entries on the most prolific artists and groups the discographies are selective; here, as in the rest of the book, singles are printed in quotation marks and albums in *italics*. Names printed in SMALL CAPITALS are the subject of individual entries. (Abbreviations: *b.* born; *d.* died; *r.n.* real name)

ABC
Pop/funk band, formed Sheffield, 1981. Previously Vice Versa. Original line-up: Martin Fry (vocal), Mark White (guitar/keyboards), Mark Lickley (bass), Stephen Singleton (saxophone), David Palmer (drums). Debut LP *The Lexicon of Love* (1982).

ADAM AND THE ANTS
New wave/pop group, formed London, 1977. Original line-up: Adam Ant (*r.n.* Stuart Goddard; vocal), Andy Warren (bass), Matthew Ashman (guitar), Dave Barbe (drums), although line-up unstable in early days. Appeared in Derek Jarman's film *Jubilee* (1978). Signed to Decca, then to independent Do It, 1979. LP *Dirk Wears White Sox* (1979). Briefly managed by MALCOLM MCLAREN; Ants left to form basis of Bow Wow Wow, replaced by Marco Pirroni (ex-SIOUXSIE & THE BANSHEES, Rema Rema; guitar), Lee Gorman (bass, later replaced by Gary Tibbs), Terry Lee Miall and Merrick (drums). Signed to CBS, 1980. 'Dog Eat Dog' heralded string of hits – 'Stand and Deliver' No 1, May 1981. Miall and Tibbs left, January 1982; Adam continued with Pirroni. Reached No 1 with 'Goody Two Shoes'. Other LPs *Kings of the Wild Frontier* (1980), *Prince Charming* (1981), *Friend or Foe* (1982).

ALLMAN, DUANE/ALLMAN BROTHERS BAND
Duane Allman (guitar), *b.* Nashville (Tennessee), 20/11/46; *d.* in motorcycle accident, 29/10/71. Founder member of Hourglass, 1968, with brother Gregg (*b.* 8/12/47; keyboards); made *Hourglass* (1968). Joined band 31st of February with Butch Trucks (drums). Duane played sessions in Muscle Shoals (Alabama) for WILSON PICKETT, ARETHA FRANKLIN, Percy Sledge, BOZ SCAGGS, establishing reputation as leading slide guitarist. Signed to Capricorn (Macon, Georgia); formed Allman Brothers, 1969. Original line-up: Duane, Gregg, Trucks, Berry Oakley (bass), Richard Betts (guitar), Jai Johnny Johanson (drums). Debut LP *The Allman Brothers Band* (1969). *Idlewild South* (1970) went gold. Duane played sessions for ERIC CLAPTON (*Layla*, 1970). *Live at the Fillmore East* (1971 double) was last to feature Duane. Berry Oakley died in motorcycle accident, 11/11/72. 'Ramblin' Man' and 'Jessica' established precedent for Southern rock, encouraging formation of Lynyrd Skynyrd, others. Other LPs *Eat a Peach* (1972), *Brothers and Sisters* (1973), *Win, Lose or Draw* (1974). Sole LPs *Duane Allman – An Anthology* (1972); Gregg Allman *Laid Back* (1974); Richard Betts *Highway Call* (1975).

ANIMALS, THE
R&B/rock band, formed Newcastle, 1962, as the Alan Price Combo; changed name, 1964. Original line-up: Eric Burdon (vocal), Bryan 'Chas' Chandler (bass), Alan Price (organ), John Steel (drums), Hilton Valentine (guitar). Played London R&B clubs, 1964, attracted cult following; record contract with Columbia, first singles and albums produced by MICKIE MOST. 'House of the Rising Sun', million-selling second release, inspired BOB DYLAN to use rock accompaniment on albums. Price left 1965, replaced by Dave Rowberry from the Mike Cotton Sound; Steel left 1966, Barry Jenkins of the Nashville Teens replacing him. Burdon broke up group late 1966, hired John Weider (guitar), Vic Briggs (guitar), Danny McCulloch (bass) and Jenkins; launched band as Eric Burdon & the Animals; took psychedelic, mystical route. Band became Los Angeles-based after 1967, enjoying sporadic hits. Burdon disbanded group, 1969, for solo career. Price had most success in '70s as leading singer/songwriter; Chandler went into management, handling JIMI HENDRIX and Slade. Reformed 1983. LPs *The Animals* (1964), *Animal Tracks* (1965), *Best of the Animals* (1966).

ARMATRADING, JOAN
Vocal/guitar, *b.* St Kitts (West Indies), 9/12/50; moved to Birmingham (England) 1958. Initially teamed up with lyricist Pam Nestor; recorded *Whatever's for Us* (1972), though Nestor uncredited. Partnership dissolved; pursued solo career. Recorded *Back to the Night* (1975) then *Joan Armatrading* (1976) providing hit 'Love and Affection'. *Show Some Emotion* (1977) gave

her success in US. *Steppin' Out* (1979; live), *Me Myself I* (1980), *Walk Under Ladders* (1981), *The Key* (1983) have consolidated worldwide success.

ATLANTIC RECORDS
Formed New York, 1947, by Herb Abramson and Ahmet Ertegun. Abramson left, Jerry Wexler in, 1953; Nesuhi Ertegun in, 1956. Main subsidiary, Atco (1955 on), run by returned Abramson. Merged with Warner Seven Arts Corp, 1967; all bought by Kinney Communications, 1969; subsequently part of WEA. Many stars, including RAY CHARLES, CLYDE MCPHATTER, THE DRIFTERS, BOBBY DARIN, SOLOMON BURKE, WILSON PICKETT, BUFFALO SPRINGFIELD, CROSBY, STILLS, NASH & YOUNG.

BACHARACH, BURT
Composer/arranger/producer, *b.* Kansas City, 12/5/29. Majored in music at McGill University, Montreal; accompanist and musical adviser to Marlene Dietrich, late '50s. Hired by LEIBER AND STOLLER to work with the DRIFTERS in New York, began songwriting partnership with lyricist Hal David. Met backing singer DIONNE WARWICK during sessions, wrote and produced numerous hit singles and albums for her, 1962-71. Perfected Latin-inflected composing/arranging style based on fusion of samba, baion, bossa nova and rock rhythms. Composed hits for GENE PITNEY, the Carpenters, Herb Alpert and many others. Married lyricist Carole Bayer Sager, 1981, with whom wrote 'Arthur's Theme' for Christopher Cross. Film scores include *Butch Cassidy and the Sundance Kid* (1969); also wrote stage musical, *Promises, Promises* (1968). Recorded several albums of own material.

BAEZ, JOAN
Folk singer long associated with political activism, *b.* New York, 9/1/41. Graduate of Boston (Massachusetts) folk-club scene; appearance at 1959 Newport Folk Festival brought national recognition. Debut LP *Joan Baez* (1960). One-time lover of BOB DYLAN: *Any Day Now* (1968) consisted entirely of Dylan songs. Married student leader and draft-resister David Harris, 1968: *David's Album* (1969) and *One Day at a Time* (1970) made a *cause*

celèbre of his imprisonment. '70s albums included much self-written material and songs by sister Mimi Farina. *Diamonds and Rust* (1975), biggest commercial success of career, included rock accompaniment and non-political songs by such writers as Jackson Browne and STEVIE WONDER. Later albums found her moving increasingly towards country music. Defiantly left-wing, has never lost campaigning zeal.

BAND, THE
Rock band formed Canada, late '50s as Hawks, backing Ronnie Hawkins on tour. Original line-up: Levon Helm (drums), Jaime Robert Robertson (guitar), Richard Manuel (piano), Garth Hudson (organ/saxophone), Rick Danko (bass); vocals by all. Moved to New York to back John Hammond, BOB DYLAN. With Dylan participated in momentous electric tour, 1965-6, including legendary London Albert Hall date. After Dylan's motorcycle crash, July 1966, recorded at Big Pink, Woodstock: double LP *The Basement Tapes* finally released 1975. First Band album *Music from Big Pink* (1968) hailed as masterpiece. Variety of American musical resources characterise subsequent LPs *The Band* (1969), *Stage Fright* (1970), *Cahoots* (1971). Other LPs with Dylan: *Planet Waves* (1974), *Before the Flood* (1975). Other LPs *Rock of Ages* (1972), *Northern Lights, Southern Cross* (1975). Thereafter worked individually; Robertson also produces. Final reunion LP *The Last Waltz* (1977) notable for guests: Dylan, VAN MORRISON, NEIL YOUNG, JONI MITCHELL, Neil Diamond, others; also filmed by Martin Scorsese. Solo LPs include *Levon Helm & the RCO All Stars* (1977), *Rick Danko* (1978), Helm's *American Son* (1980).

BEACH BOYS, THE
Vocal supergroup, formed Los Angeles, 1961. Original line-up: Al Jardine (guitar/vocal), Brian Wilson (bass/keyboards), Carl Wilson (guitar/vocal), Dennis Wilson (drums/vocal), Mike Love (vocal). Began as close-harmony group, singing Brian's celebratory songs about surfing; music became more serious and technically sophisticated as Brian (group's producer) became more ambitious. *Pet Sounds* (1966) and *Smiley Smile* (1967) showed new direction. Brian quit touring, replaced by Glen Campbell and then Bruce Johnston, 1967;

formed own label, Brother, in same year. *Surf's Up* (1971) consisted of lost 1967 tapes; *Holland* (1973) recorded in purpose-built Dutch studio. Augmented, 1972-4, by Blondie Chaplin (guitar) and Ricky Fataar (drums); joined on stage by new manager James Guercio, 1974 onwards.

BEATLES, THE
Supergroup, formed Liverpool, 1958. Original line-up: Pete Best (drums), Stuart Sutcliffe (guitar), PAUL MCCARTNEY (bass), GEORGE HARRISON (lead guitar), JOHN LENNON (guitar). Sutcliffe left for career in art (*d.* 1961); Best sacked by group on eve of breakthrough in UK, replaced by Ringo Starr. Steered by manager BRIAN EPSTEIN to phenomenal success worldwide, became major UK export; changed face of US and UK pop scene through 'progressive' approach, gave rock music artistic respectability. UK No 1 singles: 'From Me to You', 'She Loves You', 'I Want to Hold Your Hand' (all 1963); 'Can't Buy Me Love', 'A Hard Day's Night', 'I Feel Fine' (all 1964); 'Ticket to Ride', 'Help', 'We Can Work It Out' (all 1965); 'Paperback Writer', 'Eleanor Rigby' (both 1966); 'All You Need Is Love', 'Hello, Goodbye' (both 1967); 'Lady Madonna', 'Hey Jude' (both 1968); 'Get Back', 'Ballad of John and Yoko' (both 1969). Most influential albums: *Please Please Me* (1963), *With the Beatles* (1963), *A Hard Day's Night*, *Beatles for Sale* (both 1964), *Rubber Soul, Help!* (both 1965), *Revolver* (1966), *Sgt Pepper's Lonely Hearts Club Band* (1967), *The Beatles* (1968), *Abbey Road* (1969). Founded own Apple label, 1968. Group's breakup coincided with release of *Let It Be* album and film (1970); partnership officially dissolved by high court, 1971.

BECK, JEFF
Guitar, *b*. Surrey, 24/6/44. Melodic, inventive guitarist, first came to prominence in YARDBIRDS, 1964-6. Solo singles followed; subsequently formed Jeff Beck Group I (including ROD STEWART, Ron Wood, 1968-9), Jeff Beck Group II (including Cozy Powell, 1971-2), Beck, Bogert & Appice (1973), Jan Hammer Group (1977); also solo studio projects. LPs include *Truth* (1968), *Beck-Ola* (1969, with Jeff Beck Group I), *Blow by Blow* (1975), *Wired* (1976), *Live* (Jan Hammer Group, 1977), *There and Back* (1980).

BEE GEES, THE
Vocal trio/composers, formed Manchester, 1956, by brothers Barry (vocal/guitar), Maurice (vocal/keyboards) and Robin Gibb (vocal). Family emigrated to Australia, brothers became leading pop act there before returning to UK, 1966. Career fostered by Robert Stigwood, one-time associate of BRIAN EPSTEIN at NEMS; broke through, 1967, with heavily Beatle-influenced singles. Deftly assimilated novelty, psychedelic, country, and soul styles; became top US act in early '70s. Took disco route, 1974, with *Main Course*; wrote and performed score for *Saturday Night Fever*, 1977, seminal disco movie. Still major international hit-makers in '80s; brothers' production credits include albums for Barbra Streisand and DIONNE WARWICK.

BERRY, CHUCK
Guitar/vocal, *b*. St Louis (Missouri), 18/10/31. Stylish guitar work and lyrically astute compositions projected '50s rock 'n' roll into basis of '60s group boom. Nearly 20 American hits (1955-60) preceded scandal, imprisonment, renewed success as major rock influence (1964-'70s). Semi-retired and superseded as an entertainer, but still echoed by many, e.g. DAVE EDMUNDS. LPs: best original compilation *Berry Is On Top* (1959); latterly, *Motorvatin'* ('70s compilation of original hits) and *Golden Decade Vols 1, 2, 3* (ditto, but comprehensive).

BLACK SABBATH
Heavy-metal group, formerly Earth; became Black Sabbath 1969. Formed Birmingham, one of first major heavy-metal groups in both UK and US. Original line-up: Ozzy Osbourne (vocal), Tony Iommi (guitar), Geezer Butler (bass), Bill Ward (drums). Debut LP *Black Sab-* *bath* (1970); but *Paranoid* (1970) was breakthrough, title track providing hit single. Other LPs *Master of Reality* (1971), *Volume 4* (1972), *Sabbath Bloody Sabbath* (1973), and *Sabotage* (1975), delayed by management problems and label change, then *Technical Ecstasy* (1976), *Never Say Die* (1978), *Heaven and Hell* (1980). By now Osbourne had left, replaced by former Rainbow vocalist Ronnie James Dio. Ward since replaced by Vinnie Appice. Osbourne has pursued solo career with *Blizzard of Oz* (1980), *Diary of a Madman* (1981).

BLAND, BOBBY 'BLUE'
Blues/soul singer, *b*. Rosemark (Tennessee), 27/1/30. Worked in Memphis R&B circles, 1949 on; recorded for several regional black labels, notably Don D. Robey's Duke at Houston. Played club/theatre circuit, often with Junior Parker, 1954 on. Achieved nationwide recognition, late '60s; recordings (on ABC) grew away from blues roots, but turned back for reunion sessions with old friend B. B. KING. Selected LPs *Woke Up Screaming* (1981 compilation of '50s), *His California Album* (1973), *The Best of* (1981 compilation of '50s-'70s), virtually any on Duke label.

BLONDIE
Disco-pop group, formed New York, 1975, from the Stilettoes: Debbie Harry (vocal), Chris Stein (lead guitar), Gary Valentine (guitar), Jimmy Destri (keyboards), Clem Burke (drums). Debut LP *Blondie* (1977). Supported TELEVISION on British tour, summer 1977. Signed to Chrysalis 1978. Gary Valentine replaced by Frank Infante (guitar), Nigel Harrison (bass). 'Denis' began string of hit singles. *Eat to the Beat* No 1, October 1979; top-selling UK album and singles act that year. *AutoAmerican* (1981) produced by Mike Chapman. Harry made film debut in *Union City* (1980). Harry and Stein quit, July 1981, to team with CHIC for *Koo Koo*. Band reformed 1982. Other LPs *Plastic Letters* (1978), *Parallel Lines* (1978), *The Hunter* (1982).

BOOKER T & THE MGs
Soul/rock band coalesced in Memphis (Tennessee), 1961, as studio rhythm-section for STAX RECORDS. Original line-up: Booker T. Jones (keyboards), Steve Cropper (guitar), Louis Steinberg (bass), Al Jackson (drums). Steinberg soon replaced by

Donald 'Duck' Dunn. Essential foundation for majority of Stax stars throughout '60s, including OTIS REDDING. Also instrumentally successful in own right (1962-71); Jones, Cropper and Jackson doubling as producers. Jackson shot dead, 1975; others went solo, Cropper and Dunn later with the Blues Brothers (1978). LPs *The Best of* (compilation, 1972), *Time Is Tight/The Best of* (different compilation, 1978).

BOWIE, DAVID
Vocal/songwriter/producer/actor, *b*. Brixton (London), 8/1/47 (*r.n.* David Jones). First group David Jones & the Lower Third, mid-'60s. Met dancer/choreographer Lindsay Kemp. Signed to Decca, 1967: minor singles until 'Space Oddity' (1969). Retired to Beckenham (Kent) Arts Lab; returned, 1970, for *The Man Who Sold the World, Hunky Dory* (1971). Success with *The Rise and Fall of Ziggy Stardust and the Spiders from Mars* (1972), with Mick Ronson (guitar), Trevor Bolder (bass), Woody Woodmansey (drums). US breakthrough with 'Space Oddity', 1973. Retired again, July 1973. Produced LOU REED, MOTT THE HOOPLE. Comeback US tour, *Diamond Dogs* (1974). Recorded soul-influenced *Young Americans*, Philadelphia, 1975. 'Fame', written with JOHN LENNON, US No 1. *Station to Station* (1976) arguably his best. Collaborated with BRIAN ENO on trilogy *Low* (1977), *Heroes* (1977), *Lodger* (1980). Film work: *The Man Who Fell to Earth* (1976), *Just a Gigolo* (1978), *The Hunger* (1983); soundtracks for *Christiane F* (1981), *Cat People* (1982). Played title role in *The Elephant Man* on Broadway, 1980. LP *Scary Monsters and Super-Creeps* (1980) immediate UK No 1, as was *Let's Dance* (1983).

BROWN, JAMES

Vocal/keyboards/drums, *b.* Barnwell (South Carolina), 3/5/33. Leading figure of postwar black America; the first to establish self-determined superstardom while redefining '50s R&B to create funk. Southern rebel, 1956-8, national ghetto hero, 1959-63, internationally recognized phenomenon, 1964-9; success faded after mid-'70s. LPs (over 60) best represented by *Live at the Apollo* (1963), *Vol. 2* (1968), *Vol. 3* (1971), *Sex Machine* (1970), *There It Is* (1972), *Solid Gold* (compilation, 1976), *Can Your Heart Stand It?* (compilation, 1982).

BUFFALO SPRINGFIELD

Folk-rock group, formed Los Angeles, 1966. Original line-up: Stephen Stills (guitar/vocal), Neil Young (guitar/vocal), Richie Furay (rhythm guitar/vocal), Bruce Palmer (bass), Dewey Martin (drums). Debut LP *Buffalo Springfield* (1967) contained their only US Top Ten single, 'For What It's Worth'. Other LPs *Buffalo Springfield Again* (1968), *Last Time Around* (1969). Stills and Young later members of CROSBY, STILLS, NASH & YOUNG.

BURKE, SOLOMON

Vocal, *b.* Philadelphia (Pennsylvania), 1936. Wonder-boy preacher, starring in own church and radio show at age of nine, became King of Rock 'n' Soul, first Sixties soul star on ATLANTIC RECORDS (1961-8); subsequent career erratic but continuing. LPs *The Best of* (1965), *Proud Mary* (1969).

BURTON, JAMES

Guitar, *b.* Shreveport (Louisiana), *c.* 1942. Played on Dale Hawkins' rock 'n' roll hit 'Suzie Q' (1957). Joined RICKY NELSON, *c.* 1958; contributed inventive solos to many of his hits. Left *c.* 1964 for session work in Los Angeles; recorded with the Monkees, EVERLY BROTHERS, MAMAS & THE PAPAS, FLYING BURRITO BROTHERS, GRAM PARSONS, Judy Collins, and others. Worked with ELVIS PRESLEY, Las Vegas, 1969. Occasionally made instrumental records, e.g. *Corn Pickin' and Slick Slidin'* with Ralph Mooney (pedal steel). Style derived jointly from country and R&B traditions; outlived fading rock 'n' roll to become equally influential upon West Coast country rock. Worked with EMMYLOU HARRIS in Hot Band, mid- to late '70s; again with Presley. Continues to be in-demand session musician, also on dobro.

BUTLER, JERRY

Vocal, *b.* Sunflower (Mississipi), 8/12/39. Founder member of the Impressions (1957) with CURTIS MAYFIELD. Pursued solo career, 1959. Leading Chicago-based soul star (1960-5); pioneer star of the PHILADELPHIA SOUND (1968-9). LPs *Up on Love* (1980 compilation of 1958-65), *The Ice Man Cometh* (1969), *Ice on Ice* (1969).

BUTTERFIELD BLUES BAND

Blues band, formed Chicago, 1965. Original line-up: Paul Butterfield (harmonica/vocal), Mike Bloomfield (lead guitar), Elvin Bishop (guitar), Mark Naftalin (keyboards), Jerome Arnold (bass), Sam Lay (drums). Recorded for ELEKTRA *The Paul Butterfield Blues Band* (1965), *East West* (1966). Bloomfield left band to work with BOB DYLAN. Then formed the Electric Flag, later teaming up with AL KOOPER for several LPs. Other Butterfield LPs *The Resurrection of Pigboy Crabshaw* (1967), *In My Own Dream* (1968), *Keep On Moving* (1969), *The Paul Butterfield Band – Live* (1971), *Sometimes I Just Feel Like Smilin'* (1972). Band disbanded, 1973. Butterfield formed Better Days; made *Better Days* (1973), *It All Comes Back* (1974).

BYRDS, THE

Folk-rock group, formed Los Angeles, 1964. Original line-up: Roger 'Jim' McGuinn (guitar/vocal), Chris Hillman (bass/vocal), Gene Clark (guitar/vocal), David Crosby (guitar/vocal), Michael Clarke (drums). First album *Preflyte* recorded as demo before settling on seminal folk-rock style with cover of BOB DYLAN's 'Mr Tambourine Man' (1965) and LPs *Mr Tambourine Man*, *Turn! Turn! Turn!* (1966). Clark left during *Fifth Dimension* (1966). Spacier sound developed through *Younger Than Yesterday* (1967) and *The Notorious Byrd Brothers* (1968), recorded without Crosby. GRAM PARSONS joined 1968 for country-rock milestone *Sweetheart of the Rodeo* (1968). Parsons and Hillman replaced by Clarence White (guitar), John York (bass); Clarke retired, joined Firefall. With Gene Parsons (drums) new line-up made *Dr Byrds and Mr Hyde* (1969), *The Ballad of Easy Rider* (1970). Skip Battin replaced York for *Untitled* (1970). Other LPs *Byrdmaniax* (1971), *Farther Along* (1972), *Byrds* (1973 reunion). Solo LPs include *Roger McGuinn* (1973) and *Cardiff Rose* (1975); *Gene Clark with the Gosdin Brothers* (1967); *Fantastic Expedition of Dillard and Clark* (1968), *No Other* (1974); David Crosby *If I Could Only Remember My Name* (1972); with Graham Nash *Crosby & Nash* (1972) and *Whistling Down the Wire* (1975). See also CROSBY, STILLS, NASH & YOUNG.

CALE, J. J.

Vocal/guitar/songwriter, *b.* 1939; grew up in Tulsa (Oklahoma). Worked with LEON RUSSELL, late '50s on. Wrote 'After Midnight', 1965, subsequently US hit for ERIC CLAPTON, 1970. LP *Naturally* (1972) captured admirably his laidback country-rock style. Subsequent LPs *Really* (1973), *Okie* (1974), *Troubadour* (1976), *5* (1979), *Shades* (1981).

CALE, JOHN

Vocal/viola/producer, *b.* Wales. Studied avant-garde music under Lamonte Young in New York. Here met LOU REED, with whom he founded VELVET UNDERGROUND. Left, 1968, for solo career as producer, arranger, composer, performer. Produced Jonathan Richman & the Modern Lovers and Iggy Pop, early '70s; also PATTI SMITH's *Horses* (1975), Nico's *The End, Marble Index, Desertshore.* Solo career began with *Vintage Violence* (1970) and *Church of Anthrax* (1971), collaborating with Terry Riley. Returned to England; recorded *Fear* (1974) with BRIAN ENO and Phil Manzanera of ROXY MUSIC. Returned to New York. Other LPs *Paris 1919* (1973), *Slow Dazzle* (1975), *Helen of Troy* (1975), *Honi Soit Qui Mal y Pense* (1980), *Music for a New Society* (1982).

CAPTAIN BEEFHEART

Vocal/saxophone, *b.* Glendale (California), 1941 (*r.n.* Don Van Vliet). Formed Magic Band, 1964; original line-up: RY COODER (guitar), Jimmy Semens (guitar), Herb Bermann (bass), John French (drums). Debut LP *Safe As Milk* (1967). Cooder and Bermann replaced by Alex St Claire and Jerry Handley for *Mirror Man* (not released until 1973). Further changes led to *Trout Mask Replica* (1969), by Semens, Zoot Horn Rollo (guitar), The Mascara Snake (bass clarinet) and Rockette Morton (bass). Avant-garde horn-orientated work was compared to Ornette Coleman and Coltrane. Other LPs include *The Spotlight Kid* (1971), *Clear Spot* (1972), *Unconditionally Guaranteed* (1974), *Bongo Fury* (1975, with FRANK ZAPPA), *Shiny Beast (1978), Doc at the Radar Station* (1980).

CHARLES, RAY

Vocal/keyboards/saxophone, *b.* Albany (Georgia), 23/9/32 (*r.n.* Ray Charles Robinson). Principal catalyst of change in '50s American black music. West-coast style bluesman, 1949-53, became pioneer of gospel/jazz/R&B synthesis on ATLANTIC RECORDS, 1954-60, before international acclaim with commercialised variations on the theme, 1962-8. Immensely influential during his prime years; subsequently a concert performer. LPs *At Newport* (1958), *In Person* (1959), *Greatest Hits* (1962), *Ray Charles Story Vols 1-4* ('60s compilations of 1954-61). *25th Anniversary* ('70s compilation of '50s and '60s).

CHESS RECORDS

Independent label founded by brothers Leonard and Phil Chess, Chicago club-owners. Preceded by Aristocrat, 1947-50; name changed to Chess, 3/6/50. Premier label of Chicago blues; roster included MUDDY WATERS, Howlin' Wolf, CHUCK BERRY; on subsidiary Checker, BO DIDDLEY, Little Walter, Sonny Boy Williamson. Also vocal groups (e.g. Moonglows), other R&B idioms. Venerated by British R&B groups; FLEETWOOD MAC recorded *Blues Jam at Chess* (1969); ROLLING STONES set up own label in collaboration with Leonard's son Marshall. Company sold to GRT, 1969; changed hands several times since, but original recordings continue to furnish reissue series. Best documentation: three 4-LP boxed sets in *Genesis* series (UK, early '70s); individual artists LPs on UK *Chess Masters,* French *Golden Years.*

CHIC

Disco group formed New York, 1977, as working unit for Nile Rodgers (guitar) and Bernard Edwards (bass). Debut ATLANTIC single, 'Dance, Dance, Dance (Yowsah, Yowsah, Yowsah)', a Top 20 UK hit (1978), followed by 'Everybody Dance' (1979), 'Le Freak' (1979), 'I Want Your Love' (1979), 'Good Times' (1980). LPs *Chic* (1978), *C'est Chic* (1979), *Risqué* (1979), *Real People* (1980), *Take It Off* (1981), *Tongue in Chic* (1982). Rodgers also co-produces, notably DAVID BOWIE's UK No 1 single 'Lets Dance' (1983). Rodgers/Edwards scored soundtrack for *Soup for One* (1982), featuring BLONDIE and others.

CHICAGO

Jazz-rock band, formed Chicago, 1968. Originally called Chicago Transit Authority; line-up included Terry Kath (guitar/vocal), Robert Lamm (keyboards), Peter Cetera (bass/vocal) and Dan Seraphine (drums). Albums released in numerical sequence from *Chicago Transit Authority* (1969) to *Chicago 16* (1982). Top Ten UK single hits with 'I'm a Man' (1970), '25 or 6 to 4' (1970) and 'Hard to Say I'm Sorry' (1982), which featured new lead vocalist Bill Champlin.

CLAPTON, ERIC

Guitar/vocal, *b.* Ripley (Surrey), 30/4/45. Founder-member of the YARDBIRDS, 1964; subsequently with JOHN MAYALL's Bluesbreakers (1965), before joining CREAM (1966-8). In 1970

formed Derek & the Dominoes, which broke up a year later. Since then has followed solo career. LPs *Five Live Yardbirds* (with the Yardbirds, 1965); *Fresh Cream* (1966), *Disraeli Gears* (1967), *Wheels of Fire* (1968), all with Cream; *Eric Clapton* (1970), *Derek & the Dominoes* (1971), *Rainbow Concert* (1973), *461 Ocean Boulevard* (1974), *There's One in Every Crowd* (1975), *E. C. Was Here* (1975), *No Reason to Cry* (1976), *Slowhand* (1978), *Another Ticket* (1981), *Money and Cigarettes* (1983). Single hits in UK include: 'Badge' (with Cream, 1969), 'I Shot the Sheriff' (1974), 'Layla' (reissued 1982).

CLARK, DICK

TV personality, *b.* Mount Vernon (New York), 1929. Originally radio announcer; then hosted Philadelphia TV show *Bandstand,* 1956, nationally networked from 1957 as *American Bandstand.* Presented pop, rock 'n' roll with live audience of dancing teenagers; established careers of countless teen idols. Later added *Dick Clark Show.* Named most influential person in pop music in 1960 payola investigation, but career weathered crisis. Subsequent shows included *Where the Action's At, In Concert.*

CLASH, THE

New Wave band, formed London, 1976: Mick Jones (guitar/vocal), Paul Simenon (bass/vocal), Joe Strummer (vocal/guitar), Terry Chimes (drums). On SEX PISTOLS Anarchy tour, 1976; subsequently signed to CBS. 'White Riot' charted, spring 1977. Chimes replaced by Nicky 'Topper' Headon, 1978, but rejoined after Headon's departure, May 1982. Most political of New

Wave bands and one of the longest-lived. Toured America 1979, recording second album there. Starred in film *Rude Boy*, 1980. In 1982 Strummer disappeared for several weeks just before start of nationwide tour, causing speculation in media about band's future; returned, but Headon left. LPs *The Clash* (1977), *Give 'Em Enough Rope* (1979), *London Calling* (1980), *Sandinista* (1981), *Combat Rock* (1982).

COASTERS, THE
Comedy vocal team of changing personnel, developed by songwriters/producers LEIBER & STOLLER from prototype group the Robins. First line-up of Coasters proper: Carl Gardner, Leon Hughes, Billy Guy, Bobby Nunn, 1956. Hughes replaced by Young Jessie, 1957, then Cornel Gunter, while Nunn replaced by Will Jones to complete best-known line-up, 1958-61. Chart success stopped in 1961 but Coasters survived on record and tours. LPs *The Early Years* (1973 compilation), *What Is the Secret of Your Success?* (1980 compilation).

COCHRAN, EDDIE
Guitar/vocal, *b.* Oklahoma City, 3/10/38. Untypically diverse talent and attitude permeated an erratic, short-lived but influential career. Accompanied Hank Cochran (no relation), 1954-6; intermittent solo success, 1957-60; accompanied and produced others. Killed in car crash, Chippenham (Wiltshire), 17/4/60. Posthumously venerated. LPs *Memorial Album* (1960), *Singles Album* ('70s compilation), *20th Anniversary* (4-LP box set, 1980), *Rock 'n' Roll Heroes* (with GENE VINCENT, 1981).

COCKER, JOE
Vocal, *b.* Sheffield, 20/5/44. First single 'Marjorine' (1967) paved way for BEATLES-penned 'With a Little Help From My Friends' (1968), a No 1 UK hit. Followed up with another Top 10 UK hit, 'Delta Lady' (1969), and 'The Letter' (1970). LPs *With a Little Help From My Friends* (1968), *Mad Dogs and Englishmen* (with LEON RUSSELL, 1970), *I Can Stand a Little Rain* (1974), *You Are So Beautiful* (1975), *Luxury You Can Afford* (1978). Re-emerged on IS-LAND RECORDS in 1982, with a No 1 US hit, 'Up Where We Belong', a duet with Jennifer Warnes, and an album, *Sheffield Steel*.

COHEN, LEONARD
Vocal/guitar, *b.* Montreal (Canada), 21/9/34. Made reputation as poet and novelist with *The Favorite Game* (1963), *Beautiful Losers* (1966). Debut LP *The Songs of Leonard Cohen* (1967) established him as singer/songwriter; then *Songs from a Room* (1969), *Songs of Love and Hate* (1970). Toured Europe, 1970; filmed by Tony Palmer as *Bird on the Wire* (1971). *Live Songs* (1973) was collection of most famous songs. Collaborated with PHIL SPECTOR on *Death of a Ladies' Man* (1977). *Recent Songs* (1979) featured singer Jennifer Warnes.

COMMANDER CODY & THE LOST PLANET AIRMEN
Country-rock band, formed Detroit (Michigan), 1968. Core members: George Frayne (Commander Cody, vocal/piano), Andy Stein (fiddle/saxophone), Bill Kirchen (vocal/lead guitar), John Tichy (vocal/rhythm guitar), Billy C. Farlow (vocal/harmonica), Bobby 'Blue' Black (pedal steel guitar), Bruce Barlow (bass), Lance Dickerson (drums). Played anarchic amalgam of country, Western Swing, vintage rock 'n' roll. Based on West Coast, 1969 on. Outstanding LPs *Hot Licks, Cold Steel & Truckers Favorites* (1972), *Live from Deep in the Heart of Texas* (1974), *Tales from the Ozone* (1975). Norton Buffalo (harmonica/trombone/vocal) added, 1975. European tour, 1976, produced *We've Got a Live One Here!* (1976, double); disbanded afterwards.

COODER, RY
Vocal/guitar/mandolin, *b.* Los Angeles, 15/3/47. In band with TAJ MAHAL, the Rising Sons, 1966; with CAPTAIN BEEFHEART, 1967-8. Session work with ROLLING STONES (*Let It*

Bleed, 1969), Randy Newman, many others. Solo debut *Ry Cooder* (1970) featured remarkable rock readings of old blues, country songs – direction followed on *Into the Purple Valley* (1971), *Boomer's Story* (1972), also showing absorption of calypso. *Paradise & Lunch* (1974) drew on jazz and gospel strains; *Chicken Skin Music* (1976) introduced Hawaiian and TexMex music. Roots interests set aside for R&B-directed *Bop Till You Drop* (1979), *Borderline* (1980), *The Slide Area* (1982). Much film soundtrack work from *Performance* (1968) to *The Long Riders* (1980), *The Border* (1982). Brilliant instrumentalist, superb interpreter and reshaper of traditional musics. Other LPs *Show Time* (1977), *Jazz* (1978).

COOKE, SAM
Vocal, *b.* Clarksdale (Mississippi), 2/1/31; shot dead, Los Angeles, 10/12/64. Pioneer soul stylist and writer. First sang gospel with the Singing Children, the Highway QCs ('40s), the Soul Stirrers (1950-6). Pursued solo secular career 1956-64; Influenced many, including OTIS REDDING, ARETHA FRANKLIN, AL GREEN. LPs *The Soul Stirrers Featuring Sam Cooke* ('60s compilation), *The Best of* (1962), *Ain't That Good News* (1964).

COSTELLO, ELVIS
Vocal/guitar/songwriter, *b.* Liverpool (*r.n.* Declan McManus, son of Ross McManus, singer with Joe Loss Orchestra). With pub-rock band Flip City; went solo and signed to STIFF. Debut 'Less Than Zero' (1977) well received, 'Watching the Detectives' a Top 10 hit. Debut album *My Aim Is True* (1977) with US country-boogie band Clover; then formed Attractions: Steve Naive (keyboards), Bruce Thomas (bass), Pete Thomas (drums). Interest in country led to *Almost Blue* (1981), produced in Nashville by Billy Sherrill, featuring hit single 'It Was A Good Year for the Roses'. Other LPs *This Year's Model* (1978), *Armed Forces* (1979) *Get Happy* (1979), *Trust* (1980), *Imperial Bedroom* (1982).

CREAM
Rock supergroup, formed London, 1966: ERIC CLAPTON (guitar/vocal), Jack Bruce (*b.* Bishopbriggs, Lanarkshire, 14/5/43; bass/lead vocal), Ginger Baker (*b.* Lewisham, Kent, 19/8/40; drums). Blues beginnings quickly led to lengthy impro-

visations on LPs, lighter pop on singles; individual members lauded as instrumental virtuosi. LPs *Fresh Cream* (1966), *Disraeli Gears* (1967), *Wheels of Fire* (1968), *Goodbye* (1969), *Best of Cream* (1969). Farewell concert at London's Royal Albert Hall, 26/11/68. Clapton and Baker formed shortlived Blind Faith with STEVE WINWOOD and Ric Grech (ex-FAMILY), 1969; Bruce pursued solo projects.

CREEDENCE CLEARWATER RE-VIVAL
Pop-rock group, formed El Cerrito (California), 1964, as Blue Velvets, British-influenced pop band. Original line-up: John Fogerty (guitar/vocal), Tom Fogerty (guitar), Stu Cook (bass), Doug Clifford (drums). Became Creedence Clearwater Revival, 1967, releasing album of same name. *Bayou Country* (1968), *Green River* (1969) both gold albums in the US and Europe, produced several No 1 hits. Other LPs *Willy & the Poor Boys* (1970), *Cosmo's Factory* (1970), *Pendulum* (1971), *Mardi Gras* (1972 as trio without Tom Fogerty). John Fogerty solos *The Blue Ridge Rangers* (1973), *John Fogerty* (1975). Tom Fogerty worked sporadically on sessions and pursued solo career. Cook and Clifford joined Don Harrison Band.

CROSBY, STILLS, NASH & YOUNG
Supergroup formed summer 1968 by David Crosby guitar/vocal; former founding member of the BYRDS), Stephen Stills (guitar/piano/vocal; from BUFFALO SPRINGFIELD), and Englishman Graham Nash (bass/vocal; formerly with the HOLLIES). Debut LP *Crosby, Stills & Nash* (1969). NEIL YOUNG (guitar/piano/vocal; also from Buffalo Springfield) joined for *Déjà Vu* (1970), *Four Way Street* (1971, live). Young left to pursue solo career; reunion, 1974, but nothing recorded. Stills pursued solo career at same time, releasing *Stephen Stills* (1970), *Stephen Stills II* (1971), before forming Manassas, then resuming solo work, 1975. Nash and Crosby continue to work together sporadically.

CRUSADERS, THE
Jazz-rock band, formed as Jazz Crusaders, Houston (Texas), late '50s. Original line-up: Wilton Felder (bass/saxophones), Joe Sample (keyboards), Stix Hooper (drums), Wayne Henderson (trombone). Recorded frequently for Pacific Jazz

before forming seminal group the Crusaders with Larry Carlton (guitar), David T. Walker (guitar). LPs include *Crusaders I* (1972), *The Second Crusade* (1972), *Unsung Heroes* (1973), *Chain Reaction* (1975). Prolific solo artists and session players. Worldwide single hit with 'Street Life' (1979) and album of same name; all subsequent releases have topped US R&B charts.

D

DAMNED, THE
Punk group, formed London, 1976. Original line-up: Dave Vanian (vocal), Brian James (guitar/vocal), Captain Sensible (*r.n.* Ray Burns; bass), Rat Scabies (*r.n.* Chris Miller; drums). Signed to STIFF; first punk band to issue a single ('New Rose', produced by NICK LOWE, 1976). James left, 1978, to work with various bands, most recently Lords of the New Church with Stiv Bators. Damned disbanded then reassembled with Sensible on lead guitar and Paul Gray (from Eddie & the Hot Rods) bass, late 1979. Captain Sensible scored No 1 hit in summer 1982 with 'Happy Talk'. LPs *Damned, Damned, Damned* (1977), *Music for Pleasure* (1978), *Machine Gun Etiquette* (1979), *The Black Album* (1980), *Strawberries* (1982).

DARIN, BOBBY
Vocal, *b.* Philadelphia (Pennsylvania), *d.* of heart attack, 20/12/73 (*r.n.* Waldo Robert Cassotto). Stylistic chameleon; also composer; changed from pop-rock (1958-9) to cabaret (1959-61), to R&B and pop (1961-3), to acting, to folk-pop (1966). LPs *The Bobby Darin Story* (1961), *Sings Ray Charles* (1962).

DARNELL, AUGUST
Vocal/producer, *b.* Haiti (*r.n.* Darnell August Browder); brought up in Bronx (New York). Formed In Laws with brother Stony, mid-'60s; later became Dr Buzzard's Original Savannah Band, mixing soul, big band, rock cocktail; hit with 'Cherchez la Femme'. Produced various artists for ZE RECORDS. Formed Don Armando's Second Avenue Rhumba Band. With Andy (Coati Mundi) Hernandez as orchestrator, formed Kid Creole & the Coconuts, summer 1980, 13-piece playing salsa, big band swing, rock, calypso. Released *Off the Coast of Me*, 1980. Hernandez had UK hit, 'Me No Pop I', 1981.

Fresh Fruit in Foreign Places (1981) consolidated Kid Creole reputation. 'I'm a Wonderful Thing' (1982) hit, followed by *Tropical Gangsters* (1982). Live shows present precision-timed tropical mini-dramas.

DEEP PURPLE
Heavy-metal band formed London, 1968. Original line-up: Ritchie Blackmore (lead guitar), Ian Paice (drums), Nick Simper (bass), Jon Lord (keyboards), Rod Evans (vocal). Simper and Evans replaced respectively by Roger Glover, Ian Gillan, 1969. Debut single 'Hush' (1968) Top Ten US hit. First LP *Shades of Deep Purple* (1968) a Top 40 US hit. Recorded with Royal Philharmonic Orchestra at Royal Albert Hall for *In Live Concert* (1970); 'Black Night' UK No 2 same year. 'Strange Kind of Woman' (1971), 'Smoke on the Water' (1973), also reached UK Top Ten. LPs *Machine Head* (1972), *Stormbringer* (1974), *Come Taste the Band* (1975), *Made in Europe* (1976), *Powerhouse* (1978), *Deep Purple in Concert* (1980). Disbanded 1980, Ritchie Blackmore forming Rainbow and Ian Gillan fronting Gillan.

DIDDLEY, BO
Vocal/guitar, *b.* McComb (Mississippi), 30/12/28 (*r.n.* Ellas McDaniel). Eccentric genius of R&B guitar. Grew up in Chicago; varied musical experience in '40s. Recorded for Checker (CHESS subsidiary), 1955 on; notable singles include 'Bo Diddley'/'I'm a Man', 'Pretty Thing', 'Diddy Wah Diddy' (all 1955), 'Mona' (1957; later recorded by ROLLING STONES). Much touring in US, Europe, '60s-'70s; often in rock 'n' roll revival packages. Great in-

fluence on '60s UK R&B groups, e.g. Rolling Stones, YARDBIRDS. Selected LPs *Chess Masters Vol. 1, Vol. 2* ('80s doubles, compilations of later '50s-'60s).

DIRE STRAITS

Rock band formed Deptford (London), 1977. Original line-up: Mark Knopfler (vocal/lead guitar), David Knopfler (guitar), John Illsley (bass), Pick Withers (drums). Demo tape of 'Sultans of Swing' given exposure by BBC Radio London DJ Charlie Gillett; signed to Phonogram. Made *Dire Straits* (1978), *Communique* (1979). Swift US success, especially after Mark Knopfler and Withers recorded with BOB DYLAN on *Slow Train Coming* (1979). David Knopfler left, 1980, replaced by Hal Lindes (guitar), Alan Clark (keyboards). Other LPs *Making Movies* (1980), *Love Over Gold* (1982).

Dr JOHN: *see* REBENNACK, MAC

DOMINO, FATS

Piano/vocal, *b.* New Orleans (Louisiana), 26/2/28. Astonishingly consistent exponent of archetypal New Orleans R&B, especially with band led by trumpeter/arranger Dave Bartholomew. Regular success in R&B market, 1949-54, preceded wider rock 'n' roll acclaim, 1955 on; chart success lasted until mid-'60s. Subsequent recording career erratic but some good live albums and concerts. LPs *The Fats Domino Story, Vols 1-6* (1977 compilations of 1949-62), *Reelin' and Rockin'* (1983 compilation of 1963-4), *Live '65* (1965), *Live at Montreux* (1974), *Live in Europe* (1977).

DONOVAN

Vocal/guitar/harmonica, *b.* Glasgow (Scotland), 10/5/46 (r.n. Donovan Leitch). First single, 'Catch the Wind' (1965), Top 10 UK hit, followed that year by 'Colours', which also reached Top 10. UK No 1, 1966, with 'Sunshine Superman'; then 'Mellow Yellow' (1966), 'There Is a Mountain' (1967), 'Jennifer Juniper' (1968), 'Hurdy Gurdy Man' (1968), 'Atlantis' (1969), 'Babarabbajagal' (with JEFF BECK, 1969). LPs *What's Been Did and What's Been Hid* (1965), *Universal Soldier* (1967), *Gift from a Flower to a Garden* (1968), *Cosmic Wheels* (1973). In 1974 wrote a stage show, *7-Tease*. Now makes occasional tours.

DOORS, THE

Acid-rock group formed Los Angeles, 1965, as Rick & the Ravens, subsequently the Doors. Line-up: Jim Morrison (vocal), Ray Manzarek (keyboards), Robbie Krieger (guitar), John Densmore (drums). Debut LP for ELEKTRA *The Doors* (1967) contained No 1 hit 'Light My Fire'. *Strange Days* (1967), *Waiting for the Sun* (1968) topped album charts. After *The Soft Parade* (1969) Morrison became more interested in theatrics and poetry. After *Absolutely Live, Morrison Hotel* (both 1970) band toured infrequently. Prior to *LA Woman* (1971) Morrison left to live in Paris, where he died of a heart attack, 3/7/71. Posthumous release 'Riders on the Storm' a huge hit. A verse and music LP, *An American Prayer* (1978), created new interest and several old albums charted. Krieger and Densmore formed Butts Band, 1974. Ray Manzarek recorded solo *The Golden Scarab* (1974), *The Whole Thing Started with Rock 'n' Roll* (1975); has recently produced LA bands Nite City and X.

DRIFTERS, THE

Corporate identity for frequently changing groups of vocalists, the first a successful R&B act founded by influential lead singer CLYDE MCPHATTER, 1953-4, subsequently mainly featuring Bill Pinkney and Johnny Moore, 1955-8. During the Drifters' heyday as a pop-soul act Ben E. King first led an entirely new line-up, 1959-60, replaced by Rudy Lewis, 1960-3, and the returned Johnny Moore, 1963 on. After a quiet patch, in 1973 Moore's (by then different again) Drifters found new success as a British-based pop/cabaret act. In recent years several

different sets of Drifters have been simultaneously touring, one again led by Ben E. King. LPs *Clyde McPhatter & the Drifters* (1955), *Save the Last Dance for Me* (1962), *Our Biggest Hits* (1964), *24 Original Hits* ('70s compilation).

DURAN DURAN

New Wave group, formed Birmingham, 1980: Simon Le Bon (vocals), John Taylor (bass), Andy Taylor (guitar), Roger Taylor (drums), Nick Rhodes (synthesizer). Supported Hazel O'Connor on nationwide tour. Part of NEW ROMANTICS scene centred on Rum Runner Club, Birmingham. Debut 'Planet Earth' (early 1981) a huge hit, followed by 'Save a Prayer', others; promoted by lavish videos shot on location in Sri Lanka. LPs *Duran Duran* (1981), *Rio* (1982).

DYLAN, BOB

Vocal/harmonica/guitar/songwriter, *b.* Duluth (Minnesota), 24/5/41 (r.n. Robert Allen Zimmerman). Moved to New York, 1960; sang in folk clubs. Signed to Columbia; first LP *Bob Dylan* (1962). Influences then embraced country blues, old-time music, WOODY GUTHRIE. *The Freewheelin' Bob Dylan* (1963), all own songs, established him in vanguard of folk-protest movement, but *Another Side of Bob Dylan* (1964) more personal; *Bringing It All Back Home, Highway 61 Revisited* (both 1965) revolutionary electric works. Toured Britain with the Hawks (later THE BAND) to mixed response, 1966. Motorcycle accident, August 1966; retired for two years. *The Basement Tapes*, with The Band, recorded 1967 (not released until 1975). *John Wesley Harding* (1968) announced comeback; then country-flavoured *Nashville Skyline* (1969). After *New Morning* (1970), became a recluse; worked occasionally on others' records. Wrote score for and appeared in film *Pat Garrett and Billy the Kid* (1973). Signed to Asylum, 1973; toured with The Band, producing *Before the Flood* (live double), 1974. *Blood on the Tracks* (1975) reaffirmed his powers. US tour with Rolling Thunder Revue, including JOAN BAEZ, Roger McGuinn, 1976; *Desire* (1976) topped US/UK charts. Extensive European tour, 1976. *Slow Train Coming* (1979), *Saved* (1980) reflect commitment to born-again Christianity. Other LPs include *The Times They Are a-Changin'* (1964); *Blonde on Blonde* (1966, double);

Self-Portrait (1970, double); *Dylan* (1973); *Planet Waves* (1974); *Hard Rain* (1976); *Street Legal* (1978); *At Budokan* (1978, live double), *Shot of Love* (1981).

EAGLES, THE

Country-rock group, formed Los Angeles, 1971. Original line-up: Glenn Frey (guitar/vocal), Bernie Leadon (guitar/vocal), Randy Meisner (bass/vocal), Don Henley (drums/vocal). Experienced country-rock players, had Top 20 hits with debut *The Eagles* (1972), *Desperado* (1973). Guitarist Don Felder joined for *On the Border* (1974). *One of These Nights* (1975) established band in UK also. Leadon replaced by Joe Walsh (former solo artist and James Gang founder), 1976. *Hotel California* (1976), *The Long Run* (1979), *Eagles Live* (1980), *Greatest Hits 2* (1982) all topped US charts. Meisner quit for solo career; Henley and Frey have released *I Can't Stand Still* and *No Fun Aloud* (both 1982) respectively.

EDMUNDS, DAVE

Vocal/guitar, *b.* Cardiff (Wales), 15/4/44. Joined Love Sculpture, 1968, scoring Top Ten hit with 'Sabre Dance'. First solo hit, 1970, 'I Hear You Knocking'. Member of Rockpile, 1977-80, with NICK LOWE; they recorded only one LP under this name, *Seconds of Pleasure* (1980), but each performed on the other's solo albums. Edmunds' hit singles include 'Girls Talk', 'Queen of Hearts'. Has also produced albums by the Stray Cats, Flamin' Groovies, Dr Feelgood, others. LPs *Subtle As a*

Flying Mallet (1975), *Get It* (1977), *Tracks on Wax* (1978), *Repeat When Necessary* (1979), *Twangin'* (1981), *D. E. 7* (1982).

ELECTRIC LIGHT ORCHESTRA

Art-rock band, formed as parallel group to the Move, 1971, when Jeff Lynne (from the Idle Race) joined last remaining Move members Roy Wood (guitar/vocal) and Bev Bevan (drums). ELO originally Wood's brainchild but he left after *Electric Light Orchestra* (1971) to form Wizzard. Lynne and Bevan put together new group for *ELO II* (1973), employing both rock and classical musicians. Concentrated on US market, toured regularly; *Eldorado* (1974), *Face the Music* (1975) consolidated success there. 'Evil Woman' from *A New World Record* (1976) rekindled UK popularity. Line-up settled as: Lynne, Bevan, Richard Tandy (keyboards), Mik Kaminski (violin), Hugh McDowell (cello), Melvyn Gale (cello) and Kelly Groucutt (bass). Subsequent singles and albums international best-sellers. Other LPs include *Out of the Blue* (1977), *Discovery* (1979), *Greatest Hits* (1979), *Time* (1981).

ELEKTRA RECORDS

Formed October 1950 by Jac Holzman with budget of $600. By mid-'50s a specialist folk and blues label with, e.g., Josh White, Theodore Bikel; in '60s added Tom Paxton, Phil Ochs, Judy Collins. Project albums explored worlds of blues, guitar jams, and psychedelia. In folk-rock boom signed BUTTERFIELD BLUES BAND, LOVE, the DOORS, the Stooges, MC5, Clear Light. Holzman relinquished presidency, 1973; label submerged in Asylum, marketed by Warner Brothers.

EMERSON, LAKE & PALMER

Techno-rock group, formed 1969: Keith Emerson (keyboards) from the Nice; Greg Lake (bass/guitar/vocal) from KING CRIMSON; Carl Palmer (drums) from Atomic Rooster. Debut at Isle of Wight Festival, 1970. Immediate success in both UK and US with *Emerson, Lake & Palmer* (1970). Subsequent LPs *Tarkus* (1971), *Pictures at an Exhibition* (1971), *Trilogy* (1972), *Brain Salad Surgery* (1973, first for own label Manticore), *Welcome Back My Friends* (1974), *Works, Vol 1* (1977), *Works, Vol 2* (1977), *Love Beach* (1978), *In Concert* (1979). Officially disbanded 1980. Lake's solo single 'I Believe in Father Christmas'

(originally 1975) regularly charts at Xmas season. Lake now member of Asia.

ENO, BRIAN

Synthesizer / composer / producer. Founder-member of ROXY MUSIC; went solo, 1973. First LP *No Pussyfootin'* (ISLAND, 1974) collaboration with ROBERT FRIPP. Worked with Phil Manzanera (of Roxy Music), JOHN CALE, ROBERT WYATT, launched own Obscure Records, all 1975. Another Fripp collaboration, *Evening Star*, 1976. Worked with DAVID BOWIE, 1976 on; with TALKING HEADS (*Remain in Light*), 1980; with David Byrne of Talking Heads (*My Life in the Bush of Ghosts*), 1981. A great influence on '70s and '80s electric pop. Other LPs include *Here Come the Warm Jets* (1974), *Taking Tiger Mountain by Strategy* (1975), *Another Green World* (1975), *Discreet Music* (1975), *Before and After Science* (1977), *Music for Airports* (1978), *Music for Films* (1978).

EPSTEIN, BRIAN

Manager of the BEATLES, *b.* Liverpool, 19/9/34; *d.* from pills overdose, 27/8/67. Former RADA student, ran record department of family's NEMS store in Liverpool; sought out Beatles at Cavern Club after requests from customers for Beatles discs. Took charge of bookings, secured record contract with Parlophone; masterminded their UK and US breakthrough but drifted apart from group after their decision to stop touring, 1966. Formed NEMS Enterprises management agency, saw chart success with Cilla Black, Gerry & the Pacemakers, Cliff Bennett & the Rebel Rousers, others. He died just as Beatles had seemingly rejected his management in favour of career guidance from Maharishi Mahesh Yogi.

EVERLY BROTHERS, THE

Guitar/vocal: Don, *b.* Brownie (Kentucky), 1/2/37; Phil, *b.* Chicago, 19/1/39. Developed parents' country-music heritage into masterly succession of pop-rock harmony

hits, 1957-65. Personal and professional problems led to split, 13/7/73. Phil charted in duet with CLIFF RICHARD, 'She Means Nothing to Me' (1983). LPs *The Everly Brothers* (1958), *The Fabulous Style of* (1960), *Walk Right Back with* (1975 compilation of 1960-5).

FAIRPORT CONVENTION

Folk-rock group, formed Muswell Hill (London), 1967. Original line-up: Judy Dyble (vocal), Ian Matthews (vocal), Richard Thompson (guitar), Simon Nicol (guitar), Ashley Hutchings (bass), Martin Lamble (drums); recorded *Fairport Convention* (1968). Sandy Denny replaced Dyble for *What We Did on Our Holidays* (1969). Matthews left to form own group (and later Matthews' Southern Comfort). *Unhalfbricking, Liege and Lief* (both 1969) featured Dave Swarbrick (fiddle), Dave Mattacks (drums, replacing deceased Lamble). Denny and Hutchings left to form Fotheringay and Steeleye Span respectively; Dave Pegg (bass) brought in. Thompson quit after *Full House* (1970), Nicol and Mattacks after

Angel Delight (1971). Subsequent LPs dominated by Swarbrick and Pegg: *Babbacombe Lee* (1971), *Rosie* (1973), *Nine* (1973), *Bonny Bunch of Roses* (1977). *History of* (1972) is compilation of first five years.

FAMILY

Underground rock group, formed Leicester, 1966. Original line-up included Roger Chapman (vocal), Jim King (reeds), Charlie Whitney (guitar), Rick Grech (bass/violin), Rob Townsend (drums). First LP *Music in a Doll's House* (1968) firmly established group on London Underground scene. After *Family Entertainment* (1969) Grech and King quit, replaced by John Weider, John Palmer respectively; Weider replaced by John Wetton (bass), 1971. Made *Fearless* (1971), *Bandstand* (1972). Wetton and Palmer replaced by Jim Cregan (guitar/bass), Tony Ashton (keyboards), 1972. Made *It's Only a Movie* (1973), then split. Chapman, Whitney later formed Streetwalkers.

FENDER, LEO

Guitar and amplifier designer and engineer, *b.* California, 1907. Developed with others world's first commercially-produced solid electric guitar, the Broadcaster, 1948 (renamed Telecaster, 1950). Also introduced the electric bass guitar, the Precision, 1951; and the Stratocaster, 1954, incorporating tremolo-arm unit. Sold out to CBS, 1965, later producing guitar and amplifier designs for the Music Man (1972) and G&L (1980) companies.

FLEETWOOD MAC

Pop-rock band, formed as Peter Green's Fleetwood Mac, London, 1967. Original line-up: Peter Green (vocal/guitar), Jeremy Spencer (vocal/slide guitar), John McVie (bass), Mick Fleetwood (drums). Debut album *Fleetwood Mac* (1968), UK No 1, in charts for over a year. 'Albatross' (1968) also UK No 1; reissued in 1973, made No 2. Green left 1970; replaced by Christine Perfect (now McVie) from Chicken Shack (keyboards/vocal). Danny Kirwan (guitar) had joined in 1967; while Bob Welch filled in on departure of Spencer, 1971. Over next four years line-up featured other musicians, including Bob Weston (guitar). Current line-up, dating from 1975: Fleetwood, John McVie, Christine McVie, Lindsey Buckingham (guitar), Stevie Nicks

(vocal). Made *Fleetwood Mac* (1975); *Rumours* (1976) sold over 20 million copies. Other LPs *Tusk* (1979), *Live* (1980), *Mirage* (1982).

FLYING BURRITO BROTHERS

Country-rock band, formed 1968 by GRAM PARSONS, Chris Hillman (bass/guitar, of the BYRDS), Sneaky Pete Kleinow (pedal steel), Chris Ethridge (bass), also session men. *The Gilded Palace of Sin* (1968), *Burrito Deluxe* (1970) marked essence of Burritos' country style. Parsons left, 1970. Constant line-up changes followed. LPs include *Last of the Red Hot Burritos* (1972), *Flying Again* (1975), *Airborne* (1976).

FOUR SEASONS, THE

Vocal group, ex-Variatones (1953-5), ex-Four Lovers (1956-60), converted by producer Bob Crewe into Four Seasons, 1961, by then comprising lead singer Frankie Valli (*b.* Newark, New Jersey, 3/5/37), Bob Gaudio, Nick Massi, Tommy De-Vito. Immense success with falsetto-led hits, e.g. 'Sherry', 'Big Girls Don't Cry', 'Walk Like a Man', 1962-6. Valli's solo career waxed bright as group waned, 1967-75. Comeback in mid-'70s. LP *The Four Seasons Story* (1975).

FOUR TOPS, THE

Vocal group, formed Detroit (Michigan), 1954, as the Four Aims. Original, and constant, line-up: Levi Stubbs Jr (lead), Abdul Fakir, Renaldo Benson, Lawrence Payton. Low-key career until joining MOTOWN RECORDS as Four Tops, 1964. Mammoth success, mainly supervised by Holland-Dozier-Holland, 1964-7; gradual decline with other writer/producers, 1968-72. Intermittent success with other companies until chart return in 1981. LPs *The Four Tops Story 1964-72* (1973), *Tonight* (1981).

FRAMPTON, PETER

Vocal/guitar, *b.* Beckenham (Kent), 22/4/50. Came to notice with the Herd, late '60s. With Steve Marriott (vocal/guitar), Greg Ridley (bass), Jerry Shirley (drums) formed Humble Pie, 1968. Most successful LP *Rock On* (1971). Left same year to go solo; made *Wind of Change*, 1972. Formed Frampton's Camel, made eponymous LP, 1973; disbanded, 1974. *Frampton Comes Alive* (1975, live double) enormous US hit, spawning several hit singles during 1976. Later LPs *I'm in You*

(1977), *Where I Should Be* (1979), *Breaking All the Rules* (1981).

FRANCIS, CONNIE
Vocal, *b.* Newark (New Jersey), 12/12/38 (*r.n.* Constance Franconero). Powerful singer, enjoyed many singles hits, 1957-66, e.g. 'Who's Sorry Now', 'Lipstick on Your Collar', 'Stupid Cupid', 'Everybody's Somebody's Fool'. Thereafter lost ground, turned to nightclub work and middle-aged audience. Made comebacks 1974, 1978.

FRANKLIN, ARETHA
Vocal/keyboards, *b.* Memphis (Tennessee), 25/3/42. Queen of (late-'60s) Soul. Like SOLOMON BURKE, a gospel star from age of nine; recorded gospel, 1956-9. Encouraged by SAM COOKE, pursued secular career; minimal success, 1960-5, until sympathetically recorded by ATLANTIC RECORDS. Great hits, 1966-8; troubled life and career, 1969-70; rejuvenation with King Curtis band, 1971; then gradual decline. LPs include *Aretha's Gold* (1968 compilation), *Live at Fillmore West* (1971), *Best of* ('70s compilation).

FREE/BAD COMPANY
Hard-rock bands: Free formed 1968; became popular club-circuit blues group, charting with 'All Right Now', 'My Brother Jake' (both 1970). Original line-up: Paul Rodgers (vocal), Paul Kossof (guitar; *d.* 19/3/76), Andy Fraser (bass), Simon Kirke (drums). Made *Tons of Sobs* (1969), *Free* (1969), *Fire & Water* (1970) *Highway* (1970), *Live* (1971). Split, early 1971; reformed, 1972, recording *Free at Last* (1972), *Heartbreaker* (1973), latter without Fraser and, partly, without Kossof. Rodgers and Kirke re-emerged in BAD COMPANY, 1974, joined by Mick Ralphs (guitar, from MOTT THE HOOPLE), Boz Burrell (bass). Instant success in US. LPs *Bad Company* (1974), *Straight Shooter* (1975), *Run With the Pack* (1976), *Burnin' Sky* (1977), *Desolation Angel* (1979).

FREED, ALAN
Promoter/DJ, *b.* Johnstown (Pennsylvania), 15/12/22; *d.* Palm Springs (Florida), 20/1/65. Started in radio, 1942; to station WJW, Cleveland (Ohio), 1951. Presented *Moondog's Rock 'n' Roll Party*, playing R&B to rapidly growing audience. To New York, 1954, hosting *Rock 'n' Roll Party* on station WINS. Boosted black music, black artists against competition of white cover versions.

Promoted hugely popular concerts. Appeared in films *Rock Around the Clock* (1956), *Don't Knock the Rock* (1956), *Rock, Rock, Rock* (1957). Career wrecked by payola investigation; fined and given suspended sentence, 1962.

FRIPP, ROBERT
Guitar/producer/writer, *b.* Wimborne (Dorset), 1946. First group Giles, Giles & Fripp, 1967; moved to London, formed KING CRIMSON, 1969-74, 1981; produced album for experimental studio band Centipede (1971). Withdrew from musical activity 1974-7. Undertook solo projects, sessions, 1977-81, including work and collaborations with DAVID BOWIE (1977), BLONDIE, BRIAN ENO, Peter Gabriel (1977), TALKING HEADS (1979). Solo projects include self-styled 'Frippertronies' guitar/tape-recorder creations; production includes Daryl Hall, the Roches. Solo LPs *No Pussyfooting* (1973, with Eno), *Exposure* (1979), *God Save the Queen/Under Heavy Manners* (1980), *Let the Power Fall* (1981), *I Advance Masked* (1982, with Andy Summers).

GALLAGHER, RORY
Vocal/guitar, *b.* Ballyshannon, Co. Donegal (Ireland), raised in Cork. Formed blues band Taste, 1966, with Charlie McCracken (bass), John Wilson (drums). Broke into UK circuit, 1969. LPs *Taste* (1969), *On the Boards* (1970), *Live Taste* (1971), *Live at the Isle of Wight* (1972). Gallagher released *Rory Gallagher*, first solo album, 1971; subsequent LPs in his name. Specializes in small groups. *Blueprint* (1973) expanded his following to Europe and US. Selected LPs *Irish Tour '74* (1974; filmed by Tony Palmer as documentary), *Calling Card* (1976), *Photo Finish* (1978), *Stage Struck* (1980).

GAYE, MARVIN
Vocal, *b.* Washington (D.C.) 2/4/39. Sang with the Rainbows and the Marquees, late '50s, before being signed as session drummer to MOTOWN RECORDS. Later, as solo artist, had string of US R&B hits culminating in 'I Heard It Through the Grapevine' (1968), No 1 in US and UK. Move to disco sophistication has only increased Gaye's following. LPs *What's Going On* (1971), *Let's Get It On* (1973), *Marvin Gaye Live* (1974), *I Want You* (1976), *Here My Dear* (1980), *Midnight Love* (1982).

GENESIS
Art-rock band, founded mid-'60s. Original line-up: Peter Gabriel (vocal), Tony Banks (keyboards), Mike Rutherford (bass). Recorded *From Genesis to Revelation* (1969), *Trespass* (1970); then joined by Phil Collins (drums), Steve Hackett (guitar). Steadily built strong UK and US following with *Nursery Cryme* (1971), *Foxtrot* (1972), *Live* (1973), *Selling England by the Pound* (1973), *The Lamb Lies Down on Broadway* (1974). Gabriel left, 1975; Collins took over as singer; writing duties, which Gabriel had dominated, now shared. Group's success continued with *A Trick of the Tail* (1976), *Wind and Wuthering* (1976), *Seconds Out* (1977), *And Then There Were Three* (1978, following Hackett's departure), *Duke* (1980) and *Abacab* (1981). All three have also released solo material; Collins has worked with jazz-rock outfit Brand X, and also produced.

GIBSON

Guitar company founded by Orville Gibson (1856-1918), Kalamazoo (Michigan), 1902. Original reputation grew from excellence of carved-topped guitars and mandolins; more recently name synonymous with top quality guitars widely used in rock. Innovations include ES150 semi-acoustic guitar (1935) and LES PAUL model (1952), reissued in late '60s after use by blues-rock guitarists created renewed demand. Company is still in production.

GRATEFUL DEAD, THE

Acid-rock band, formed 1965 (originally the Warlocks). Line-up: Jerry Garcia (guitar/vocal), Bob Weir (guitar/vocal), Phil Lesh (bass), Ron 'Pig Pen' McKernan (harmonica/organ; d. 8/3/73), Bill Kreutzman (drums). Later added Mickey Hart (drums), Tom Constanten (organ). Line-up augmented 1973 by Keith (piano) and Donna (vocal) Godchaux, who left in late '70s; latest keyboards player is Brent Mydland. Many offshoot bands; all members have undertaken extensive solo and session work. LPs include *The Grateful Dead* (1966), *Anthem of the Sun* (1967), *Aoxomoxoa* (1968), *Workingman's Dead, Live Dead, American Beauty* (all 1970), *Wake of the Flood* (1973), *Blues for Allah* (1975), *Terrapin Station* (1976), *Shakedown Street* (1978), *Wake of the Flood* (1979), *Reckoning, Dead Set* (both 1981). Garcia has recorded solo and with Merle Saunders, Howard Wales, JEFFERSON STARSHIP; Bob Weir formed Kingfish, 1975, and later Bobby & the Midnites; Hart worked on soundtrack of *Apocalypse Now;* Lesh works with electronic artist Ned Lagin.

GREEN, AL

Vocal, *b.* Forest City (Alabama), 13/4/46. Sang with the Creations before turning solo, 1967. Signed to Willie Mitchell's Hi Records, Memphis, 1969. Respected soul artist. Soon established as best-selling singles and albums act. LPs include *Back Up Train* (1967), *Green Is Blues* (1969), *Al Green Gets Next to You* (1970), *Let's Stay Together* (1971), *I'm Still in Love with You* (1972), *Call Me* (1973), *Living for You* (1974), *Explores Your Mind* (1974), *Al Green Is Love* (1975), *Greatest Hits* (1975), *Full of Fire* (1976), *Have a Good Time* (1976), *The Belle Album* (1977), *Truth 'n' Time* (1979), *Precious Lord, Higher Plane* (both 1982).

GUTHRIE, WOODY

Vocal/harmonica/guitar/songwriter, *b.* Okemah (Oklahoma), 14/7/12; *d.* Queens (New York), 3/10/67. Country singer, late '30s; became songwriter, political activist, 1939 on; father of Arlo. Recorded for Library of Congress, 1940; for various New York labels, '40s to early '50s, often in company of blues artists Leadbelly, Sonny Terry & Brownie McGhee, or country singer Cisco Houston. Poet of dispossessed, author of 'This Land Is Your Land', 'Pastures of Plenty', 'So Long, It's Been Good to Know You', many others; also children's songs. Described Okie migration from Southwest (late '30s) in song-cycle *Dust Bowl Ballads.* Enormous influence on BOB DYLAN, JOAN BAEZ, most of US folk movement in '50s-'60s. Incapacitated by nervous disease from mid-'50s. Subject of film *Bound for Glory* (1976); of book, *Woody Guthrie: A Life,* by Joe Klein (1981). Selected LPs *Dust Bowl Ballads* (originally recorded 1940, often reissued, also as *A Legendary Performer*), *This Land Is Your Land,* most others on Folkways.

HALEY, BILL

Guitar/vocal, *b.* Highland Park (Michigan), 6/7/25; *d.* Harlingen (Texas), 9/2/81. First rock 'n' roll star. Country and Western Swing artist until gradual incorporation of R&B into sound, 1951-3. New style consolidated with new record deal, 1954; international breakthrough and colossal success, 1955-7, with the Comets: (best known line-up) Rudy Pompilli (saxophone), Johnny Grande (piano/accordion), Fran Beecher (lead guitar), Billy Williamson (steel guitar), Al Rex (bass), Ralph Jones (drums). LPs *A Tribute to* (1981 compilation of 1954-9), *Rockin' Rollin'* (definitive 5-LP box set).

HARRIS, EMMYLOU

Vocal/guitar, *b.* Birmingham (Alabama), 1947. Unsuccessful folk and country singer until she met GRAM PARSONS; worked with him on *G.P.* (1972), *Grievous Angel* (1973). After Parsons' death went solo; debut *Pieces of the Sky* (1975). Formed Hot Band, including JAMES BURTON. Backup vocalist with BOB DYLAN (*Desire,* 1976), LINDA RONSTADT, others. Albums moved away from country roots, then back with *Blue Kentucky*

Girl (1979), *Roses in the Snow* (1980). Later Hot Band members included Albert Lee, Ricky Skaggs. Other LPs *Elite Hotel* (1977), *Luxury Liner* (1977), *Quarter Moon in a Ten Cent Town* (1978), *Evangeline* (1981), *Last Date* (1982).

HARRISON, GEORGE

Guitar/vocal/songwriter with the BEATLES, *b.* Liverpool, 25/2/43. After group's breakup, *All Things Must Pass* (1970) revealed emergence from songwriting shadow of JOHN LENNON and PAUL MCCARTNEY; *Living in a Material World* (1973), *Dark Horse* (1974), *Extra Texture* (1975) showed similar preoccupation with Eastern values and Indian music. Organised and appeared in the Concert for Bangla Desh, New York (1972) to raise money for famine relief. Financed films (*Monty Python's Life of Brian, The Long Good Friday);* became a recluse, re-emerged with *George Harrison* (1979). *Somewhere in England* (1981) a homage to Liverpool roots in memory of John Lennon. Records for own label, Dark Horse.

HENDRIX, JIMI

Guitar/vocal, *b.* Seattle (Washington), 27/11/42; *d.* from inhalation of vomit, London, 18/9/70. One of the most creative guitarists in rock. Took electric guitar in new directions; used studio-treated sounds, feedback. First came to prominence in Jimi Hendrix Experience, 1966-9, after being 'discovered' in New York by Chas Chandler (of the ANIMALS) and brought to England. Initial recording and performances in UK led to wider acclaim in US, particularly after appearing at Monterey festival, 1967. Three LPs with the Experience *Are You Experienced* (1967), *Axis: Bold As Love* (1967), *Electric Ladyland* (1968). Performed at Woodstock festival, 1969; later formed Band of Gypsys. Selected posthumous LPs *Cry of Love* (1970), *Rainbow Bridge* (1971), *The Jimi Hendrix Concerts* (1982).

HOLLIES, THE
Pop-rock group, formed Manchester, 1962, from amalgamation of local groups Deltas and Dolphins. Line-up: Allan Clarke (vocal), Eric Haydock (bass), Tony Hicks (guitar), Graham Nash (rhythm guitar), Don Rathbone (drums). Rathbone replaced by Bobby Elliott from Shane Fenton's Fentones, 1964; Bernie Calvert replaced Haydock, 1966. Dispute over commercial direction caused Nash to leave, 1968; became part of Crosby, Stills & Nash (subsequently CROSBY, STILLS, NASH & YOUNG). Replaced by Terry Sylvester, ex-Swinging Blue Jeans. Clarke left for solo career 1971, replaced by Michael Rickfors; Clarke rejoined 1973. Always a singles rather than album band, but LPs *Evolution* and *Butterfly* (both 1967) notable.

HOLLY, BUDDY
Vocal/guitar, *b.* Lubbock (Texas), 7/9/36; *d.* in plane crash, Iowa, 3/2/59 (*r.n.* Charles Hardin Holley). Country artist, 1954-5, inspired by local shows by ELVIS PRESLEY to develop personalised variation of rock 'n' roll. First professionally recorded 1956; international success 1957-8, with the Crickets: best known line-up Joe Maudlin (bass), Jerry Allison (drums), earlier also featuring Son-

ny Curtis, then Niki Sullivan (guitar). Influential posthumous releases revealed wealth of demos. LPs *Buddy Holly Lives* (1978 hit compilation), *The Complete Buddy Holly* (definitive 6-LP box set).

HUMAN LEAGUE
Electro-disco group, formed Sheffield, 1977: Martyn Ware, Ian Craig Marsh, Phil Oakey (vocal). Adrian Wright (synthesizer/visual director) recruited, 1978. Signed to Fast Product, releasing 'Being Boiled' (1978, reissued 1982). Signed to VIRGIN, 1979, releasing *Reproduction* (1979), *Travelogue* (1980). Marsh and Ware left, 1980; Oakey recruited Joanne Catherall and Susanne Sulley (dancers/vocal), Ian Burden (keyboards). 'Love Action' (1981) a hit; 'Don't You Want Me' (1981), with Jo Callis (synthesizer), reached No 1, as did *Dare* (1981), 'Mirror Man' (1982).

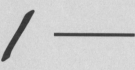

ISLAND RECORDS
Independent label formed by Chris Blackwell, a white Jamaican; London office set up, 1962. Distribution deal with US R&B label Sue, 1964, provided hits by JAMES BROWN, Bob & Earl, Inez & Charlie Foxx. First rock hit Traffic's 'Paper Sun' (1967). Subsequent signings included BOB MARLEY, FREE, JETHRO TULL, FAIRPORT CONVENTION, Cat Stevens, ROXY MUSIC and, more recently, GRACE JONES and Kid Creole & the Coconuts (see AUGUST DARNELL). Scored first US No 1 with 'Up Where We Belong' (1982) by JOE COCKER and Jennifer Warnes.

ISLEY BROTHERS, THE
Originally a Cincinnati (Ohio) vocal trio: lead singer Ronald (*b.* 21/5/41), Rudolph (*b.* 1/4/39), O'Kelly (*b.* 25/12/37). Recordings 1956-66 typified by 'Shout' (1959), 'Twist and Shout' (1962). Success on MOTOWN RECORDS, 1966-8 beginning with 'This Old Heart of Mine'. Revived own label, T-Neck, for progressive rock-soul hits (1969 on); singers augmented by younger brothers Ernie (lead guitar/percussion), Marvin (bass) and cousin Chris Jasper (keyboards). Success with *3+3* (1973) established pattern of annual follow-ups. Other LPs *Super Hits* ('70s compilation of 1966-8), *Timeless* (1978 compilation of 1969-72), *Forever Gold* (compilation of post-'72 hits).

JAM, THE
Mod-revival band, formed Woking (Surrey), in '70s. Original line-up: Bruce Foxton (bass), Paul Weller (vocal/guitar), Rick Buckler (drums). Breakthrough, 1976, with punk explosion, though neat haircuts, Rickenbacker guitars and allegiance to the WHO, KINKS, STONES made them uncharacteristic of period. Signed to Polydor, releasing 'In the City' (1977). Weathered demise of punk and Mod revival, producing many hit singles: 'Going Underground' (1981), 'A Town Called Malice' and 'Beat Surrender' (both 1982), all No 1s. Broke up, November 1982; Weller embarked on solo career. LPs *In the City, The Modern World* (both 1977), *All Mod Cons* (1978), *Setting Sons* (1979), *Sound Affects* (1980), *The Gift, Dig the New Breed* (both 1982).

JAMES, ELMORE
Vocal/guitar, *b.* Richland (Mississippi), 27/1/18; *d.* Chicago, 24/5/63. Early musical experience in Mississippi Delta area; moved to Chicago, *c.* 1952. Recorded for various small labels, 1952 on. Impassioned singer, slide guitarist, best known for 'Dust My Broom'; further developed work of ROBERT JOHNSON in 'Standing at the Crossroads'. Important model for British R&B bands of '60s. LPs *One Way Out* (1980), *The Best of Elmore James* (1981), *Got to Move* (1981) – all compilations of 1952-63.

JEFFERSON AIRPLANE/
STARSHIP
Acid-rock band, formed San Francisco, 1965. Original line-up: Signe Anderson (vocal), Jorma Kaukonen (guitar), Paul Kantner (guitar/vocal), Marty Balin (vocal), Jack Casady (bass), Skip Spence (drums). Debut LP *Takes Off* (1966) established band at forefront of Bay Area movement. Anderson replaced by Grace Slick, Spence by Spencer Dryden for *Surrealistic Pillow* (1967), including hits 'Somebody to Love', 'White Rabbit'. Balin left, 1970, but rejoined, 1974, for first Jefferson Starship. Kaukonen and Casady formed embryonic Hot Tuna, 1969, with veteran Papa John Creach (fiddle); finally left Airplane, 1972. Hot Tuna albums include *First Pull Up, Then Pull Down* (1971), *Burgers* (1973), *Double Dose*

(1978). Dryden replaced by Joey Covington, 1970. Kantner and Slick recorded, outside the group, *Blows Against the Empire* (1970), *Sunfighter* (1971), *Baron Von Tollbooth & the Chrome Nun* (1972). 1973 Starship line-up: Slick, Kantner, Balin, David Freiberg (bass), Creach, Johnny Barbata (drums), Pete Sears (bass), Craig Chaquico (guitar). Despite turbulent '70s history (Slick leaving on several occasions), Starship survived into '80s. Airplane LPs include *After Bathing at Baxters* (1968), *Crown of Creation* (1969), *Volunteers* (1970), *Long John Silver* (1972), *Thirty Seconds Over Winterland* (1973). Starship LPs include *Dragon Fly* (1974), *Red Octopus* (1975), *Spitfire* (1976), *Freedom at Point Zero* (1979), *Earth* (1980). Grace Slick solo: *Welcome to the Wrecking Ball* (1981).

JETHRO TULL
Electric folk-rock group, formed London, 1968. Original line-up: Ian Anderson (flute/guitar/vocal), Mick Abrahams (guitar), Glenn Cornick (bass), Clive Bunker (drums). Initial performances and debut LP *This Was* (1968) caused sensation. Abrahams left, late 1968, to form Blodwyn Pig and continue blues direction Anderson no longer favoured; replaced by Martin Barre for *Stand Up* (1969). *Benefit* (1970) broke them in US. John Evans (keyboards) joined for *Aqualung* (1971); Cornick replaced by John Glasscock (bass), Bunker by Barriemore Barlow (drums): this line-up remains. LPs include *Thick As a Brick* (1972), *Passion Play* (1973), *War Child* (1974), *Minstrel in the Gallery* (1975), *Songs from the Wood* (1977), *Heavy Horses* (1978), *Stormwatch* (1979). (Below: Ian Anderson)

J. GEILS BAND
Rock 'n' roll band, formed Boston, 1969, as J. Geils Blues Band, later J. Geils Band Original line-up: Peter Wolf (vocal), J. Geils (guitar), Magic Dick (*r.n.* Richard Salwitz; harmonica), Stephen Jo Bladd (drums), Seth Justman (keyboards), Daniel Klein (bass). (Maintained to present day.) LPs include *J. Geils Band* (1971), *The Morning After* (1972), *Bloodshot* (1973), *Blow Your Face Out* (1976), *Centrefold* (1982).

JOHN, ELTON
Vocal/piano/composer, *b.* Pinner (Middlesex) 25/3/47 (*r.n.* Reginald Dwight). Pianist with R&B band Bluesology at age 14; took office job with song publishers Dick James Music while writing songs in spare time with lyricist Bernie Taupin. Became full-time songwriting team, wrote for Cilla Black, Eurovision Song Contest heats; also undertook session work. Signed by James's label DJM, 1969: *Empty Sky* (1969), *Elton John* (1970) big critical successes, inspired singer/songwriter vogue of early '70s. *Don't Shoot Me, I'm Only the Piano Player* (1973) signalled end of cult status, beginning of acceptance as superstar; developed extravagant tongue-in-cheek stage personality in keeping with new role. *Goodbye Yellow Brick Road* (1973), *Captain Fantastic and the Brown Dirt Cowboy* (1975) explored early days as struggling songwriter; started Rocket label, 1974, with self and Kiki Dee main acts. Cut down drastically on touring and recording after 1977, when elected chairman Watford Football Club; broke up partnership with Bernie Taupin, same year, to write with Gary Osborne.

JOHNSON, ROBERT
Vocal/guitar, *b.* Hazlehurst (Mississippi), prob. 8/5/11; *d.* (murdered) Greenwood (Mississippi), 16/8/38. Intinerant musician in '30s, travelled widely; crossed paths of many other blues artists, including ELMORE JAMES, Howlin' Wolf, Johnny Shines. Recorded 29 blues for ARC, 1936-7: most influential body of work in blues history. Versatile, innovative guitarist; singer of great passion and directness. Vast influence upon postwar blues and rock musicians, e.g. ERIC CLAPTON, JIMI HENDRIX, TAJ MAHAL, JOHNNY WINTER. Entire repertoire reissued on *King of the Delta Blues Singers* (1961), *King of the Delta Blues Singers Volume II* (1970).

JONES, GRACE
Vocal, *b.* Jamaica. Moved to New York to become a model, then to Paris. Svengali-figure Jean-Paul Goude fashioned image of black amazonian goddess, sexy and androgynous. Signed to ISLAND, releasing 'I Need a Man'; became queen of New York's Studio 54 high-society scene with version of classic 'La Vie en Rose'. Known for brilliantly designed stage sets, costumes; shows are more theatrical events than gigs. LPs *Portfolio* (1977), *Fame* (1978), *Warm Leatherette* (1980), *Nightclubbing* (1981), *Living My Life* (1982).

JOPLIN, JANIS
Vocal, *b.* Port Arthur (Texas), 19/1/43; *d.* of drug overdose 4/10/70. Had blues and bluegrass act in early '60s before joining San Francisco's Big Brother & the Holding Company: Sam Andrew (guitar), James Gurley (guitar), Pete Albin (bass), David Getz (drums). Debut LP *Big Brother & the Holding Company* (1967). Came to real fame at Monterey Pop Festival (1967). After *Cheap Thrills* (1968) went solo, later fronting her Full Tilt Boogie Band: John Till (guitar), Ken Pearson (organ), Richard Bell (piano), Brad Campbell (bass), Clark Pierson (drums). Died before release of *Pearl* (1971), which included posthumous No 1 US single 'Me and Bobby McGee'. Documentary film *Janis* released, 1974. Other LPs *I Got Dem Ole Kozmic Blues Again Mama!* (1969), *In Concert* (1972), *Greatest Hits* (1973), *Janis* (soundtrack 1975).

JORDAN, LOUIS
Saxophone/vocal/bandleader, *b.*

Brinkley (Arkansas), 8/7/08; d. Los Angeles, 4/2/75. With Chick Webb's band, 1936-8. Formed own Tympany Five, gradually adapted swing and blues, 1939-41, into very influential prototype urban R&B. Solid success, 1942-50, typified by 'Caldonia' (1945), 'Choo Choo Ch'Boogie' (1946). Outpaced by successors during R&B-to-rock era; continued to record and tour sporadically until his death. LP *The Best of* ('70s compilation of '40s hits), *Choo Choo Ch'Boogie* ('70s compilation of '50s 'rock' re-recorded hits).

JOY DIVISION
New Wave group, formed Manchester, (England), 1977: Bernard Albrecht (guitar), Stephen Morris (drums), Peter Hook (bass), Ian Curtis (vocals). Matured into purveyors of intensely introverted Gothic gloom. Signed to Factory, released *Unknown Pleasures*, which topped independent label charts, 1979; follow-up *Closer* (1980). Curtis committed suicide, May 1980. Uncharacteristically commercial 'Love Will Tear Us Apart' (1980) and double live album *Still* (1981) consolidated success. Carried on as three-piece, renamed New Order.

KID CREOLE: *see* DARNELL, AUGUST

KING, B. B.
Vocal/guitar, *b.* Indianola (Mississippi), 16/9/25 (*r.n.* Riley B. King). Sang with gospel quartets, early '40s. Moved to Memphis, 1946; worked locally with BOBBY 'BLUE' BLAND, Sonny Boy Williamson, others. Own radio show, 1949-50; DJ on black-owned station WDIA, 1950-3. Recorded for regional labels, 1949-61; R&B hits with 'Three o'Clock Blues' (1952), 'You Upset Me Baby' (1954), 'Sweet Little Angel' (1956), others. Signed to ABC, 1962. Made classic *Live at the Regal*, 1965. Incessant nationwide touring throughout '60s; exposed to rock audience, emerged as leading figure in blues in '70s. Numerous European tours. Pop hit with 'The Thrill Is Gone', 1969; made *Indianola Mississippi Seeds* with rock musicians, including CAROLE KING, 1970. Subsequent LPs alternated between familiar blues and new, often nonblues, material. Most influential of

modern blues artists, on contemporaries and younger artists alike. Selected LPs *The Best of B. B. King* (1981 reissue of 1956 LP) *Live and Well* (1969), *Love Me Tender* (1982). *The Great B. B. King* (1978) is good '60s-'70s hits collection.

KING, CAROLE
Vocal/composer, *b.* New York, 9/2/42 (*r.n.* Carole Klein). Joined Aldon Music publishing firm from high school, teamed up with future husband Gerry Goffin to write pop songs full-time. Wrote for DRIFTERS, Dusty Springfield, Tony Orlando, Bobby Vee, Shirelles, many others; also recorded for Aldon-owned label Dimension and arranged and produced tracks for other acts. Moved to California, 1966, contributed songs to Monkees TV shows. Returned to recording with *Writer* (1970) and multi-million selling *Tapestry* (1971), both featuring more personal style of songwriting. Became leading early-'70s singer-songwriter. Next to JOHN LENNON and PAUL MCCARTNEY, the most recorded songwriter in rock music.

KING CRIMSON
Art-rock band, formed London, 1969, from nucleus of Bournemouth-based musicians: ROBERT FRIPP (guitar/mellotron), Ian McDonald (reeds/keyboards), Greg Lake (bass/vocal), Mike Giles (drums), Pete Sinfield (lyrics/synthesizer). In this form cut only one LP, *In the Court of the Crimson King* (1969). Among musicians who passed through group: Gordon Haskell (brass/vocal), Mel Collins (reeds), Boz Burrell (bass/vocal), Bill Bruford (drums), John Wetton (bass). LPs *In the Wake of Poseidon* (1970), *Lizard* (1970), *Islands* (1971), *Earthbound* (1972, recorded live on tour in US), *Lark's Tongues in Aspic* (1973), *Starless and Bible Black* (1974), *Red* (1974), *USA* (1975, also live). Fripp himself compiled double compilation *A Young Person's Guide to King Crimson* (1975). In 1981 Fripp released a further LP as King Crimson, *Discipline,* featuring Bill Bruford and Adrian Belew (ex-TALKING HEADS), then *Beat* (1982).

KING RECORDS
Independent label, founded by Sydney Nathan, Cincinnati (Ohio), 1944. Quickly established itself as leading urban blues/R&B company with Roy Brown, JAMES BROWN, Earl Bostic, Freddy King, others. Also important country, Western Swing,

bluegrass, and rockabilly label: Delmore Brothers, Hank Penny, Moon Mullican, others. Subsidiaries included DeLuxe, Federal. Major hit with Bill Doggett's 'Honky Tonk', 1956. Influential in genre markets until mid-'60s. Catalogue sold to Starday, subsequently Gusto, which has reissued much vintage material.

KINKS, THE
R&B/pop group, formed London, 1962, by brothers Ray (vocal/guitar) and Dave Davies (lead guitar). Joined Pete Quaife (bass), Mick Avory (drums), 1963, to back blues singer Robert Wace. Moved from primitive R&B style to quaint, ironic Ray Davies songs about suburban life; became astute commentators on 'Swinging London' scene. After 1967, forsook singles for concept albums *The Village Green Preservation Society* (1968), *Arthur* (1969, first conceived as TV musical), *Lola Versus Powerman and the Moneygoround* (1970), *Everbody's in Showbiz — Everybody's a Star* (1972). Augmented by John Gosling (keyboards), Laurie Brown (trumpet), Alan Holmes (saxophone), John Beecham (trombone), 1971 onwards. Formed own Konk label, 1974. Later albums *Preservation Act 1* (1973), *Preservation Act 2* (1974), *Soap Opera* (1975), *Schoolboys in Disgrace* (1976), *Sleepwalker* (1977), *One for the Road* (live album, 1980).

KNIGHT, GLADYS, & THE PIPS
Vocal, *b.* Atlanta (Georgia), 28/5/44. Child gospel/secular star. Pips formed in 1952: brother Merald, cousins William & Elenor Guest; Elenor later replaced by cousin Edward Patten. Smalltime act, 1952-

60; recording stars of 'chittlin circuit', 1961-6; breakthrough with MOTOWN RECORDS, 1967-73. Continuing success, occasionally without Pips. LPs *Teen Anguish* (1981 compilation of 1961-6), *Anthology* (1973 compilation of 1967-73), *Memories of the Way We Were* (1979 compilation of 1973-9).

KOOPER, AL
Keyboards/guitar, *b.* New York, 5/2/44. Had hit, 'Short Shorts', with Royal Teens, 1958. Became writer, session musician. Played organ on BOB DYLAN's 'Like a Rolling Stone' (1965), *Highway 61 Revisited* (1965), *Blonde on Blonde* (1966), *New Morning* (1970); guested on Dylan's Rolling Thunder Revue, late Seventies. Formed Blues Project with Steve Katz; selected original Blood, Sweat & Tears and produced/played on debut *Child Is Father to the Man* (1968). Involved in supersession projects: *Super Session* (1968) with Mike Bloomfield and Stephen Stills, *The Live Adventures of Al Kooper and Mike Bloomfield* (1969). Despite string of solo albums, better known as highly regarded session musician and producer with JIMI HENDRIX, Nils Lofgren, TOM PETTY, TAJ MAHAL, the Tubes, Lynyrd Skynyrd, others.

KORNER, ALEXIS
Vocal/guitar, *b.* Paris (France), 1928. Played with Chris Barber Jazz Band in Forties (and subsequently). Worked with English singer/harmonica-player Cyril Davies, with whom formed Blues Incorporated 1961. Pioneered British R&B club circuit, early Sixties. Many associates went on to rock careers, e.g. Charlie Watts, Mick Jagger, Eric Burdon, Paul Jones, Ginger Baker, Graham Bond, JOHN MCLAUGHLIN. Led series of bands, late '60s-early '70s; CCS, produced by MICKIE MOST, had several hits, 1970-1. Generally more popular in Europe than UK. Latterly has worked as DJ, TV presenter, voice of many TV commercials. LP: some early material on *The Great British Rhythm & Blues Barrelhouse and Boogie Bonanza 1962-68* (1982 compilation).

KRAFTWERK
Electro-disco band, formed by Ralf Hutter (vocal/keyboards/ synthesizers) and Florian Schneider (ditto) out of remnants of Organisation, of Düsseldorf (W. Germany), about 1971. Early albums influenced by John Cage and Stockhausen, reflecting industrial and urban life through electronic soundscapes. After *Ralf and Florian* (1973), had commercial success in US and UK with *Autobahn* (1974), having added Klaus Roeder (violin/guitar), Wolfgang Flur (percussion). Flur remained for *Radio Activity* (1975), then replaced by Karl Bartos. Inclined towards Euro-disco, with occasional tongue-in-cheek deadpan humour. 'The Model'/'Computer World' (1982) a No 1 hit. LPs *Kraftwerk* (1972), *Trans-Europe Express* (1977), *Man Machine* (1978), *Computer World* (1981).

LED ZEPPELIN
Heavy-metal band, formed 1968 by JIMMY PAGE on breakup of YARDBIRDS. Original line-up: Page, John Paul Jones (bass/keyboards), John Bonham (drums), Robert Plant (vocal). Instantly hugely successful, first in US, then UK and worldwide. LPs *Led Zeppelin I* (1969), *II* (1969), *III* (1970), *IV* (1971), *Houses of the Holy* (1973), *Physical Graffiti* (1975), *Presence* (1976), *The Song Remains the Same* (1976, double soundtrack

to film), *In Through the Out Door* (1979), *Coda* (1982). Bonham died September 1980. Plant released a solo LP (1982).

LEE, BRENDA
Vocal, *b.* Atlanta (Georgia), 11/12/44. Debut appearance at Ozark Mountain Jubilee, 1956; career nurtured by country star Red Foley. Became child-star after first hit, 'Sweet Nuthins' (1959); many transatlantic hits before chart decline in Beatle era. Retired 1967; reemerged in country music field (1971) with *Brenda*. Other albums (selective) *Memphis Portrait* (1970), *New Sunrise* (1974), *Now* (1975).

LEIBER & STOLLER
Songwriters/producers: Jerry Leiber (*b.* Baltimore, Maryland, 25/4/33) and Mike Stoller (*b.* New York), collaborators since 1949. Wrote countless blues/R&B numbers, initially for black artists. Signed to ATLANTIC as independent producers, 1955; handled the COASTERS, ISLEY BROTHERS, CLYDE MCPHATTER, DRIFTERS; formative influence as producers on PHIL SPECTOR, BURT BACHARACH. Worked with many other acts, black and white, for other labels, including ELVIS PRESLEY ('Jailhouse Rock'). Formed Red Bird/Blue Cat labels, 1964; had hits with Shangri-Las, Dixie Cups, others. Sold out; bought Starday/King, 1970, but had little success. Returned to production in '70s with Stealers Wheel, Procol Harum, Elkie Brooks. Relatively inactive since, but assured immortality for huge contribution to rock 'n' roll.

LENNON, JOHN
Vocal/guitar/songwriter with BEATLES until 1970 split, *b.* Liverpool, 9/10/40; *d.* (murdered) New York, 8/12/80. Became US resident from 1971, recorded solo and with wife Yoko Ono as Plastic Ono Band. Albums *Plastic Ono Band* (1970), *Imagine* (1971, produced by PHIL SPECTOR), *Sometime in New York City* (1972), *Mind Games* (1973). Successfully fought deportation order to become US citizen, 1975. Retired from recording scene after *Rock 'n' Roll* (1975); broke silence with *Double Fantasy* (1980).

LEWIS, JERRY LEE
Piano/vocal, *b.* Ferriday (Louisiana), 29/9/35. Second rock superstar of SUN RECORDS, 1956-63. Spectacular breakthrough (1957) preceded scandal and hard times until 'What'd I Say' (1961) and wildly acclaimed European tours (1962-3-4-6) led to revitalized career as country star, 1968-70s. Critically ill, July 1981; survives as rock 'n' roll legend. LPs *The Original JLL* (1976 compilation of Sun tracks); *The Essential JLL* (1978 compilation of Sun tracks), *The Sun Years* (definitive 12-LP box set, 1983), *Live at the Star Club* (1964), *The Greatest Live Show on Earth* (1964), *Vol. 2* (1966), *The Best of* (1970 compilation of 1968-70), *The Killer Rocks On* (1972).

LITTLE FEAT
Rock band, formed mid-1970. Original line-up: Lowell George (guitar/vocal), Roy Estrada (bass), Bill Payne (keyboards), Ritchie Hay-

ward (drums). Debut LP *Little Feat* (1970). After *Sailin' Shoes* (1972), Estrada joined CAPTAIN BEEFHEART; band expanded with Paul Barrere (guitar/vocal), Sam Clayton (congas/vocal), Kenny Gradney (bass/vocal). George, Hayward and Payne played as session musicians before recording *Feats Don't Fail Me Now* (1974). George went solo, made *Thanks I'll Eat It Here* (1978); died shortly after its release. Other LPs *Dixie Chicken* (1973), *The Last Record Album* (1975), *Time Loves a Hero* (1976), *Down on the Farm* (1978), *Hoy Hoy!* (1981).

LITTLE RICHARD
Piano/vocal, *b.* Macon (Georgia), 5/12/35 (*r.n.* Richard Penniman). The wildest rock 'n' roll originator. Regional notoriety, unexceptional R&B recordings, 1951-4; colossal success with great rock hits, 1955-7; retired to church, 1957; recorded gospel, 1959-62. Second successful career as rock 'n' roll legend, 1962-72; rapid deterioration until late-'70s return to church. LPs *Here's Little Richard, LR Vol. 2, The Fabulous LR, Well Alright!* (all four covering 1955-7), *Get Down with It* (1982 compilation of 1966-7).

LOVE
Psychedelic-rock group, formed Los Angeles, 1965: Arthur Lee (guitar/vocal), Bryan MacLean (guitar/vocal), John Echols (guitar), Ken Forssi (bass), Don Conka (drums); Conka soon replaced by Alban 'Snoopy' Pfisterer. Debut LP *Love* (1966). For *Da Capo* (1967) Pfisterer switched to keyboards and Michael Stuart (from Sons of Adam) played drums. After *Forever Changes* (1968), new line-up: Lee, Jay Donellan (guitar), Frank Fayad (bass), George Surano-

vitch (drums). Lee cut unreleased album with JIMI HENDRIX (1970); made solo *Vindicator* (1971); reformed more soulful Love, 1974: Melvan Whittington (guitar), John Sterling (guitar), Robert Rozelle (bass), Joe Blocker (drums). Album *Reel To Real* (1975). Other LPs *Four Sail* (1969), *Out Here* (1969), *False Start* (1971), *Best of Love* (1980), *Love Live* (1982). (Above: Arthur Lee)

LOVIN' SPOONFUL, THE
Pop-rock group, formed New York, late 1965. Original line-up: John Sebastian (vocal/guitar/harmonica/songwriter), Zal Yanovsky (guitar), Joe Butler (drums), Steve Boone (bass). Prototype good-time music, typified by US No 1 'Do You Believe in Magic' (1965). UK hits, 1966, with 'Daydream', 'Summer in the City'. By final LP, Yanovsky left to go solo, replaced by Jerry Yester. Only Sebastian has enjoyed real success since group's 1968 breakup. LPs *Do You Believe in Magic?* (1965), *Daydream* (1966), *What's Up Tiger Lily?* (1966, soundtrack LP), *Hums* (1967), *You're a Big Boy Now* (1967, soundtrack LP), *Everything's Playing* (1968).

LOWE, NICK
Bass guitar/vocal, *b.* Walton-on-Thames (Surrey), 24/4/49. Founder member of Brinsley Schwarz, 1969-75. House producer/artist, STIFF RECORDS, 1966, working with ELVIS COSTELLO, the DAMNED, Wreckless Eric. Also produced GRAHAM PARKER & the Rumour, Dr Feelgood, the PRETENDERS. Joined Radar Records, 1977, touring world as member of Rockpile (which also featured DAVE EDMUNDS). Rockpile disbanded, 1981; Lowe resumed solo career. LPs *Jesus of Cool* (1977), *Labour of Lust* (1979), *Seconds of Pleasure* (as Rockpile, 1980), *Nick the Knife* (1981). 'I Love the Sound of Breaking Glass' Top Ten UK hit, 1978. Bass-player on many hits by Dave Edmunds, including 'Girls Talk', 'Here Comes the Weekend'.

McCARTNEY, PAUL
Vocal/bass/songwriter with BEATLES, *b.* Liverpool, 18/6/42. Recorded *Paul McCartney* (1970) just prior to group's break-up; formed Wings, 1971, with wife Linda, Denny Laine (ex-MOODY BLUES, guitar),

Henry McCullough (guitar), Denny Seiwell (drums). Albums: *Ram* (1971, solo), *Wild Life* (1971), *Red Rose Speedway* (1972). McCullough and Seiwell left, 1973; depleted line-up cut *Band on the Run* (1974) in Nigeria. Continuing chart success, late '70s, with albums *Venus and Mars* (1975), *Wings at the Speed of Sound* (1976), *London Town* (1978), and best-selling single of all time, 'Mull of Kintyre' (1977). Laine left, 1978. Reunited with Beatles producer GEORGE MARTIN for *Tug of War* (1982).

McDONALD, COUNTRY JOE
Vocal/guitar/harmonica/songwriter. *b.* El Monte (California), 1/1/42. Folksinger around Berkeley (California), early '60s; recorded *The Goodbye Blues* (1964). Member of various local bands. Formed Country Joe & the Fish, 1965: Barry Melton (guitar), David Cohen (keyboards/vocal), Chicken Hirsh (drums), Bruce Barthol (bass). LPs *Electric Music For the Mind & Body* (1967), *I Feel Like I'm Fixin' to Die* (1967), *Together* (1968), *Here We Are Again* (1969). Since 1970 McDonald has assumed solo career, though the Fish regrouped for *Reunion* (1977). Solo LPs include *Hold On – It's Comin'* (1971), *The Paris Sessions* (1973), *Paradise with an Ocean View* (1976), *Goodbye Blues* (1978).

McLAREN, MALCOLM
Promoter/manager, *b.* London, 1946; art student and political activist, late sixties. Made film about London's Oxford Street. Opened Let it Rock, Fifties rock 'n' roll memorabilia shop, in World's End (London), 1971; subsequently changed its name (Too Fast to Live, Too Young to Die; Sex; Seditionaries; World's End) and style throughout '70s and early '80s. Managed NEW YORK DOLLS, 1974-5. Created SEX PISTOLS, 1976, fomenting punk 'rebellion'; skilfully managed group, media coverage, record deals (with EMI, A&M, VIRGIN). Group broke up 1978; McLaren lost control of affairs, 1979. Involved (and appeared) in Pistols film project *The Great Rock 'n' Roll Swindle* (originally titled *Who Killed Bambi?*), 1977-9. Created Bow Wow Wow, 1980 – another platform for his Situationist-based theories such as opposition to work ethic, celebration of 'instant' cassette technology. Charted with 'Buffalo Girls' (1982). Own LP *Duck Rock* (1983).

McLAUGHLIN, JOHN

Guitar, *b.* Yorkshire, 1942. Played with R&B groups in mid-Sixties, notably Graham Bond Organisation and Brian Auger Trinity. LP *Extrapolation* (1969) proved virtuosity. Joined Tony Williams Lifetime, 1970. LPs *Emergency* (1970), *Turn It Over* (1971). Then played with Miles Davis on *Bitches' Brew* and *In a Silent Way*. Further solo LPs *Devotion* (1970), *My Goal's Beyond* (1971). By now a convert to philosophy of Bengal mystic Sri Chinmoy; formed Mahavishnu Orchestra. Released *The Inner Mounting Flame* (1972), *Birds of Fire* (1973). Teamed up with fellow-convert CARLOS SANTANA on *Love Devotion Surrender* (1973) before disbanding Mahavishnu Orchestra after final live LP *Between Nothing and Eternity* (1973). Formed Mahavishnu Mark II. LPs *Apocalypse* (1974), *Visions of the Emerald Beyond* (1975), *Inner Worlds* (1976). Returned to more acoustic music, with Indian group Shakti for their LP, *A Handful of Beauty* (1977).

McPHATTER, CLYDE

Vocal, *b.* Durham (North Carolina), 15/11/32; *d.* 13/6/72. Immensely influential high tenor, preceding soul stars like SMOKEY ROBINSON. First sang gospel with the Mount Lebanon Singers, '40s, then R&B with the Dominoes, 1950-3 and his own group the DRIFTERS, 1953-4. After army service, in 1956 pursued successful solo career that faded during rise of '60s soul stars. LPs *Clyde McPhatter & The Drifters* (1955), *The Best of* ('60s compilation), *Live at the Apollo* (1964).

MADNESS

Ska-based pop group, formed Camden Town (London), 1978. Line-up: Chas Smash (vocal/trumpet), Mike Barson (vocal/keyboards), Lee

Thompson (vocal/saxophone), Chris Foreman (guitar), Suggs (vocal), Mark Bedford (bass), Dan Woodgate (drums). Quirky band with good-natured, 'nutty' humorous image. First single 'The Prince' (TWO-TONE), 1979. Signed to STIFF; enjoyed unbroken run of 14 hit singles, backed by imaginative videos, enthusiastic shows. Made feature film *Take It or Leave It* (1981) about early years. LPs *One Step Beyond* (1979), *Absolutely* (1980), *Complete Madness* (1981), *Seven* (1981), *The Rise and Fall* (1982).

MAHAL, TAJ

Vocal/guitar, *b.* New York, 17/5/42. Founder member of Rising Sons with RY COODER, 1966. Began solo

career as folk blues practitioner. LPs include *Taj Mahal* (1968), *Giant Step/De Ole Folks at Home* (1969). *The Real Thing* (1971), *Music Keeps Me Together* (1975), *Evolution* (1978), *International Rhythm Band Live* (1980).

MAMAS & THE PAPAS, THE

Vocal group, formed Los Angeles, 1965. Original line-up: John Phillips, Michelle Phillips, 'Mama Cass' Elliott, Denny Doherty. John Phillips helped arrange Monterey Festival (1967), in which band featured, and film *Monterey Pop*. After several gold singles and albums group split up, 1968; members undertook solo and session work. Brief reunion for *People Like Us* (1971). 'Mama Cass' died 29/7/74. LPs include *If You Can Believe Your Eyes and Ears* (1967), *The Mamas and the Papas Deliver* (1967), *The Papas and the Mamas* (1968). Solo LPs John Phillips *The Wolfking of LA* (1969); 'Mama Cass' *Dream a Little Dream*

(1968); *Dave Mason and Cass Elliott* (1970).

MANFRED MANN

R&B/pop group, formed by Manfred Mann (keyboards) and Mike Hugg (drums) 1962. Other members: Mike Vickers (saxophone), Paul Jones (harmonica/vocal), Dave Richmond (bass). Richmond left, 1964, replaced by Tom McGuinness. Jones, focal point of group, left for acting career, 1966, replaced by Mike D'Abo from Band of Angels; Vickers also left 1966, replaced (briefly) by Jack Bruce and former Hamburg associate of BEATLES, Klaus Voorman. Numerous UK/US hits, film score for *Up the Junction* (1968). Group broke up, 1969; Mann and Hugg formed Manfred Mann Chapter III with new personnel. Hugg left, 1971; Mann formed Manfred Mann's Earth Band later same year. Notable albums *Mann Made* (1964), *Mighty Garvey* (1968), *Chapter Three* (1969).

MARLEY, BOB

Vocal/guitar/songwriter, *b.* Jamaica, 6/4/45; *d.* Florida, 11/5/81. Began to record 1961. Formed the Wailers, 1964. Had local hits in '60s, e.g. 'Rude Boy' (1966). *Soul Rebel, Soul Revolution* (both 1969) produced by Lee Perry. Espoused Rastafarianism. *Catch a Fire* (1972) began association with ISLAND. Toured US, UK; released *Burnin'* (1973), including 'I Shot the Sheriff', later hit for ERIC CLAPTON. *Natty Dread* (1975) included some of his best-known songs, e.g. 'No Woman, No Cry'. Leading voice of Jamaican music, Rasta philosophy. Made *Live* (1975), *Rastaman Vibration* (1976), *Exodus* (1977); 'Jamming', from *Exodus*, was UK Top Ten hit. Returned to Jamaica, toured Africa, 1978. Played for Zimbabwean independence celebrations, toured Europe, 1980. Other LPs include *Rasta Revolution, African Herbsman* (both 1973), *Kaya* (1978), *Babylon by Bus* (1978, double), *Survival* (1979), *Uprising* (1980).

MARTIN

Guitar company. Founded by Christian Frederick Martin (1796-1873), New York, 1833; moved to permanent base in Nazareth (Pennsylvania), 1839. Has built reputation for superb hand-crafted acoustic guitars, and will be remembered as innovator of large 'Dreadnought' shape, designed by Frank Henry Martin and Harry L. Hunt *c.* 1915.

MARTIN, GEORGE

Record producer, renowned for association with BEATLES; b. London, 3/1/26. Classically trained at Guildhall School of Music; joined EMI, 1950, becoming youngest-ever

label head when placed in charge of Parlophone. Recorded mainly ballad singers and comedians (Temperance Seven, Peter Sellers, Matt Monro); signed Beatles, 1962, fostered their growth as musicians and songwriters, contributed innovative arrangements to songs on *Revolver* and *Sgt Pepper*. Left EMI organization, 1965, to form own Air company; produced most acts signed by BRIAN EPSTEIN, notably Gerry and the Pacemakers (1962); later worked with JEFF BECK (1971-6), and with groups Seatrain, Stackridge, America. Produced albums for ULTRAVOX and PAUL MCCARTNEY, 1982.

MAYALL, JOHN

Vocal/harmonica/guitar/keyboards, b. Manchester, 29/11/33. Moved to London, 1963; formed first Bluesbreakers. Subsequent line-ups included many leading figures of British R&B: ERIC CLAPTON, Jack Bruce, Peter Green and other members of what became FLEETWOOD MAC, Mick Taylor (later to join ROLLING STONES), nucleus of Colosseum. Recorded regularly for Decca, including classic *Blues Breakers* (1965) with Clapton. New band, 1969, leaned more to jazz. Began to use US musicians, 1970; thereafter worked mainly in America with US musicians from jazz, soul backgrounds. Recorded with ALLEN TOUSSAINT, 1975. Selected LPs *A Hard Road* (1966),

Bare Wires (1968), *The Turning Point* (1969), *Thru the Years* (compilation of '60s).

MAYFIELD, CURTIS

Guitar/vocal, b. Chicago, 3/6/42. Founder member of the Impressions (1957) with JERRY BUTLER. Accompanied (1959-60) and wrote hits for Butler, then many others while rejoining Impressions as creative leader, 1961. Over 30 hits written and latterly arranged/produced by Mayfield, 1963-70; Sam Gooden, Fred Cash lent vocal support. Formed own record company, 1968; pursued solo career, 1970 on. Careers of both Mayfield and revamped group slumped in late Seventies; renewed success for Impressions in 1981. LPs (with Impressions) *Your Precious Love* (1981 compilation of 1958-9), *Originals* (1976 compilation of 1961-8), *This Is My Country* (1968), *The Young Mods' Forgotten Story* (1969); (solo) *Curtis* (1970), *Live* (1971), *Roots* (1971), *Superfly* (1972), *Move On Up/The Best of* (late '70s compilation); group without Mayfield: *Finally Got Myself Together* (1974), *First Impressions* (1975).

MERSEYBEAT GROUPS

Attention focused on Liverpool beat group scene in 1963 after success of BEATLES. Bands with most commercial potential signed to BRIAN EPSTEIN's management company, including Gerry & the Pacemakers, Fourmost, Billy J Kramer & the Dakotas. Most other local groups were commercial failures, owing to inability to recapture live excitement on disc, lack of charisma, unsympathetic record companies, and inadequate material. Notable failures: Dennisons, Rory Storm & the Hurricanes, Seniors, Undertakers, Kingsize Taylor & the Dominoes. Exceptions included the Swinging Blue Jeans, Merseybeats (later relaunched as the Merseys), and Searchers; last-named were most instrumentally accomplished of all Merseybeat bands, rivalled Beatles in chart status until personnel changes (1965) led to popularity decline. Merseybeat fad ended about 1965 – most groups forced into night-club work. Searchers celebrated 20th anniversary in 1982, other Liverpool bands still together with much-changed line-ups.

MILLER, STEVE

Vocal/guitar, b. Dallas (Texas), 5/

10/43. Formed the Ardells (early Sixties), with BOZ SCAGGS, Ben Sidran. Formed Goldberg/Miller Blues Band, then Steve Miller Band. Original line-up: Miller, Lonnie Turner (bass/vocal), Curley Cooke (guitar), Tim Davis (drums). Jim Peterman (organ) joined, 1967. Cooke replaced by Scaggs (guitar/vocal), 1967. LPs *Children of the Future* (1967), *Sailor* (1968), *Brave New World* (1969), *Your Saving Grace* (1969). Turner replaced by Bobby Winkelman for Nashville-produced *Number Five* (1969). New trio formed with Miller, Ross Vallory (bass), Jack King (drums); LP *Rock Love* (1971). Most recent regular band is Miller, Turner, Gary Mallaber (drums), Norton Buffalo (harmonica/vocal), David Denny (guitar). Other LPs include *The Joker* (1973), *Fly Like an Eagle* (1976), *Abracadabra* (1982).

MITCHELL, JONI

Vocal/guitar/piano/dulcimer/songwriter, b. Alberta (Canada), 7/11/43 (r.n. Roberta Joan Anderson). Emerged from acoustic music scene of Sixties as distinctive vocal stylist, songwriter of great poetic skill. 'Big Yellow Taxi' UK Top 20 hit, as was 'Both Sides Now', written for Judy Collins (both 1970). These and other compositions covered by many artists throughout popular music. LPs *Joni Mitchell* (1969), *Clouds* (1969) *Ladies of the Canyon* (1970), *Blue* (1971), *For the Roses* (1972), *Court and Spark* (1974), *Hissing of Summer Lawns* (1975), *Miles of Aisles* (1976), *Hejira* (1976), *Don Juan's Reckless Daughter* (1978), *Shadows and Light* (1980), *Mingus* (1980), *Wild Things Run Fast* (1982).

MOODY BLUES, THE

Art-rock group, formed Birming-

ham, 1963. Original line-up: Graeme Edge (drums), Denny Laine (guitar/vocal), Mike Pinder (keyboards), Ray Thomas (vocal/harmonica), Clint Warwick (bass). 'Go Now', UK No 1, 1964. Laine and Warwick left, 1967; replaced by Justin Hayward and John Lodge. Changed from R&B to 'cosmic-progressive' rock with *Days of Future Passed* (1967), fusing rock, classical, and electronic styles. Set up own record label, Threshold, 1969. Massive worldwide following peaked with *Seventh Sojourn* (1972); group members involved in solo projects, notably Hayward and Lodge in Blue Jays vocal/instrumental duo, 1975. Reformed, 1977; *Octave* issued a year later.

MOOG, ROBERT
Inventor, *b*. New York, 1934. First person to apply technique of voltage control to musical instruments; with Herbert Deutsch, developed idea to produce prototype electronic music synthesizer, 1964. Vast publicity followed Walter Carlos' *Switched On Bach* (1968) using Moog system. Popular Minimoog, condensed instrument, launched 1970; Polymoog, one of first polyphonic synthesizers, 1975.

MORODER, GIORGIO
Producer, *b. c*. 1945. Popularised use of synthesizers, particularly repetitive sequencer patterns, at his Munich studio to produce so-called 'Eurodisco', late Seventies. Made name with hypnotic, rhythms for Donna Summer's hit 'Love to Love You Baby' (1976). One of first producers to exploit potential of extended mixes on 12 in singles. Solo LPs include $E=MC^2$; several film scores, e.g. *Midnight Express* and *Cat People*.

MORRISON, VAN
Vocal/guitar/saxophone/songwriter, *b*. Belfast (Northern Ireland), 31/8/45 (*r.n*. George Ivan Morrison). Formed the Monarchs, 1960. Formed Them, 1963: Billy Harrison (guitar), Alan Henderson (bass), Ronnie Millings (drums), Eric Wicksen (piano). Recorded several R&B LPs including *Them* (1965), *Them Again* (1966), *Now and Them* (1968), *Time Out, Time In for Them* (1968). Went solo; built reputation with haunting lyrics, varied and adventurous musical settings. LPs include *Astral Weeks* (1968), *Moondance* (1970), *His Band and the Street Choir* (1970), *Tupelo Hon-*

ey (1971), *St Dominic's Preview* (1972), *Hard Nose the Highway* (1973), *It's Too Late to Stop Now* (1974), *Veedon Fleece* (1974), *A Period of Transition* (1977), *Wavelength* (1981), *The Common One* (1981), *Beautiful Vision* (1982), *Inarticulate Speech of the Heart* (1983).

MOST, MICKIE
Producer, *b*. Aldershot (Hants), 1938 (*r.n*. Michael Hayes). Formed the Most Brothers with Alex Murray, 1958; moved to South Africa and covered US hits for African market. Back in UK, 1962, produced debut disc for the ANIMALS, then major international hits for Herman's Hermits, Nashville Teens, DONOVAN, JEFF BECK, Lulu and BRENDA LEE. Formed own label RAK, 1969, became most successful independent label of early '70s; artists included Mud, Suzi Quatro, New World, Smokie, Hot Chocolate. Took over career management of Kim Wilde, 1981. Regular panellist on ITV talent contest show, *New Faces*.

MOTORHEAD
Heavy-metal band, formed London, 1976. Line-up: Ian 'Lemmy' Kilminster (bass/vocal; previously with Hawkwind), 'Phast' Eddie Clarke (guitar), Phil 'Philthy Animal' Taylor (drums). LPs include *Motorhead* (1977), *Bomber* (1979), *Overkill* (1979), *Ace of Spades* (1980), *No Sleep Till Hammersmith* (1981), *Iron Fist* (1982). Clarke left group and no steady replacement found. Kilminster has worked with Girlschool and Plasmatics.

MOTOWN RECORDS
Formed Detroit (Michigan) 1960 by Berry Gordy Jr. Main subsidiaries Tamla, Gordy. Moved to Hollywood (California), 1971; still going strong. Major writer/producers included: SMOKEY ROBINSON, Holland-Dozier-Holland, Norman Whitfield. Very many stars included: SMOKEY ROBINSON & the Miracles, FOUR TOPS, TEMPTATIONS, DIANA ROSS & the Supremes, MARVIN GAYE, STEVIE WONDER, Lionel Richie, Rick James.

MOTT THE HOOPLE
Glam-rock group, formed Herefordshire, 1969, adding Ian Hunter in London. Original line-up: Hunter (vocal/guitar), Overend Watts (bass), Dale 'Buffin' Griffin (drums), Verden Allen (keyboards), Mick Ralphs (guitar). Recorded *Mott the Hoople* (1969), *Mad Shadows*

(1970), *Wildlife* (1971), *Brain Capers* (1971). Split up, early 1972, but encouraged to reform by DAVID BOWIE, who wrote/produced their first hit 'All the Young Dudes' and LP of same name. Allen and Ralphs left, 1972; latter formed BAD COMPANY, but returned to play on *Mott* (1973); replaced during US tour by 'Ariel Bender' (Luther Grosvener from Spooky Tooth). Morgan Fisher replaced Allen. Recorded *The Hoople, Live* (both 1974); finally split up, early 1975. Latterly Mick Ronson had briefly replaced Bender; went on to work further with Hunter. Watts, Griffin and Fisher recruited Nigel Benjamin (vocal), Ray Major (guitar) for two final LPs as Mott: *Drive On* (1975), *Shouting and Pointing* (1976).

MUDDY WATERS
Vocal/guitar, *b*. Rolling Fork (Mississippi), 4/4/15 (*r.n*. McKinley Morganfield), *d*. 30/4/83. Grew up around Clarksdale (Mississippi), played with local musicians, '30s-1943; moved to Chicago. Recorded for Aristocrat (later CHESS), 1947 on; gradually formed classic Chicago blues band with Little Walter or Walter Horton (harmonica), Jimmy Rogers (guitar), Otis Spann (piano). 'Rollin' Stone' (1950), 'Hoochie Coochie Man' (1953), 'Got My Mojo Working' (1957), others, became source-book of British R&B in '60s. Many collected on superb *The Best of Muddy Waters* (repeatedly reissued). Toured Britain, 1958; played Carnegie Hall, 1959; Newport Jazz Festival, 1960 (LP *At Newport* a key item in British R&B development). Found wider audience, '60s-'70s; recorded 'psychedelic' *Electric Mud*, 1968. *London Sessions* (1972) featured admirers RORY GALLAGHER, STEVE WINWOOD, Rick Grech, Georgie Fame (as Georgie Fortune). Appeared at many festivals, United States and Europe. Albums produced by JOHNNY WINTER, 1977 on. Long established as King of Chicago Blues, maintained remarkable

standards of personal performance, band-leading, recording. Selected LPs *Hard Again* (1977), *Live* (1979), *Chess Masters Vol 1, Vol 2* ('80s compilations of '40s-'50s).

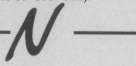

NELSON, RICK(Y)
Vocal, *b.* Teaneck (New Jersey), 8/5/40. Appeared with parents in TV series, *The Ozzie and Harriet Show,* mid-Fifties; launched as first of many imitations of ELVIS PRESLEY, 1956, with cover version of FATS DOMINO hit 'I'm Walkin''. Chart success continued until 1964, by which time had abbreviated first name to Rick. Re-entered limelight, 1969, with hit version of BOB DYLAN's 'She Belongs to Me'; became significant figure in late '60s/early '70s country-rock movement. Notable LPs *Bright Lights and Country Music* (1966), *Country Fever* (1967), *Perspective* (1969), *Rick Sings Nelson* (1970), *Rudy the Fifth* (1971), *Garden Party* (1972), *Playing to Win* (1981).

NEW LIVERPOOL BANDS
Concept first discussed about 1977, then embracing Pink Military, Big in Japan, Dalek I. Centred upon Eric's nightclub, groups such as Orchestral Manoeuvres in the Dark, Echo & the Bunnymen, The Teardrop Explodes, and Wah! Heat shared influences (LOVE, DOORS, Stooges, others) but little else. Independent label Zoo gave Teardrop Explodes recording debut, 'Sleeping Gas', 1977. Band split, November 1982, singer Julian Cope going solo. Echo & the Bunnymen relatively stable. OMD had huge hits with 'Enola Gay' (1980), 'Souvenirs' (1981), 'Joan of Arc' (1981). LPs Echo & the Bunnymen *Crocodiles* (1980), *Heaven Up Here* (1981); Teardrop Explodes *Kilimanjaro* (1980), *Wilder* (1982). Wah! *Nah-Poo – the Art of Bluff* (1981), *The Maverick Years* (1982). OMD *Organisation* (1980), *Architecture and Morality* (1981).

NEW ROMANTICS
General label applied to bands such as Visage, Spandau Ballet, DURAN DURAN, ULTRAVOX, Landscape influenced by electro-disco, funk; emphasised glamorous appearance as much as music. Used promotional videos inventively. Attracted acutely fashion-conscious fans; conse-

quently much media attention also. Had own circuit of nightclubs, many overseen by Steve Strange.

NEW YORK DOLLS
Glam-rock band, formed New York, 1973: Johnny Thunders (guitar), Sylvain Sylvain (guitar/piano), David Johansen (lead vocal), Arthur Kane (bass), Jerry Nolan (drums). Described as poor man's Rolling Stones (mainly because of Johansen's and Thunders' looks); evoked world of drugs, junk food. First album *New York Dolls* (1973) produced by TODD RUNDGREN; *Too Much Too Soon* (1974) by George 'Shadow' Morton. MALCOLM MCLAREN managed them, 1974-5, attempting relaunch with new look. Split 1977; Thunders and Nolan formed the Heartbreakers. Only Johansen, with set of under-recognized solo albums, made good.

ORBISON, ROY
Vocal/guitar, *b.* Vernon (Texas), 23/4/36. Performed locally with the Wink Westerners and own Teen Kings, early '50s; recorded rockabilly for SUN RECORDS, 1956-8; international success as dramatic pop balladeer, 1960-6. LPs *At the Rockhouse* (1958, reissued 1981), *All-Time Greatest Hits* (compilation of 1960-6), *Regeneration (1977).*

PAGE, JIMMY
Guitar, *b.* Heston (Middlesex), 9/1/44. London-based session player

from teens, joined JEFF BECK in the YARDBIRDS, 1966. Founder-member of LED ZEPPELIN, formed 1968. Classic 'Stairway to Heaven' guitar part became beginners' standard reference. Investigated guitar synthesizer, resulting in film soundtrack for *Death Wish II* (1981).

PARKER, GRAHAM
Vocal/guitar/songwriter, *b.* east London. Formed Graham Parker & the Rumour, early 1976, from remnants of various pub-rock groups: Brinsley Schwarz (guitar), Bob Andrews (keyboards, from Brinsley Schwarz), Martin Belmont (guitar, from Ducks Deluxe), Andrew Bodnar (bass), Steve Goulding (drums). NICK LOWE produced *Howlin' Wind* (1976), *Heat Treatment* (1977). Then *Parkerilla* (1978, live), *Squeezing Out Sparks* (1978, produced by Jack Nitzsche), *The Up Escalator* (1980).

PARLIAFUNKADELICMENT
Corporate name for troupe created by George Clinton, *b.* Kanapolis, (New Jersey), 22/7/40. Clinton led black doo-wop-to-soul vocal group the Parliaments, 1956-66, until first hit '(I Wanna) Testify' (1967), coincided with incorporation of backing band, Funkadelic. During late '60s-early '70s developed bizarre variations on rock-soul. Cult stars by 1975; later, major force of black music. Most important (of many) LPs: Funkadelic – *America Eats Its Young* (1972), *Cosmic Slop* (1973), *Standing on the Verge of Getting It On* (1974), *Let's Take It to the Stage* (1976), *Tales of Kidd Funkadelic* (1976), *One Nation under a Groove* (1978); Parliament – *Chocolate City* (1975), *Mothership Connection* (1976), *Motor Booty Affair* (1978).

PARSONS, GRAM
Guitar/vocal, *b.* Winterhaven (Georgia), 5/11/46; *d.* of drug overdose, 19/9/73. Pioneer of country rock. Formed International Submarine Band, 1966. LP *Safe at Home* (1966). Joined BYRDS for *Sweetheart of the Rodeo* (1968), then left to form FLYING BURRITO BROTHERS. Left to assume solo career, 1970. LPs *G.P.* (1973), *Grievous Angel* (1974) (both with EMMYLOU HARRIS), *Gram Parsons with the Flying Burrito Brothers* (1975).

PARTON, DOLLY
Vocal/songwriter, *b.* Locust Ridge (Tennessee), 19/1/46. First recorded at 11. Went to Nashville (Tennessee) to make career in country music, 1964. Recordings for Monument, 1964-7, unnoticed. Signed to RCA, worked as duo with established singer Porter Wagoner, 1967-74. Went solo, 1974. Many country hits, mostly own compositions, e.g. 'My Tennessee Mountain Home', 'Coat of Many Colours', 'Jolene'. Moved towards rock with *New Harvest – First Gathering* (1977), *Here You Come Again* (1978), *Heartbreaker* (1978). Poignant, deeply expressive singer; skill extends beyond country music. Has sung on sessions with EMMYLOU HARRIS, LINDA RONSTADT. Selected LPs: several *Best of* collections (RCA), *9 to 5 and Odd Jobs* (1980), *Heartbreak Express* (1982; includes remarkable hit 'Single Women'), *Greatest Hits* (1982 compilation of 1977-82).

PAUL, LES
Guitar/inventor, *b.* Waukesha (Wisconsin), 9/6/16 (*r.n.* Lester William Polfus). Avid inventor, fine guitarist in jazz and country fields. Began experiments with electric guitars, '30s; built studio to develop innovative multitracking ideas, '40s. Released some of the earliest multitracked records, including 'Lover' (1948), recorded on his home equipment. Teamed up with Mary Ford (*r.n.* Colleen Summers), 1949, to produce multitracked vocal/guitar hits. As progression from Paul's early guitar-making experiments, GIBSON eventually produced now famous Les Paul model, 1952, widely used in rock since late '60s. LPs Les Paul & Mary Ford *All Time Greatest Hits* (1978). Paul & Chet Atkins *Chester and Lester* (1978).

PERKINS, CARL
Guitar/vocal, *b.* Ridgely (Tennessee), 9/4/32. Briefly successful but highly influential rockabilly originator with SUN RECORDS, 1954-7. Slumped until 1964 British tour heralded comfortable future. Intermittently with Johnny Cash revue, 1967-76; now records and tours with sons. LPs *Dance Album* (1957, reissued 1981), *The Original CP* (1976 compilation of Sun tracks), *The Sun Years* (definitive 3-LP box set, 1981), *King of Rock* ('60s compilation of 1958-63), *The Man Behind Johnny Cash* ('70s compilation).

PETTY, TOM, & THE HEARTBREAKERS
Rock band, formed Los Angeles, mid-'70s: Tom Petty (vocal/guitar), Benmont Tench (keyboards), Ron Blair (bass), Stan Lynch (drums), Mike Campbell (guitar). Teamed with British producer Denny Cordell for eponymous debut album (1976); well received in UK before US. Influenced by British beat, with penchant for All-American imagery and large nod towards the BYRDS. Other LPs *You're Gonna Get It* (1977), *Damn the Torpedoes* (1979), *Hard Promises* (1980), *Long After Dark* (1982).

PHILADELPHIA SOUND
Philadelphia was always a source of much talent but distinct soul success began with writers/arrangers/producers Kenny Gamble and Leon Huff's work with the Intruders (1966 on) and Thom Bell's with the Delfonics (1968 on). First major successes with JERRY BUTLER (1968-9), Archie Bell (1968 on), WILSON PICKETT, Joe Simon (1971) the Stylistics (1971 on), the Spinners (1972 on). Gamble-Huff founded Philadelphia International label, 1971; international hits, 1972-3, through hits by the O'Jays, Harold Melvin & the Blue Notes (featuring Teddy Pendergrass), Billy Paul, the Three Degrees, others. Continued success exemplified by McFadden & Whitehead's 1979 smash, 'Ain't No Stoppin' Us Now'.

PICKETT, WILSON
Vocal, *b.* Pratville (Alabama), 18/3/41. Raised in Detroit, where first recorded with the Falcons, 1961-2. Pursued solo career, 1962; first hits 1963 ('The Midnight Hour') led to soul stardom on ATLANTIC RECORDS, 1965-72; thereafter faded. LPs *Greatest Hits* (compilation).

PINK FLOYD
Psychedelic rock band, formed London, 1966. Original line-up: Syd Barrett (vocal/guitar), Roger Waters (bass), Rick Wright (keyboards), Nick Mason (drums). Barrett wrote all group's early material, including Top Ten hit 'See Emily Play' (1967), debut LP *Piper at the Gates of Dawn* (1967). Dave Gilmour (guitar) brought in, 1968; Barrett quit soon afterwards, subsequently recording, with members of group, *The Madcap Laughs* (1970), *Barrett* (1971); also featured on some of second PF LP *A Saucerful of Secrets* (1968). Group steadily built up reputation to become one of most successful in recording history, through LPs and well-timed, spectacular tours, stage shows. LP *More* (1968, film soundtrack), *Ummagumma* (1969), *Atom Heart Mother* (1970), *Meddle* (1971), *Obscured by Clouds* (1971; film soundtrack), *Dark Side of the Moon* (1973), *Wish You Were Here* (1975), *Animals* (1977), *The Wall* (1979). 'Another Brick in the Wall', first single since Barrett era, No 1, 1980. *The Wall* subsequently staged, 1981; filmed, 1982. All members have participated in solo projects as performers/producers.

PITNEY, GENE
Vocal, *b.* Hartford (Connecticut), 17/2/41. Successful American pop star of the Sixties. Consistent run of international hits (1961-6) gave way to intermittent success until career slumped around 1970. LPs: many hit compilations.

PLATTERS, THE
Vocal group, formed Los Angeles, 1953. Original line-up: Tony Williams (lead singer), Alex Hodge, David Lynch, Paul Robi. Hodge replaced by Herb Reed, Zola Taylor

added to group. Consistent success 1955-62; Williams, pursuing solo career about 1960, replaced by Sonny Turner. Brief revitalization with changed line-up and sound, 1966-7. Subsequently cabaret act. LP *The Original Platters/20 Classic Hits* (1978 compilation of 1955-60).

POLICE, THE
Rock band, formed London, 1976: Sting (*r.n.* Gordon Sumner, bass/vocal), Stewart Copeland (drums/vocal), Henri Padovani (guitar/vocal). 'Fall Out' released on Illegal, 1977. Padovani left after Andy Summers (guitar/vocal) added. Signed to A&M, releasing 'Roxanne', debut album *Outlandos d'Amour* (both 1978). After successful US tour 'Roxanne' and 'Can't Stand Losing You' re-released to chart, 1979. *Reggatta de Blanc* (1979) awarded them superstar status. 'Message in a Bottle', 'Walking on the Moon' (both 1979) both reached No 1. *Zenyatta Mondatta* (1980) badly received by critics but huge seller. Extensive world touring throughout 1980 brought universal accolades. *Ghost in the Machine* (1981) another smash, providing three hit singles, 'Every Little Thing She Does Is Magic' a No 1. Sting's film-acting career began, 1979, with cameo as Ace Face in *Quadrophenia*; also featured in Chris Petit's *Radio On* the same year; first starring role in *Brimstone and Treacle* (1982).

PRESLEY, ELVIS
Vocal, *b.* Tupelo (Mississippi), 8/1/35; *d.* Memphis, 17/7/77. First of the great rock 'n' roll stars. Moved to Memphis at age 13; audition by SUN RECORDS head Sam Phillips, 1954, led to tour dates billed as 'the Hillbilly Cat'. 'Colonel' Tom Parker took over personal management, 1955, in same week that Phillips sold Presley's contract to RCA in record $35,000 deal. Began RCA career with Chet Atkins as producer; appeared in first film, *Love Me Tender*, 1957. After stint in US Army (1958-60), retired from performing to concentrate on movie work; also forsook rock material for preponderance of ballads. Standard of discs declined markedly in '60s, but made a triumphant return to form with TV special (1968), *From Elvis in Memphis* (1969), and Las Vegas appearance (1969); performed frequently in early '70s.

PRETENDERS, THE
Rock group, formed London, 1979.

Line-up: Chrissie Hynde (vocal/guitar), James Honeyman-Scott (keyboards/guitar/vocal, *d.* '82), Pete Farndon (bass; *d.* '83), Martin Chambers (drums). 'Brass in Pocket' (1979) UK No 1, January 1980. Debut LP *Pretenders* immediate No 1, 1980. Made US, European tours; *Pretenders II* (1982).

QUEEN
Heavy-metal band, formed London, 1972. Line-up has remained unchanged: Freddy Mercury (vocal/piano), Brian May (guitar), John Deacon (bass), Roger Taylor (drums). Gradually developed away from strictly heavy-metal image, ensured longevity by well-crafted singles, notably 'Bohemian Rhapsody' (1975), and spectacularly staged tours, live shows. LPs *Queen* (1973), *Queen II* (1974), *Sheer Heart Attack* (1974), *A Night at the Opera* (1975), *A Day at the Races* (1976), *News of the World* (1977), *Jazz* (1978), *Live Killers* (1979), *The Game* (1980), *Flash Gordon* (1980, film soundtrack), *Greatest Hits* (1981, including No 1 single with DAVID BOWIE, 'Under Pressure'), *Hot Space* (1982).

QUICKSILVER MESSENGER SERVICE
Psychedelic-rock band, formed El Rey (California), 1966. Original line-up: John Cippolina (guitar/vocal), Gary Duncan (guitar/vocal). David Freiberg (bass/vocal), Jim Murray (harp/vocal), Greg Elmore (drums). LPs *Quicksilver Messenger Service* (1968), *Happy Trails* (1969),

Shady Grove (1970). Line-up augmented by Dino Valenti (vocal) and occasional piano from Nicky Hopkins. Freiberg left to join JEFFERSON STARSHIP. Other members reunited for *Solid Silver* (1976). All play sessions except Elmore. Other LPs *Just for Love* (1970), *What About Me* (1970), *Quicksilver* (1971), *Comin' Thru* (1972).

— R —

REBENNACK, MAC (DR JOHN)
Vocal/piano/guitar, *b.* New Orleans (Louisiana), 1941 (*r.n.* Malcolm John Rebennack; *alias* John Creux). Began as session musician backing Professor Longhair, Frankie Ford, JOE TEX. Graduated to sessions and production with Minit, All-for-One. Moved to Los Angeles, early '60s; worked with PHIL SPECTOR, SAM COOKE, Harold Battiste; returned to New Orleans. LPs include *Gris Gris* (1968), *Babylon* (1969), *Sun, Moon & Herbs* (1971), *Gumbo* (1972), *In the Right Place* (1973), *Desitively Bonaroo* (1974), *Cut Me While I'm Hot* (1975), *Tango Palace* (1979), *Plays Mac Rebennack* (1982).

REDDING, OTIS
Vocal, *b.* Dawson (Georgia), 9/9/41, *d.* in private aircraft crash, Lake Monona, Wisconsin, 10/12/67. Outstanding soul artist. First US hit single, 'These Arms of Mine' (1963), followed by 'Mr Pitiful' (1965), 'I've Been Loving You Too Long' (1965), 'Respect' (1965). First UK hit single 'My Girl' (1966). '(Sitting on the) Dock of the Bay' (1968) topped charts in US, UK. LPs *Otis Blue* (1966), *King and Queen* (with Carla Thomas, 1967), *History of Otis Redding* (1968), *Dock of the Bay* (1968), *Immortal Otis Redding* (1968).

REED, JIMMY
Vocal/harmonica/guitar, *b.* Dunleith (Mississippi), 6/9/25; *d.* Oakland (California), 29/8/76. Played in Chicago area from late Forties. Recorded for Vee Jay, Chicago, 1953-65; many R&B chart hits, e.g. 'You Don't Have to Go' (1954), 'Ain't That Lovin' You Baby' (1956), 'You Got Me Dizzy' (1956), 'Honest I Do' (1957), 'Baby What You Want Me to Do' (1959), 'Big Boss Man' (1960). Trademarks lazy, slack-mouthed delivery, piercing harmonica breaks, hypnotic rhythms. Worked on club/concert circuit '60s-'70s, gradually finding new white audience; often

off scene through illness. Selected LPs *Upside Your Head* (1980 compilation of 1955-64; includes many hits), *Got Me Dizzy* (1981 compilation of 1953-64).

REED, LOU
Vocal/guitar/songwriter. Leader of VELVET UNDERGROUND, 1966-70. Quit; went to England to record eponymous debut album, 1971. Collaborated with DAVID BOWIE on *Transformer* (1972), yielding UK hit 'Walk on the Wild Side'. Failure of ambitious operetta *Berlin* (1973) resulted in Reed adopting coarse heavy-metal approach on live *Rock 'n' Roll Animal* (1974). Except for electronic *Metal Machine Music* (1976), continued to perform in primarily mainstream rock setting, exploring his youth and past, excelling in *Street Hassle* (1978). Retired from live performance, 1981. Other LPs *Sally Can't Dance* (1974), *Coney Island Baby* (1976), *Rock 'n' Roll Heart* (1977), *The Bells* (1979), *Growing Up in Public* (1980).

RICH, CHARLIE
Vocal/piano, *b.* Colt (Arkansas), 14/12/32. Frustrated jazz stylist, joined SUN RECORDS (1957) as session pianist/composer. Wrote songs for JERRY LEE LEWIS, others. From 1959 sporadic hits in own right; big success as country star, 1973 on. Ironically, his greatest songs are blues, e.g. 'Who Will the Next Fool Be', 'No Headstone on My Grave'. LPs *The Original CR* (1976 compilation of Sun tracks), *The Many New Sides of CR* (1965), *Behind Closed Doors* (1973).

RICHARD, CLIFF
Vocal, *b.* Lucknow (India), 14/10/40 (*r.n.* Harry Webb). UK's most consistent hit-maker since late '50s. Grew up in Cheshunt (Herts); played in skiffle group but switched to rock 'n' roll after seeing BILL HALEY perform. Formed rock group, the Drifters; spent month at Butlin's holiday camp, Clacton, 1958, before being signed for *Oh Boy!* TV show by producer Jack Good. Went solo, Drifters became the SHADOWS and his long-time backing group; soon dropped rock 'n' roll for more general pop appeal, starred in several high-grossing films. Huge UK and European success '60s-'70s not matched in US until 1979, when 'We Don't Talk Anymore' was breakthrough hit. Notable LPs *I'm Nearly Famous* (1976), *Every Face Tells a Story* (1977), *Green Light* (1978), *Rock 'n' Roll Juvenile* (1979).

ROBINSON, SMOKEY
Vocal/songwriter/producer, *b.* Detroit (Michigan), 19/2/40 (*r.n.* William Robinson). Formed group, 1956, evolved into the Miracles; discovered by Berry Gordy, 1957. Wrote, recorded numerous US hits; produced many sessions for Mary Wells, TEMPTATIONS, others. Appointed vice-president of Gordy's MOTOWN corporation, 1968. Left Miracles, 1972. Solo albums include *Smokey* (1973), *Pure Smokey* (1974), *Quiet Storm* (1974), *Where There's Smokey* (1979), *Being with You* (1981).

RODGERS, JIMMIE
Vocal/guitar/songwriter, *b.* Pine Springs (Mississippi), 8/9/1897; *d.* New York, 26/5/33. 'Father of Country Music', pioneer country recording artist, 1927-33. Developed white blues idiom in series of 13 *Blue Yodel* compositions, also others; further themes include railroads, hobos, cowboys. Many became country standards, e.g. 'Any Old Time', 'Mississippi Moon', 'Waiting for a Train'. Profound influence on country music, Western Swing, bluegrass, from '30s on. Admired by many US rock musicians, e.g. DUANE ALLMAN, Maria Muldaur; subject of tribute albums by country singers, e.g. Merle Haggard, Hank Snow, Ernest Tubb. LPs: virtually entire output reissued on seven RCA albums, 1956-64; these or others intermittently available.

ROLLING STONES, THE
Rock 'n' roll band. Original line-up: Mick Jagger (vocal), Keith Richard (guitar), Brian Jones (guitar), Ian Stewart (piano), Dick Taylor (bass), Mick Avory (drums). Played first gig together, 1962, at London's Mar-

quee club. Avory soon left (later joined KINKS); replaced by Charlie Watts. Bill Wyman took over from Taylor, late 1962. Andrew Oldham became manager, 1963, sacked Stewart and publicised group as anti-Establishment figures: drug busts, sexually ambiguous songs, statements against marriage fuelled controversial image. Recorded fine series of R&B-based albums: *Out of Our Heads* (1965), *Aftermath* (1966), *High Tide and Green Grass* (1966). Ridiculed over pseudo-psychedelic *Their Satanic Majesties Request* (1967), but *Beggar's Banquet* (1968) renewed status as rock figureheads. Jones left, June 1969, died following month; replaced by Mick Taylor. Launched own Rolling Stones label, 1971, with *Sticky Fingers*. Band moved to France, made sporadic albums: *Exile on Main Street* (1972), *Goat's Head Soup* (1973), *It's Only Rock 'n' Roll* (1974), *Made in the Shade* (1975), *Some Girls* (1978), others. Taylor left, 1974; replaced by Ron Wood of Faces. Still touring in '80s, still widely regarded as best live rock 'n' roll band in world. Eighties albums: *Emotional Rescue* (1980), *Tattoo You* (1981), *Still Life* (1982).

RONSTADT, LINDA
Vocal/guitar, *b.* Tucson (Arizona), 15/7/46. Accomplished country-rock singer. Joined Stone Poneys, 1965. Top 20 US hit, 1967, with 'Different Drum'. Went solo and cut *Hand Sown, Home Grown* (1969), *Silk Purse* (1970). Signed to Asylum, 1973. LPs *Don't Cry Now* (1973), *Heart Like a Wheel* (1974), *Prisoner in Disguise* (1975), *Hasten Down the Wind* (1976), *Simple Dreams* (1977), *Living in the USA* (1978), *Mad Love* (1980), *Get Closer* (1982).

ROXY MUSIC
Art-rock band, formed London, 1971. Original line-up: Brian Ferry (vocal/keyboards), David O'List (guitar), Andy Mackay (saxophone/oboe), Paul Thompson (drums), Graham Simpson (bass), BRIAN ENO (synthesizer/effects). Debut LP *Roxy Music* (1972) consolidated by hits 'Virginia Plain', 'Pyjamarama' same year. Immediately won popular and critical acclaim. O'List replaced by Phil Manzanera, 1972. After *For Your Pleasure* (1973) Eno replaced by Eddie Jobson (violin/keyboards). Released *Stranded* (1973), *Country Life* (1974), *Siren* (1975). Members also engaged in solo projects: Ferry with *These Foolish Things* (1973),

Another Time Another Place (1974), singles success; Mackay with *In Search of Eddie Riff* (1974), music for TV series *Rock Follies* (1976); Manzanera with *Diamond Head* (1975) and reformation of his old group Quiet Sun (also 1975). Further solo efforts followed and still continue; group itself returned with *Manifesto* (1979), *Flesh and Blood* (1980), *Avalon* (1982).

RUNDGREN, TODD
Vocal/guitar/keyboards, *b.* Philadelphia (Pennsylvania), 22/6/48. First recorded with the Nazz before becoming producer/engineer at Bearsville Records, working with THE BAND, Badfinger, Jesse Winchester; then went solo. LPs *Runt* (1970), *Ballad of Todd Rundgren* (1971), *Something/Anything* (1972), *A Wizard, a True Star* (1973), *Todd* (1974). Formed Utopia: John Siegler (bass), Ralph Powell (Moog), Ralph Shuckett (keyboards), Moogy Klingman (keyboards), John Wilcox (drums). Utopia LPs include *Utopia* (1974), *Initiation* (1975), *Another Live* (1975). Other LPs *Faithful* (1976), *Hermit of Mink Hollow* (1978), *Back to the Bars* (1981), *Swing to the Right* (1982).

RUSSELL, LEON
Vocal/piano/guitar/other instruments/composer, *b.* Oklahoma, 2/4/41. One of the original super-session men, played with, e.g., JERRY LEE LEWIS, Ronnie Hawkins in Tulsa before moving to Los Angeles in '50s. Worked on many PHIL SPECTOR 60s hits, among others. Re-emerged among Delaney & Bonnie's Friends on *Accept No Substitute* (1969). Through JOE COCKER recording his song 'Delta Lady' (1969), he struck up relationship that led to Russell organizing Mad Dogs and Englishmen group for Cocker; double live LP *Mad Dogs and Englishmen*

(1970) followed. Set up Shelter Records with English producer Denny Cordell, recorded first solo LP, *Leon Russell* (both 1969). Subsequent solo records highly successful in US up to mid-'70s when backed by popular tours. Also worked with BOB DYLAN, producing 'Watching the River Flow', 'When I Paint My Masterpiece' (1971). Selected LPs *Carney* (1972), *Hank Wilson's Back* (1973), *Americana* (1978).

SAHM, DOUG
Vocal/guitar, *b.* Texas, 6/11/41. Recorded for small Texas labels in youth. Moved to San Francisco, 1965, forming Sir Douglas Quintet, featuring seminal garage-band organ style of Augie Meyer; had classic hit 'She's About a Mover'. Maintained quintet through five LPs, including *Mendocino* (1969), title track providing further singles hit. Recommended: *Best of the Sir Douglas Quintet* (1965). In '70s Sahm recorded under own name, *Doug Sahm and Band* (1973) attracting attention through presence of BOB DYLAN, DR JOHN. Pioneered TexMex/Austin 'cosmic-country' style. Selected LPs *Texas Tornado* (1973), *Groovers Paradise* (1974), *Hell of a Spell* (1980).

SANTANA, CARLOS
Guitar, *b.* Autlan de Navarro (Mexico), 20/7/47. Formed eponymous group playing fusion of rock with Latin American and African rhythms, coming to attention through performance at Woodstock festival, 1969. Recorded huge-selling first LP; line-ups have changed since, but Santana's fluid, melodic guitar lines define group's sound. LP (with JOHN MCLAUGHLIN) *Love Devotion Surrender* (1973). Selected Santana LPs *Santana* (1969), *Abraxas* (1970), *Caravanserai* (1972), *Inner Secrets* (1979), *Zebop* (1981).

SCAGGS, BOZ
Vocal/guitar, *b.* Ohio, 8/5/44 (*r.n.* William Royce Scaggs). Raised in Texas, where teamed up with STEVE MILLER; joined Miller band, heavily featured on *Children of the Future* (1967), *Sailor* (1968). First solo album, *Boz Scaggs,* featuring DUANE ALLMAN, among others, won acclaim, but after *My Time* (1972) found a more commercial white-

soul direction. *Slow Dancer* (1974) with MOTOWN producer Johnny Bristol clinched new style. *Silk Degrees* (1976) provided UK and US singles success with 'Lido Shuffle', 'What Can I Say'; featured group Toto, now successful in their own right. Subsequent LPs include *Down Two Then Left* (1977), *Middle Man* (1980), *Hits* (1980).

SCOTT-HERON, GIL
Vocal/songwriter, *b.* Chicago, 1950. Recorded rap verse for Flying Dutchman label in late '60s with Brian Jackson before signing to Arista, 1974, to record black consciousness lyrics with funk backing by the Midnight Band (later, Amnesia Express). LPs *Small Talk at 125th and Lennox* (1970), *Pieces of a Man* (1971), *Winter in America* (1973), *The First Minute of a New Day* (1974), *From South Africa to South Carolina* (1975), *It's Your World* (1976), *Bridges* (1977), *Secrets* (1978), *Reflections* (1981), *Moving Target* (1982).

SEDAKA, NEIL
Vocal/songwriter, *b.* Brooklyn (New York), 13/3/39. Classically trained, joined Aldon Music in 1960 as house songwriter; teamed with high-school friend Howard Greenfield for Bobby Vee, CONNIE FRANCIS, others. Groomed by RCA as teen idol, recorded string of self-written hits including 'Oh Carol' (1959), 'Breaking Up Is Hard to Do' (1962), 'Next Door to an Angel' (1962). Retired to write for the Monkees, Tom Jones, Fifth Dimension, others; re-emerged 1970 encouraged by success of former Aldon colleague CAROLE KING. Enjoyed renewed chart success; recorded *The Tra La*

Days Are Over (1973) with 10CC at group's Stockport studios.

SEGER, BOB
Guitar/vocal, *b.* Detroit (Michigan) 1947. Debut single 'Heavy Music' (1966). LPs *Smokin' O.Ps* (1970), *Back in '72* (1972), *Seven* (1973), *Beautiful Loser* (1975), *Night Moves* (1976), *Live Bullet* (1976), *Stranger in Town* (1978), *Against the Wind* (1980), *Nine Tonight* (1981), *The Distance* (1983). Tours frequently with his Silver Bullet Band.

SEX PISTOLS, THE
Punk band. Founding group of punk rock, formed from the Swankers: Johnny Rotten (*r.n.* John Lydon) (vocal), Steve Jones (guitar), Glen Matlock (bass), Paul Cook (drums). Managed by MALCOLM MCLAREN. First gig at St Martin's School of Art, 6/11/75. Signed to EMI for £40,000, October 1976, releasing 'Anarchy in the UK', December. Furore over group's bad language on TV caused widespread cancellation of gigs on subsequent nationwide tour. Band dropped by EMI; signed to A&M for £150,000; dropped the following week for £75,000. Matlock fired, February 1977; replaced by Sid Vicious. Signed to VIRGIN, May, for £50,000, releasing 'God Save the Queen', which just missed No. 1. Debut LP *Never Mind the Bollocks . . . Here's the Sex Pistols* (November 1977). Split between Lydon and McLaren over publicity, animosity caused by film *The Great Rock 'n' Roll Swindle*. Band split after US tour, January 1978.

SHADOWS, THE
Guitar group, formed 1957 as Drifters, backed CLIFF RICHARD on first hit, 'Move It'. Line-up: Hank Marvin (guitar), Bruce Welch (guitar), Ian Samwell (bass), Terry Smart (drums). Samwell and Smart replaced by Jet Harris and Tony Meehan, 1959; group changed name to avoid confusion with US DRIFTERS. Became UK's top instrumental outfit. Meehan left, 1961, replaced by Brian Bennett; Harris left, 1962, replaced by Brian Locking. John Rostill replaced Locking, 1963. Group disbanded, 1969. Marvin and Welch formed instrumental trio with John Farrar, 1970; Bennett joined them, 1973, for reunion album, *Rockin' with Curly Leads*. Welch has produced albums for Cliff Richard. Notable LPs *Specs Appeal* (1975), *20 Golden Greats* (1977).

SIMON, PAUL
Vocal/songwriter, *b.* New York, 13/10/42. Formed high-school duo with classmate Art Garfunkel, 1957; turned to folk music, early '60s; was performing solo in UK when 'Sounds of Silence' (1965) became surprise US hit. Teamed again with Garfunkel; they survived initial folk-rock owing to sophistication of songs and production, and became unofficial spokesmen of student America with *Bookends* (1967), *The Graduate* (film soundtrack, 1968), vastly successful *Bridge Over Troubled Water* (1970). Garfunkel moved into films, partnership ended, 1972. Simon's solo albums featured reggae, gospel, jazz styles: *Paul Simon* (1972), *There Goes Rhymin' Simon* (1973), *Still Crazy After All These Years* (1975), *One Trick Pony* (1980). Reunited with Garfunkel, 1981, for Central Park (New York) concert and live album.

SIOUXSIE & THE BANSHEES
Punk/art-rock group, formed 1976 by 'Bromley Contingent' members Siouxsie Sioux (vocal), Steve Severin (bass). Debuted with Sid Vicious and Marco Pirroni (later of ADAM & THE ANTS, Rema Rema) at London's 100 Club Punk Festival with 20-minute version of Lord's Prayer. Added Kenny Morris (drums), John McKay (guitar), 1977. Toured Europe; signed to Polydor, 1978, releasing 'Hong Kong Garden'. Debut album *The Scream* (1978). McKay and Morris left during UK tour, September 1979; replaced by John McGeoch (guitar), Budgie (drums). Other LPs *Join Hands* (1979), *Kaleidoscope* (1980), *Juju* (1981), *Once Upon a Time: The Singles* (1981), *A Kiss in the Dreamhouse* (1982).

SMALL FACES, THE
Mod-rock group, formed east London, 1965. Original line-up: Kenny Jones (drums), Ronnie Lane (bass), Steve Marriott (guitar/vocal), Jimmy Winston (organ). Marriott was former child actor, wrote group's material with Lane; heavily promoted as having mod beginnings, many UK hits resulted. Winston replaced by Ian McLagan, 1966. Excellent concept album with novelty round sleeve, *Ogden's Nut Gone Flake* (1968), mirrored Marriott's artistic ambitions. Marriott left, 1968, to form Humble Pie with PETER FRAMPTON of the Herd. Others joined with Ron Wood and ROD STEWART to form the Faces.

SMITH, PATTI
Poet/rock critic/songwriter/vocal/guitar, *b.* Chicago, 12/46. Published volumes of poetry, *Seventh Heaven*, *Witt*; contributed to *Creem* magazine, 1971. Started performing, 1974, with Lenny Kaye (guitar), Richard Sohl (piano), Ivan Kral (bass/guitar), Jay Dee Daugherty (drums). Released 'Piss Factory'/'Hey Joe' (1974, rereleased 1977). Debut album *Horses* (1976) produced by JOHN CALE. Second album, *Radio Ethiopia* (1977), not well received. Out of action for a time after accident on stage. Comeback album *Easter*, 1978. Collaborated with BRUCE SPRINGSTEEN, who co-wrote 'Because the Night', massive hit for Smith in 1978. Retired 1979.

SOFT MACHINE
Underground/jazz-rock band, formed Canterbury (Kent), 1966. Original line-up: Mike Ratledge (keyboards), ROBERT WYATT (vocal/drums), Daevid Allen (guitar), Kevin Ayers (vocal/bass). Has since had 15 line-up changes. Initially adopted by London Underground, but only debut 'Feelin' Reelin' Squeelin'' and *The Soft Machine* (1968), recorded without Allen, reflect this period. Allen went on to form Gong in France; Ayers left before second LP (later to form Whole World); Hugh Hopper (bass) joined. Through *Volume Two* (1969), *Third* (1970), *Fourth* (1971) this line-up remained, though often augmented. Group experimented with structures, harmonies, free-form improvisation; after Wyatt's departure, 1971, moved further towards jazz. Influence more widely felt on European rock scene of early '70s than in UK. *Triple Echo* (1977) is excellent compilation; most recent LP is *Land of Cockayne* (1981).

SPECTOR, PHIL
Producer, *b.* New York, 26/12/40. Spent teens in California, formed high school trio the Teddy Bears, 1957; international hit with own song, 'To Know Him Is to Love Him' (1958). Worked in Phoenix studio of producers Lee Hazlewood and Lester Sill, learned record production at first hand; moved back to New York, 1960, worked with LEIBER & STOLLER. Formed own Philles label, 1961, with Sill, developed 'wall of sound' production technique on records by Ronettes, Crystals, Bob B. Soxx & the Blue Jeans, Darlene Love, Righteous Brothers, IKE & TINA TURNER, others. Bought out Sill,

1962, became youngest-ever label head at 21. Retired from recording, 1966, incensed by the failure of Ike & Tina Turner's 'River Deep – Mountain High'. Re-emerged, 1970, with work on BEATLES' *Let It Be* soundtrack and solo albums for JOHN LENNON, GEORGE HARRISON. Produced for Dion, Cher, others in mid-'70s; financed film projects (*The Last Movie, Enter the Dragon*), but has remained out of public eye during the '80s.

SPRINGSTEEN, BRUCE
Vocal/guitar/harmonica/songwriter, *b.* Freehold (New Jersey), 23/9/49. Signed with Columbia 1972; *Greetings from Asbury Park, N. J.* released 1973. With *The Wild, the Innocent and the E-Street Shuffle* began media campaign that was to vex career. E Street Band became backing group. *Born to Run* (1975) broke Springsteen in UK as well as US. Hiatus in career when locked in litigation with manager Mike Appel. Brooding *Darkness at the Edge of Town* (1978) revealed obsession with his father as well as familiar escape-on-wheels imagery. Retired into studio for 18 months; released double album *The River*, 1980. Big European tour, 1981. Solo acoustic album *Nebraska* (1982) evinced interest in US 'roots' music, particularly WOODY GUTHRIE.

STATUS QUO
Heavy-metal band, formed London, 1966. Original line-up: Francis (then Mike) Rossi (guitar/vocal), Alan Lancaster (bass), Rick Parfitt (guitar/vocal), John Coughlan (drums), Roy Lynes (keyboards). Achieved hits, 1968, with 'Pictures of Matchstick Men', 'Ice In the Sun'. Changed direction in '60s building steady following on club/college circuit. Lynes left; no further

changes till Coughlan left, 1982; replaced by Pete Kirchner (from Original Mirrors). In '70s pursued hard-rock style, enjoying success as live, LP, singles group; peaked 1975 when *On the Level*, and 'Down Down' topped respective charts. Selected LPs *Piledriver* (1973), *Rockin' All Over the World* (1977), *Gold Bars* (1980, hits collection), *Never Too Late* (1981).

STAX RECORDS
Formed near Memphis (Tennessee) as Satellite Records, 1959, by Jim Stewart and Estelle Axton. Moved into Memphis, 1960; renamed Stax, 1961. Main subsidiary, Volt (1962 on). Distributed by ATLANTIC RECORDS, 1961-8; bought by Gulf & Western Corp, 1968; bought back for distribution by Columbia, 1972; bankrupt, 1976. Stars included: BOOKER T & THE MGS, OTIS REDDING, Rufus & Carla Thomas, Johnnie Taylor, Isaac Hayes, Albert King.

STEELY DAN
Electric jazz-rock group, formed early Seventies by Donald Fagen (keyboards/vocal), Walter Becker (bass). First LP was soundtrack for *You Gotta Walk It Like You Talk It* (1971). Moved from New York to Los Angeles, recruited original line-up: Denny Dias (guitar), Jeff Baxter (guitar), David Palmer (vocal), Jim Hodder (drums). Group split up, 1974, Baxter joining Doobie Brothers. Recent Steely Dan comprises Becker, Fagen, session musicians. LPs *Can't Buy a Thrill* (1972), *Countdown to Ecstasy* (1973), *Pretzel Logic* (1974), *Katy Lied* (1975), *The Royal Scam* (1976), *Aja* (1977), *Greatest Hits* (1978), *Gaucho* (1980), *Gold* (1981). Fagen solo *The Nightfly* (1982).

STEWART, ROD
Vocal, *b.* Highgate (London), 10/1/45. Joined Long John Baldry's Hoochie Coochie Men (1963), singing and playing harmonica (featured latter on Millie Small's No. 2 UK hit, 'My Boy Lollipop, 1964). Debut solo single 'Good Morning Little Schoolgirl', (1964). Joined Steampacket 1965; Shotgun Express 1966. Founder member of JEFF BECK Group, 1967, recording *Truth* (1968), *Beck-Ola* (1969). With fellow-member Ron Wood left to form the Faces, releasing *First Step* (1970), *Long Player* (1971), *A Nod's As Good As a Wink to a Blind Horse* (1972), *Ooh La La* (1973). Pursued solo recording career at same time,

releasing *An Old Raincoat Will Never Let You Down* (1969), *Gasoline Alley* (1970), *Every Picture Tells a Story* (1971), *Never a Dull Moment* (1972), *Smiler* (1974). Faces disbanded, 1974, Wood joining the ROLLING STONES. Stewart continued with LPs *Atlantic Crossing* (1975), *A Night on the Town* (1976), *Footloose and Fancy Free* (1977), *Blondes Have More Fun* (1978), *Foolish Behaviour* (1980), *Tonight I'm Yours* (1981), *Absolutely Live* (1982). Hit singles include 'Maggie May' (1971), 'Stay with Me' (with Faces, 1972), 'You Wear It Well' (1972), 'Cindy Incidentally' (with Faces, 1973), 'Sailing' (1975), 'This Old Heart of Mine' (1976), 'Tonight's the Night' (1976), 'D'Ya Think I'm Sexy' (1978), 'Tonight I'm Yours' (1981).

STIFF RECORDS
Independent label, formed autumn 1976 by Jake Riviera (Andrew Jakeman) and Dave Robinson. Both previously involved in pub rock, hence early roster included Sean Tyla, Pink Fairies, Ian Dury. Aimed to sign anything majors rejected; released first punk single, by the DAMNED. Revived '60s idea of package tour, putting together ELVIS COSTELLO, Wreckless Eric, Ian Dury, others for two nationwide trips. Riviera left, 1979, taking Costello and NICK LOWE with him to Radar, formed with Andrew Lauder (subsequently turned into F-Beat). Robinson continued signing one-off novelties and inconsistently successful acts Lene Lovich, Belle Stars and Tenpole Tudor, relying on MADNESS to produce unbroken line of hits. Known for brilliant promotional videos.

STONE, SLY
Keyboards/vocal, *b.* Dallas (Texas), 15/3/44 (*r.n.* Sylvester Stewart). First noted as San Francisco DJ and record producer, mid-Sixties. Formed first group, 1966, soon replaced by Family Stone, combining revitalized JAMES BROWN-style soul inspiration with West Coast psychedelic rock innovations. Heyday was brief, 1968-71, but very influential; helped by appearance in movie *Woodstock*, 1969. LPs *Greatest Hits* (1970 compilation of 1968-9), *There's a Riot Going On* (1971), *Ain't But the One Way* (1983).

STRANGLERS, THE
New Wave band, formed London, 1975: Hugh Cornwell (guitar/vocal), Jean-Jacques Burnel (bass/vocal),

Dave Greenfield (keyboards), Jet Black (drums). Built up strong following by consistent gigging. Punk in attitude only – music more influenced by garage bands of early '60s. *Rattus Norvegicus* (1977) first New Wave LP to score high chart position. Solo efforts, e.g. Burnel's *European Son*, Cornwell's collaboration with Robert Williams on *Nosferatu* (1979), led to rumours of split, unjustified. Cornwell jailed for drug possession; released, April 1980. *La Folie* (1982), featuring a new soft-focus romantic approach, charted, as did 'Golden Brown'. Other LPs *No More Heroes* (1977), *Black and White* (1978), *The Raven* (1979), *The Gospel According to the Meninblack* (1981).

SUN RECORDS
Formed Memphis (Tennessee), February 1952, by Sam Phillips. Main subsidiary, Phillips International, 1957 on. New Memphis studio, 1960; second studio in Nashville, 1961. Company dormant during mid-'60s; bought by Shelby Singleton, 1/7/69, becoming Sun International Corp of Nashville. Initially mainly an R&B label, 1952-4; hits with Rufus Thomas, Jr Parker, etc. Thereafter essential source of rockabilly/rock 'n' roll: ELVIS PRESLEY, CARL PERKINS, JERRY LEE LEWIS, others; also country: Johnny Cash.

TALKING HEADS
Minimalist/funk-rock group, formed New York, 1974: David Byrne (vocal/guitar), Tina Weymouth (bass), Chris Frantz (drums). Toured Britain with Jerry Harrison (keyboards) several times, 1977-8. New look line-up, concentrating on funk, 1980: Bernie Worrell (keyboards), Adrian Belew (guitar), Steve Seales (percussion), Busta 'Cherry' Jones (bass), Dolette McDonald (bass/vocal). African accent on *Remain in Light* (1980). Byrne collaborated with BRIAN ENO on *My Life in the Bush of Ghosts* (1981). Tom Tom Club, formed by Frantz, Weymouth, Monte Brown and Steve Stanley, released 'Wordy Rappinghood' (1981): hit everywhere except in US; LP *Tom Tom Club* followed. Byrne produced B52s' *Mesopotamia*. Other LPs *Talking Heads: 77* (1977), *More Songs About Buildings and Food* (1978), *Fear of Music* (1980) (these three produced by

Eno); *The Name of This Band Is Talking Heads* (1982, live double).

TELEVISION
New Wave band. Tom Verlaine (*b.* 13/12/49; vocal/guitar), Richard Hell (bass), Billy Ficca (drums), formed Neon Boys, New York, early '70s. With addition of Richard Lloyd (guitar/vocal) became Television, 1974. Part of Max's Kansas City/CBGB's club circuit in New York. BRIAN ENO made unsuccessful attempt to record group for ISLAND, 1974. Hell left to form the Voidoids; recorded seminal 'Blank Generation' (1976), three LPs for Sire. Replaced by Fred 'Sonic' Smith. This line-up signed to ELEKTRA; released classic *Marquee Moon*, 1977. Follow-up *Adventure* failed to achieve similar critical credit. Disbanded 1978. Verlaine since recorded *Tom Verlaine* (1979), *Dreamtime* (1981), *Words from the Front* (1982).

TEMPTATIONS, THE
Soul vocal/instrumental group, formed Detroit, 1959, as the Distants; renamed by MOTOWN head Berry Gordy, had many hits, 1960-73. Original line-up: Eddie Kendricks, Otis Williams, Paul Williams, Melvin Franklin, David Ruffin. Changed from familiar Motown sound to psychedelic soul, 1968, when Dennis Edwards of the Contours replaced Ruffin; new producer, Norman Whitfield. Kendricks left for solo career, 1971; Ricky Owens took over as lead singer, replaced six months later by Damon Harris. Paul Williams found shot, 1973. Group now records mainly in sophisticated soul/disco vein, having left motown for ATLANTIC, 1977. Notable albums: *Sing Smokey* (1965, all SMOKEY ROBINSON songs), *Cloud Nine* (1969), *Together* (1970, with DIANA ROSS and the Supremes), *Masterpiece* (1973), *A Song for You* (1975), *Bare Back* (1978).

10CC
Art-rock band, formed Manchester, 1972. Original line-up: Eric Stewart (vocal/guitar), Graham Gouldman (vocal/bass), Lol Creme (vocal/guitar), Kevin Godley (vocal/drums). All thoroughly grounded in Sixties UK pop scene; Stewart set up Strawberry Studios, Stockport, where group came together to record. Initial success (without Gouldman) as Hotlegs with No 2 hit 'Neanderthal Man' (1970). 'Donna' first effort as four-piece, picked up by Jonathan King for new label UK. LPs *10CC* (1973), *Sheet Music* (1974), *Original Soundtrack* (1975), *How Dare You* (1976). Godley and Creme left to pursue more experimental direction; Stewart and Gouldman continued as 10CC. Further LPs *Deceptive Bends* (1977), *Live and Let Live* (1977, live double), *Bloody Tourists* (1978). Stewart suffered serious car accident, January 1979. *Greatest Hits* released that year; comeback LP, *Ten Out of 10*, 1981.

TEN YEARS AFTER
Blues/hard-rock band, formed Nottingham, mid-'60s; became Ten Years After, 1967, adopting then popular British blues style. Original line-up: Alvin Lee (vocal/guitar), Leo Lyons (bass), Chick Churchill (keyboards), Ric Lee (drums). Debut *Ten Years After* (1967); built up following after *Undead* (1968, live), *Stonedhenge* (1969). Concentrated efforts on US; by demise had completed 28 US tours, more than any British group. Superstardom achieved by appearance in *Woodstock*. Made supposed final appearance, 1974, releasing last LP *Positive Vibrations*. Lee already working outside TYA: *Alvin Lee & Co/In Flight* (1974). Contract required final TYA US tour, 1975. Lee continued to release solo LPs, tour. Other selected TYA LPs *Ssshh* (1969), *Cricklewood Green* (1970), *Watt* (1970), *Rock and Roll Music to the World* (1972).

TEX, JOE
Vocal, *b.* Rogers (Texas), 8/8/33 or 35 (*r.n.* Joseph Arrrington Jr). Derivative R&B/rock 'n' roll recordings, 1955-60, until developing distinctive, often humorous 'rap'-style soul. 'Chittlin circuit' favourite, 1961-4; major soul star, 1965-72. Retired to become Muslim minister; returned to charts, 1977. Died of heart attack at home, 13/8/82. Select LPs *Greatest Hits* ('60s compilation),

I Gotcha (1972), *Bumps and Bruises* (1977).

THIN LIZZY

Hard-rock group, formed Dublin (Ireland), 1970; moved to England, mid-1971. Original line-up: Phil Lynott (vocal/bass), Eric Bell (guitar), Brian Downey (drums). Recorded *Thin Lizzy* (1971), *Shades of a Blue Orphanage* (1972), *Vagabonds of the Western World* (1973); also achieved surprise hit with 'Whisky in the Jar' (1973). Bell left, 1973; replaced first by Gary Moore (left, mid-1974), then Brian Robertson and Scott Gorham. Major international status followed 'The Boys Are Back in Town', *Jailbreak* (both 1976). Robertson left after *Johnny the Fox* (1976), replaced temporarily by Moore again, then Snowy White. Subsequent LPs *Bad Reputation* (1977), *Live & Dangerous* (1978), *Black Rose* (1979), *Chinatown* (1980), *Renegade* (1981). Lynott released *Solo in Soho,* 1980.

TOOTS & THE MAYTALS

Vocal group—Fred 'Toots' Hibbert, Raleigh Gordon, Jerry Matthias—formed Jamaica, early '60s. Became major local act, though career interrupted by Toots's absence in jail, 1965-7. With producer Byron Lee made *Funky Kingston* (1973), *In the Dark* (1974). Signed to ISLAND, 1975; released *Reggae Got Soul,* toured UK, 1976. Became one of best-known reggae groups in international market. Subsequent LPs include *Pass the Pipe* (1979), *Best of* (1979), *Just Like That* (1980), *Toots Live* (1980), *Knockout* (1981).

TOUSSAINT, ALLEN

Producer/vocal/piano, *b.* New Orleans (Louisiana), 14/1/38. Began career as session player for Shirley & Lee, Lloyd Price, Smiley Lewis. Became producer at Minit Records

with Ernie K. Doe, Jessie Hill, Meters, Wilbert Harrison, Lou Johnson, Lee Dorsey, Chris Kenner, others. Also wrote and played with these artists. Recent productions include DR JOHN, Labelle, Frankie Miller, JOE COCKER, Albert King, Etta James. Solo LPs *Toussaint* (1971), *Life, Love & Faith* (1972), *Southern Nights* (1975), *Motion* (1978).

TRAFFIC

Rock supergroup, formed London, 1967, after STEVE WINWOOD had left Spencer Davis Group; first signing to new ISLAND RECORDS. Original line-up: Steve Winwood (guitar/keyboards/vocal), Dave Mason (guitar/vocal), Chris Wood (sax/flute), Jim Capaldi (drums). Immediate success with 'Paper Sun', 'Hole in My Shoe' (both 1967); released *Mr Fantasy* same year. Mason quit, December 1967 (though rejoined on several occasions). Group had officially split up by end of 1969, having released *Traffic* (1968), *Last Exit* (1969), *Best of* (1969). However, Winwood called in Wood and Capaldi for solo project *John Barleycorn Must Die* (1970), actually released as Traffic. Thereafter reborn group began heavy touring schedule, occasionally augmented by Rick Grech (bass/violin), Reebop (percussion), Jim Gordon (drums), Mason and Muscle Shoals session-men David Hood (bass), Roger Hawkins (drums). Final Traffic LP, 1974. Capaldi has enjoyed intermittent solo success; Winwood made first solo LP *Winwood,* 1977. Additional Traffic LPs *Welcome to the Canteen* (1971), *The Low Spark of High-Heeled Boys* (1971), *Shoot-Out at the Fantasy Factory* (1973), *On the Road* (1973), *When the Eagle Flies* (1974).

T REX

Glam-rock band; originally Tyrannosaurus Rex, formed London, 1969 by Marc Bolan (acoustic guitar/vocal), Steve Peregrine Took (percussion). On fourth LP, *Beard of Stars* (1970), Took replaced by Micky Finn (drums/percussion), Bolan introduced electric guitar. Name abbreviated to T Rex, 1970; achieved surprise No 2 hit with 'Ride a White Swan'. At peak of popularity, 1971-3, enjoying mass hysteria at live shows, string of hits, e.g. 'Hot Love', 'Get It On', 'Telegram Sam'. Disbanded, 1975; Bolan moved to US; formed new (but unsuccessful) T Rex, 1976. Own TV series (1977) championed new UK punk groups. Killed in car crash, 16/9/77. Selected T Rex LPs *T Rex* (1970), *Electric Warrior* (1971), *The Slider* (1972), *Tanx* (1973).

TURNER, IKE & TINA

Ike Turner (guitar/piano), *b.* Clarksdale (Mississippi), 5/11/31; Tina Turner (vocal), *b.* Brownsville (Tennessee), 26/11/38 (*r.n.* Annie Mae Bullock). Throughout '50s Ike led Kings of Rhythm; also talent scout for Modern Records. Discovered Tina; 'A Fool in Love' (1960), her debut, was US hit and led to formation of Ike & Tina Turner Revue, with Ikettes (among whom have been Bonnie Bramlett, Merry Clayton, P. P. Arnold). Have recorded over 30 LPs for various labels. Hits include: 'It's Gonna Work Out Fine' (1961), 'River Deep Mountain High' (1966, produced by PHIL SPECTOR; hit outside US only), 'Proud Mary' (1971), 'Nutbush City Limits' (1973). Marriage broke up, 1976; Tina has since pursued successful solo career.

TURNER, JOE

Vocal, *b.* Kansas City (Missouri), 18/5/11. Blues shouter prominent in '30s Kansas City jazz scene with boogie pianist Pete Johnson, recorded prolifically from 1938. Untypically survived changing times to find greater success with R&B/rock 'n' roll on ATLANTIC RECORDS, 1951-9. Hits covered by BILL HALEY, ELVIS PRESLEY, JERRY LEE LEWIS and other rockers. LPs *Have No Fear, Big Joe Turner Is Here* (1977 compilation of 1945-7), *His Greatest Recordings* (1971 compilation of 1951-7).

TWO-TONE RECORDS

Independent label, founded by Jerry Dammers of the Specials, 1979. Dedicated to dance-floor music by racially mixed bands with reggae roots. Released Specials' 'Gangsters', March 1979. Signed distribution deal with Chrysalis. Subsequent singles regularly charted, e.g. MADNESS's 'The Prince', the Selecter's 'On My Radio', both autumn 1979. First Specials LP *The Specials* (1979) produced by ELVIS COSTELLO. The Beat, from Birmingham (formed 1979), charted with 'Tears of a Clown'. Specials EP 'Too Much Too Young' No. 1, February 1980. The Selecter left, 1980. Replaced by Swinging Cats; suffered from constant line-up changes. Film *Dance Crazy* (1981) combined live footage of Two-Tone bands and news commentary. Specials' 'Ghost Town' No 1, July 1981; then split up, ex-members forming Fun Boy Three, same year. LPs include: Specials *More Specials* (1980); Selecter *Too Much Pressure* (1980), *Celebrate the Bullet* (1981).

—U—

UB 40
Pop-reggae band, formed Birmingham (England), 1978. Line-up: Jim Brown (drums/vocal), Ali Campbell (rhythm guitar/vocal), brother Robin Campbell (lead guitar/vocal), Earl Falconer (bass), Norman Hassan (percussion), Brian Travers (saxophone), Mickey Virtue (keyboards), Astro (percussion). Debut LP *Signing Off* and first single 'Food for Thought' (both 1978) substantial UK hits. Formed own label, Dep International, 1980. Other LPs *Present Arms* (1980), *UB 44* (1982).

ULTRAVOX
New Romantics group, formed 1976; originally called Tiger Lily

(and other names). Line-up: John Foxx (vocal), Chris Cross (bass), Stevie Shears (guitar), Warren Cann (drums), Billy Currie (keyboards/violin). Shears left, early 1978; replaced by Robin Simon. Signed to ISLAND; third LP, *Systems of Romance*, produced by Connie Plank, affirmed allegiance to contemporary European sound. During US tour Simon and Foxx left, latter to continue solo career on VIRGIN. Remaining members brought in Midge Ure (vocal/synthesizer) of Slik, the Rich Kids, leading to more formal electronic approach; signed to Chrysalis, 1980. Released *Vienna*; title track No 2, 1981. Associated with NEW ROMANTICS but withstood their passing. Subsequent LPs *Rage in Eden* (produced by Plank, 1981), *Quartet* (1982). Ure also member of Steve Strange's band Visage.

—V—

VANGELIS
Composer/keyboards, *b.* Volos (Greece), *c.* 1943 (*r.n.* Vangelis Papathanassiou). Played in Greek jazz-rock group Aphrodite's Child, '60s (also featuring vocalist Demis Roussos). Gradually overstepped limitations of pop format. Moved to London, mid-'70s, building own Nemo studio. Recorded series of solo albums, including collaborations with singer/lyricist Jon Anderson of YES notably the well-received *Short Stories* (1979). Huge success with soundtrack of film *Chariots of Fire* (1981); also composed soundtrack for *Blade Runner* (1982). Selected LPs *Heaven & Hell* (1975), *Albedo 0.39* (1976), *Spiral* (1977), *Beauborg* (1978), *China* (1979), *See You Later* (1980).

VELVET UNDERGROUND
Art-rock group, formed New York, 1966: JOHN CALE (vocal/viola), LOU REED (vocal/guitar), Sterling Morrison (guitar), Maureen Tucker (drums). Became part of Andy Warhol's Exploding Plastic Inevitable touring show, adding Warhol 'superstar', female vocalist and songwriter Nico. Explored decadence of urban life, sex, drugs. Recorded *The Velvet Underground and Nico* (Verve, 1967, produced by Warhol); Nico left shortly afterwards for solo career. Cale left, 1968; replaced by Doug Yule. Tucker replaced by Billy Yule, 1970. Reed left

same year, just before critically acclaimed *Loaded*. Yule brothers kept group going for a time with new members; released *Squeeze* (1972). Other LPs *White Light/White Heat* (1967), *The Velvet Underground* (1969), *Live at Max's Kansas City* (1972).

VINCENT, GENE
Vocal, *b.* Norfolk (Virginia), 11/3/35; *d.* California, 12/10/71 (*r.n.* Vincent Eugene Craddock). After debut international hit 'Be-Bop-a-Lula' (1956) lack of chart success belied enduring popularity and influence. Seminal rockabilly with the Blue Caps (Mk.1, 1956; Mk. 2, 1957-8); renewed career in Britain, 1960-4; returned to States for 1967 album. LPs *Singles Album* (1981 compilation of 1956-60), *Rock 'n' Roll Legend* (4-LP box set), *Gene Vincent* (1967, recently reissued), *Rock 'n' Roll Heroes* (with EDDIE COCHRAN, 1981).

VIRGIN RECORDS
Independent label founded by Richard Branson, 1973. First release, MIKE OLDFIELD's *Tubular Bells* (May), was spectacular worldwide best-seller. Label grew steadily with mainly progressive rock by Oldfield, Steve Hillage, others, but proved adaptability by signing SEX PISTOLS, 1977. Subsequent New Wave signings include HUMAN LEAGUE, XTC. Previously album-oriented label, now competed in singles market. Also acquired Japan, Simple Minds. Has shown considerable interest in African pop music. (Below: Richard Branson)

—W—

WALKER, T-BONE

Vocal/guitar, *b.* Linden (Texas), 28/5/10; *d.* Los Angeles, 16/3/75 (*r.n.* Aaron Thibeaux Walker). Moved to West Coast, 1934. His 'I Got a Break Baby'/'Mean Old World' (1942) probably first blues record with electric guitar. Recorded with small band for various labels, 1946-54; most famous song 'Call It Stormy Monday' (1947), later covered by BOBBY 'BLUE' BLAND. Consistently hip lyrics; guitar-playing influenced many younger bluesmen, e.g. B.B. KING. On first blues package tour of Europe, 1962; many subsequent visits. Selected LPs *T-Bone Jumps Again, Plain Ole Blues* ('80s compilations of 1942-8 classics), *Classics of Modern Blues* (1975 double compilation of 1950-3), *T-Bone Blues* (ATLANTIC, 1960), *Very Rare* (1973, produced by LEIBER & STOLLER).

WARWICK, DIONNE

Vocal, *b.* East Orange (New Jersey), 12/12/41. Became session singer in New York, where discovered by BURT BACHARACH, 1962. Made many million-selling singles, albums before 1971 break-up. Move to Warner Bros, 1973, marked return to soul field: *Just Being Myself* (1973) included songs by MOTOWN writers Holland and Dozier; *Track of the Cat* (1975) produced by PHILADELPHIA SOUND specialist Thom Bell. Single 'Then Came You' (1974), teamed with Detroit Spinners. *Heartbreaker* (1982) produced by Barry Gibb of BEE GEES.

WEATHER REPORT

Jazz-rock band, formed 1970. Original line-up: Joe Zawinul (keyboards), Wayne Shorter (saxophones), Miroslav Vitous (bass), Airto Moreira (percussion). Nucleus of Zawinul and Shorter unchanged to date, sidemen come and go: one of most notable, Jaco Pastorius, revolutionised jazz-rock bass playing. Selected LPs *Sweetnighter* (1973), *Mysterious Traveller* (1974), *Black Market* (1976), *Heavy Weather* (1977), *Night Passage* (1980).

WHO, THE

Mod-rock band, formed Shepherds Bush (London), 1963, as the High Numbers. Original line-up: Roger Daltrey (vocal), John Entwistle (bass), Keith Moon (drums), Pete Townshend (guitar). Became top band of mod era, Townshend's songs stressing strong identification with working-class teenagers. *The Who Sell Out* (1967) and *Tommy* (1969) both experiments in concept albums: latter given stage and film treatment in '70s. *Quadrophenia* (1974) celebrated mod lifestyle, also filmed (1980). Other key albums *Live at Leeds* (1970), *Who's Next* (1971), *Who by Numbers* (1975), *The Kids Are Alright* (1979). Keith Moon died, 8/9/78, replaced by Kenny Jones of the Faces. Band decided to quit touring, 1982.

WILLIAMS, HANK

Vocal/guitar/songwriter, *b.* Mt Olive (Alabama), 17/9/23; *d.* (prob.) West Virginia, 1/1/53. Country music's greatest figure; one of the most gifted songwriters in popular music. Signed to MGM, 1947. Recorded extraordinary series of immediate classics, mostly own compositions: 'I Saw the Light' (1948), 'There'll Be No Teardrops Tonight' (1949), 'Lovesick Blues' (1949), 'I'm So Lonesome I Could Cry' (1949), 'Cold, Cold Heart' (1950), 'I Can't Help It (If I'm Still in Love with You)' (1951), 'Jambalaya' (1952), 'You Win Again' (1952), 'Your Cheatin' Heart' (1953). Lovesongs of despair and blues alternated with rowdy honky-tonk, novelty songs; small-band accompaniments featured fiddle, steel guitar. Also gospel songs; under name 'Luke the Drifter', tales, lay sermons. Led wild life (subject of several biographies, also sanitised film account *Your Cheatin' Heart*). Selected LPs *Greatest Hits Vol. 1, Vol. 2* ('70s compilations of 1947-52).

WILSON, JACKIE

Vocal, *b.* Detroit (Michigan), 9/6/34. Influential 'operatic' soul tenor. First sang gospel with the Ever Ready Singers, 1950, then R&B with the Dominoes, 1952-6. Solo career of about 50 American hits, 1957-70s, only represented internationally by 'Reet Petite' (1957), 'Higher and Higher' (1967). Collapsed, Camden (New Jersey), 29/9/75; survives as brain-damaged invalid. LPs *My Golden Favorites* ('50s compilation), *Sings the Blues* (1960), *Greatest Hits* ('60s compilation).

WINTER, JOHNNY

Guitar/vocal, *b.* Leland (Mississippi), 23/2/44; brought up in Beaumont (Texas). Blues enthusiast; backed local bluesmen on small local labels in '60s. His debut album for Columbia, *Johnny Winter* (1969), was followed by *Second Winter* (1970), *Johnny Winter And* (1970), *Live* (1971), *Still Alive and Well* (1973), *Saints and Sinners* (1974), *Johnny and Edgar Together* (brother Edgar Winter on keyboards/saxophone, 1976), *Nothin' but the Blues* (1977), *Raisin' Cain* (1980). Produced (and often played on) MUDDY WATERS' later LPs.

WINWOOD, STEVE

Keyboards/guitar/vocal, *b.* Birmingham, 12/5/48. Joined Spencer Davis Group, 1964; single hits included 'Keep On Running' (1965). With TRAFFIC, 1967-9. Briefly involved with Blind Faith (*see* CREAM), 1969. Traffic reactivated 1970-4. Produced several finely crafted solo LPs on which he plays all instruments: *Steve Winwood* (1977), *Arc of a Diver* (1981), *Talking Back to the Night* (1982).

WISHBONE ASH

Rock group, formed London, 1969. Original line-up: Andy Powell (guitar), Ted Turner (guitar), Martin Turner (bass/vocal), Steve Upton (drums). Debut *Wishbone Ash*, 1970. Popular club band, at its best on *Argus* (1972). Laurie Wisefield (guitar) replaced Ted Turner, 1974. Recorded *There's the Rub* (1974) in US; thereafter US residents. Subsequent LPs include *Locked In* (1976), *New England* (1976), *Front Page News* (1977), *No Smoke Without Fire* (1978), *Just Testing* (1980). Extensive world tour, 1980. Martin Turner replaced by John Wetton (ex-FAMILY), then Trevor Bolder. Now firmly established international group. Most recent LPs *Number the Brave, Hot Ash* (both 1981).

WONDER, STEVIE

Vocal/keyboards/guitar/drums, *b.* Saginaw (Michigan), 13/5/50 (*r.n.* Stephen Judkins). Blind from birth, signed by MOTOWN in 1960; launched as 'Little Stevie Wonder', matured from child-star into middle-of-the-road entertainer. Changed direction with *Where I'm Coming From* (1971), specialising in roots-conscious black rock with jazz/Latin inflections. *Talking Book* (1972), *Innervisions* (1973), *Fulfillingness First Finale* (1974) established him as '70s superstar. Re-signed to Motown, 1975, for record-breaking $13m advance. Other major LPs *Music of My Mind* (1972), *Songs in the Key of Life* (1976), *The Secret Life of Plants* (1979), *Hotter than July* (1980).

WYATT, ROBERT

Vocal/drums, *b.* Bristol, brought up in Dulwich (London). Drummer with the SOFT MACHINE; left, 1971. First solo LP, *The End of an Ear,* released that year. Formed own band Matching Mole (name loosely derived from French for Soft Machine); released *Matching Mole, Little Red Record;* disbanded, 1972. Suffered accident, summer 1973; paralysed from waist down. Composed *Rock Bottom* while in hospital; produced by PINK FLOYD's Nick Mason, 1974. Surprise hit with new version of Monkees' 'I'm a Believer', 1974. *Ruth Is Stranger Than Richard* (1975) well received. Composed music for *The Animals Film* (1982). Recent records on Rough Trade, e.g. 'Shipbuilding' (1982).

YARDBIRDS, THE

R&B band, formed Kingston (Surrey), 1963. Original line-up: Chris Dreja (rhythm guitar), Jim McCarty (drums), Keith Relf (vocal/harmonica), Paul Samwell-Smith (bass), Anthony Topham (lead guitar). Precursors of progressive-rock movement. ERIC CLAPTON replaced Topham late 1963. *Five Live Yardbirds* (1964) established reputation as leading live R&B group; Clapton left, 1965, replaced by JEFF BECK. Samwell-Smith departed, 1966, replaced by JIMMY PAGE, while Dreja switched to bass. Beck left, late 1966; continued as foursome until 1968 break-up. Page formed LED ZEPPELIN, 1968; Relf and McCarty co-founded Renaissance, 1969.

YES

Art-rock group, formed London, 1968. Original line-up: Jon Anderson (vocal), Chris Squire (bass), Peter Banks (guitar), Tony Kaye (organ), Bill Bruford (drums). Recorded *Yes* (1969), *Time and a Word* (1970). Banks left, early 1971, replaced by Steve Howe; made *The Yes Album* (1971). Kaye replaced by Rick Wakeman (from the Strawbs), also 1971; group achieved most fully realised sound on *Fragile* (1971), *Close to the Edge* (1972), massive sellers in UK and US. Bruford left to join KING CRIMSON; replaced by Alan White for triple live *Yessongs* (1973). Wakeman had released solo *The Six Wives of Henry VIII* (1973), but completed *Tales from Topographic Oceans* (1974) before quitting; replaced by Patrick Moraz for *Relayer* (1974). This line-up stable for 18 months, individual members meanwhile engaging in solo projects. Wakeman returned, 1976. Anderson and Wakeman left, 1981, former to work with VANGELIS; replaced by Trevor Horn (vocal/guitar), Geoff Downes (keyboards), from Buggles. Recorded *Drama* (1981); completed UK/US tour. Howe and Downes then teamed up with Carl Palmer (from ELP) and John Wetton to form Asia.

YOUNG, NEIL

Vocal/guitar, *b.* Toronto (Canada), 12/11/45. Played in folk-rock groups, mid-'60s. Moved to Los Angeles, joined BUFFALO SPRINGFIELD, 1966. Became last member of CROSBY, STILLS, NASH & YOUNG, 1969, then resumed solo career with Crazy Horse: Danny Whitten (guitar), Billy Talbot (bass), Ralph Molina (drums). Later group the Stray Gators used, briefly, Jack Nitzsche (keyboards) Ben Keith (pedal steel guitar), Tim Drummond (bass), Johnny Barbata (drums). After death of Whitten Young formed new Crazy Horse with Talbot, Molina, Keith, Nils Lofgren (guitar). Lofgren later assumed solo career; replaced by Frank Sampedro. LPs *Neil Young* (1969), *Everybody Knows This Is Nowhere* (1969), *After the Goldrush* (1970), *Harvest* (1972), *Journey Through the Past* (1972), *Time Fades Away* (1973) *On the Beach* (1974), *Tonight's the Night* (1975), *Zuma* (1976), *American Stars & Bars* (1977), *Decade* (1977), *Comes a Time* (1978), *Live Rust* (1979), *Rust Never Sleeps* (1979), *Hawks & Doves* (1980), *Reactor* (1981), *Trans Music* (1982).

Z

ZAPPA, FRANK & THE MOTHERS OF INVENTION

Frank Zappa (guitar/vocal) *b.* Baltimore (Maryland), 21/12/40. Joined Soul Giants, mid-'60s, which later became the Mothers of Invention. Original line-up: Zappa, Elliot Ingber (guitar), Roy Estrada (bass), Jimmy Carl Black (drums), Ray Collins (vocals), Dave Coronada (saxophone). First LP *Freak Out* (1966). Mothers augmented by Don Preston (keyboards), Bunk Gardner (saxophones), Billy Mundi (drums), Jim Sherwood (saxophones). Line-up has included CAPTAIN BEEFHEART, Jean-Luc Ponty, Ian Underwood, George Duke, Max Bennet, Lowell George, Shuggy Otis. With manager Herb Cohen, Zappa set up Straight and Bizzarre labels, 1969. LPs include *Absolutely Free* (1967), *Ruben and the Jets* (1968), *Uncle Meat* (1968), *Hot Rats* (1969), *Weasels Ripped My*

Flesh (1970), *200 Motels* (1971), *The Mothers: Fillmore East – June 1971* (1971), *Just Another Band from LA* (1971), *Overnite Sensation* (1973), *Roxy and Elsewhere* (1974), *Bongo Fury* (1975), *Studio Tan* (1978), *Joe's Garage* (1979), *Tinsel Town Rebellion* (1981), *Ship Arriving Too Late to Save a Drowning Witch* (1982).

ZE RECORDS

Founded by ex-New York theatre critic Michael Zilkha and Michel Esteban, late '70s. Reflected Manhattan nightlife world. LP *Mutant Disco* (1981) featured AUGUST DARNELL in various guises; also Material, Was (Not Was). Distributed by ISLAND RECORDS.

Index

Acknowledgements

The publishers wish to thank the following organizations and individuals for their kind permission to reproduce the photographs in this book:
Ace Photo Agency 3, 115 above left, 119, 153 above, 161 left, 162, 173; Air Studios Ltd 176 left; Arista Records 166 left; John Atkins 13, 21 below; Tony Bacon 141; Camera Press 105, 114, 133 below; CBS Records 182 right; Courtesy of the Country Music Foundation Library and Media Center, Nashville, Tennessee 19; Geoff Dann 126, 127, 128 below right, 128-9, 130; De Monde Ad Agency/George Bodnar 122-3; Ralph Denyer 124, 128 above left, 129 131, 134, 135 above, 136, 139, 144, 147, 148 above; EMI Records 151 above, 186 right; Grassroots Records 24 below; Harbinson 22, 25; Martin Hawkins 26 left; London Features International 2 above and below right, 4 right, 5 centre and right, 6-7, 11, 24 above, 28, 29, 31-3, 34 below, 36, 37, 41, 42, 43 below, 44-5, 45 above right, 46, 48 below, 51, 52-3, 55, 56, 58, 59 below, 60, 62-3, 64-5, 65 right, 66-7, 68 right, 69, 71, 73, 74 left, 76 77 above, 78-82, 83 below, 85, 86 above, 87, 90, 92, 93 above, 94 left, 95, 96, 98-9, 100 below, 101-2, 104, 108, 110 below left, 111 right, 113, 115 below left, 115 right, 116-7, 120, 125, 137, 151 below, 153 below, 155, 156, 159, 160, 161 right, 163, 166 right, 168 right, 169, 171, 174, 176 right, 177-9, 186 left, 187-9; Iain MacMillan 2-3, 100 above; Moog Music Inc 132, 133 above; *Music Week* 150; Michael Ochs Archive 26-7; Sylvia Pitcher 18, 20-1, 34 above; RCA Records 8-9; David Redfern endpapers, half title, 2 above left, 4 left, 4-5, 7 right, 10, 12, 14, 16, 17, 23, 35, 43 above, 44, 45 below, 49, 50, 52 below, 54, 57, 59 above, 61, 64 below, 68 left, 70, 72, 74-5, 75, 77 below, 83 above, 86 below, 88-9, 91, 93 below, 94 right, 97, 103, 106, 107 above, 109, 110-11, 118 above left, 121 left, 140, 142-3, 157, 158, 164, 167, 172, 175 right, 180, 181, 182 left, 184, 185; Rex Features 2 below left, 39, 47, 48 above, 107 below, 110 above left, 118 below left, 118 right, 121 right, 154, 170; Stiff Records 175 left; Studio Sound/Richard Elen 145, 146, 148 below, 149; Courtesy of Thames Television 30-1, 40; John Topham Picture Library 84; Universal Pictorial Press Agency Ltd 152; Dave Walters 112; Warner Brothers 165; Zefa Picture Library/SKO Systems 135 below.